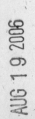

MY CENTURY IN HISTORY

Thomas D. Clark

My Century in History

—⁓—

Memoirs

Foreword by Charles P. Roland
Introduction by James C. Klotter

THE UNIVERSITY PRESS OF KENTUCKY

Publication of this volume was made possible in part by
a grant from the National Endowment for the Humanities.

Scholarly publisher for the Commonwealth, serving Bellarmine University, Berea College, Centre College of Kentucky, Eastern Kentucky University, The Filson Historical Society, Georgetown College, Kentucky Historical Society, Kentucky State University, Morehead State University, Murray State University, Northern Kentucky University, Transylvania University, University of Kentucky, University of Louisville, and Western Kentucky University.

The Press is grateful to Georgiana Strickland for her role in preparing this book for publication. She assembled the computer scans of Thomas D. Clark's original typescript; edited the text; conferred with Dr. Clark's family, friends, and colleagues; and acted as a consultant to the Press editors. Ms. Strickland also provided the annotations found in this book, clarifying references to events and terms that may not be familiar to the reader, and wrote captions for the photographs. The Press wishes to acknowledge Loretta Clark, Bennett Clark, and Elizabeth Stone for reading and commenting on drafts of the manuscript, and for providing photographs for reproduction in this book.

Thomas D. Clark's article "Our Roots Flourished in the Valley," copyright © Organization of American Historians, was first printed in the *Journal of American History* 65 (June 1978): 1, and parts of it appear here in slightly different form; reprinted with permission. Parts of "The Book Thieves" chapter of this book were first printed in slightly different form in the *Kentucky Review* 15 (winter 1984), 27–45.

Frontispiece: Thomas D. Clark holds an early printing of Lincoln's Gettysburg Address, selected as the two millionth book to be added to the University of Kentucky Library in 1986. (University of Kentucky Special Collections and Digital Programs)

Editorial and Sales Offices: The University Press of Kentucky
663 South Limestone Street, Lexington, Kentucky 40508-4008
www.kentuckypress.com

10 09 08 07 06   5 4 3 2 1

Library of Congress Cataloging-in-Publication Data

Clark, Thomas Dionysius, 1903-2005
  My century in history : memoirs / Thomas D. Clark ; foreword by Charles P. Roland ; introduction by James C. Klotter.
    p. cm.
  Includes index.
  ISBN-13: 978-0-8131-2400-1 (hardcover : alk. paper)
  ISBN-10: 0-8131-2400-X (hardcover : alk. paper)
  ISBN-13: 978-0-8131-2401-8 (leatherbound ed. : alk. paper)
  ISBN-10: 0-8131-2401-8 (leatherbound ed. : alk. paper)
  1. Clark, Thomas Dionysius, 1903-2005. 2. Historians—Kentucky—Biography. 3. Kentucky—Biography.
  4. Kentucky—Historiography. I. Title.
  E175.5.C56A3 2006
  976.90072'02—dc22

This book is printed on acid-free recycled paper meeting the requirements of the American National Standard for Permanence in Paper for Printed Library Materials.

Manufactured in the United States of America.

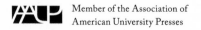

Member of the Association of
American University Presses

For Loretta

CONTENTS

Illustrations follow pages 108 and 300

FOREWORD

I AM PLEASED AND HONORED to have been asked to prepare a brief foreword for this memoir by Thomas D. Clark. Here, in the author's own words, the reader learns of the countless vicissitudes surrounding the extraordinary life of one of the most distinguished American scholars of the twentieth century. His memoir is written with commendable modesty, yet it demonstrates the ability of an individual to soar above his origins.

Tom, as his multitude of friends and admirers knew him, carried out to an astonishing measure an axiom set forth by the renowned Confederate general Stonewall Jackson. When Jackson was young, he wrote, "You can be whatever you resolve to be." Tom was born and reared on a hardscrabble cotton and subsistence farm in east-central Mississippi at the dawn of the twentieth century. As a child he experienced the demanding life that has traditionally been associated with such a childhood. He hoed and picked cotton, split firewood, butchered hogs and beeves, harvested fruit and vegetables, and cared for the animals that provided the motive power for the farm as well as much of the food for the family's table. He lived intimately with nature.

Though he received little formal schooling in his early years, he was imbued somewhere along the way (doubtless by his mother, a teacher in a one-room country school) with a desire for an education. This desire was powerfully stimulated by more than two years of grinding labor on a dredgeboat when he was a teenager. On leaving the boat, as he puts it, he stumbled away "headed only God knew where." After three days of walking through the Mississippi forest he reached his Grandmother Clark's home. "I did not know where or how I would find a school to attend," he wrote, "but I was determined to find one."

Find a school he did, and eventually he made his way through the University of Mississippi ("Ole Miss") and earned a master's degree in history at the University of Kentucky and a doctorate in the same field at the newly established Duke University. As a graduate student he learned the secrets of his discipline, that it entailed research in primary sources as well as the study of published books. He was destined to become one of the leading collectors of primary historical sources. As Tom colorfully put it, his embrace of higher education took him "out of the cotton patch."

At Duke, Tom met and fell in love with Elizabeth "Beth" Turner of South Carolina, a librarian. The two were married in June 1933 and lived a happy life together for sixty-two years. Beth died at the end of July 1995, leaving Tom in a state of "almost overpowering loneliness." Two years later, in his ninety-third year, he was married to Loretta Gilliam Brock, whose previous husband had died some years earlier. In his memoir he pays Loretta this tribute: "I can say with joyous certainty that my marriage to gentle, talented Loretta has been one of those turns of fortune that give fundamental meaning and spice to life."

In 1931 Tom joined the faculty of the University of Kentucky as a part-time history teacher and part-time searcher for manuscripts for the newly founded Special Collections Department of the library. In his more than three decades at Kentucky he fulfilled an extraordinary professional career: he produced more than forty books, a number of them now classics. He became the major force behind the creation of the University Press of Kentucky, the state archives, and the state History Center, as well as the university's Special Collections Department. He served as president of two of the nation's major professional historical associations. He also served for several years as managing editor of the *Journal of Southern History* and for another several years as the executive secretary of the Organization of American Historians. In the late 1960s

Tom left Kentucky to join the faculty of Indiana University, where he was appointed Distinguished Service Professor and wrote the history of the university. Meanwhile he taught as a visiting professor at numerous American universities and several abroad.

Tom's early experience as a farmer and laborer left an indelible imprint on his character, personality, speech, and writing. He was a quintessentially earthy individual, a quality that he imparted fully to his scholarship as well as his everyday conversation. I first met him in the spring of 1947 when I was a graduate student at Louisiana State University, where he participated in a distinguished series of lectures. I vividly recall my surprise and pleasure at the southern tone of his speech and the down-home nature of his metaphors and examples. One comment especially stuck in my mind. He said he first recognized the element of common humanity among all people when he shared drinking water with black laborers on the dredgeboat where they all worked. They drank directly from the same bucket.

We enjoyed a close and warm friendship of almost sixty years. He frequently hailed me as "the lad from the canebrakes of West Tennessee." Because we were products of the same general part of the country, I possessed a special insight into his rustic illustrations of human characteristics. He once told of an incident in which a woman approached him in a state of considerable perturbation. He said, "I could see she had her tail caught over the spatterboard." I understood instantly because I could recall as a boy seeing the agitation of a horse whose tail was caught over the spatterboard of the buggy it was pulling. On another occasion he told me about discovering that a colleague was engaged in what Tom considered a compromising situation. "I caught him with wool between his teeth," he said. As a youth I had often heard that expression used to describe a sheep-killing dog.

Though Tom was some fifteen years my senior, our careers as historians overlapped for such a long period that we shared countless experiences and acquaintances in the profession. Both of us immensely enjoyed discussing them when we got together. To my mind, one of his most intriguing stories was that of accompanying Professor John Crowe

Ransom to the post office in Memphis, where both were temporarily teaching, to mail off the manuscript of the famed Southern Agrarian manifesto *I'll Take My Stand*.

Tom was a deeply serious scholar, but he leavened his seriousness with a wry and pungent sense of humor and a complete appreciation of the ubiquitous irony of the human condition. He never missed the laughable or ridiculous aspect of a situation, and his books are peppered with whimsical expressions and evocative rustic metaphors. My favorite among his works, the one that most prominently displays these qualities, is *Pills, Petticoats, and Plows: The Southern Country Store*. In it he pictures the stores as symbols of the creation of a new economic system rising out of the wreckage of the old system destroyed by the Civil War. These "crossroads emporiums of cheap merchandise" instantly sprang up at innumerable rural road intersections and often formed the nuclei of new settlements. "They quickly became the heartbeat and pulse of a good portion of American business," he said. "In their own communities they were centers of every sort of neighborhood activity. Everything of importance that ever happened either occurred at the store or was reported there immediately."

Tom was a man of astonishing vigor and longevity. He was also a man who held a grand intellectual vision. To him, history was far more than a mere narrative of events; it was a galvanizing force in the life of society. He agreed with a statement made by General Robert E. Lee shortly before his death: "It is history that teaches us to hope." Tom believed that education is the key to progress and, of course, that history is an indispensable ingredient of education. One of the things that attracted him to the Kentucky students was their abiding sense of history.

His travels and work overseas immensely broadened his perspective and deepened his understanding of the universality of human characteristics. The chapter in this memoir on his Indian experience is riveting. His commentary demonstrates both deep understanding and compassion and his own profound and humorous sense of irony. He was particularly impressed by what he observed in India, "An Ancient Land in the Grip of History," as he called it. He gives the reader his views of the indescribable poverty and squalor that he witnessed, as well as the sublime beauty of the Taj Mahal.

Tom loved his native South even as he was sharply cognizant of its shortcomings. He viewed its development with optimism. In the midst of the civil rights friction of the 1950s and 1960s he followed his head and heart and supported the desegregation of the university and the public schools. He had confidence that the increasing urbanization and prosperity of the region would solve its racial problems. He enthusiastically welcomed the turn of southern agriculture from cotton farming to tree farming, grazing, and diversified crops. He owned extensive woodlands in Kentucky, South Carolina, and his native Mississippi. He also welcomed the growth of southern industry, and he wrote eloquently about these matters in many of his books.

Tom lived an incredibly long, full, and productive life; he died on June 28, 2005, a few days short of his hundred and second birthday. Two years before, he had received an American Historical Association Award for Scholarly Distinction. The citation read, in part: "He stands as a model historian, leader, advocate, teacher, and person. [He] continues to remind us what historians should be, and what they should do." All who knew him would utter an earnest "Amen" to that tribute.

Tom is sorely missed by a host of Kentuckians and others. The scene feels emptier for his departure. His was a comforting presence. He was the guardian angel, the driving spirit, of worthy causes; his name lent legitimacy and force to any endeavor. In 1992 Governor Brereton Jones described Tom as "Kentucky's greatest treasure," and the Kentucky legislature designated him the state's first and only Historian Laureate "for the period of his natural life." He remains the historian laureate in the hearts of his fellow scholars.

Charles P. Roland
Emeritus Professor of History
University of Kentucky

INTRODUCTION

THOMAS D. CLARK DIED IN Lexington, Kentucky, on June 28, 2005, just days before his hundred and second birthday. The governor ordered flags flown at half mast over the state capitol in Clark's honor. Earlier, the legislature had directed that the Kentucky Historical Society's new building be renamed the Thomas D. Clark Center for Kentucky History. The Kentucky Department for Libraries and Archives was already operating out of the Clark-Cooper Building, and the University Press of Kentucky calls the Thomas D. Clark Building home. A bas-relief of Clark stands at the History Center, and a bust of him holds a place of prominence at the Lexington History Museum. Numerous endowments, scholarships, and prizes bear his name. Three books have chronicled his career, including *Thomas D. Clark of Kentucky: An Uncommon Life in the Commonwealth* (2003). And Clark himself had written or edited some four dozen books, taught at several universities during a career of more than forty years, and served as president of two of America's major historical organizations. Clearly his was no ordinary historian's life.

Clark's life was extraordinary in many ways. Named Kentucky's Historian Laureate for Life in 1990, he apparently took the "for Life" designation seriously. When asked the secret of his longevity, he frequently told younger scholars, "Never stop working." He never did.

Clark worked hard all his life. Born July 14, 1903, in Louisville, Mississippi, in a double log cabin built by his great-grandfather, he was the son of a cotton farmer and a teacher. Even though the Wright Brothers took their first flight five months after his birth, signaling the changes that lay ahead in the new century, it was the trappings of the old century that first surrounded him. He spoke with ex-slaves and former Civil War soldiers. Pictures of famous Confederate leaders covered the walls of his home. In fact, his life seemed to be typical of others of his time and place. Clark would soon grow beyond the bounds of that society in many ways. First, however, he had to leave school to toil in the cotton fields, later to labor in a sawmill, and then to work on a boat that dredged Mississippi swamps.

At age eighteen Clark finally restarted his educational pursuits, and four years later he graduated from high school. In 1925 he entered the University of Mississippi, where he came under the influence of historian Charles S. Sydnor and began to study history. He also helped operate the Ole Miss golf course to earn money for tuition. In that job Clark spent considerable time, not all of it pleasant, with William Faulkner. A summer session at the University of Virginia earned him enough credits to graduate from Ole Miss, and he accepted a fellowship for graduate study at the University of Kentucky.

As Clark said later, in coming to Kentucky he found a state new to him and saw his first Republican. After earning his master's degree a year later, he entered Duke University's Ph.D. program. Under William K. Boyd's rather loose direction, he received one of that institution's first doctorates, in 1932. He also met there his first wife, Elizabeth Turner. Married sixty-two years at the time of her death in 1995, they had two children, Thomas Bennett Clark and Ruth Elizabeth Clark Stone. Clark subsequently married Loretta Gilliam Brock, and their union joyfully endured until his death.

While in graduate school, Clark first held temporary, Depression-era teaching posts at what are now the University of Memphis and the University of Tennessee. He then accepted a position at the University of Kentucky, where he taught for thirty-seven years, from 1931 to 1968, and chaired the history department from 1942 to 1965. A hard-driving chair, he developed an ulcer but forged a top-twenty department by the time he retired in 1968. Particularly strong in southern history, the department included such scholars as Clement Eaton, Holman Hamilton, A. D. Kirwan, and Bennett Wall. After leaving the University of Kentucky, Clark taught for six years at Indiana University and wrote a four-volume history of that institution.

During his teaching years, Clark also lectured at some twenty other schools, both in the United States and abroad, including ones in Austria, Greece, India, England, and what was then Yugoslavia. As he later recalled, "The classroom is the thing I treasure the most."

Tom Clark also played a key role in the growth of professional organizations devoted to Clio. After he attended his first such historical meeting in 1928 and spoke at length with U. B. Phillips about researching slavery, Clark grew increasingly involved. He served as president of the Southern Historical Association from 1947 to 1948, and was managing editor of the *Journal of Southern History* from 1948 to 1952. The history honorary society, Phi Alpha Theta, named him its president in 1957. In 2004 Clark received the American Historical Association's Award for Scholarly Distinction.

Clark had an especially strong impact on what is now the Organization of American Historians (OAH). His presidency of the then–Mississippi Valley Historical Association in 1956–1957 was followed by six years as chairman of the Executive Committee. After that tour of historical duty, Clark was named chair of the Committee on the Future of the Association. In that capacity he proposed the new name for the organization—the OAH—and helped in its transition from a regional to a national group. He served as executive secretary of the OAH from 1970 to 1973. In that position he established the organization's new offices at Indiana University, cleared the bats out of the building, pushed for a newsletter, and helped transform the OAH into a productive, modern historical organization. It honored him with its Distinguished Service Award in 1984 and its inaugural Centennial Award two decades later.

And across the years, Tom Clark continued to write, using a two-finger technique on a battered manual typewriter. The first of forty-some books that bear his name appeared in 1933; the last—this book of memoirs—is being published in 2006. Almost all of his previous works received favorable scholarly reviews; many used sources previously untouched by academic hands; most were written in a style that made them accessible to wide audiences. The core of his most influential work came in the thirty years following 1937 and represented his interests in southern, western, frontier, and state history.

Clark's interest in the movement west brought forth his rollicking and readable *The Rampaging Frontier* (1939) and two decades later his much-used work *Frontier America* (1959). *Frontiers in Conflict* (with John D. W. Guice, 1989) completed that trilogy. Writing initially at a time when the Frederick Jackson Turner thesis held sway, Clark proclaimed his distance from it and represented the transitional position between the Turner school and newer interpretations.

That same interest in the frontier involved Clark in studying the "First West" that was Kentucky. His *History of Kentucky*, written at age thirty-four, represented a major feat of scholarship, given the poor state of Kentucky's archives at the time. It remained a standard text for some six decades. *The Kentucky* (1942), his volume in the Rivers of America series, and his excellent *Kentucky: Land of Contrast* (1968) in the Regions of America series offered both fresh examinations and solid interpretations of their subjects.

Clark's strongest and in some ways most enduring work was in the field of southern history. In fact, his first major foray into the study of the land of his birth may have been his best book. *Pills, Petticoats, and Plows: The Southern Country Store* (1944) remains a classic. The author tramped across the region, personally gathering country store records, many on the verge of destruction, and then used that storehouse of research to fashion a readable and even touching portrait of an institution crucial to the South. His next two works, both published in 1948, performed the same service for newspapers in the region—*The Rural Press and the New South* and *The Southern Country Editor*. Three important books followed in the 1960s, representing his mature scholarly judgment and understanding of the South's evolving Second Reconstruction. *The Emerging South* (1961), *Three Paths to the Modern South* (1965), and *The South since Appomattox* (with A. D. Kirwan, 1967) presented a southern way of life "caught in the great web of revolt against the past." They told of revolution while "the ghost of the past stalked the land trying to reincarnate itself." That same discussion of change continued in his pathbreaking 1984 work, *The Greening of the South: The Recovery of Land and Forest.*

Clark edited numerous other works—for instance, his important, multivolume *Travels in the South,* travel diaries, and other works on the frontier and on the South. He also wrote a series of Kentucky-based studies, particularly in the last three decades of his life. Many in the historical profession rediscovered Tom Clark only recently, when he gave wonderful talks, all without notes or prepared text, at meetings of the Southern Historical Association in 2003 and 2004. After hearing him, new generations of scholars revisited his books, to their pleasure.

This memoir—his last book—was completed shortly before his death. Parts of it had appeared earlier, in such places as the *Journal of American History,* the *Western Historical Quarterly,* and the *Kentucky Review,* or had been given as talks, but much of it was new and fresh when he submitted the manuscript for publication in January 2005. Fresh from talking that day to a group of what he called "wriggly" first graders, he turned over the typed pages to the director of the University Press of Kentucky with the words "I promise you . . . that I won't be at all upset if you think it's not worth publishing." The manuscript then underwent the publisher's usual formal review process and received final Editorial Board approval in March 2005.

After its acceptance by the Press, Clark wrote additional material as requested by the three outside readers and worked with Georgiana Strickland, an editor he greatly respected, to integrate the new material into the earlier manuscript. He had approved the first six edited chapters before his short illness and death in June brought his participation to a close. After he passed away, Georgiana Strickland continued her yeoman work in putting together the diverse parts to make the book here presented. Loretta Clark helped her in many crucially important ways,

Dr. Clark's children perused material relevant to the family for accuracy, and historians Terry Birdwhistell, John E. Kleber, Charles P. Roland, and the individual he called "Young Jim Klotter" looked over the work at various times to ensure that it remained true to Tom Clark's voice and did full justice to its author. At the Press, director Steve Wrinn, together with Anne Dean Watkins, Lin Wirkus, and David Cobb, shepherded it through the publication process.

Despite writing a shelfful of books, despite all his scholarly production and professional service, in the end Thomas D. Clark may be best remembered for his efforts in the field of public history. Seldom has a member of the academic community been so revered by so many, in any state. Part of that resulted from his efforts to build accessible research collections for scholars and the interested public alike. He played a major role in organizing the Special Collections at the University of Kentucky, the University Press of Kentucky, the State Archives, and the Kentucky History Center. A translation of an inscription in St. Paul's Church in London, England, is entirely apt for Clark: "If you would see the man's monuments, look around you."

But his monuments also include the people he touched. Simply said, Clark became "the people's historian." He did not confine himself to reading dusty tomes or faint microfilms behind some ivy-covered library wall. Tom Clark also walked the land and talked with the people around him. He did oral history before it became fashionable, and his books and talks reflected the stories he heard. Moreover, the often critical but usually optimistic Clark became an advocate for constitutional change, educational reform, conservation, and a future-oriented public agenda. If Kentuckians had done all the things that Tom Clark sought for his adopted state, they would have a better commonwealth now and a brighter promise for the future. In a sense, he stood as the unofficial conscience of Kentucky and, by extension, of America.

Tom Clark argued that current generations have unparalleled access to centuries of knowledge and experience. But when a *New York Times* survey revealed how little history Americans knew, Clark agreed, saying, "They know too little to wander safely out on Main Street alone."

Yet he placed much of the fault at the feet of historians: "We haven't fed them." Clark sought to remedy that and accepted nearly every invitation to speak, no matter the group or the size of audience. He gave hundreds of such talks after he "retired." While he spoke well the language of academe, Clark could also talk—and write—so that all could understand and learn from history. He continued to teach long after he left the classroom.

Thus, though Clark lived a long life, he made each year count. This memoir shows that while our world will be a much poorer place historically without Tom Clark the historian, it will be an even poorer place, in all respects, without Tom Clark the man.

James C. Klotter
State Historian of Kentucky and
Professor of History
Georgetown College

My Century in History

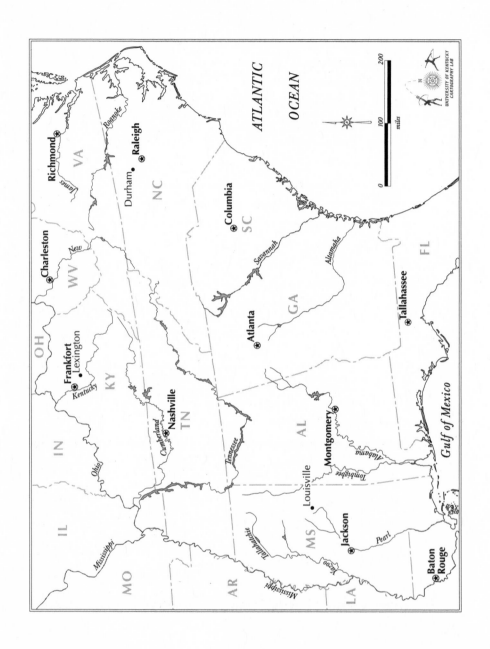

The Land of the Dancing Rabbit

I WAS BORN AND SPENT THE FIRST QUARTER CENTURY of my life in the heart of the former Choctaw Nation, which, since 1817, has been known as the State of Mississippi. During my youth I oriented almost as well with Choctaw nomenclature and legend as with that of "Old Carolina." The personal names of Choctaw chiefs Pushmataha, Mushulatubbee, and others were almost household names. My home county of Winston was surrounded by Noxubee, Oktibbeha, Choctaw, and Neshoba Counties. I attended high school in Choctaw County. In the vicinity were to be found such place names as Mushulaville, Noxapater, Shuqalak, Wahalak, and Scooba. Headstreams bore the names Noxubee, Tombigbee, and Tallahega, as well as Pearl and Big Black. For me, these Choctaw names were as commonplace as Winston or Louisville, the seat of Winston County.

The Choctaw homeland originally extended from central western Alabama across the broad waist of what is now Mississippi to the great river. Probably no historian can say positively when the tribal Choctaws first appeared in the area. Whenever they came and wherever they came from, in their new home they adapted to an arboreal-agrarian way of life. Generally they lived in reasonable peace with their Chickasaw and Creek neighbors and tolerated white intruders.

The extensive scope of the Choctaw territory was drained by a multiplicity of streams, including the Noxubee-Tombigbee, Tallahega, Pearl, and Big Black–Mississippi systems. The land—swamp and ridge—was both virginal and fertile and was generously dotted with freshwater springs. In the eyes of subsequent settlers it was highly adaptable to the growing of cotton, corn, sugar cane, and other crops. The opening of this land to white settlers during the decades 1820–1840 slipped the latch for a regional land rush of emigrants fleeing the rapidly depleting soils of the upper Piedmont South. Their arrival generated almost irresistible pressure on the federal government to remove the Indian population.

The history of this era and region comprises a fascinating but complex chapter in the history of American folk movements. Documentary sources are fairly plentiful for the political aspect, but there is a paucity of personal materials. No doubt an overwhelming majority of the emigrants to the Old Southwest were completely ignorant of the incidents that had opened the region to settlement. While they looked upon Andrew Jackson as the hero of the Battle of New Orleans, and knew of the crushing battles against the Creek Indians at Horse Shoe Bend and the inhumane and murderous actions on the Tallapoosa River in Alabama, most had probably never heard of the Treaty of Dancing Rabbit Creek.

That document resulted from a council gathered on the sloping shoulder of the creek on September 27, 1830. There Generals John Eaton and John Coffee secured the reluctant signature of Chief Greenwood LeFlore. Drafted in Washington, the treaty required the Choctaws to surrender their lands in Mississippi and cleared the way for their removal to territory west of the Mississippi River. So high-handed was the action of the federal negotiators that they fled the treaty ground immediately after the halfhearted signing of the document.

The Treaty of Dancing Rabbit Creek removed the Indian barrier to settlement and marked the opening chapter in the brutal suffering and death that would befall the Choctaws along the "Trail of Tears." Yet by no means were all the Choctaws removed from their homeland. Many took refuge in the almost impenetrable Noxubee and Pearl River swamps. All left a heritage of nomenclature, folk medicine, and folk history. A sizable number, in fact, are still on the land. They maintain their attachment to the great Nanih Waiya Mound and Cave, constant sources of regret about the past. Much of their swampland is still intact.

The opening of Mississippi found surveyors ready to lay out counties, establish township, range, and section boundaries, and welcome claimants. Among their number was Colonel Louis Winston who, equipped with a compass, a four-pole chain, and a tomahawk, carved out a large square block of land and named it Winston County. To stroke his ego further he located its seat and named it Louisville (pronounced Lewisville), ignoring the more applicable Choctaw names of Tallahega, Noxubee, Neshoba, Mushulaville, and Nanih Waiya. After 1830 there descended upon these lands a veritable horde of emigrants, largely from South Carolina. They came in search of fortune, peace, and a new start in life. Within two decades 4,650 settlers, some thousand of whom were black slaves, arrived in Winston County alone.

Among those making the long and arduous journey into the Old Southwest were my Clark and Bennett ancestors. In the mid-1830s four Clark brothers loaded up their families and meager household furnishings and set out from Anderson County, South Carolina, in search of fertile lands, timber, and fresh spring water. My Bennett ancestors made the trek west from Charleston. In time both of my ancestral lines settled in Winston County.

Of all the American land rushes, the one to the Old Southwest offered perhaps the most dynamic challenges. The dollar cost per acre was low, but to bring these lands to settlement condition required an enormous expenditure of human energy. This was the age of large families and the indenture of sons until they reached the age of majority. So it was with the Clarks, the Bennetts, and their collateral families.

For three-quarters of a century I have gone back to the homeland of the Choctaw Nation and that of my immediate ancestors. I have visited the lonely scene of the meeting of the Choctaws with the wily Jacksonian manipulators, the Nanih Waiya Mound, and Colonel Louis Winston's county and town. All of these monumental sites stir deeply in my soul an everlasting fealty to place. Time has dimmed the history of the region, and so-called progress gnaws at the very heart of the land. Where once my great-grandfather laid claim to land and built his house beside a muddy stretch of earth, there is now projected a four-lane concrete highway leading straight to the Choctaw casino, where tribesmen have the last victory by stripping the sons and daughters of the old emigrants of their cash. For me, however, the land of the Dancing Rabbit is burned deeply in memory as a place of origin.

I

~

The Long Road Home

My ANCESTORS BEGAN THEIR JOURNEYS FAR AWAY from their final destinations. En route they passed through several layers of human culture and were well seasoned by rugged environmental conditions. It is doubtful that any of my forebears had any clear notion of what they were really seeking. Like thousands of eighteenth-century immigrants to North America from the British Isles, the Clarks and Bennetts were caught up in a state of restlessness created by economic depression and the diminishing quality of land, as well as by political and religious pressures.

Information about the Clark family is sparse and sometimes conflicting. According to one source, two brothers, John and Joseph Clarke, sons of Thomas and Rose Kerrich Clarke, emigrated from Suffolk County, England, and settled in Rhode Island Plantation in 1637 or 1638. Dr. John Clarke (1609–1676) became an important figure in the political and cultural affairs of Rhode Island Plantation, enough so that he merited an extensive sketch in the *Dictionary of American Biography*.

John's younger brother, Joseph (1618–1694), settled in Newport, Rhode Island. He and his wife, Margaret, produced eight children. Their oldest son, Joseph (1642–1726), and his wife, Bethia Hubbard (1646–1717), had nine children, of whom the oldest son was again named Joseph. This third Joseph (born 1694) married Elizabeth Nichols, and together they migrated to the James River Valley of Virginia and later to Prince Edward County, where their only son, the fourth to bear the name Joseph, was born in 1732. Together with one or two of his sons, this fourth Joseph is believed to have been present as a militiaman in Yorktown at the surrender of Lord Cornwallis in 1781.

Another source of genealogical information says that the third Joseph was in fact the first in my Clark line to immigrate from England to the colonies and came directly to Virginia in the 1730s. Information on the remaining generations is the same in both sources.

Matthew, my direct ancestor and grandson of the third (or first) Joseph, was born in Goochland County, Virginia, in 1763. Because he was an underage volunteer during the Revolution, he probably never formally joined the Virginia militia, a fact he regretted the rest of his life, since he was unable to claim a military pension. In 1790 Matthew married Abigail Baldwin of Prince Edward County, Virginia, and they later migrated to the hilly Savannah River backcountry of Anderson County, South Carolina. There, along with their four Virginia-born sons and another son born in South Carolina, they cleared a homestead and established a subsistence way of farm life. Abigail died in 1811 and Matthew married twice more, but I am descended from his first marriage.

Like American backcountry folk in general, the Clarks (somewhere along the way they dropped the *e*) either made or kept few family records or personal diaries and letters. It must be assumed that Matthew's family heard by the grapevine about the Indian territorial cessions in Alabama and Mississippi. Certainly they were aware of the great folk movement in that direction. However they learned about the Treaty of Dancing Rabbit Creek and the Jacksonian removal of the Choctaws, Matthew's four sons contracted emigration fever.

Like all trail emigrants, four of the Clark brothers, together with their families, loaded their wagons with household plunder and what farm implements they could carry, and herded and flocked their cattle, hogs, sheep, and poultry. Thus equipped, they set forth to the far-off Eden. There were long stretches of hill pine and swamp hardwood forest to penetrate and myriad bridgeless streams to ford. In general the Clark caravan followed the well-worn emigrant route across Georgia and Alabama, halting long enough in the latter state to grow a crop. Near the end of their trek they arrived at the central western boundary of Pickens County, Alabama, just east of the flatlands of the Noxubee River drainage system. Just over the river and in the heart of the Choctaw lands, Thomas Baldwin Clark (born 1791), Matthew's oldest son and the leader of the family, like Moses of old, came to the edge of the promised land but never moved on. He died in 1847 and lies today in an unmarked but identified grave plot. The other three sons of Matthew and Abigail Clark either remained in Alabama or moved on to the opening frontiers in Arkansas and Texas. In time their family clans grew numerous, if not wealthy or famous.

My great-grandfather John Collingsworth Clark (1815–1900), oldest son of Thomas Baldwin Clark and Jane McClure Clark, moved on to higher ground to locate and establish a permanent homestead on a fertile tract of cotton land along the Hughes Creek, a branch of the Pearl River, in the newly organized Winston County, Mississippi. He located his home on the winding dirt road south of the county seat town of Louisville. There he and his wife, Matilda Pee Clark of Fairfield County, South Carolina, created a fixed family base. He was home at last.

Like his ever-gathering neighbors, John C. made only a modest claim, to a quarter section (160 acres) of land. No doubt the difficulty of clearing this wild land was a central fact in his limiting the size of the claim. On this land the Clark family put down permanent roots. It would be occupied by several generations of the family to come.

John C. and his sons constructed a log house beneath the shade of an unusually large "black Spanish" variety pecan tree. The house stood close beside the road, which had no doubt once been a Choctaw trail through the pine and swamp wilderness. In time it would become part of the road connecting Middle Tennessee with the Gulf of Mexico. The size of the rooms in the house was governed by the availability of long, straight timbers and the capability of the builders to hew, notch, and lift the logs into place. The Carolina-type house had two large rooms with the traditional hall, or dogtrot, dividing them. The rooms were laced together in the rear by a long hip-roofed shed and on the front by a full-length piazza, or veranda.

In this building there was space enough to house the members of the rapidly expanding family. John C. and Matilda had need of ample space to bed down their eleven children. The big "front room" of the homestead might well have been labeled a birthing center. My grandfather, my father, and I were born there, as were many other family members. The rambling old house was a comfortable family haven. When John C.'s nephew Micajah rode back to Mississippi after a return visit to Anderson and Pendleton Counties, South Carolina, he made note of a pleasant visit with his uncle's family and their thriving homestead.

John and Matilda were diligent and thrifty settlers. In time John and his maturing sons cleared the heavy forest growth from the land, burned and destroyed the canebrakes, and planted fields of corn and cotton. They grew ribbon, or Louisiana, sugar cane and sorghum, planted fruit trees, and cultivated generous family-sized vegetable gardens. They built a large log barn, a molasses mill, a blacksmith shop, and a cabin to house a Choctaw Indian tenant. The family drew almost all of their subsistence from the land. Cattle and hogs ranged the woods, bearing earcrops signifying their ownership. Fields were enclosed within split-rail fences to keep the animals on the outside. In general outline the original Clark homestead was a duplicate of the ancient English enclosure system of land management.

When Matilda Pee Clark died in 1884, John sent his sons to locate a gravesite in the outer limits of the orchard. There they buried the pioneer mother who had made the arduous journey southwestward, and erected at her head a slender stone shaft on which were carved the year and place of her birth and the year of her death. In time other members of the family and neighbors were buried alongside her. They named the burying ground Flower Ridge.

Along with their folkways and culture, the Clark family brought with them a strong commitment to the teachings of John Wesley and the evangelism of circuit riders. The Clarks and their neighbors built a Methodist church alongside the graveyard, an institution that has endured through changing times. My grandfather Thomas Whitfield Clark was representative of the traditional Virginia-Carolina social bearing. His courtship notes to Janie Elvira Cagle are all in "dripping" Victorian prose.

Janie, my grandmother, was from a third-generation German immigrant family that had become Americanized in western North Carolina. Her father, Charles Cagle, was attracted to the opening of the southwestern Choctaw lands. He and his family traveled south through eastern Tennessee to Mississippi. In the first part of their journey they followed the old hog road, and in Mississippi they reached Winston County by way of the road Andrew Jackson had opened during the War of 1812 and before the Battle of New Orleans. Charles established a blacksmith shop in Louisville and settled down for good.

After a courtship of socially acceptable length, Thomas Whitfield Clark married Janie Elvira Cagle and took her to live on a tract of land adjoining his father's place. Following in his father's footsteps Thomas established a subsistence farm and built a log house and barn, a blacksmith shop, a smokehouse, and a cotton house. He hired a "jack leg"* carpenter to fashion some household furniture from heart pine and swamp-grown oak. On that land Thomas and Janie became the parents of twelve offspring, a homegrown labor force within itself. The family, like its pioneering ancestors, drew its living and a limited amount of cash from the land. Thomas's cotton was processed on a horse-powered gin, then hauled away on a two-day journey to the nearest cotton buyer in Meridian.

Almost overlooked by historians of the South is the fact that nonslaveholding plain folk of the region depended for labor upon their numerous male offspring. There prevailed an almost unspoken folk rule that sons would remain with their parents until they reached the major-

---

* Self-taught

ity age of twenty-one years. This concept was a strong one in both my ancestral families.

My Bennett maternal ancestors shared many experiences with the Clarks, but there were also differences. They, too, were of English origin, having reached Charleston, South Carolina, by way of the Barbados trade route, probably in the late 1700s. Little is known about this immigrant family that landed in North America. John Adam Bennett was born probably before 1790 and grew up in Charleston. He seems to have been a blacksmith, a tinkerer, and a merchant in a modest way. In 1818 he married the widow Eliza Shelbaback. Sometime in 1830 the Bennett family moved to Autauga, Alabama, probably by coastal ship from Charleston to Mobile. A son, Joseph Mason Bennett, my great-grandfather, was born in Charleston, moved with his family to Autauga, and later moved to Winston County, Mississippi. Somewhere in his moves he met the widow Sarah Clark Eatman and married her. Sarah had been married to Duncan Eatman, a Charlestonian who had contracted the Choctaw land fever and begun the long trek southwestward. In Elberton, Georgia, he became ill and died, leaving Sarah and their two children stranded without funds or friends. Fortunately a family named Oliver befriended her. Male members of the Oliver family for several generations back had borne the name of the ancient god Dionysus, which they spelled Dyonicious.

Joseph and Sarah Bennett settled in Winston County and built a home on the "Wire" Road near Louisville. Joseph Mason Bennett was not a farmer and seems to have had little desire to own land. He moved into town and became a merchant. When my maternal grandfather was born, Sarah named him Dyonicious in gratefulness to her Oliver benefactors. Later, when I was born, my mother named me for my two grandfathers. She could never have imagined the burden that middle name has been for me over the years. It seems that certain ignoramuses introducing me as a speaker think it humorous that I bear such an outlandish name. Many times I have had grave doubts about my indebtedness to that ancient Greek god or to the five generations of Georgia Olivers. On one occasion I did have an opportunity to come close to my namesake when

I stood in the pleasant valley in Thebes where legend says Dionysus was born. Another time I caught up with Dionysus when I visited the site of the great Alexandrian palace and saw the wonderful mosaic that had been dug out of the sands of the Aegean Sea. In that setting he was riding a tiger, which seemed more in keeping with his lifestyle.

Dyonicious was the only one of the five sons of Joseph and Sarah Bennett who became a farmer. He was successful, within the context of time and place, as both a dirt farmer and a livestock breeder. He was willing to experiment in both fields. While a young man opening new fields and becoming a farmer, he met Alice McGee, a Methodist who lived in adjoining Choctaw County. Alice was a third-generation Scotch-Irish daughter of John McGee, the son of John and Edna Field McGee, who were married in Ireland on the eve of their departure for the Carolinas. Dyonicious and Alice produced a family of ten children, of whom my mother, Sallie Jesse, was the second.

Thus both my paternal and my maternal families settled in Winston County and remained there for four generations. From earliest memory I have carried in my mind an unsolved puzzle. Though the Clarks and Bennetts lived only five miles apart as the crow flies, they apparently never had social or business interrelations until my parents met and married in 1902. My father, John Collingsworth Clark, named for his grandfather, met my mother when she became a teacher in the one-room Flower Ridge School. She had attended the Southern Female College in West Point, and this was her first teaching assignment.

Both the Clarks and the Bennetts had remained within the southern thermal belt that reached from the Carolinas to the Gulf of Mexico, and favored the soil types and general environmental conditions they had known in the Upper South. Socially and culturally both families clung rather faithfully to folk customs and ways of life that had their origins in other times and places. Family blood and kinship reached far out into cousinships. They were profoundly committed to the Methodist faith, perhaps without actually knowing who John Wesley was or what he believed. They were fully literate, but no branch of my family had any zeal for formal learning beyond the fourth grade. My grandfather Bennett's "blueback" speller virtually documents this fact. Both families read the Bible, but none seems to have kept personal diaries or engaged in more than limited amounts of letter writing. None were poets or artists. Curiously, none of them was a wood craftsman despite the fact that they had available a wide variety of wood specimens. Their focus was on the land and its agricultural promise.

Perhaps one of the most distinguishing characteristics of both pioneering families was their ability to make quick adjustments to place and environment. Their adjustment to forest and field proved a powerful force, setting new standards of domestic life and economy. Both the Clarks and the Bennetts were forced by geographical and commercial conditions to extract their livelihood from the land. This included a long list of products that ranged from house-yard chickens to ribbon and sorghum molasses and brown sugar. Both ridge and swamplands were highly adaptable to the production of short-staple cotton, but the distance to market for cotton meant that transportation almost absorbed the capital returns from the cotton crop.

FROM THE LATE 1830s TO THE closing years of the nineteenth century the populace of Winston County was geographically, sociologically, and commercially isolated from the rest of America. Only winding and muddy or dusty dirt road umbilical cords connected the people with the world outside. In the twenty-first century it is challenging to try to visualize the community as it was then: a gaggle of general-store merchants who carried limited stocks of supplies that had been hauled in on two-horse wagons over distances of fifty or sixty miles. There existed no bank, no credit facilities of any kind, no warehouse, and no industries more complex than a small three- or four-man "peckerwood" sawmill or a one-horse cotton gin. Cotton farmers bought only the essential metal parts for creating wooden plow stocks, made collars out of corn shucks to harness their plow mules, and relied on hand-shaped tools for harvesting and processing grain crops. Hand tools were at best crude and required considerable skill to use. For instance, a phenomenal amount of muscle and skill were required to hew flat sides on logs and then notch them and lift them into place to build a log house, barn, or smokehouse. Wagons and buggies were crude vehicles in which to travel. Much of the traveling, however, was done on horseback, with ample saddlebags flung across the saddles. Horseback-riding women rode in cumbersome side saddles, many times holding one child up front, with another clinging behind.

Clearing land from virgin forest was a major undertaking in Winston County until the era of World War I. It took stout arms, legs, and backs to fell trees, cut them into short logs, pile the brush, and get ready for a communal logrolling. Fields and pastures were opened a few acres at a time. These tasks might never have been performed so frequently had there not been festival aspects to the logrollings.

By 1850 Winston County had accumulated a population of 5,175 individuals, 2,768 of whom were black slaves. By that date most of the population lived on 551 so-called "improved" farms covering 40,627 cleared acres out of a total land area of 160,672 acres. Still in the wilderness, the cotton farmers of the county could in no way claim status with the famous cotton snobbery of the older settled region around Natchez. They produced in 1849 only 3,091 bales of cotton.

Some of my Clark and Bennett ancestors owned a few slaves, but none took a strong position in the great controversy over that institution. In fact, few individuals in Winston County in the waning antebellum years developed a burning passion over the issue of slavery or later secession. But soon after the firing on Fort Sumter young Clark, Cagle, and Richardson volunteers joined the ranks of the Confederate army. The Richardsons were cousins on my grandmother's side. Two of my youthful great-uncles joined a Confederate command and marched north just in time to get caught up, untrained and poorly armed, in the battle of Shiloh Church. One of them received a bullet wound in the stomach and died on the steps of the church. My great-uncle Pinckney Cagle was in the first battle of Bull Run. Later he was bugler in Nathan Bedford Forrest's command, and then he rode with "Fighting" Joe Wheeler.

Winston County itself was too isolated and primeval to be invaded by anybody, except for one frightening appearance by Benjamin Grierson's Illinois raiders, who were riding south hell-for-leather in 1863 to cut the Confederate rail supply line at Newton. The people of Louisville literally boarded and locked up the town, including great-grandfather Cagle's blacksmith shop. Just outside town the raiders overtook a luckless Confederate messenger who was carrying saddlebags full of Confederate monetary notes and confidential communications from Vicksburg and Jackson. No harm was done to the town. The command was in too big a hurry to get on to Newton and the railroad to stop and steal horses or silverware or burn houses. But Grierson's raiders fell victim to the legendary wrath of Chief Mushulatubbee. The heavens opened up and sent a flood roaring and swirling down Tallahega Creek just in time to catch the Yankees. A *New York Times* reporter described the scene as resembling Edgar Allan Poe's "Descent into the Maelstrom." Horses were drowned, but miraculously no human lives were lost. This was perhaps the only time Winston County ever received notice in the *New York Times*. I can claim a slight trace of fame from Grierson's raid. He and his cavalrymen rode by within a hundred yards of the room in which I would later be born.

Almost miraculously, Winston County and Louisville suffered no physical harm in the war aside from a creekful of cavalry horses. None of my families had slaves to lose, and my grandfathers were too young to join the Confederate army, though my grandfather Bennett had to hide in the woods on one occasion to avoid guerrilla raiders, known as "bushwhackers."

Life in most respects went on at its accustomed pace after the war. The most significant ripple was the fact that a large slave population was freed almost overnight. In some of the former slaveholding families there remained a close sentimental attachment between former masters and their ex-slaves, an attachment that in some cases endured for two or three generations.

My grandfather Bennett later described for me some of the postwar racial incidents during the disturbing years of Radical Reconstruction. On one occasion he witnessed the brutal whipping of a black youth for no reason other than imagined impudence. There was organized in the county a klavern of the Ku Klux Klan. Only my great-uncle Pinckney

Cagle and my grandmother Bennett's cousin Bogg Ellis joined the Klan. When the Congressional Reconstruction Commission came to Winston County in 1865–1866 because of reported incidents of racial brutality, the visit generated a generous amount of anger and fear. The testimony of some of the "testifiers" gave insight into local reactions to the issue of the freedmen. The commission's visit, however, brought an end to Ku Klux Klan activities. No longer did headless horsemen ride along country roads, sending up ungodly screams and waving flaming torches.

Thus my immediate and extended families lived through the Civil War and Radical Reconstruction with little disruption of their lives. They were, however, sensitively aware that the state of Mississippi had suffered severe losses and experienced radical changes in its politics and way of life. There followed a bitter period of political chaos. I was not born until decades later but gained a spiritual sense of the era through often-told fireside accounts—accounts that made a deep impression on my youthful memory. Changes during this period came rapidly to the Choctaw lands, if not necessarily for the Clarks and Bennetts. By the sterile postwar era they had long established their way of life and were bound by folkways and devotion to place. There was almost no outmigration of family members. Instead, an overpowering provinciality set in that bonded man and land.

IF I COULD HAVE CHOSEN the time and place of my birth, I might have chosen Louisville and Winston County, if for no other reason than to experience the seminal changes that came to the area at the turn of the twentieth century. In 1903, the year of my birth as my parents' firstborn child, railway surveyors were slogging their way through the bogs of Tallahega Swamp, locating a ground-level right-of-way for a railroad that was slowly creeping north from Mobile. The plan was to link up with Colonel J. W. T. Falkner's road into middle Tennessee. Merchants in dusty Louisville were reluctant to subscribe for stock in the line, so the engineers developed a plan to build a depot five miles out of town on the banks of the Tallahega. This bluff produced a subscription of $17,000, and the depot was built in town.

In 1904 a banker appeared in Louisville seeking a place to establish a branch bank. On his heels came the organizer of a telephone company, and new stores were built on Main Street. But no change had a greater impact than the organization of a stock company cotton warehouse. No longer need farmers make long journeys to find cotton buyers. Mississippi was now part of the national cotton market, and the opening up of the timberlands brought new prosperity to the state.

Progress in Louisville mirrored the expansion in the life of the nation. Teddy Roosevelt was president, and the success of the recently concluded Spanish-American War led to the expansion of American power into Puerto Rico, the Caribbean, and the Philippines. These events would ultimately have an impact in Mississippi. It was an exciting time in which to be growing up.

The lapse of seventy years between the signing of the Dancing Rabbit Treaty and the dawning of a new Progressive age was by many standards a relatively short interval. But in the case of my homeland it was an extended age of shedding a frontier image and becoming a reluctant part of the new age of American modernization. In many respects it was a glorious experience to be born in that transitional historical moment. The old order ended, for example, when patrons no longer had to ride substantial distances to inquire for their mail at the Louisville post office. In my second year of life a rural free delivery carrier passed by my home. It was now possible to subscribe to a newspaper and learn what was happening in the world out beyond county boundaries.

In 1903 one could figuratively look back to County Suffolk in England, to New England, Virginia, the Carolinas, and the great emigrant road that had led into the Choctaw homeland, and to my family's final settlement in a permanent place as a long road home. Johnnie Collingsworth's big old rambling double log house stood intact until the mid-twentieth century, home to generations of Clarks.

2

~

OLD PLACE, NEW PLACE

AFTER THE ELAPSE OF A CENTURY, I BELIEVE I STILL have a clear memory of the plain houses that sheltered my family and a strong sense of connection to those places. Consciously or unconsciously, migrants to Mississippi transported to the Old Southwest their memories of Virginia and the Carolinas. None were more tangibly demonstrated than those of simple domestic architectural forms. Even the big old double log, or dogtrot, structures reflected more than a whim of earlier home design. At the time of my birth and early years, a good proportion of the Mississippi white population was housed in plain, unpainted, framed-board buildings that somewhat resembled the more refined features of the so-called "plantation" houses in the older settled regions of the Upper South.

Early in my life my father and mother pursued the eternal southern dream of owning a piece of land and settling down on it in a first-stage house. When I was born, in 1903, they were living with my grandfather

Clark in the old family homestead. When I was about one year old they bought a farm known as the "Watson Place" (Watson had been a major in the Confederate army) and constructed their first house. Three of my siblings were born there—brothers John Marvin in 1904 and Ernest Lester in early 1908. My first sister, Ellia Brown, was born there in 1906 but died at just under one year of age. We lived on the Watson Place until 1908, when my parents sold that farm and, on the same day, bought a farm from the Smith Boswell family near my grandfather Bennett's home. There they built what came to be called the "New Place." My remaining siblings were born there—Walter Ervin in 1909, Wilma Effie in 1911, and Ethel Lou in 1913.

Deed records indicate that my mother and father cleared a profit on the exchange of farms. They may still have owed something on the "Old Place," but if so it does not appear in their papers. They paid five dollars an acre for the Boswell place and were left with $400.00, which they doubtless used to build the new house.

Both houses were reduced shadows of the pioneer log structure built by my grandfather Clark, with two rooms divided by a dogtrot hall and a long shed at the back that housed the kitchen, the dining room, and a catchall room. Across the entire front was an ample veranda, sometimes referred to as a piazza or gallery, and there was another on the back. This appurtenance was as much a part of the southern home as the family sitting-bedroom. I am certain no member of my family or our neighbors ever conceived of the front porch as a sociologically significant open-air parlor, but climate and folk custom made it so.

On the afternoon of July 15, 1953, as I sat in a faculty assembly called by Dean Giles Alington of University College, Oxford University, a messenger appeared at the door and handed Dean Alington a telegram from my brother Ernest informing me that my father had died. I was unable to return home in time for the funeral. When I did return to Mississippi to visit my mother, I was told that my father had sat on the front veranda talking to visitors until a late evening hour, a thing he thoroughly enjoyed doing. His last moments had been spent in a pleasant southern environment. Possibly to a majority of rural southern householders, the front porch was as much a cherished social center as their church, a place where neighbors came to "set awhile," to gossip, to do their verbal farming, and to argue politics and religion, topics of endless veranda forums. Thus in my childhood and youth I was bonded to the porch as a place for baring the soul and embracing the freedom of the land that spread out before us.

Sometime in the late 1890s or the early years of this century an ingenious folk craftsman introduced to the southern veranda an angular wooden creation called a "porch swing." If a young man could "shy" the old folks away and persuade a country girl to sit beside him in a swing, there was no better courting place. It far outdid even an overstuffed "front room" with all its colored glass ornaments and fake china statuary. The swing was even more conducive to hand-holding than looking through travelogue brochures or family photograph albums.

The Mississippi country veranda of my boyhood was truly what modern sociologists have come to call "place." Aside from the congenial evening folk gatherings, the courtings, the watermelon cuttings, and the swinging, it was a place of soft southern twilight with all the subtleties of life itself. Here was the ideal place to sense the changing rhythms of nature. As darkness came on and temperatures dropped, the whippoorwills would open their symphony of mating calls and territorial declarations, and the July bugs and katydids would awaken to carry on their ceaseless night songs. Occasionally a great horned owl would send up bloodcurdling hootings from a nearby tree, or its little sister the screech owl would utter its mournful notes reminiscent of the inevitability of death, and the nocturnal flying squirrel would join in the chorus with its squeakings. The veranda was the box seat from which one literally absorbed the mysteries of nature and the night.

We lived in harmony with the creatures of wild nature, declaring war only upon snakes and chicken hawks. In my boyhood there were numerous coveys of quail, a bountiful population of cottontail rabbits, dens of opossums and raccoons, and fleeting glimpses of foxes. All of these established territorial rights, with runs and special hiding places. Some of the animals burrowed dens under the clay roots of storm-tossed trees or in the numerous sinkholes created by underwater veins. It was a common experience to come on roosting circles where quail had bedded down, tails inward and heads pointed outward in every quarter of the compass for unimpeded flight if danger threatened. I came to know the ranges of the wild creatures and their habits. I never ceased to be thrilled at finding a quail's nest filled with a prodigious number of small, pointed eggs tucked away securely in a tuft of broom sedge. In early spring we would find the fur-lined nurseries of the sedge-field rabbits harboring their clutches of defenseless young.

Most of the animals had instinctive modes of self-preservation. From the moment baby quail cracked the egg case, they were alert to the dangers that lurked in their grassy world. What they did not inherit instinctively they quickly learned from their parents in the process of scurrying for food. I was always amazed by the fact that a covey of twenty marble-sized brown bodies could flatten themselves against the ground so thoroughly as to become virtually invisible when an intruder was near.

Our new farm was located west of the Tallahega Swamp, and the springbranch streams on the land drained into it. The lush swampland supported a dense stand of virgin trees interspersed with reed brakes and occasional sloughs. The lateral creek that ran nearby contained a couple of good swimming holes and several good fishing spots. Big buck-toothed, cane-cutter swamp rabbits flourished in the undergrowth, and raccoons and mink beat out trails to the water's edge, searching for minnows and crawfish. This wilderness was not without its dangers. Large timber rattlesnakes flourished in the moist brakes. For young boys the swamps were places of constant adventure, with just enough threat of danger to keep invaders ever alert.

A most agreeable neighbor owned the cotton farm through which Reedy Creek ran, and he was generous in giving us free access to the swamp. We regarded this neighbor with both respect and a sense of humor. By a fortuitous political maneuver of the sort for which Mississippi was famous, he got himself elected to the Mississippi House of Representatives, and forever afterwards we called him "Senator." The "Senator's" parents and a large tribe of younger siblings lived less than a mile away on the opposite side of our place. They enlivened things for the neighbors by joking and tormenting the "Senator." The Carters had emigrated some years earlier from Chester County, South Carolina, and they regaled us with comparisons of life in Chester and Winston Counties.

Thus it was in that place and time that my mother and father set out to establish a stable way of life for their growing family. My father literally chopped a cotton farm, a few acres a year, out of the woods. The year 1908 was a far from propitious one in which to begin the growing of cotton. That year Mississippi produced a bumper crop, leading the South in yield of lint cotton per acre. Never in a moment of his life was my father an optimist. He read the sparse stories that appeared in the *Winston County Journal* begging local farmers to reduce their cotton acreage and to hold their crops off the market until prices went up. That year a group of farmers and businessmen organized a warehouse company in Louisville, and for the first time bales of cotton could be stored indoors away from the weather and thieves. Too, there were employed official cotton weighers who, for ten cents a bale, assured farmers an honest weighing of their cotton.

I am certain that my father never stored his cotton or waited for a rise in price. He was at the mercy of both the merchant-cotton buyer and the far-removed cotton manipulators and speculators. How slender was our cash income. If we had depended on cotton alone we would have starved to death. My mother and father were truly subsistence farmers. In the first decade of the new century there was little need for any considerable amount of cash money in order to enjoy a fairly comfortable living on the reasonably fertile cotton farms in central Mississippi. My mother had a great love for the outdoors and possessed a magical green thumb. Her big vegetable gardens supplied generous varieties of vegetables year-round. Outside the garden fence were potato and pea patches that produced bountifully in that sandy soil. Ribbon and sorghum cane patches supplied our annual syrup need. My grandfather Bennett set an excellent example of "living off the land." He operated a cane mill that we used. Even yet I cringe at the memory of feeding cane stalks into the rollers and being splattered with juice, making me a perfect target for yellow jackets.

Despite the fact that we moved into a community with a fairly large school-age population, there was no nearby school. One summer neighbors built a brush arbor in which to hold a revival meeting. When the last echo of the hellfire preaching had died away and the shouters had calmed down, the arbor was turned over to my uncle Albert Bennett, a college sophomore, to teach a summer subscription school. That fall nearby parents built a rough one-room boarded house on the site of the brush arbor and called it Providence, no doubt because it was a providential miracle that it was built at all. Under the roof of that crude house I received my first exposure to formal education and gained my first taste for literature. The Mississippi Department of Education had adopted a series of modern readers to replace the hallowed McGuffey books. The new readers covered the common school curriculum from the primer to the tenth grade and were truly lineal descendants of the McGuffey readers. The Baldwin readers held great fascination for me. It was from them that I learned to read. Those for the early grades were liberally illustrated in color, which instantly caught childish attention. Like the McGuffeys, the Baldwin series was eclectic, with selections becoming more mature through the advancing grades. Through them I got my first sampling of American and English literature, along with a taste of ancient folklore and legend. I still own a set of these books, given to me by the American Book Company when I was a publishing author with them. Occasionally I look through these old readers and get a vicarious enjoyment from their modest challenges to pursue the gradual process of learning.

Over the years of a professional life, and even in retirement, I have sat for almost endless hours listening to committee discussions, to legislative hearings, and to private conversations about educational problems and inadequacies, and have spent more hours going through a mountain of local, state, and national educational reports and newspaper and periodical editorials, all decrying the low state of American public school education, the fact that "Johnny can't read." Teachers are reined up short for their inadequacies. Personally I cannot recall when I did not have an interest in and respect for books. My mother had a modest collection, and the Bennett family had several shelves up a stairway filled with miscellaneous books. My Bennett grandparents undertook to steer their grandchildren onto the road of success. One Christmas they gave each of us a ten-cent copy of Horatio Alger's moral and success offerings. I read that it paid to be industrious, frugal, honest, and vigilant, and that someday I could marry the boss's daughter and own his business.

My mother was a reader of books and magazines in a community where many people regarded such "foolishness" as a waste of time. They thought she should be running a spinning wheel or knitting socks—something "practical." I can say with certainty that she inspired in me a sense of the importance of reading. We subscribed to clubs of newspapers, an arrangement that allowed us to take several publications at a reduced rate. We took *Progressive Farmer* and the family magazine *Comfort*, published in Augusta, Maine. I was blessed indeed to have exposure to these materials. However poor were the Mississippi common schools in 1908–1916, I did get some elementary grounding and taste for learning. No doubt teachers, schools, and textbooks were working hard to prepare students to live by nineteenth-century standards as the twentieth pressed hard upon them.

I never completely mastered the intricacies of spelling many English words, but I had good elementary exposure. We never used the revered Webster's *Blue Back Speller*, but I had access to it. I own my grandfather Bennett's copy, with his boyish drawings and doodlings on every page. Mr. Webster would have sent him to the foot of the class to remain there until he erased his marks. The speller we used was less moralistic and didactic in tone and organization. All of my grade school teachers, including my mother, had students stand in line and spell against one another, and when you missed a word you went to the "foot of the line" to stay there until a faltering classmate took your place. Some teachers asked their pupils not only to spell words but also to break them down by syllables. Many Friday afternoons parents were invited to the school to attend spelling bees. Once a year several schools joined together to have field days in which spelling contests were principal events.

Teachers seldom taught more than a single term at Providence School. In 1915 my mother applied for the teaching position and was elected. By that time, however, the schoolhouse had burned under somewhat suspicious circumstances. Some said a black farmer, provoked by schoolboys muddying his spring and chasing his goats, was the villain. Whoever was responsible, when the building caught fire that summer afternoon the community was left without a place to hold school, and there was no will to build a new one. After that my mother taught in a vacant tenant house on our place. She taught four months a year for forty dollars a month, and often she was paid in county warrants that had to be discounted to receive cash. This meant she earned little more than the average cotton picker. She supplied a water bucket and dipper, painted the blackboard, bought crayons and erasers, and even rustled up the wood with which to fire the stove.

Nothing about a one-room schoolhouse caused so much trouble as a cheap cast-iron wood stove. One moment the room was too hot, and the next it was freezing. The stove consumed wood by the cord, the pipe was forever tumbling down, scattering soot everywhere, and even the stove itself might totter off its shaky legs and turn over. Parents were indifferent about furnishing firewood, and much of the time, boys were in the woods gathering fuel when they should have been attending to their studies in a properly heated room.

Poor, isolated Providence School was typical of the primitive rural Mississippi educational effort of that time. Funds for building and maintaining schoolhouses were meager indeed, and conditions under which instruction was given were almost never conducive to serious learning. My mother's teaching experience could well be considered a microcosm of teaching in general in Mississippi public elementary schools. She faced problems of disciplining obstreperous farm boys and girls. Frequently she sent a boy to the nearby woods to cut a switch with which to thrash a recalcitrant. After such whippings we waited with bated breath to see if there would be an angry parental reaction. I recall once when a contentious old neighbor came riding up through our cotton field at a furious gallop just after my mother had whipped his overgrown daughter for misbehaving. We virtually had my father's shotgun cocked and ready to defend our hearth when the old man dismounted and shouted, "Miss Sallie, I have come to thank you for whipping Minnie Lee."

TEACHER'S LICENSE.

No. *19* ———— *First* ————— Grade.

Office of County Superintendent,

...... *Winston* ...... County, Mississippi.

This Certifies that on 2̶1̶.8̶.2̶2̶ *R April* ...180*9*

...*Miss Sallie Bennett*...

Was examined according to law, and that ___*her*___ papers written on that day and now on file in this office, entitle ___*her*___ to a ___*1st*___ GRADE LICENSE, with the per cent. on each subject as marked below:

SPELLING	*90*	GRAMMAR	*80*
READING	*75*	COMPOSITION	*70*
GEOGRAPHY	*75*	UNITED STATES HISTORY	*85*
HISTORY OF MISSISSIPPI	*75*	ELEMENTS OF PHYSIOLOGY & HYGIENE	*80*
PRACTICAL ARITHMETIC	*90*	ELEMENTS OF NATURAL PHILOSOPHY	*50*
MENTAL ARITHMETIC	*94⅔*	CIVIL GOVERNMENT	*75*

GENERAL AVERAGE *86 ¾₄*

Upon satisfactory evidence that ___*she*___ possesses a good moral character, aptness to teach and ability to govern, I hereby authorize ___*her*___ to teach in the public schools of ___*Winston*___ County, for a period of ___*two*___ years from date of this examination.

J. T. McIntosh } Examiners. _____ Superintendent of *Winston* County.

☞ This License is not valid unless it shows the per cent. made on each subject and on the general average and is signed by the Examiners.

Sallie Bennett's 1899 teacher's license.

My mother taught at Providence, White Hall, and Scotts Springs. White Hall was too far from our farm to drive back and forth every day over the miserable dirt roads, so we would rent a shabby house near the school and camp there during the five-day school week. Mother would drive there in the buggy, taking with her Ernest and Wilma, while Marvin and I walked through Reedy Creek Swamp. Meanwhile my father would keep the home fires burning.

My mother was a dedicated classroom teacher. She saw to it that her pupils got down to business with their books and behaved themselves in the process. She made role models of her own children, and our father placed a threat over our heads if we caused our mother trouble in school. She kept us involved in some form of learning twelve months a year. I probably got as far as eighth grade under her tutelage.

THE OPENING DECADES OF THIS century were hard and uncertain years, especially for rural Mississippians. Hardly had my family settled on the new farm before there began to appear in the columns of the local newspaper, and in its ready-print columns, vague hints of future troubles for cotton farmers. Like subtle flashes of heat lightning, stories warned that the Mexican boll weevil had invaded Texas. In the following years reports described the insects' slow but certain migration toward Mississippi. Our neighboring cotton farmers, however, were more concerned about low prices, overproduction, and limited marketing facilities than the rumors of an unseen weevil. The *Winston County Journal* reported meetings of farmers in Louisville in which they discussed their plight, emphasizing the necessity to reduce cotton acreage. Actually these gatherings appeared only to boost production; greedy farmers believed their neighbors would reduce their crops and they themselves would make a killing by planting more. Paradoxically the *Journal* carried a story bragging that the United States Department of Agriculture said Mississippi had led the South the year before in the production of cotton, with 3,395,000 bales, or 283 pounds of lint per acre.

Despite the instability of cotton prices and the failure of farmers to take the advice of the Agricultural Extension Service to diversify their crops and produce more foodstuffs, life in hill country Mississippi in this era was not without color and excitement. Baptists and Methodists blended religion with recreation in a memorable way. No matter how long or how dull the sermons, there were great expectations for better things to come on "dinner-on-the-ground" Sundays. Annually at crop laying-by time there were revival meetings. Many times I have recalled the excitement of weeklong meetings in which relays of high-powered preachers and song leaders undertook to insulate our souls against all temptations during the coming year. I can only vicariously relive those days when we tore around in the afternoons, milking the cows, feeding the mules and hogs, and getting dressed for church. We could always count on some good Methodist sisters receiving a full measure of grace and prancing up and down the aisles uttering incoherent outbursts of joy at having been anointed with the spirit. I recall a chronic shouter who was said to be able to make a figure 8 with her arms and hug both the preacher and the song leader in a single lunge.

There also prevailed the custom of inviting families to go home with a neighbor for dinner and to spend a lazy summer afternoon on a front veranda gossiping about crops, politics, and local scandals. Big-meeting weeks were disastrous times for watermelons and yellow-legged, frying-size chickens. We often accepted invitations, and I found the visits exciting, not only because of the sumptuous midday dinners and afternoon suppers, but also because of association with neighborhood boys. I remember once we discovered a hole in the creek that contained a lot of catfish, and we muddied our Sunday clothes catching them, to the consternation of our mothers.

Ninety years later I vividly recall several incidents that occurred during big-meeting time. A transient horse trader, one of civilization's most cunning rascals, came riding up to our farm astride a good-looking sorrel mare. My father, never an expert trader, swapped a good plow mule for the little mare. Everything about the animal proved satisfactory except for one basic trait—she was balky. She never indicated when she would stop stone still and refuse to move except to toss her head up and down. Owning a balky horse in that community was almost as humiliating as having a daughter become pregnant out of wedlock. On one occasion we drove our balky mare in a mixed team to a Methodist revival meeting at White Hall. Several preachers had a go at the sinful congregation, pleading with us to mend our ways. That night at least a half dozen shouting females turned the meeting into babbling chaos. When the preachers could think of no more sins to charge us with and the shouters lay in the aisles, exhausted from their leapings and flailings, it was way past farmers' retirement hour, and church was adjourned. We went to our wagon in pitch darkness, expecting to get under way home as soon as we could hook up the traces of our team. Our balky mare chose that moment to set her feet and refuse to move. There we sat in stygian darkness and frustration. Suddenly there went up an anguished cry as if all the imps of hell had come to undo the work of the revival. A family discovered that a child of theirs was missing, and for an hour the mother shrieked and moaned while the father called the boy's name in a shrill hog-calling shout. There we sat listening to those blood-curdling yells, unable to move our balky beast. Later we learned that the child, bored with the proceedings, had gone home and was found sound asleep and perfectly safe in bed.

One day in 1910 my family was bustling around to get off to a revival meeting. That day we had company, one of whom was "Uncle" Joe Keen, an ancient neighborhood character chock full of folklore and superstitions. Some of us were in the yard when we spotted Halley's Comet hovering over our western woods; its bright, fiery tail seemed barely a few feet above the treetops. Uncle Joe said it was a sign of the wrath of God and that He would dip the great fiery streamers down to set the world on fire and burn us all to cracklings. We had one grim satisfaction from this prospect: when that happened we would be in church.

Halley's Comet never dipped quite so low as to sweep our woods, but other disasters did beset Mississippi in 1910 and 1911. In July 1910, Jack Johnson, a black man, whipped Jim Jeffries in a national boxing bout. As news of the outcome of this fight drifted down to us, there was much local discussion of it, mostly of a racial nature. The *Journal* carried a story that said that across the country black reaction to the fight had been bold and impudent, and this had caused several race riots. Later, feelings became especially heated when Jack Johnson was reported to have married a white woman.

Hardly had talk died down about the Johnson-Jeffries fight than there occurred a horrendous murder in the backwoods of Winston County. In August 1910 Janie Sharp, a young girl, walking alone over a woodland trail, was murdered. I recall vividly a strange man coming to our house early in the morning and asking my father to call the sheriff on our telephone. Whether or not ours was the first call I never knew. A young neighbor of the Sharps', Swinton Permenter, was accused of the murder, and there followed a long series of trials in which he was found guilty and sentenced. After several appeals and retrials he was set free for lack of conclusive evidence. This crime shocked the people of the county and to this day remains unsolved.

The following year was equally eventful. In early May, in the midst of cotton-chopping season, our community became highly agitated over the lynching of two black tenants who lived on the adjoining Johnson Pearson farm. Bruce White and Cliff Jones had worked through at least two crop seasons on "Cap" Pearson's place, and at settling up time he either lost his account book or, more likely, never kept one. The tenants always came out in debt. That spring Cap had sought to rid his corn crib of rats by poisoning them with strychnine. He kept the poison tucked away between the logs of the crib door, and the tenants knew about its location. Angered by their state of peonage, from which there appeared no escape, they took the bottle of poison and dosed the landlord's coffee pot, his meal and flour barrels, the water bucket, and a snuff dipper with which Cap Pearson habitually washed out his mouth before supper. This day he detected the bitterness of the water before he swallowed it. An excitable man, he sent for my grandfather Bennett and an uncle to come and help him determine what had happened. They found the missing bottle of poison in a log heap, and the tenants confessed their crime. My grandfather called the sheriff to come and take charge of them. In the meantime word of the crime spread about the town, and a lynch mob of vicious men and boys set out to intercept the sheriff. They hanged the prisoners over the middle of the "big road" without giving them the remotest semblance of a trial. Perhaps most of the mobsters did not even know what crime their victims had committed. My mother refused to permit my father to go near the Pearson place, nor did any of our neighbors go there. The basic truth was that no one condoned Cap Pearson's treatment of his tenants any more than the tenants' clumsy attempt to seek vengeance. This incident introduced me to the horrors of the widespread southern crime of mob lynching. I was early made acutely sensitive to and repulsed by the inhumane brutality and bestiality of the crime, as well as the prevalence of intense racial fears and hatreds.

Our county had not really recovered its composure after the White-Jones lynching before its reputation was further besmirched by a barbaric public hanging in the latter part of 1911. Bell Gage, a mulatto cocaine addict, murdered his wife while under the influence of the drug. Bell and my father had grown up together, and my father showed him kindness during his imprisonment and trial. Somehow the murder weapon came into the possession of one of my Bennett uncles, and my brother Marvin still owns it. On the morning of the hanging over three thousand people congregated about the jail. Pocket knife traders and hawkers of soda pop, popcorn, peanuts, fried fish, cheap tableware, and patent medicines made a field day of the occasion. Just before 1:00 P.M. a black minister addressed the jeering, disorderly company of rednecks. Promptly at 1:00 Sheriff Archie Hull sprang the gallows trap, and a few moments later Drs. W. W. Parkes and Albert Dempsey pronounced Bell Gage dead. The victim left a pathetic note, later published, in which he expressed gratitude for the way he had been treated. The grass rope noose was cut into bits and peddled to spectators. I remember that a Bennett uncle brought home one of the grisly souvenirs, which he exhibited with pride. Immediately there appeared editorials in neighboring weeklies denouncing the medicine-show aspect of the snuffing out of the man's life. I do not recall that there was ever another hanging in the county, certainly not another one that so affronted the dignity of human life. Bell Gage the cocaine addict indelibly inscribed a morbid footnote on Winston County's history.

A pessimist would most surely have concluded in 1910–1912 that a parlous moon shone on us. We were made to feel morally debauched by the lynching and public hanging. There was more trouble to come, however. Even as Bell Gage's body writhed in its death throes, news was already being spread across the South that the Texas fever tick threatened calamity to our cows. A campaign was mounted to halt this menace by dipping every cow and calf at regular intervals in a vile-smelling and poisonous creosote solution. The Mississippi Extension Service designed an uncomplicated concrete vat, to be constructed in a pit. These were located in convenient locations about the county, and "dipping days" were scheduled. The eradication campaign was supervised by tick inspectors, some of whom could not have identified the parasite if one had crawled across their hands. I recall driving our unruly cows through the pole-lined chute to the vat and helping shove them into hell's own ill-smelling brew. The dipping vat raised almost as much of a storm as the race issue. Many a rednecked old farmer argued that the vat injured his cows and the solution poisoned the milk. Some claimed they had searched the scriptures and nowhere found mention of the Texas tick or dipping vats. These were the ignorant and cussed who denied the existence of the tick. They knew, however, about hollow tail and hollow horn, and about the nauseous grubs that raised great welts up and down the backbones of starveling cattle in the spring. The first two of these ailments were folk myths; the trouble was hollow bellies. Many times I saw bony old cows switching slit tails wrapped with turpentine-soaked rags.

The smart-alec scientists were not satisfied to declare our cows stumbling symbols of certain death. They declared that hookworms were literally gnawing us into the grave. We had never heard of Charles Warder Stiles, who had headed a commission to eradicate the hookworm, or the writer Walter Hines Page, who promoted his efforts, or the St. Gotthard Tunnel in Italy, where the dread parasites had caused the death of many of the workers. The crusade against our unseen enemy was sprung on us suddenly. In August 1912 the *Winston County Journal* ran a bloodcurdling illustration of a greatly enlarged female hookworm that resembled a diamondback rattlesnake more than a worm. We were told the worm laid 3,000 eggs a day, but without an explanation of who counted them. Alongside the illustration of the voracious monster was that of an emaciated boy teetering on the brink of the grave. The *Journal* listed times and places when a representative of the Rockefeller Sanitary Commission and the Mississippi Department of Health would be on hand to gather fecal specimens for hookworm tests. I became so frightened at the prospect that I was constipated for a week. In the end my test proved negative, and I could look forward to a healthy existence, provided the scientists did not discover some other deadly menace.

Somehow we survived reasonably happily the depressed cotton prices, Texas ticks, hookworms, and the disgrace of a lynching and a public hanging. My brothers and I were fortunate to have young neighbors who shared our country-boy adventures. We fished and hunted together, swam in the creek, played marbles and town ball, ran semi-wild (feral) cats with our dogs, raided cane and watermelon patches, aggravated our black neighbor about his goats, and did a thousand and one things. Those were days of extended leisure time in certain seasons of the year. We knew little about organized recreation. We had no community baseball team or any other form of so-called organized sports.

At an early age I became an admirer of my father's double-barrel shotgun and longed for the day when I could shoulder it and go on the popular Thanksgiving Day hunts. Before I was permitted to hunt, however, I had to learn to shoot. One Thanksgiving morning my Bennett uncles decided the time had arrived for me to take the first step toward becoming a hunter. We went into the woods, and they cocked a single-barrel choke-bore gun loaded with a black powder shell. When I fired it, the gun kicked me back against a log and I fell head over heels, sure that I had shot myself.

There were fortunately less life-threatening sports than shooting a kicking gun. Our black neighbor who owned the goats was of a lovable nature. Besides the herd of goats, he owned two things we admired greatly: a well-stocked fish pond and a pack of lean and hungry pot-licker hounds. When persimmons ripened in the fall and possum grapes hung in heavy bunches, we nagged Arthur Kennedy to take us possum hunting. Luckily we never stepped on a rattlesnake, fell into a sinkhole, or cut ourselves with the ax. We had nothing to guide us but Arthur's instinct and his smoky lantern. Possum hunting took considerable patience, but there came that thrilling moment when the dogs struck a hot trail and sent up their throaty tree baying. You could almost guess the size of the game by that of the tree it climbed. A young possum seemed invariably to climb a large tree, while a fat old boar took to a slender sapling. I remember a night when the dogs bayed and pawed up a slender sapling, but as soon as we cut it they bayed up another one. By the time we had chopped down a half dozen trees, Arthur said it was time for us to get out of the woods. We had treed a "hant." Other times, having brought home a big fat possum at night, we would discover the next morning that overnight a half dozen young ones had crawled out of their mother's pouch.

Swamp woods viewed in the flickering glare of a kerosene lantern presented a spooky appearance. A wholly different host of nocturnal creatures lived apart from those of the day. There were great swamp owls, flying squirrels, and brigades of frogs. Occasionally a bobcat sent up its bloodcurdling scream.

Patterns of economic and social life in Mississippi prior to World War I were shaped largely by basic human needs. Gaining a livelihood on a subsistence farm necessitated performing many tasks in the old ways. All across the South cornbread was a dietary staple. Serving a meal of fresh vegetables without cornbread would have been almost as unthinkable as a blue hole creek baptizing without a convert. In our case, when corn on the stalk became dry and hard enough to grind, we observed the weekly ritual of shucking and shelling a bushel of corn to take to the grist mill on Saturdays. Often I rode a mule to the mill seated atop a sack of corn. The miller operated a steam mill, and just a little before daybreak he would blow the whistle to let his patrons know he was ready to grind their grist. Corn sacks would be lined up across the mill floor in the order of their arrival. The miller would dip his toll dish into every "turn" to extract his pay.

When I first started going to the grist mill I was too young and weak to lift a bushel of meal onto a mule. One of my youthful humiliations occurred when my sack fell to the ground and I had to get a girl to help me lift it back across the saddle. Years later, when I went to live in Lexington, Kentucky, I boarded a few blocks from Henry Clay's home, Ashland, and later I served on its board of trustees. I discovered that Clay had made some political headway as the "mill boy of the Slashes." I could relate firsthand to him in this experience, if not in its political ramifications.

Those were days of extended family and neighborly visitations. There were several elderly ladies, some of them kinswomen, who came to our house for visits and stayed several days at a time. Then there were pack peddlers selling books, Bibles, and fruit trees, who came for overnight visits. The Bible salesmen were in many cases self-ordained preachers who peddled a strong dollop of sanctimony along with their sales talk. Sometimes a whole wagonload of distant kinfolk would drive up unannounced and spend a week with us. This meant we had to deplete our diminishing supply of mule feed further, slay a yardful of frying-sized chickens, and raid the garden to feed the guests.

We did some visiting ourselves, but mostly for a day and a night. Almost every month we went to see one or the other of our grandparents. The Bennetts took great pleasure in having their children and grandchildren come for visits. My grandfather raised bountiful supplies of crops that appealed to country youth. He followed a rather strict ritual in serving his fine melons. On the veranda at 3:00 each summer afternoon he would deftly slice a melon lengthwise with a large butcher knife, then carefully present a slice to each family member. We never heard of eating watermelons with meals. My grandmother Bennett was an excellent old-fashioned type of southern cook, preparing food as much by instinct as by recipe. She was heavy-handed in the use of cream and butter. My father's family lived farther away, and it took more effort to visit them. We almost always spent the night and sometimes two or three days at a time.

Over the years we attended three Methodist churches from time to time, but the one at Flower Ridge, on the old Clark homestead, was our mother church. Many times we combined church meetings with visitations to our relatives. There were subtle but sometimes distinct differences between the Clark and Bennett families. My grandmother Clark was a small woman who raised a large family almost single-handedly. She lived into her nineties, living proof that worry will not necessarily kill a person. She was afraid we would get too near the bee gums, or that we might step on a snake in the honeysuckle vines, or that a mule might kick us into kingdom come. The Clark women were good cooks, but never with the zest of my grandmother Bennett, nor did the Clarks make a mid-afternoon ceremonious occasion of cutting a watermelon.

Louisville in 1910 was a small, dusty county seat with its main street lined with shabby wooden stores. On Saturdays farm wagons and teams lined up from one end of the commercial area to the other. The town maintained a well in the middle of the street from which men and beasts scotched their thirst. Almost every man and boy in the county went to town on Saturdays to pick up the news, talk about crops, and groan about hard times. Saturday was also a day when country lawyers were highly visible, along with the perennial crop of political candidates. Even doctors often walked the streets in hopes of acquiring patients. Peddlers selling every sort of nostrum imaginable, "cheap john" merchandise, and their special brand of religious gospel took their stand along the street. They resorted to every kind of antic to draw a crowd. I remember once my father came home with a bright new penny, which he said a medicine-show man had thrown out to draw suckers. My father was a very proud man, and he said the coin had landed on his shoe and stuck there.

As a boy in town on Saturdays I never ceased to be amused by the hawkers, many of whom came with one-horse wagons or buggies equipped with collapsible tailgates from which they shouted their spiels. On one occasion I watched a doctor selling a strong liniment for tired feet. The nostrum was powerful enough, he claimed, to be poured on the feet without removing the shoes. The "doctor" would spot a plowhand shod in cast-iron-like brogans and ask him if his feet hurt. It was a safe question. The feet of every human being who wore the old-style rough brogans ached almost as a matter of course. The old faker would douse a generous amount of liniment on the plowman's feet, give it time to soak in, and then ask him if his feet felt better. The penetrating liquid would have had a cooling effect, and the demonstration would assure the old quack several sales at a dollar a bottle. On other occasions I saw a quick-talking hawker sell "genuine" silver tableware at a ridiculously low price. I wondered how many of the pieces turned green before the gullible purchaser got home with them.

There were few Jews in Winston County until the opening of the twentieth century, and then only two or three pack peddlers who made regular rounds through the country. I never heard an anti-Semitic remark, but countrymen were amused at the Eastern European accents and manners of the visitors. I remember with considerable nostalgia the emigrant peddlers who trod the miserable, muddy or dusty country roads burdened with their striped canvas backpacks of merchandise. There were J. Morris, J. Gordon, Louis Glazer, and one named Kaplan. They spoke broken English and used quaint phrases. The visitations of these men introduced us to the fact that not all the peoples of the world spoke the same language. I am certain there prevailed the local notion that Christ was white Anglo-Saxon and spoke English with a southern drawl.

All the Jewish merchants in Louisville had started out as peddlers, building up their trade from backpack to one-horse wagon to a corner store on Main Street. During their peddler days they built up an enormous amount of goodwill that ensured them customers for their stores. When these itinerant merchants unrolled their packs before our fireside, all the wonders of the commercial world seemed to pop up before our eyes. The Italians could not have been more entranced by the exotic goods Vasco da Gama brought home from the East. Laid out to tempt us was a variety store full of cheap merchandise. I never catch the scent of a cosmetic counter without being reminded of the marvelous wares of the Jewish pack peddlers of my boyhood.

In 1912 Louis Glazer advertised that he and his partner, Mr. Kaplan, had rented a store and now enjoyed the status of town merchants. They invited their country customers to come in and see their stock of shoes with indestructible soles, implying that a wearer could walk all the way to Jerusalem and back without his feet ever touching bare earth. We bought clothes from Louis Glazer, and in 1917 my father bought me my first long suit, a blue serge, from him. When I put on the trousers and vest I was performing a minor ritual that indicated I had entered the first stages of manhood.

Successors to the general merchandise peddlers were the agents of the proprietary remedies made by J. R. Watkins and W. T. Raleigh. Their lines ranged from liniments and colic remedies for livestock to vanilla extract and spices. The agents lived in the county and no doubt knew every road and pig trail, as well as every man, woman, and colicky plow mule. The Raleigh man, "Dr. Osborne," was obese and a great trencherman. I remember him as the cook at the annual fish fries on Hemphill Lake and the Duckpond. He would heat a cast iron pot half filled with lard and deep-fry fish in it. Though he punished his waistline, he won an array of highly satisfied customers. Along with the peddlers of remedies were the sellers of fruit trees, rosebud salve, and insurance. Neighborhood women came around selling sweet-scented cloverine salve, which had a thousand uses. Fruit tree salesmen were as reliable as the hawkers of the Brooklyn Bridge.

Just as certain as spring broke, there would appear neighbor women with their plan books. If they sold a certain amount of merchandise from a catalog they would win a porch swing, a rocking chair, or even a phonograph. Sometimes the plan-book ladies became so numerous that they had to buy from one another in order to find enough local customers.

The community in which I spent my youth was composed of two distinct human societies. Almost from my first moments of realization, I became aware of the hard and fast facts—that there were two worlds revolving about me, one white, the other black. The latter were always spoken of as "Negroes" by my family and most of polite society. The boundaries between the two worlds were distinguished almost by instinct. I played with black children and had good and enduring black friends, yet there was the eternal code of relationship and behavior that my family observed always with punctiliousness. Never did I feel at ease addressing an elderly black person by his or her first name. I always used the respectful prefixes "uncle" or "aunt." This custom, so far as I was concerned, had not the slightest implication of social inferiority or denigration. Black landowners adjoining our farm remained cherished neighbors and friends to my father and mother for at least two generations, yet the code of interracial relationships separated us in many areas. Thus we lived in the pre–World War I decades, our two worlds revolving about each other with reasonable harmony, both races experiencing the economic disappointments and setbacks of the times. Historians no doubt will go on ad infinitum writing about slavery, liberated blacks, social conflict, lynchings, discrimination, and the dramatic march to modern freedom. Perhaps not all the sources or all the facts of our biracial southern society will ever be exhaustively explored and interpreted. As times and conditions change, so will the perspective on the South's past.

My second recollection of racial relationships was the nagging fear of both whites and blacks that a race riot would occur. No one ever seemed to know either the source of the rumors or the reasons for their currency. On one occasion the tenants on my grandfather Bennett's farm gathered in his kitchen because they feared a race riot was about to occur and they did not wish to be victimized by rumors and suspicions. There was a rumor afloat that L. B. Graham, a crusty hardware merchant, had offered to supply guns and ammunition to blacks but with the hitch that he would be waiting for applicants with his own weapon. Those were troubled years in Mississippi. I am sure that many incidents were blown out of all proportion. There was much discussion of the story that earlier in the century President Theodore Roosevelt had entertained Booker T. Washington at a dinner at the White House, and of his appointment of a black woman, Effie Cox, as postmistress at Indianola. There were other stories, largely apocryphal no doubt, about "biggeded northern niggers." Men like James K. Vardaman and other self-serving Mississippi politicians kept the pot of racial prejudice well stirred. The two most deeply seated facts in all of our lives, however, were the failing of hill country cotton farming and the intense bitterness and guilt created all across the South by the frequent lynchings.

By 1911 there began an outflow from Winston County of blacks going to the big sawmill camps. When the mills moved into the county to lay low the virgin forests, they drew hundreds of cotton tenants to their camps. This was the first era in county history when workers could draw considerable wages from nonfarm work. Blacks deserted the tenant shacks and cotton fields to live in tar-paper houses and accept the arduous work in mills and woods. There also began the migration of blacks up the Illinois Central Railroad to East St. Louis and Chicago. A boy from a neighboring farm went to Chicago and never came home again.

Between 1911 and 1914 the boll weevil was well on its way to stinging us out of our cotton crops. Because of this infestation my father found it hard to make ends meet. For two or three years we produced scarcely enough cotton to pay the tax and fertilizer bills. Today I marvel at the fact that we survived as well as we did. We could not have done so if my mother had not taught school, however meager her salary.

In 1913 my father and several of our neighbors were enticed by a total stranger into joining a truck-growing cooperative. No one knew much of anything about the background of the persuasive rascal named Manning, nor did they take the trouble to make inquiries. Manning painted a glowing picture of profits to be made growing vegetables for the Chicago produce market. Farmers were told they could buy materials, seeds, and fertilizer through the cooperative at greatly reduced prices. In our case we built cold frames and grew our own onion, tomato, and cabbage plants but had to purchase other seeds and fertilizer. Our sandy land was adaptable to the growing of vegetables, and we grew bumper crops of turnips and greens, onions, cabbages, beans, and enough tomatoes to feed the county. Rabbits almost gnawed us out of the cabbage business. We attempted to poison them by placing apples laced with strychnine around the patch, made newspaper cones to frighten them, and even resorted to use of the shotgun, yet nothing seemed to help. Nevertheless, in spite of the rabbits we harvested a surprisingly good crop of cabbage to be consumed by hungry Chicagoans. We spent days making crates, but none of us had the slightest notion about how to prepare produce for a city market. I remember when we pulled and washed our turnips and greens we stood back and admired the beautiful vegetables. We hauled our produce to a railway siding and packed it in refrigerator cars alongside that of our neighbors. Then came word from Chicago that brokers claimed our shipments were of inferior quality and had been damaged in shipment. Little money was ever forthcoming. Manning vanished, and we were left with staggering bills for materials and fertilizer. Amazingly my family survived this failure, which compounded our already troublous economic problems. Somehow my father paid his bills, but as a member of the cooperative he was left responsible for defaulting debtors. No hill country farmer ever exerted greater willpower and determination to survive adversity than my father. Fortunately our family farm was never mortgaged as were many of those of our neighbors.

We learned from the trucking debacle that we could extract a respectable subsistence from the land without making much money. Home demonstration agents instructed farm wives in the modern arts of canning and preserving vegetables and fruits. The active interest in the canning clubs no doubt resulted in greater changes in our dietary habits than we realized. Year-round our dining table was laden with a hardy countryman's diet of home-grown viands. We knew nothing of the nutritional analysis of sweet potatoes and black-eyed peas. We ate them without question.

National and world events in 1914 portended phenomenal changes for us. No prophet was at hand to tell us about the social and economic revolution that would occur in our immediate future. In that year our region stood on the great historical divide that would see many of the old ways of the South sloughed off into oblivion.

3

A World in Change

If any single year can be said to be one of transition for a region and its people, 1914 was that year for the South. Our lives in central Mississippi, molded in an unprogressive age of faltering agrarianism, never again got pieced together. The coming of the automobile to the rest of America had made little or no impression on our way of life. The machine was still a curiosity in Winston County. I recall distinctly the first automobile I ever saw. We were visiting my father's brother, who lived beside the "big road." We had just seated ourselves in the wagon to go home when there roared up the hill a mechanical monster that frightened our mules so badly they almost upset the wagon. After that an occasional car would be driven onto the primitive dirt roads, become mired up to the hubs in mud, and have to be towed by mules onto high and dry ground.

By 1914 a neighbor or two had bought a car but could drive it only in dry weather, and then in summer the dust would smother the passengers.

In the winter months the roads became almost too muddy to be used even by mules and wagons. In time, however, Henry Ford's Model T made buggy sheds obsolescent, and gas pumps crowded the public watering trough off Main Street; hitching racks and wagons with spring seats became as archaic as side saddles. Occasionally an affluent member would charge onto church grounds in his gas buggy and cause half the horses and mules hitched to trees to break away and run off. Following such incidents there was little evidence of brotherly love or Christian charity.

The automobile held before us a powerful glass revealing how primitive our road system was. With a team and wagon one could make compromises with the mudholes, but not so with an automobile. In time Ford cars crammed their noses into the curbs along Main Street, their boxy hind ends sticking out like fattening hogs at the trough. On many occasions immediately after World War I, I saw the so-called "poor white trash" of the county driving round and round the Confederate monument in town. They were barefooted and ragged, but the sides of the car concealed their poverty. In a significant fashion the machine was lifting many of them out of their almost congenital social status and into a new age of technological egalitarianism.

At the same time other changes in our traditional way of life were occurring. County and state Extension agents scolded us for wasting our soil, for our stubborn loyalty to cotton as a main crop, and for our deficient diet. They were even critical of our clothing. Nevertheless, they found it difficult to wean Winston County farmers away from the ways "paw and grandpaw" had done things. Early my father became convinced that terracing his land was necessary if he expected to continue farming sandy hillsides. He became adept at using the model "A-frame" level developed by the Extension Service, and we were among the first to terrace our land. I recall that an ignorant and bullheaded neighbor asked my father to level his land, but when he backed off and took sight on the stakes, he declared water would not run off in terraces built along such circuitous lines. In a fit of temper he kicked the stakes down and laid new courses by his expert eye. I saw that farm gradually waste away in deeply eroded gullies.

I fell under the influence of the Smith-Lever Act of 1914, which established the Agricultural Extension Service and, later, the Smith-Hughes Act and the Four-H Club movement. I grew an acre of corn and specially fertilized it, bought and fed a purebred Duroc Jersey pig, and kept a record of my activities. I never won a prize or attracted farmer attention of any sort, but I did demonstrate in a modest way that better results could be achieved on our farm by the more scientific use of improved seeds and more generous application of fertilizers. I doubt, though, that my Four-H Club zeal in any way changed my father's mode of farming as the agricultural reformers had hoped it would. As it turned out, my destiny was not to be on a cotton farm.

We began to read news accounts in the *Memphis Commercial Appeal,* the *Tri-Weekly Atlanta Constitution,* and even the *Winston County Journal* about a European conflict. I doubt if there was a person in Winston County who could have described accurately the whereabouts of the Balkans or who had heard the name Sarajevo, where the Austrian crown prince was assassinated in late June 1914. We surely were unaware that the gathering storm of war, like a Gulf hurricane, would in time have a direct bearing on our course of life. We felt that the Atlantic Ocean and the great North American land mass were sufficient buffer between ourselves and the conflicts in Europe. Our focus was upon immediate threats to our domestic happiness from evils nearer at hand. Cotton had rapidly failed as a mainstay cash crop. The boll weevil in the field and the cotton brokers in the markets were prime offenders. Even the old credit-granting general mercantile system with its sins, real and imagined, teetered on the brink of oblivion.

By late 1915 the rising conflict in Western Europe was beginning to have a significant impact on industry, on fortunes, and on our post–Civil War way of life. We felt it first in rising prices for cotton and in the increasing amounts of pine and hardwood lumber being harvested and shipped out of the area. I remember vividly when the first of the old exploitative "cut out and get out" mills went into operation in Winston County. A Yankee from Chicago built one of his mills in our community, a big mill capable of producing as much lumber in a day as a "peckerwood" could saw out in a fortnight. I can yet recall the shrill commanding shrieks of the four o'clock morning wake-up call of the mill. Until then, we had never seen a sawmill more complicated than the peckerwood ones, which did well to saw out four or five thousand board feet a day. Mr. Shriver's big mill sawed logs into lumber in a blue streak. It was equipped with a "shotgun" carriage, which the block setter rode strapped to a security stanchion. Lumber poured from the saw in a continuous stream, mounting up more than fifty thousand board feet a day.

In the wake of this technological marvel I witnessed the harvest of a virgin forest. I saw tall rosemary pines that had stood a century or more, their tops reaching up to gather the rays of the sun just the day before, cut down and turned into logs up to the first limbs. Hundreds of thousands of feet of sound timber were left in the woods to rot away in sinful waste. The international demand for lumber and heavy construction timber in 1914 and after was insatiable. Lumber from the Shriver mill was hauled to the railway siding in town by an almost continuous train of mule-drawn wagons. I saw the already poor dirt roads churned into bottomless mudholes during the winter months and dustbowls in summer. Former cotton tenants were turned into day laborers, living with their families in crowded and crude tar-paper shacks. The motto of millmaster Shriver was "Kill a mule, buy anothern, kill a nigger, hire anothern." The world at war screamed for lumber in billions of board feet.

On a minuscule scale my uncle Lester Bennett formed a partnership with our neighbor Ernest Boswell to buy and operate a "peckerwood" sawmill in 1917. They worked almost frantically, producing yellow pine lumber for the military camps and shipyards. I went to work for them "doodling" sawdust. This meant I used a large grain scoop to shovel sawdust onto a wheelbarrow and roll it up an incline to be dumped. I still shudder when I think of the ordeal of trying to keep the sawdust pit to a level where the saw would not blow it back in the sawyer's face. There was not one labor-saving or safety device present in that mill. I worked with the saw buzzing just over my head for ten hours a day. The work was hot, the days long, and the pay low, a dollar a day. I quickly learned that working in a sawmill was far more arduous than farming. The sputtering steam engine and circular saw were more heartless slave drivers than Harriet Beecher Stowe's Simon Legree. Sawmill work was too exhausting for me, and I went back to the farm.

At that time we were clearing away the woods on ten acres in the most fertile area of our land preparatory to planting the traditional fallowing crop of corn. In the most pressing moment of clearing away the woods, splitting fence rails, piling brush in heaps, cutting the heavier logs into manageable lengths, and even bird thrashing before we burned the brush heaps, my father contracted measles, and the rest of my family fell victim to Spanish influenza, part of a local outbreak that resulted in several deaths in Winston County. News stories told of the deadly effects of this disease, both in the military camps and among the civilian population. A neighbor boy on an adjoining farm died from the disease, causing much local anxiety. Luckily my family survived both influenza and measles without fatalities. Nevertheless, that was a dread moment for us. The local doctors were almost wholly ignorant of proper treatment for their influenza patients, and the frequent accounts of death were almost as unsettling as the frightful news reports from the Western Front. For some miraculous reason I escaped contracting both diseases and worked alone, serving as nurse and performing the daily farm chores, with the exception of milking the cows, which was left to the calves. I continued working in the new ground, trying to get it far enough along for the spring logrolling. Not until I read a biography of Abraham Lincoln did I learn that this might be a step toward the White House.

By hard struggle we got the ground ready for an all-day March logrolling. Our neighbors came with their prized hand sticks and piled the logs in heaps to be burned. A logrolling in the hill country South was little short of a spring festival, with a lot of joking, pranking, bragging, and sometimes loss of tempers. It was a real joy to lift up a hand stick in such a way that the opposite partner got the short end. Thus did the term "short end of the stick" enter the American lexicon.

We kept up with the progress of the war in Europe. So thoroughly propagandized were we about German atrocities that we became convinced that the time was near at hand when the Kaiser's troops would invade our county, with Louisville a strategic objective. One night during this period of war hysteria there occurred a thunderous explosion that blew out windows and rattled every door in town. People were certain the awful moment had arrived and the Germans had begun blowing up our defenseless community. At daybreak, however, no track of the Hun was found, no building had been wrecked, and no citizen injured. The cause of the explosion remained a mystery. Three years later, when I was working on a dredgeboat, our dynamiter admitted that he had set off the explosion. He and his girl had had a falling out, and in a fit of anger he had piled crossties on several sticks of dynamite, lit a long fuse, and left town, glorying in the speculative chatter about the "German attack."

As events on the European front became more ominous, southern militancy became more pronounced. The local and regional newspapers published sensational stories of what was happening on the Western Front. We were placed under a heavy barrage of pro-British and anti-German propaganda. Our views of the Germans paralleled those the preachers painted of the devil every big-meeting week.

We remained staunch in our faith in the righteousness of the Democratic Party. The voters of Winston County had gone to the polls in 1912 to cast an overwhelming vote for Woodrow Wilson. He was a southerner, a Democrat, and in our minds a "fine Christian" man. Again in 1916 we rejoiced when our idol was reelected, this time because he had "kept us out of war."

Well before the United States declared war, we had come to feel the impact of the European conflict. The opening of the Gulf coastal shipyards with their insatiable demand for lumber and carpenters, as well as the building of the great Wilson Dam and the nitrate plant at Muscle Shoals and Sheffield, Alabama, drained our neighborhood of men, boys, and entire families leaving to work at the carpenter trade. The boys with whom I had played in earlier years moved to Mobile and never returned to Winston County. Almost anybody who could even vaguely distinguish a hammer from a nail could find a job in the government works. My father, however, was not attracted by the more lucrative public jobs and remained on the farm to fight the boll weevil.

With the declaration of war in April 1917, the military draft began gathering neighbor boys into the various branches of the service. One of the first local draftees was a boy from an adjoining farm. He could neither read nor write, and his family was left totally in the dark for almost two years as to whether or not he had fallen in battle. War fever ran high in the county. The newspapers carried stories of both battles and human atrocities in Belgium and France. They literally screamed damnation on the Kaiser and his iron-heeled Hunnish minions. I read these stories with deep interest. In this era there appeared, in ready-print serialized form in the *Winston County Journal,* Arthur Guy Empey's book *Over the Top.* He graphically portrayed the tortures of trench warfare—the mud, the killing, the cooties, and the tensions of war. Years later as a graduate student in history I discovered that if Empey's book was not pure fraud, it was at least without factual substance.

Life during wartime was both exciting and trying, even though we were far removed from the centers of military activity. Tension and nagging fear kept us aware that times were highly abnormal. I have vivid memories of several incidents that occurred in those years. I saw my first airplane in the summer of 1917 when a squadron of Jenny planes* took off from Payne Field in West Point, Mississippi, to boost the war savings and bond drive. A crowd lined a level cow pasture strip to watch the great flying armada swoop down out of the skies. At noon the dramatic moment arrived when six tiny biplanes, barely larger than turkey buzzards, came into sight and then landed one behind the other. The helmeted and begoggled flyers gave the appearance of being from another world. Their machines, however, were very much of this one. Three or four of them were unable to rise and fly away to their home base and had to be hauled away ingloriously on army trucks. On another occasion a plane landed in the middle of a Four-H Club boy's corn patch, and gawking sightseekers trampled his crop into the ground.

Wartime patriotism bubbled to fever pitch in Winston County. I bought savings stamps with the little money I could spare, never enough

---

* Military training planes

to stock a rifle with a bayonet. Women of all ages set to knitting socks and sweaters for the soldiers. They had little notion of sizes or precise matches of socks, but their garments were no further off in this respect than were those issued to recruits by the army and navy. Under Mr. Hoover's austerity food program we dutifully observed meatless, wheatless, and sugarless days. We ate a lot of corn bread and had our own supply of soggy brown sugar. I recall hearing one of our female "fasting neighbors" whimper about "how good a pan of hot biscuits would taste," downed no doubt with a cup of coffee sweetened with "real" sugar.

In a less sensational vein we responded to every war drive. In one such campaign, my mother and I drove far into the "back country" of Winston County soliciting materials that could be sold at auction in town to raise money for the Red Cross. We loaded our mule-drawn wagon with donations of all sorts—remnants of lint cotton, coops of chickens, baskets of eggs, bundles of rich pine kindling wood, lots of firewood, sacks full of hickory nuts and black walnuts and other salable produce, and even a long-legged fighting gamecock. When we hauled our collection to town to be auctioned before the door of the Methodist church, the auctioneer named the rooster "Woodrow Wilson." Woodrow captured the interest of the bidders and may have sold for the highest price any rooster had ever brought in the past—or in the future for that matter. He was sent to Jackson and then to Memphis to be sold. Louisville managers of the drive were so pleased with the popularity of the little rooster that they asked the school superintendent to write President Wilson explaining how nobly his namesake had supported the war effort. Superintendent Rundle received a note of thanks from Joseph Tumulty, Wilson's private secretary.

In early November 1918 came the frustrating news of the false armistice, the capitulation of the Austro-Hungarian forces. Then, on November 11, came word to Louisville by telegraph that the German army had surrendered. I was working in the middle of our new ground field when I heard whistles blowing, bells ringing, and guns firing. The end of the war had come, and we hoped that our lives would take up where they had left off in 1914.

I could not possibly have foreseen at that moment the vast and sweeping changes that would come in the American way of life. Already forces were at work thrusting us into an unsettled age that would affect every aspect of our lives. Following the war our economic condition deteriorated mightily. Farmers who had persisted during the war believed in 1918 that a new and golden age for cotton was opening. Wartime needs had driven cotton prices to an all-time high, and production levels had remained stable. The end of the war drove prices to a level below the cost of production. We faced an extremely uncertain future on our farm. I continued to work intermittently in the sawmill and log woods. I bought a team of horses and an old ramshackle wagon and hauled lumber to Louisville during several months. It seemed in those days that my life would be spent atop a creeping lumber wagon or lifting heavy lumber. The work was arduous, and the monetary returns were inverse to the labor demands.

Other sorts of irreversible change were upon us. I recall the return of the veterans to our community, callow youths who had left the farm having never before crossed the county line. Now they returned as world travelers who had been exposed not only to the hardening influences of the battlefield but to new and alien cultures. Many of them came back spouting French phrases and bragging about their exploits among the mademoiselles, to the shock of their elders. Their tales were never printed in family newspapers, especially not in the *Winston County Journal*.

ON JULY 12, 1919, I WENT WITH my father and mother to attend the funeral of an aunt, who was to be buried in the first grave opened behind the new Calvary Baptist Church. That morning we were deeply touched not only by the death of our much-loved aunt, but almost as much by the emotional strain of our economic dilemma. We already knew that our cotton crop was going to be largely a failure. The rows were strewn with squares and bolls punctured by the weevils. When the funeral was concluded and my mother and father and I were in our wagon on the way home, we heard the ringing of a bell, a new sound that differed from any farm bell we knew. The bell was on a newly built quarterboat anchored underneath the old iron bridge across Tallahega Creek. We knew by then that sometime soon work would begin on the canalization of the winding Tallahega Creek from near its head to its juncture with the Pearl River. A dredging company had been organized immediately after war's end for the purpose of draining two or three flood-prone areas. We had only the vaguest information about the dredging project or the Winston Dredging Company. Nevertheless, on July 14, 1919, my sixteenth birthday, I walked to the iron bridge, climbed over the railing onto the top deck of the boat, and went downstairs. The foreman, his wife, and the small crew were at breakfast, but that did not deter me from making application for a job to whoever was in charge of hiring men. The captain was a tall, gaunt Kentuckian from the Purchase area named H. L. Lewis. I was hired as cabin boy at a salary of $20.00 a month and board. This meant I peeled potatoes, washed dishes, swept the boat, made beds, and did every other domestic chore. My parents were concerned that I would be exposed to evil influences aboard that boat. As it turned out, the other crew members were also farm boys, most of them from the eastern part of the county. They were hardly old salts or Mississippi River deckhands and gamblers.

For most of a year we lived close to raw nature on the virgin swamp. One hazard was snakes. In my earliest memories I recalled hearing tales of the huge water moccasins that infested the Tallahega Swamp, but I had never conceived of either their size or the numbers we found. It seemed too that most of the beech trees harbored nests of the wicked baldheaded hornets. A third menace, swamp mosquitoes, attacked us in swarms, and I developed a full-blown case of malaria, which I had difficulty in curing. Every day, precisely on time, my body was racked in a violent chill, followed by a raging fever.

During that time the dredge was being manufactured in Ohio, but there was no indication as to when it might be shipped to Louisville. New crew members were set to clearing the right-of-way for the canal and cutting and stacking cordwood along the way to be used in firing the dredge's boiler. I was soon moved from cabin boy to the right-of-way cutting crew. While we waited for the dredge to arrive we also constructed a barge on which to deliver wood to the boiler. In the process of constructing this big and clumsy vessel, we came to have some notion of Noah's problems in constructing the ark. I learned how to use a caulking chisel and long oakum ropes to seal the seams on the boat. We installed a Model-T Ford engine in the boat. Once in the process of cranking the motor, it kicked back and broke my arm.

After an interminable wait, during which we cut miles of right-of-way and opened access roads, the dredge finally arrived in Louisville. There were flatcar loads of steel plates cut and drilled to precision for the hull of the boat, a heavy steel boom, a dipper boom, and a yard-and-a-half-long shovel, as well as a large boiler, two big engines, a pair of heavy spud feet, rolls of heavy cables, and barrels of bolts, nuts, and rivets. With the exception of Captain Lewis and maybe one or two of the crew, none of us had ever seen a dredge boat, let alone helped assemble one.

In cool December weather we set to work putting together the fifty-foot hull, a task that necessitated setting hundreds of bolts and molding rivets. When it was complete, we spent a grisly day and night getting the hull to slip down the wooden ways. Just at sunup the monster slipped into the water, and we went to bed to sleep off the nightmare of its launching. When we finally awoke we went out to inspect our handiwork. That big clumsy hull was two-thirds full of water and on the verge of sinking. A bolt had been left out of one seam and a geyser of water gushed up from the creek. That day was one of the dreariest I had ever spent. For more than a week we pumped bilge water down to a level where the leak could be bolted shut. Finally we were able to tug the engines and boiler aboard, hoist the huge boom and dipper arm, and string the cables.

When at last the dredge was complete, the first head of steam had been raised in the new boiler, and the engines, shives,* cables, and lever controls were tested, we were ready to scoop up the first yard and a half and be on our way to digging a thirty-foot-wide canal. I was assigned the distinguished position of lone deckhand. I oiled the engines, greased the booms and pulleys, drilled holes in replacement plates for the spud feet, and kept the deck cleared of debris.

---

* Steel-encased pulleys

Night and day for more than a year, furiously jerking and tossing, we clawed and slashed a broad swath through the dense swamp, cutting magnificent virgin trees into lowly cordwood to be fed into the dredge's ravenous furnace, and leaving behind towering embankments of soggy swampland. Every sweep of the dredge's big dipper brought us two and a half yards of dirt closer to our ultimate destination, the meeting point of the Tallahega and the Pearl River.

As time passed, the gabfest around the big old wood-burning stove turned to speculation about the crew's future. Vaguely I dreamed for a time of becoming a civil engineer. All along the way we had worked with engineers who outlined the course of the canal and established its elevations. Someone had brought some college mathematics textbooks on board, and I turned through them but could not comprehend their complexities.

I worked on that pitching monster, greasing engines, repairing cables, drilling an interminable number of holes with an old-fashioned hand-turned drill. I climbed the boom to grease ratchet tracks and point shives, and did all sorts of other chores on deck. On one occasion I waded winter floodwaters up to my chin carrying a stadia rod and dragging a surveyor's chain. I lived perpetually smeared with grease and mud with little or no promise of future advancement. I was eighteen years old and becoming disillusioned.

On one occasion in 1920 I saw a boy I knew well working on a school assignment. This, plus my mother's interest in education, stirred in me a strong impulse to take leave of the grease, the roaring, the drilling of holes in steel plates, and the eternal mud. I had not the slightest notion about how to seek entrance to a college, but I bundled up my grease- and mud-soaked clothes, quit the job on the dredgeboat, and stumbled down the landing board, headed only God knew where. I trudged through several miles of virgin hardwood forest, heavily populated by cottonmouth moccasins and timber rattlesnakes, while overhead there gathered black waves of Gulf rainclouds. After three days of walking and soul searching, I reached my Grandmother Clark's home. I did not know where or how I would find a school to attend, but I was determined to find one.

4

~

THE ROAD TAKEN

By THE TIME I REACHED MY GRANDMOTHER CLARK'S
home late in the afternoon of September 12, 1921, a record-smashing Gulf
rainstorm was roaring in, strong enough to douse any dreams I had for
the future. Yet by sunup the following morning I began the seven-mile
walk to my home. Midway there I came to the ancient iron bridge that
spanned the Tallahega. For a brief, meditative moment I stood staring
down, just as I had done precisely two years and two months before.
Beneath me and winding away into the distance lay two miles of canal
channel that I had helped create. Turning and walking off that bridge, I
crossed one of the major divides of my life.

Back home my mother washed and ironed my limited supply of
clothes, and three days later I was on my way to seek entrance to the
A&M College at Starkville, twenty-five miles distant. Sometime in the
past an uncle in the Bennett clan had attended the preparatory department there, and I thought I could do the same thing, not knowing that

the school had discontinued its preparatory program. I had never heard of high school units or high school preparation to enter college. When I presented myself to the crusty old registrar, seeking admission, he was so rude in his response that I developed a lifelong antipathy for registrars. He seemed to look upon me as some strange, archaic creature that had crept out of the mud of Tallahega Swamp. And perhaps I was.

That was surely one of my most frustrating moments. I had no job and knew of no high school I could afford to attend. One thing was certain: I would stay as far away from A&M College as time and distance would permit. In my befuddled state of mind I wandered off the campus to a restaurant near the dilapidated little Illinois Central depot. There I poured out my tale of woe to the young combination cook and waiter, who told me about the Choctaw County Agricultural High School in his hometown of Weir. He said I could go down on the westbound afternoon train and in the hour between trains I could see the school superintendent, T. A. Patterson. Luck favored me. On my arrival in Weir the first man I saw was T. A. Patterson. When I explained to him my situation, he then and there admitted me to the school without asking about my preparation to enter the ninth grade. He remarked that I appeared to be a big, stout boy—and I was. I was as brown as a Choctaw Indian, and obviously I was in good physical condition. Mr. Patterson said he thought I would make a good football player. Even at that time, and in a poor county agricultural high school, football seemed to be important. In my case, being a prospective player seemed to be far more important than being prepared to do high school work or even read and write. In less than thirty minutes my fortune had taken a decided turn for the better.

I rushed home to Louisville, gathered up the remainder of such clothes as I possessed, and returned to Weir on Sunday afternoon, ready to enter classes the next day. Two years aboard a dredgeboat in close association with a crew of rugged workmen had prepared me in many ways for adapting quickly to life in a crowded dormitory. I had learned early to observe certain mores in living with others and to adapt to hard physical labor. My health, except for the attack of malaria, was sound, and I had developed a strong muscular system.

On Monday afternoon I went out for football practice, never having seen a football and only vaguely recalling anything I had heard about the game. The coach assigned me to the position of right guard, with instructions to knock down and run over anybody who got in my way. The following Friday afternoon we played the Kosciusko High School team and won. I was no doubt as physically well conditioned as any boy on either team, but I knew nothing about the fundamentals of the game. During my four years in high school I played alternately right guard and center. How I escaped serious injury is still a mystery to me. The school was too poor to buy suitable and safe uniforms. I wore a little old cloth helmet, thin shoulder pads, inadequately staved pants,* and common plow shoes to which an old bachelor cobbler in the village nailed cleats. During the four years we played other agricultural high schools, we won a fair number of the games.

The Choctaw County Agricultural High School was a part of Mississippi's attempt to provide rural boys and girls access to a high school education. The various schools had a linkage at least with the federal Smith-Hughes Act. They maintained dormitories, dining halls, and work programs. The school at Weir consisted of two buildings, a big old brick structure that housed all twelve grades, and a barnlike, yellow-pine, two-story dormitory in which both boys and girls were housed. The rooms were heated by coal fires, privies were located safely out of smelling range, and there were no bathing facilities. Living in that dormitory was little different from living in a Mississippi farmhouse. The place was so highly flammable that it was a miracle we escaped a fiery holocaust. There was a dining room in which a country cook prepared farm-style meals, which the girl students served. Our monthly board bills ranged from eight to ten dollars, and there were no room charges. Almost every student had some kind of self-sustaining job, and in addition we were required to give the school ten hours a week of our "free time." Much of the "free time" work consisted of plowing, hoeing corn and cotton, gath-

---

* Pants with padding in the legs and over the buttocks, with the padding held in place by stiffening bands

ering crops, and caring for the school's livestock. For me this was a veritable "Brer Rabbit in the briar patch" situation. The system functioned without students complaining or "soldiering"* on the job. Besides work for the school, boys often found Saturday jobs working for villagers and local farmers. My first year at Weir I worked as a janitor in the classroom building and also as janitor for as straitlaced a Presbyterian congregation as ever rubbed two dimes together. I swept their church house, then rang the bell to let John Knox's disciples know that I had the fire in the heater going and it was time for them to foregather. When this was done I scampered across the village to commune with the Methodists.

At Weir I lived in the crowded coed dormitory, with the girls occupying the first floor and the boys the second. I never heard even a whisper of gossip about any misconduct between the sexes. In later years, when the issue of coed college dormitories stirred moralistic horror, I recalled that for me it was an old, old story. There was not a drop of running water in that dormitory, not a single lavatory or commode. How we escaped contracting hepatitis is a matter I still wonder about. Not a farm or tenant house in Choctaw County was more primitive than that dormitory and school building. Social life was almost as barren as dormitory life, but on occasions when there was some form of entertainment in the school auditorium, boys and girls could have dates, walking to the school building under the eagle eyes of the teachers.

Under the terms of the Smith-Lever and Smith-Hughes acts, boys were required to take four years of agriculture and girls to take home science courses that taught them to be good farm wives. We were all being prepared to go back to the farm at a time when farming in Mississippi faced a dismal future. The teacher of agriculture was a Methodist minister's son who had no practical farming experience and imparted to us such little information as he had garnered in classes in A&M College. He did teach us how to operate a Bostrom level, an instrument for measuring the elevation of terraces, and to identify the various varieties of field crops and breeds of domestic animals.

---

* Slacking off

In late spring of my freshman year Superintendent Patterson asked me to remain in Weir during the summer to run the school farm. He promised me that if I would do so I could have first choice of a job in the fall. That summer I worked six days a week plowing cotton and corn and performing general farm chores, which included feeding a drove of hogs, looking after the cows, and caring for a pair of horses. For all of this I received my board and room and $20.00 a month. I saved almost enough to pay my next year's board bill.

One night during that summer I observed a queer-seeming assembly of men entering the school building. This, I soon learned, was a gathering of the local Ku Klux Klan. It included the leaders of the dusty little village in which no crime greater than chicken stealing had ever occurred and racial relations were normal in the Mississippi sense of the term. The superintendent of the school seemed to be a ringleader. Ku Kluxes were out to "keep the niggers in their place" and to raise the moral tone of the village by clamping down a curfew when all God-fearing citizens should be at home and in bed. Ironically, while the Klansmen were meeting, the blacks were holding a shouting, singing revival only a half mile down the road in the Rosenwald-endowed schoolhouse.

During the following two summers I returned home to work on my father's farm. In the summer of 1924 my brother Marvin and I managed to find a purchaser for pine crossties, provided we could produce two freight-car loads a week. The Burlington Railroad was one of the few companies still buying ties. We hired two experienced crews of black tie-makers, bought a good stand of pine timber, and went to work. We operated two wagons and fulfilled our weekly contract. In those post-1920 agricultural depression years we were lucky to find a buyer for our ties at any price.

An event occurred during that summer at home that made a profound impression on me. My father rented his upper farm to a white tenant, violating his long-standing distaste for white sharecroppers. The son of that family, Ansel Baines, wandered into the town of Weir, where people went to bed with the chickens, and was lolling aimlessly about the main street, violating a curfew proclaimed by the Ku Klux Klan. Patrolling Klansmen brutally assaulted the harmless and ignorant boy, causing him serious head injuries. After he hobbled home he went into a coma from what a local doctor diagnosed as a brain tumor. I sat up parts of nights with that comatose boy. His sister had briefly attended classes in nursing and decided to take her brother to a charity hospital in St. Louis for an operation. The boy died on the operating table, and his body was sent home in a flimsy cardboard coffin. I hauled Ansel Baines's corpse from Louisville out to our upper farm in a crosstie wagon, then to a backcountry church. Just before we reached the grave the bottom of the flimsy coffin gave way, and we barely got it into the ground without spilling the body. I developed a bitter antipathy for the hooded brotherhood of Ku Klux Klan bullies. The criminals preyed shamefully upon Mississippians during those years.

Today I look back in an effort to recall what I did to earn the mandated sixteen units of credit necessary to enter college, or what I actually learned in Choctaw County Agricultural High School. I know that I had a double dose of agriculture, some history, far too little English, and plane and solid geometry. I took algebra in the last period of the day, and half the time the teacher dismissed the class. I came away from that class knowing about as much about algebra as a goat. In that school I had some good and some extremely poor and indifferent teachers. Many of them were young girls just out of college. The library was scarcely worthy of the name, and many of its books had little relevance to the school's teaching program. All were as safe and moral as the Elsie Dinsmore series. The Ku Klux Klan superintendent sought to curb our access to "undesirable" books. *Huckleberry Finn* and *Tom Sawyer* were deemed unfit for high school students to read. I read Mark Twain's masterpieces under my bed covers after all lights in the dormitory were expected to be out. I read other books the same way, including the sweet nature-oriented Limberlost books by Gene Stratton Porter, some Greek legends, and a little safe Eddie Guest–type poetry. I think the classroom building would have crumbled to the ground if I had accidentally discovered and read Walt Whitman's *Leaves of Grass*. I did get smatterings of

English, history, Latin, geometry, and a subject called expression. I got a glimmer too that there was something more exciting in the field of learning to be found in college.

One thing was firmly fixed in my mind from the outset. I wanted nothing to do with A&M College, its agricultural courses, or its registrars. Like many a rural Mississippi lad I aspired to be a lawyer, not knowing any more about that profession than I was able to observe on Saturday trips to town, when every notary public shyster walked the streets in search of clients. I had visions of being in the courtroom arguing cases before jurors and judges. My senior year I settled on the fact that I was going to the University of Mississippi. I knew no more about that school than what my mathematics teacher had told me. He had dropped out a year to teach school and earn enough money to complete his senior year in engineering. In addition to advising me to enroll at the university, he said I should apply for the job of keeping up the university golf course. He thought it would be very much like the outdoor work I had done at Weir.

THE YEARS WHEN I WAS IN school in Mississippi have been labeled "Progressive" by historians. In some essential institutional areas they no doubt were, because previous conditions could hardly have been less promising. There were, however, so many negative facts associated with that era in Mississippi that it seems a profanation of the word to describe it as "Progressive." There had come a dividing line between the tumultuous years of James Kimble Vardaman's governorship, 1904 to 1908, and those of Theodore Gilmore Bilbo, governor from 1916 to 1920. Vardaman, though a racist, had some progressive ideas. Bilbo was, in contrast, a thoroughgoing racist and demagogue. Both men personified the deterrent forces at work in Mississippi that created such an unfortunate image of the state.

A limited statistical profile indicates that Mississippi during the Vardaman-Bilbo years was fully a quarter of a century behind many of the newer agrarian industrial states. Its population was well nigh static, increasing only slightly more than 7,000 in the decade 1910–1920. Outmigration of both blacks and whites cut sharply into population growth. In addition, Mississippi was overwhelmingly rural. Only 13.4 percent of its people could be classified as urban dwellers, and these few lived in small towns, none with a population of more than 50,000. The rest of us, numbering 1,550,407, lived in the country on 272,101 farms, which averaged less than seventy acres. There was a decided racial imbalance, with 826,752 born of native white parents and 935,184 black. Only approximately half of the school-age children maintained an average daily attendance in the 138-day schools. Slightly more than 5,000 students were enrolled in all the colleges in the state the year I entered the University of Mississippi as a freshman, and slightly more than 20 percent of the population of voting age were too illiterate to mark a ballot. Even more disheartening was the fact that perhaps three times as many persons were functionally illiterate. This was the sociopolitical climate in which I spent my youth, and Bilboism flourished.

Locally Mississippians were entrapped in an archaic system of government that kept us divided and almost continuously involved in tumultuous political campaigns and elections. Counties were divided into beats, each presided over by a supervisor who, as a member of the county board, had broad fiscal and road maintenance responsibilities. The results almost always were picayunish financing and a system of patchwork dirt roads.

In 1916 the U.S. Congress enacted the first federal aid-to-highways law and the first gasoline and automobile taxing law. Between that date and 1921, Governor Bilbo committed Mississippi to participation in the federal aid program, but he lacked legislative support and funds with which to make more than a token gesture. In the year federal aid was enacted, roads in Mississippi were muddy streaks, largely unmarked, and disconnected at county borders. An occasional signboard provided only vague directions between towns. There were no highway maps, and gasoline pumps were far between, most of them located in front of hardware and country stores. To attempt to cross the state in any direction was a confusing if not hazardous ordeal. I do not recall, however, hearing any teacher mention any of these negative facts about Mississippi. We endured our lack of progress with traditional fortitude and cherished any changes, however minuscule, that promised improvement. There was political interference with every institution, from the insane asylum to the public universities and colleges. The years in which I struggled to secure an education coincided with the heyday of rednecked control over the people of Mississippi.

IN MID-APRIL 1925 I GRADUATED from high school at twenty-one years of age, having been admitted to the incoming freshman class in Ole Miss. The finishing gesture of the high school was its commencement. It is almost an academic axiom that commencement speakers are to be listened to politely and promptly put out of mind. I still recall, however, the address delivered by Professor A. B. Butts, a political scientist from A&M College. He came with carefully made charts to reinforce his message. These demonstrated the monetary worth of high school and college education. I do not recall that the professor uttered one word recommending the process of education as a means of maturing the intellectual man. His well-charted message was harmonious with the main currents of the Harding-Coolidge era in American history. It was indeed encouraging to be told that we had attended high school for four years so we could make money and enjoy the good life, and that if we went to college life would be even richer and more enjoyable. But on some vague intellectual level I refused to accept the professor's preachment. Making money as a central objective in life seemed to me too shallow a reward for expending so much energy and time in pursuit of a solid education. Anyway, after the shattering depression of 1920–1921, Mississippi hardly seemed a likely place to make money.

I had no more cash in hand in the spring of 1925 than I had had in 1921, but I did have a high school diploma. The season for planting a cotton crop was well advanced, almost too far to mature a crop before frost. Already weeds in the field were knee-high. Generously my father allowed me to plant ten of the best acres of his land. I plowed almost day and night until fertilizer and seed could be put in the ground. Season and insects were merciful to me, the soil was rich and warm enough to sprout seeds quickly, and a heavy application of nitrogen caused the plants to grow rapidly. That was in many respects the happiest summer of my life to date. I was a cotton farmer in my own right, weevil damage was minimal, and cotton prices remained stable.

My cotton opened early, and I was able to get most of it picked by mid-September. My yield was a little over a bale to the acre, and I was assured sufficient funds to pay my first year's expenses at Ole Miss, whether or not I got the job on the golf course. I hauled cotton pickers to the field at dawn and cotton to the gin night and day, sleeping atop the loaded wagon until it was my turn under the gin's suction pipe. I must have been the weariest freshman to enter Ole Miss that fall, but I had my cotton money in the bank. I almost never go back to visit in Mississippi that I don't go out to that field to pat the earth with a sense of reverence. Perhaps I was the only entering freshman who came to the campus directly from the cotton patch.

GOING AWAY TO COLLEGE BROUGHT a nearly complete separation from my family and the old and ailing agrarian way of life that had held my people in its unrelenting grip for the past century in rural Mississippi. Never again would I be a farmer or be trapped in the complex economic and sociological peonage of the old and dying hill-country cotton routine. Little did I appreciate, however, how fundamental were the post–World War I changes in creating demarcations between two distinct eras in the history of the South.

With my departure for Ole Miss in the fall of 1925, I learned that separating oneself from nearly two centuries of a traditional agrarian way of life involves deep emotions. Anyone who has never lived and worked on a farm probably cannot appreciate how intimately one can become attached to simple, everyday things. There is always the affection for the land and its seasonal moods, the woods, and the age-old landmarks, including roads and footpaths.

There also prevailed an affection for domestic animals. In my family's case there was only a thin line between attachment to members of the family and to our farm animals. In early spring 1922, when Missouri,

Kentucky, and Tennessee mule traders made their annual appearance in Louisville, I went with my father to purchase a pair of light cotton mules. My father was a poor horse trader, but we selected a mismatched pair of young mules, one black, the other light tan. We came in time to cherish these animals as if they had human personalities. They faithfully responded to whatever calls we made on them, never balking or acting up. When I came home from my high school graduation in April 1925, my father allowed me to use not only some of his best cotton land but also the services of black Kate. She pulled my plows, and with her teammate, Nell, hauled cotton choppers in the spring, pickers in the fall, and cotton to the gin. In leaving the farm I was saddened at having to leave these animals behind. Kate lived out an unusually long, mulish life span of thirty-five years, surviving until I had become a full professor in the University of Kentucky.

There were also the farm dogs with their distinct personalities, always on hand to see what was going on. They followed us to the fields, ran rabbits and feral cats, and killed snakes. Once Jack, the fox terrier, jumped ahead of my sister Wilma and killed a big copperhead. For days his head was badly swollen, a bitter reward for his heroism.

I left behind that September day not only the land with its familiar hills, field patterns, and timberlines, but the annual renewal of life in the blooming of the dogwoods, wild azaleas, plums, red haws, and cucumber trees. There were the fishing and swimming holes in the creek, the sedge fields populated with rabbits, quail, and brown field rats, the woods that concealed the haunts of squirrels, foxes, raccoons, and opossums. All of these were indelibly impressed upon my memory and emotions. The most painful part of my separation from the land was the realization that I was leaving behind my father and mother with limited help to work the farm, destined to live out their lives in a badly declining farm economy.

5

Out of the Cotton Patch

On Sunday Morning, September 13, 1925, I loaded onto a cotton wagon a brand-new trunk containing most of my worldly possessions and hauled it to town to be deposited with the Gulf, Mobile, and Northern Railway's baggage master. At the same time I purchased a ticket for Oxford to be used the next day. While I was there the northbound passenger train arrived with two or three Ole Miss boys aboard. One of these was Dees Stribling of Philadelphia, Mississippi, a boy with whom I soon became well acquainted. These acts began my entry into the world of the university.

Monday morning I set forth for Oxford, less than a hundred miles away, in company with two other Mississippi boys, Henry Lee Rogers of Louisville and Will Brantley of Philadelphia. That day I began a tiring, circuitous railway journey to the university and, figuratively, set out on a much longer one into the future. It took us all day and into early evening to make the trip. We changed trains three times, each change involving boring waits in run-down, dusty Mississippi country villages. When we boarded the mainline Illinois Central train in Winona it had on board a fairly large and noisy crowd of Ole Miss students from Jackson and southern Mississippi. Upperclassmen ran up and down the aisles hazing freshmen, and there was a general hullabaloo, people shouting inanities, laughing, and some misbehaving rowdily. Henry Lee Rogers claimed Will and me as his freshmen and protected us from being paddled, or "tallied," as it was called.

On that train ride I had impressed upon me an important lesson about college and life in general. People who made the loudest noise on the train or on campus, proving themselves to be collegiate, would be among the poorest students. Later I observed that many of them were not on the Oxford-bound train following the Christmas holidays. I recall distinctly one girl, who must have been the belle of her high school, shouting "Hey, hey!" to everybody and everything. Later on the campus her jenny-like mating call rang through the ancient oak grove. She was one of the early fail-outs.

The battered little Illinois Central station in Oxford was more befitting a crossroads landing than a university town. It rested sleepily at the foot of the long wooded hill path that led to the center of the university campus. When we arrived that September evening it seemed that everybody in the university had come down in good Mississippi country style to meet the train. There was more whooping and shouting, with upperclassmen greeting returning friends and black trunk hostlers chanting their solicitations. Dees Stribling was there to meet us, and he and Henry Lee Rogers escorted Will Brantley and me up the hill, fending off paddle-happy sophomores. We were safely deposited in our rooms, which in a sense were for that night our fortresses.

The Ole Miss campus in 1925 was out in the wooded countryside of Lafayette County. Student baggage was hauled onto the campus by "country Negroes," who supplemented their sharecropper incomes by using their cotton mules and wagons as drays. One of the more aggressive hostlers solicited patronage by crying around the circle drive, "I never missed a train, I never lost a trunk." I quickly learned that although blacks were unable to enroll for classes in the university, they ran most of the service functions. Waiters in the cooperative dining halls were black, as were the bedmakers and janitors; and the chancellor's right-hand man, Calvin, served as timekeeper and rang the big bell signaling class changes. Electronic time was still well off in the future.

Aside from these functionaries, there were the black campus characters who hung around the students and were as much a part of the institutional tradition as were the professors or the Confederate monument at the foot of the circle. Two of these were "Blind Jim" and Strawberry. Jim was "dean" of the freshman class, periodically exacting tuition fees from his charges. Each entering class was under moral obligation to buy their "dean" a new suit of clothes, sometimes dressing him up in a senatorial swallowtail coat. He was always around places where students congregated, countering their crude jokes, selling peanuts, and sometimes scolding his tormentors. He was present at athletic events, sometimes leading freshman cheers and always attracting attention. Strawberry was a campus fixture without portfolio. His only stock in trade was a good-natured clownishness. He was the butt of harmless banter and jokes and the beneficiary of modest alms. The place of these blacks in university life was one of the first things we learned about the traditions of the institution. Blacks had been an intimate part of the university's history since its founding, and it may have been a black who gave it the name Ole Miss.

That night in September 1925 when we climbed the hill to the campus, most of us, I am sure, knew nothing of the moral and political turmoil that had recently wrought injury to the university, any more than most of us were aware of other events in the state's history during the past quarter of a century. At that moment the university was enjoying a fairly stable administrative period after a blustery moment of scandal. The former chancellor, Joseph Neely Powers, a thoroughgoing political hack of the old demagogic Mississippi machine, had been dismissed from office. He was a glad-hander who had been appointed by Governor Theodore G. Bilbo and supported also by Bilbo's successor, Lee M. Russell. Powers apparently had never graduated from college and lacked the academic experience to direct the administrative affairs of a progressive university.

In 1923 the acting dean of education, Roswell W. Rogers, charged that Chancellor Powers was immoral and had been involved in a clandestine affair with an auburn-haired woman. Like a Faulknerian character, he was said to have honored the Chisca Hotel in Memphis with his romantic trysts, and had even invited his lady-love to the campus when his family was absent. This was not necessarily a moral lapse in the eyes of Bilbo and Russell. In fact, Chancellor and Mrs. Powers were houseguests in the governor's mansion the night before his hearing before the Board of Trustees. The case stirred up considerable newspaper publicity. The sycophantic Board of Trustees exonerated Powers, but not before his reputation was besmirched, if not permanently sullied. When "Granny" Henry L. Whitfield was elected governor in 1924 he appointed a new board of trustees for the university, and Chancellor Powers was retired from office.

Alfred E. Hume, a civil engineer and mathematician, was made chancellor to succeed Powers. He had a distinctly Calvinistic turn of mind about personal and academic decorum. He kept a watchful eye on the campus, helping to make rules and personally overseeing their enforcement. One of the chancellor's rules ran counter to the changing times. Students were forbidden to have automobiles on the campus, or anywhere in Oxford for that matter. There was also a rigid rule about once-a-week chapel attendance, in which students no doubt were supposed to recharge their spiritual tanks in quarter-hour sessions. Outwardly, at least, there seemed to prevail on the campus a democratic spirit. In 1912 Lee M. Russell, subsequently governor, had prevailed upon the Mississippi legislature to ban fraternities from the campuses of the university and public colleges.

Over the years, perhaps from its founding, Ole Miss had the reputation in the state of being an elitist or, in 1920s lingo, a "jelly bean" school. I knew little or nothing of this when I arrived on the campus. I am certain that, with the exception of a few insecure snobs, the great majority of students in the 1920s were pretty much of a common social and economic stratum of Mississippi society.

In time I came to know Chancellor Hume in a somewhat formal

way. I covered his office for a year or two as a reporter for the student newspaper, the *Mississippian*. Early in my academic career I was amazed to learn how little students knew or cared about the background and personnel of their university. I think students entering Ole Miss in the 1920s were too naive and overawed in making adjustments to campus life to be concerned with the university's history and politics. The University of Mississippi was small, with fewer than a thousand students enrolled in 1925. We were gathered from almost every section of the state. I am sure that most of us did not know that there existed on the campus *sub rosa* chapters of several Greek-letter fraternities. But we quickly learned that the university administration was strongly committed to its role *in loco parentis,* apparently thinking that students should take vows of sobriety and celibacy.

The faculty and instructional staff numbered fewer than a hundred, only nine of whom had the doctor of philosophy degree. Chancellor Hume had only a bachelor's degree, in civil engineering. Partly because of financial stringency and partly from a strong provinciality, there had developed over the years a considerable amount of academic inbreeding. Too, the faculty exhibited a preponderance of graduates of southern universities and colleges. On the credit side, there existed a core of older faculty members who were good teachers and men dedicated to their fields. With the exception of the dean of women, who taught genteel courses in clothing design and food preparation, Ole Miss was a man's world. The student body was overwhelmingly male, so the coeds enjoyed a highly favorable advantage in their wide choices of dates and even in seeking prospective husbands.

Although by tradition the university was a liberal arts institution, its library contained fewer than 40,000 volumes and few or no rare books or manuscripts. The catalogs of that era made no mention of academic counseling for students. I recall vividly my anguishing experience in getting registered for my first semester's work. I obtained a registration card from the registrar's office and set forth to find the necessary professorial offices to procure course approvals. So far as I had an adviser, it was Dees Stribling, a senior law student who knew the procedures and undertook to help me make out my schedule. There prevailed a near panic on the campus over freshman English and algebra. Some unidentified campus freehand artist had adorned the bathrooms and toilets with the likenesses of mathematics professor Torrey and English professor Wallace, labeling them all-American sons-of-bitches. Upperclassmen told ghoulish stories about their crucifixions in these professors' courses. In addition Dees strongly advised me to avoid taking freshman English under Professor Arthur Palmer Hudson. To do so, he said, would be akin to committing academic hara-kiri. We spent much of registration day juggling my program so as to avoid Hudson, but finally I had no alternative but to lay my neck on the Hudson chopping block. At one point in the process of trying to bypass the professorial ogre, we walked past his office door, and I saw a tall, bony man, the perfect counterpart of Ichabod Crane. Later, when we had exhausted our choices, Dees walked in with my card, explaining to Professor Hudson that we had spent much of the day trying to schedule his section of English 1A. Later I learned that Dees himself still had to repeat freshman English. I could not have imagined at that gloomy moment that I was to profit mightily from Professor Hudson's teaching in freshman English and in several other courses, or that we would enjoy a warm friendship that lasted throughout his life. I came away from Ole Miss deeply in debt to him for his demanding instruction.

SINCE I HAD NOT BEEN GIVEN the job on the golf course before arriving on the campus, I planned to go out for freshman football. Before I did so, however, I went out to the golf course to see if there was still a possibility of employment. I saw standing in the middle of the ninth green a tall, dignified, gray-haired man holding the shaft of a broad coco-mat drag. I introduced myself, and before I could inquire about the job he thrust the shaft into my hand and told me to start work. This man was Dr. Peter Rowland, professor of pharmacology in the two-year medical school. He told me my pay would be twenty dollars a month. I was to rake the sand greens, cut the fairways, rake leaves, fill in gullies, and occasionally oil the sand on the greens with cast-off motor oil. In my spare moments I was to watch out for poachers and collect dues.

Used in connection with the University of Mississippi's nine-hole cow-pasture golf course in 1925, the title "greenskeeper" was a misnomer. I doubt if there existed another course as primitive this side of the highlands of Scotland. Doubtless the fairways had once been a hillside cotton field in the heyday of Lafayette County plantations. In its abandoned and eroded state the site must have been haven to an abundance of cottontail rabbits. The designer of the course had had to plan fairways that wound in and around clumps of scrub oak trees, across gullies, and along slanting hogback hills. In many places it was almost impossible to distinguish fairways from the rough—most of the ground was rough. The "greens" were well tamped clay hardpans surrounded by sloped embankments to trap drifting sand, which followed the natural laws of physics and gathered in the lowest levels in rain and windstorms. The course was barren of green sod in about the same degree as my ignorance of the game of golf. Fortunately the basic needs of the course pretty well synchronized with my skills. I did know how to use a hoe and shovel, operate a lawnmower, rake leaves, and dam up gullies. I kept the golf course job the entire time I was at Ole Miss. At the beginning of my junior year I quit and got a job as a library assistant, but I had hardly checked out my first book before Professor A. L. Bondurant came and asked me to go back to the golf course at double my former pay, and said that I could employ a part-time assistant.

The three years in which I worked on that course were years of seasoning for me in the field of human nature. They brought me into association with many faculty members. The president of the club, "Uncle" Peter Rowland, as his friends and medical students called him, was a thoroughly fine, old-fashioned southern gentleman with gracious and courtly manners. His son Herron was proprietor of Rowland's Drug Store on a prominent corner of the courthouse square uptown, later to become famous as a Faulkner hangout. "Uncle" Peter was a brother of Dunbar Rowland, an old organizational pioneer in the field of state and regional history. There was also the foursome of deans Milden, Bondurant, Shaw, and Swan, who dropped their official duties promptly at three o'clock most days and played golf until dinnertime. None of them was a prime golfer, and their scores were in the vicinity of the horse latitudes. Occasionally I would see one of them improve his lie, sneak an ill-driven ball out of the rough, or perform other mayhem on course rules.

Among the students who often came out to play was George Healy, later editor of the New Orleans *Times Picayune.* He was always decked out in proper golf togs, as became a hep college sports reporter of the 1920s. Then there was the varied assortment of professionals and townspeople. Some of them were friendly, while others appeared too haughty to notice a college boy in overalls working on the course—unless it was to ask him if he had seen where a badly sliced ball had landed. I was eventually able to acquire a cheap set of clubs for myself and played the course every week or so.

Often I had as a volunteer helper a young black named Willie. I never knew Willie's last name or where he lived. Like the morning dew he would appear and disappear silently. My other occasional volunteer helper was William Faulkner. Bill occasionally played the course but also worked on it spasmodically, perhaps partly for exercise, partly because he wished to help improve it, and possibly because he liked to be off with a couple of lads who asked no prying questions and engaged him in no high-flown literary conversation. A more compelling reason may have been the three sizable waterholes on the course that Willie suggested were productive spots from which to rescue golf balls that had gone astray. Bill was not averse to granting asylum to a few of the maverick balls to replenish his own supply.

Sometimes Bill was talkative, and we discussed the ever-nagging subjects of scrubby grass, shedding oak leaves, and the rescue of errant balls. At other times he was as silent as the Confederate monument. Never do I recall his saying anything about writing, showing any curiosity about what I was studying, or discussing anything intellectual related to the university. Our relationship was confined narrowly to the never-ending chores of maintaining the greens and fairways and seining the waterholes for wayward balls. He at least tolerated our unintrusive company.

I knew that Bill was the author of a couple of slender books, and the gossip was that he aspired to be a literary man, but that is practically all

I knew about him at that time. I now wonder how many aggravating situations connected with the writing of his novels that he was resolving in his mind as he worked on the course. His brothers John and Dean were students in the university, and on one or two occasions I had to appeal to his father, Murray Falkner, the university's registrar, to permit me to delay payment of my registration fees, a thing granted with the greatest kindness and understanding. Bill, however, was, so far as I knew, simply a man about the town and campus. There were times when he would appear on the course with the Oxford lawyer Phil Stone, and occasionally he would play with Ella Somerville or Dorothy Oldham. Ella Somerville was the mother figure of the artistically inclined on campus and in town. Dorothy Oldham was the sister of Estelle, Faulkner's future wife, and later was custodian of his papers and memorabilia, which were placed in the university's library. She was a beautiful girl and a fair golfer. Sometimes, not often, Bill filled in as a fourth player for the deanly duffers who daily hacked and divoted their way around the course. They were as dubious of being caught in Bill's company as he was of being seen fraternizing with them.

As time passed I heard amusing stories about the antics of my "gray" friend of the golf course. The stories of his dismissal as branch postmaster for inattention to duty were told and retold around the campus. He was said to have distributed letters to various postal boxes without regard to the addressee. Apparently he passed a lot of time playing poker with the athletes of the east wing of Gordon Hall, and on many late evenings could be seen in the university power plant fraternizing with the workmen. As Winston Churchill said about Russia, for me Bill was an "enigma wrapped in a mystery." I sensed one thing with some certainty—Bill Faulkner possessed qualities that set him apart from other members of the golf set, an indefinable sophistication that belied his shabby dress and the general disregard in which some people held him.

One afternoon just before the end of my last year at Ole Miss, Bill came to me to report that he had suddenly and mysteriously lost his golf clubs while playing the course, which meant that he was out of play until he could recover them because he was too poor, he said, to buy new ones.

For two months after that Willie and I searched high and low for Bill's clubs without success. When I left the university in June 1928 to attend summer school in the University of Virginia, I resigned my job as "greens-keeper" of that old cow pasture course with genuine nostalgia. That stretch of well-trampled ground had helped sustain me during my three years in Oxford. As with the cotton field on my father's farm back in Winston County, I had developed a deep affection for the course, poor as it was. I parted with Bill Faulkner and Willie with a pang of nostalgia. I realized, however, that I was leaving behind a bit of unfinished business. I had been unable to solve the mystery of Bill's disappearing golf clubs.

Soon after I arrived in Charlottesville there came a crumpled and soiled envelope that contained a letter from Bill Faulkner. He came close to charging me with a capital felony. Bill had spotted his golf clubs in the hands of a geology professor who said he thought I had loaned them to him. In a fit of anger Bill suggested that I had "loaned" the professor his clubs for a price. That letter made me as angry as Bill seemed to be. With my temper in full bloom, I wrote a forthright denunciation of both Bill and the professor. It must have singed his mustache, for in about ten days I received an apologetic reply. Apparently the professor had "played through" Bill and absentmindedly picked up his clubs while Bill was taking a drink of water, then was unable to account for the remarkable fact that he did not own the clubs with which he was playing. All these years I have wondered where the professor left his own clubs.

The following summer I was back in Oxford for a brief visit with Professor Charles S. Sydnor, and for old times' sake I played a round of golf on that barren wasteland. Near the fourth green I caught up with the ever-present foursome of university deans, still chipping away at the fairways and wrinkling the sandy surfaces of the greens. Like Rip Van Winkle, they seemed hardly to have left the fairways since 1925. I remarked to one of them that I had been reading reviews of "Our Bill's" novels in very sophisticated journals. He approached me, hand hollowed around his mouth, and whispered audibly, "We don't talk about him here."

I saw William Faulkner only once after leaving Ole Miss. In November 1955, Phi Alpha Theta, the honorary history fraternity, hosted a dinner at the annual meeting of the Southern Historical Association in Memphis. Three after-dinner speakers were to address the recent *Brown v. Board of Education* decision by the Supreme Court that ended school segregation. Bill, who had been awarded the Nobel Prize for Literature in 1950, was one of the speakers, and I was toastmaster. The topic was highly controversial and produced rumors of a possible disruption, though none occurred. During a quiet moment I approached Bill and reminded him of our three-year association on the Ole Miss golf course. His response was a blow to my ego. He gave me a cold stare of nonrecognition. I might as well have addressed myself to the stone Confederate soldier on the Lafayette County Courthouse lawn.

Back when Bill was dismissed as branch postmaster in Oxford, he is said to have remarked that he "did not want to be at the beck and call of every son-of-a-bitch with two cents in his pocket." In 1987, some years after his death, the U.S. Postal Service issued a stamp in his honor in its Prominent Americans series. It portrayed Bill in a literary pose, pipe in hand. Now the "sons-of-bitches" in Oxford and elsewhere would have to pay twenty-two cents to take his likeness home with them.

LIFE ON THE OLE MISS CAMPUS in the jazzy, flapperish 1920s was much like that throughout American academia. Students reacted exuberantly to the social impulses of the times, with an especially overenthusiastic sense of being partially free of parental control. Despite the strictness of the university administration concerning campus social and behavioral mores, there was after all a considerable latitude in response to the times. Prohibition on the campus, as in the rest of Mississippi and the nation, did not curb drinking. Some of the dormitory basements emitted mash odors more nearly resembling a German brewery than the traditional musty scent of student dwellings. An appreciable amount of alcoholic spirits was brought onto the campus, some from Memphis bootleggers and a lot from Lafayette County moonshiners.

In such a congregation of southern boys there was bound to be a fascination with the regional pastime of shooting craps. On occasion I saw boys kneeling on a quilt spread on a dormitory room floor rolling bones. I recall once happening on a game and seeing a boy with dollar bills folded and tucked between his toes. The dice were rolling in his favor, and he was raking in the next month's board money. William Faulkner surely had himself and a host of Ole Miss boys in mind when he wrote *The Reivers*. In fact, there are many touches of the university community in his books and short stories. The Memphis hotels, especially the Chisca, were frolicsome centers for weekend student adventurers. In those years Beale Street was at its peak as a center of jazz. The famous black bandsman W. C. Handy on occasion brought his musicians to play for campus dances. For a majority of students, however, life was lived at a much tamer pace, often being little more exciting than attending a literary society smoker, participating in a YMCA crusade, or gathering in a dormitory room for a bull session.

There was also a great deal of pranking and practical joking, some of which got a little out of control at times. I once perpetrated a practical joke on a law school senior. In some way I had become Otho Magee's freshman mail boy. I went into the post office every morning on my way to breakfast, but there was never a letter for his box. Yet he always greeted me as if I bore a letter telling him he had suddenly fallen heir to a rich estate. I became bored with this futile business and proceeded to remedy the situation. The *Memphis Commercial Appeal* ran a weekly page of letters, supposedly from children, on its eighth page. I sent a letter to the editor of this page saying that Otho was a handsome black-haired basketball player who was pining away on the Ole Miss campus for lack of love, and promising that he would send a photograph of himself to the first ten girls who wrote him. About a week after the letter appeared in the newspaper, the university postmaster placed a slip in Otho's box asking me to call at the window for his mail. When I presented the slip the postmaster hoisted up to the window one of Uncle Sam's famous striped bags filled with letters. When I delivered Otho his mail that morning he all but went into a state of shock. And that was only the beginning. Letters kept coming for weeks, and Otho's social correspondence became a matter of general dormitory interest. No one, I am sure, had ever imagined there were so many amorous females out in the hinterlands. I was found out and retired summarily as Otho Magee's mail boy because of this bit of good samaritanism.

I lived my freshman year in Taylor Hall, a dilapidated pre–Civil War dormitory, much of which had been used as an infirmary and morgue during the war. The old building contained thirty rooms as dreary as any to be found in an academic dwelling on the North American continent. Approximately seventy of us all but formed a closed union of poverty isolated from the rest of the campus. My first semester I roomed with a quiet and exceedingly neat lad from the wild Vinegar Bend section of southeast Mississippi. The rugged life in Taylor Hall, however, was too arduous for him, and he moved to more modern quarters. During the second semester I roomed with James F. Hopkins, also from Winston County, and we roomed together off and on during the remaining time I was at Ole Miss.

The general pattern of my college career was basically set in my freshman year. Professors and their courses varied widely in quality and interest. For example, the first class I met was in political science and was taught by the freshman football coach, fresh out of Grinnell College in Iowa with an A.B. degree. He practically recited the textbook to us, but in a charming manner. Later he moved to Louisville, Kentucky, and I saw him often. He held various positions ranging from professor of political science in the University of Louisville to chairman of the Kentucky Elections Commission.

True to the horrifying early predictions, Hudson's freshman English course proved a grueling ordeal, but in the end a rewarding one. No one ever seemed to realize the trauma Hudson must have suffered because of our homegrown brand of Mississippi English. He published in mimeograph form a weekly freshman theme review, which contained samples of the best and the worst of the week's offerings. I still have my file, a revealing document as to public school teaching in the state in the 1920s.

During my years in the university I sat through several courses that were intellectual time-wasters. The professors would have been of greater practical service to the teaching profession as hoe hands on a cotton farm. No course I sat through, however, could have excelled in mediocrity one dealing with the history of modern Europe. Fortunately for future generations of students, that professor recognized his inadequacy and moved to Birmingham to become a real estate agent. There were nevertheless some truly bright and intellectually dedicated professors on the Ole Miss faculty. There arrived on the campus in the fall of 1925 one of the ablest young scholars ever to serve the institution. Charles S. Sydnor had only recently received his doctorate in history from the Johns Hopkins University. He came to the campus a well-prepared and motivated historian. By some chance I became acquainted with him early, and on frequent occasions I had conversations with him about the study of history. Sydnor was a gentle-mannered Virginian, son of a Presbyterian minister, and perhaps an idealist. He inspired me to abandon my intention to study law and become instead a historian. As with Palmer Hudson, my friendship with Charlie Sydnor lasted throughout his lifetime. I took only one of his courses, and that in English history. It was outside the classroom that he was in many ways my most inspiring teacher. I was happy in later years to see him achieve a national reputation as a sound historical scholar.

The first semester at Ole Miss was a period of some uncertainty for me. I lived in mortal fear of falling a victim to that institution's academic yellow peril, a midterm warning that my work was not up to the desired university standard. The dean had a less than subtle way of informing students that unless they improved their grades during the latter half of the semester they should purchase a one-way railway ticket home. I escaped this dreaded fate, but I was witness to the downfall of several victims, including my friend Will Brantley, who had ridden to Oxford with Henry Lee Rogers and me. Will returned to Philadelphia and later was elected sheriff of Neshoba County. The university was culpable for its failure to provide counseling to struggling students. An entering student was on his own except for such fellow student assistance as he could muster.

During my first two years at Ole Miss there prevailed a friendly, almost intimate family relationship among students. There were, as a matter of human nature, some snobs. Many of the boys from the Delta area behaved the way cotton planters' sons had ever behaved in the South. But most of us were either small-town or rural boys and girls. Boys took their meals in a large cooperative dining hall, paying a relatively low pro rata monthly bill. The whole time I was at Ole Miss there persisted some conflict between students who wanted to have a blessing before meals and those who wanted to get down to the business of eating without that formality. Once the dining hall manager took a vote on whether to have the blessing or not, and the majority favored it. The first time after this vote the manager called on what he thought would be a safe lad to initiate the new dispensation. The boy stepped forth, raised his hand, and called on the Lord to bless everything and everybody in Mississippi in a ten-minute invocation. From then on we began our meals without ceremony.

The insidious idiocy of hazing freshmen continued. This consisted of paddling them, cutting their hair, and making them run errands. The hair cutters seemed to be lineal descendants of bushwhackers, night riders, and Ku Klux Klansmen. I saw a poor, homesick freshman paddled unmercifully, an act that almost sent him home in defeat. Possibly because I was older than the average freshman I escaped the hazing. I looked upon the practice as barbaric, and I think the university administration shared my views.

I went home only twice a year, at Christmas and in June. The rest of the time I was campus-bound. Except for my mother's weekly letters, I was almost completely out of communication with my family. On my first Christmastime visit I arrived in Louisville a full-fledged college man with proof of my new station in life painted across the back of my yellow slicker. I spent the night with my uncle Walter Bennett in town, and the next morning in a heavy downpour of rain I mounted a mule and rode home on the same muddy road over which I had hauled lumber, crossties, and cotton. This indeed was a less than dignified homecoming for a lad who had been to Ole Miss.

The mid-1920s was the era of jazz and flapperdom. The current popular songs shaped student fancies and reactions. The jazz music of New Orleans and Memphis set the social and musical tempo of the times. During these years the university catalogs gave no evidence that the faculty recognized music as an essential ingredient of the liberal arts. I do not recall that there were concerts or any other type of formal musical performances on the campus. Thus we were left wandering in a morass of jazz, the Charleston, rolled-stockinged flappers, slender beaded dresses, and bobbed hair. This was a watershed era when southern girls struck their first full blows for social deliverance. So shocking was this revolt to some that the editor of the *Mississippian* in 1927 wrote an editorial in praise of the old-fashioned girl. It was republished in the country weekly press of the state. There were, however, some barriers the coeds still had to smash. I do not recall ever seeing one smoke a cigarette—the tobacco companies had not yet penetrated our campus fortress with their subtle advertising.

Just as coeds threw corsets and garters to the wind, college men marched in lockstep with the style fads of the age. Their bell-bottom trousers, pointed shoes, narrow braided ties, crepe de chine shirts, yellow rain slickers, and feather-edge haircuts dated them. They read *College Humor,* the local campus humor magazine, *The Scream,* and the sports pages of the *Commercial Appeal.* The poets, musicians, and self-announced writers among us were set apart.

This was a period in southern history in which the Ku Klux Klan, "sawdust-trail" evangelists, and William Jennings Bryan and his rabble-rousing fundamentalists were hot on the trail of sinners and evolutionists. The fundamentalists had just stampeded the Tennessee legislature into passing an anti-"monkey" law, and John Thomas Scopes had been tried in Dayton for breaking that law. They had secured the passage of a similar law in Mississippi. On my first visit home one of my Clark uncles, whose mind was set in the anti-monkey groove, asked me if the Ole Miss professors had tinkered with my soul. I assured him that none had mentioned my soul but that some of them were playing havoc with my peace of mind with their tests and impending examinations.

At the time the Mississippi anti-evolution law went into effect in January 1927, I was enrolled in a course in eugenics and heredity in which we were concerned with chromosomes and other physical matters in an orthodox way. Just before the law went into effect and intellectual freedom in Mississippi went out the window, Professor L. E. Thatcher delivered a provocative lecture on evolution. I think under no other circumstance would I have been so keenly alerted about the subject or so completely repulsed by the nonsensical antics of the southern fundamentalists. Remarkably, no one on the university faculty seems to have gone to Jackson to appear before the legislature to protest passage of the law. One reason, I think, was that no professor was engaged in research and writing in the biological sciences. Too, the turgid history of high-handed political interference in university affairs had had an intellectually stifling effect.

Mississippi, along with its neighboring southern states, was a happy hunting ground for such barnstorming evangelists as Gypsy Smith and Mordecai Ham. In a revival meeting in Jackson, Smith had brought about a rash of conversions of self-proclaimed hardened sinners. One of these was Frederick Sullins, editor of the *Jackson Daily News,* who by his own confession at the altar had sinned prodigiously. Readers of his editorials were quick to support this statement. Sullins took to the sawdust trail, preaching his brand of redemption. On one occasion he left an audience in Charlotte, North Carolina, in tears after describing his turning away from the fleshpots of Mississippi politics. He came to Ole Miss and lectured to us about our prodigal ways and suggested that we follow in his steps. Less sensationally, the Oxford churches and the campus YMCA asserted prior claims on our religious activities. Each fall W. D. Weatherford, southern regional secretary of the YMCA, spent a week or two in Oxford emphasizing the moral mission of that organization. Certainly my uncle Clifton had little reason to fear I had fallen among the heathens just because I had gone to college.

In retrospect I am convinced that some of the extracurricular activities in which I participated were far more rewarding than some of the courses I sat through. Though only marginally successful as a debater, I nevertheless profited from the experience. During my entire time at Ole Miss I was active in the Phi Sigma Literary Society, serving one term as president. This gave me experience in debating and speaking. I think, however, that my most rewarding activity was serving as a reporter on the campus newspaper, the *Mississippian.* In my junior year I was an associate editor and reported on the activities of the chancellor's office; that is, I wrote stories from whatever information the chancellor saw fit to give me. I developed a high regard for Chancellor Hume, and he came to know at least who I was.

In the fall of 1927, on the eve of the Ole Miss–A&M College football game, the night watchman, the university's sole security guard, either resigned or was fired. Chancellor Hume asked me to enlist ten dependable students to form a campus ranger squad to manage traffic and to keep some semblance of order among pugnacious drunks at the game. We were undeputized, unarmed, and unmarked. Our only weapon was our power of persuasion. Fortunately there were no serious incidents, and the football fans left the campus without provoking fights or bullying the callow student guards. I, however, came desperately close to committing one of life's more embarrassing blunders. Someone parked a big black car in the middle of the driveway in front of the Lyceum Building, completely blocking traffic. I rushed up officiously to order the car moved, but before I could do so I saw Dean Alfred M. Milden of the College of Arts and Sciences emerge through a side door accompanied by a man I did not know. Before I could say anything he turned to the man and said, "Senator Stephens, I want you to meet one of our students." The driver of the car was U.S. Senator Hubert D. Stephens.

During the remainder of that year Bob Davis, a burly football player, and I patrolled the campus. This was a risky business for us and for the university. We had little or no constabulary authority. So far as I can now recall the university had no visible fire protective devices, and certainly no motor vehicle in which we could move about the campus. Our pay as watchmen was minimal.

Though my expenses were modest, even for the 1920s, my cotton money was almost exhausted by the end of my sophomore year, and I was wholly dependent on my earnings, except for a small loan from the Field Co-operative Fund. This fund had been established by B. B. Jones, a Mississippi native, who had struck it rich in the oil business. He lived in Virginia but came to the campus occasionally to lecture us on the importance of keeping a precise record of everything we spent throughout life.

Near Christmas each year he sent the student borrowers a gift of apples from his Virginia orchard.

My golf course job was a great boon but fell short of paying all my expenses. My roommate, James Hopkins, was much younger and much smarter. He came from the little Winston County village of Noxapater. His father was a rural mail carrier, and his mother worked in the village post office. He never seemed to be under financial stress. While I was struggling to earn enough money to pay my bills and still keep up with my classwork, Hop seemed unruffled, making all A's. Little could either of us have imagined that a decade later we would be colleagues in the Department of History in the University of Kentucky, and that he would write two significant books and organize and edit the first six volumes of *The Papers of Henry Clay*.

At the end of my junior year I lacked only twelve hours of completing course work for a degree. My uncle Albert Bennett was superintendent of the Albemarle County schools in Virginia and a part-time professor in the University of Virginia. Once when he came back to Mississippi to visit his family, while I was still at Ole Miss, he expressed the opinion that I was not getting a good education. He proposed that I attempt to salvage a part of my wasted academic career by attending a session at the University of Virginia, though he was doubtful that I could pass the courses in that superior institution. Under ordinary circumstances the University of Mississippi would have refused permission for a senior student to complete work for a degree in another institution. I am certain that my acquaintance with the famous foursome of deans on the golf course worked in my favor. In addition, Dean A. L. Bondurant was a Virginian who thought highly of that state's university, so permission was granted and I was accepted at Virginia.

Once again I boarded the Gulf, Mobile, and Northern train to set forth on a fresh educational adventure. I left Louisville in June 1928, bound for Charlottesville, Virginia. That town might as well have been located on another continent so far as my travel and geographical experience was concerned. I had crossed the Mississippi border only once in my life, in 1919 when I went on an excursion and visited with our old neighbors the Boswell boys in Mobile. I knew next to nothing about the Upper South, except that most of the Civil War had been fought there. And I knew that the Southern Railway train that I had boarded in Middleton, Tennessee, ran past Chattanooga. Beyond that point I was in *terra incognita*. Riding the day coach on a Southern local train for the better part of two days and a night was not an exhilarating experience. By the time the train reached Spartanburg, South Carolina, where I had to change, I was worn out and no doubt exasperated the conductor and porter by asking them how far it was to Charlottesville. They did not know precisely, only that it was a long way ahead and beyond their run.

In the morning of my second day I arrived in Charlottesville to begin the challenge of doing university work in an institution that was said to have much higher academic standards than Ole Miss. Soon after I was settled in my uncle's apartment, he and my aunt went away for much of the early summer, and I was left on my own to sink or swim in that more rarefied university atmosphere. Luckily I had met on the train a boy from Georgia who was going to summer school, and soon we became acquainted with several other students from the Lower South. As a group we were well insulated against the fraternity snobbishness that prevailed in that day on the University of Virginia campus.

When I registered for classes at Virginia I felt much the same as I had at Ole Miss in the fall of 1925. My uncle had talked so emphatically about the superiority of Virginia that I wondered if I could possibly meet the challenges of the courses I was required to take, three in Shakespeare and two in sociology. Four of the professors proved to be excellent lecturers, and one was poorer than the weakest one I had had at Ole Miss. Fortunately three of the ablest professors were scholars with good reputations and the authors of published books. Professor Hench of the English Department, I discovered, had a campus "graveyard" reputation similar to that of A. P. Hudson at Ole Miss. I found him an exciting instructor who made Shakespeare's tragedies understandable for me.

When I completed the remaining academic hours for my bachelor's degree and my final grades were available, my uncle went with me to the registrar's office to receive the report, which showed that I had an all-A record. That startled him. As we walked down the Colonnade toward Cabell Hall he said that if I would go to medical school he would pay my expenses. I had not the slightest inclination to become a doctor of medicine, nor were my courses at Ole Miss planned to meet the requirements for entry into a school of medicine.

That summer the University of Virginia had more extracurricular programs than Ole Miss had had during my years on that campus. There were musical and lecture programs. One speaker was an economist from Vanderbilt University who placed more emphasis on folksy humor than on his science. Part of his discussion had to do with his ups and downs as a chicken farmer just outside Nashville. I am convinced that his economics were as outmoded in the waning days of Coolidge prosperity as those of the Ole Miss professor who translated all the processes of economics into the simplified terms of rural Pontotoc County. He had perhaps never taken the pains to digest the writings of John Stuart Mill or T. R. Malthus.

Two of the lecturers who visited Virginia that summer were Senators Alben W. Barkley of Kentucky and James W. Wadsworth Jr. of New York. Accompanying them was John L. Lewis, president of the United Mine Workers union. The presiding master of ceremonies said the three had come to Charlottesville in a small plane. I could hardly concentrate on the senators' speeches for speculating on how those three could have crowded themselves into the plane and then how the plane could have gotten off the ground. Barkley was the first Kentucky politician I was to see. Little did I know that night that in future years I would develop a friendship with his son, grandchildren, and second wife, Jane. After his death I helped with the removal of his papers to the University of Kentucky Library, an act that gave me a fairly intimate view of his family life.

Of almost as much meaning to me as the courses I took at the University of Virginia were opportunities to visit several parts of that state. My aunt Katherine Bennett was from the village of Fairfield in the Shenandoah Valley just south of Lexington, Virginia. I accompanied her several times on visits to her family, the Fultzes, who lived in the old Governor Clark home. This was close by the birthplace of John Breckinridge, Caleb Wallace, Ephraim McDowell, and many other Kentucky pioneers.

One could not live even briefly in Charlottesville without becoming aware of the influence of Thomas Jefferson. I had classes along his colonnade, used the library in the Rotunda, and even had a class in the little Jeffersonian theater. That outmoded building was furnished in ancient country-school style with wooden benches and desks, strongly reminiscent of the ones in my mother's Scotts Springs schoolhouse. It appeared that every young man who had attended the University of Virginia had carved his initials on the benches and desks. One morning in the midst of a sociology class, a dog jumped a rabbit out behind the building and treed it just outside the back door. The dog set up such a howling and commotion that he drowned out the professor, who asked me to go down and see if I could quieten the animal. I felt right back home in Mississippi with my dog Jack and a rabbit up a hollow tree rather than on my uncle's highly vaunted University of Virginia campus. Mr. Jefferson might have preferred it that way.

At the time of my brief enrollment, the University of Virginia was undergoing a social revolution, one that seemed to me, however, to follow only a natural course of civilized life. For the first time women were admitted to the sacrosanct halls of masculinity in graduate and professional courses. This proved to be an unsettling moment for the Virginia gentlemen. When a woman entered the classroom they stamped their feet, clawed the tops of their desks, and uttered other sounds of derision. For those of us who had been coeducationally housebroken during our academic careers, the protests seemed a rare form of adolescent paranoia. I wondered if Virginia males had even accepted the fact of motherhood. In later years the old order at Virginia suffered a further modification as a result of the democratization program instituted by President Colgate Darden.

IN THE FALL OF 1928 I COULD look back on my undergraduate experience and raise the question of how much my intellectual status had been improved. How good an education had I actually received? Was I well enough prepared to find a job and grow in it? What had I learned in my classes and extracurricular college associations? My grade record at Ole Miss was strictly average. I had spent three years trying to overcome an inadequate high school preparation and striving to make intellectual advancement at the university level.

Only a corporal's guard of my Ole Miss professors had made genuine contributions to my educational maturity. Too many of the courses I took were of an introductory nature and gave me only a faint glimmer of their fields. For instance, I took an introductory course in sociology taught by a droning professor who leaned heavily on E. A. Ross's pioneering textbook in the field. In psychology I was introduced to the Jukes and Callicack families, the Helmholtz theory of color vision, and little else. My courses in history (with one exception), English literature, folklore, Greek, French, and biology were indeed enlightening. I had little talent for languages, but I did learn enough French to pass my doctoral language examination handily. Throughout my post-baccalaureate years I have deeply regretted my ignorance of chemistry, mathematics, physics, and music. I got a grounding in both biology and geology, but not in geography. As a matter of fact, the latter subject was not listed among the courses of study at Ole Miss. The University of Mississippi's undergraduate course offerings were largely limited to the basics in the liberal arts and in three or four professional areas.

The faculty, as noted, was sparse in numbers and limited in training and scholarly experience. Few members made any pretense of doing research or writing. Few had published significant articles or books. There was a dedicated core of professors and students who sought to charter a chapter of Phi Beta Kappa, but the senate of that organization refused a charter on grounds of political interference with university administration, racial discrimination, overemphasis on athletics, and lack of greater scholarly accomplishment. Despite that denial the university produced a commendable number of leaders for Mississippi and other parts of the nation, Rhodes scholars, and undergraduates who went on to graduate schools and became able scholars.

Personally my years at Ole Miss were cardinal ones in which I became aware of the world of scholarship, was intellectually stimulated, and profited from extracurricular activities and rich human associations. During these years I was enabled to sever the stifling bondage of rural provinciality that had held my family and its neighbors in thralldom for generations. Much of the factual information that was peddled in the classroom may have been already archaic, but my undergraduate years were a necessary seasoning time that formed an intellectual passage to further academic growth.

6

~

BIG RIVER

I RECEIVED THE MORE RUGGED PART OF MY EDUCATION in human relations well beyond the bounds of a university campus. As I approached the end of my freshman year at Ole Miss, I needed to find a summer job that would allow me to remain in college. I had two close friends who were graduating in engineering that spring and were going to work with the United States Corps of Engineers in the Fourth District. They suggested that I apply to Captain Sam Hornsby in Natchez for a summer job on a Mississippi River quarterboat. I did so and was instructed to report for work on May 26, Confederate Memorial Day, 1926. I had read several of Mark Twain's books but not *Life on the Mississippi*. One could not live in the state of Mississippi, however, without being aware of the great mile-wide river that flowed so authoritatively along most of the state's western boundary.

Natchez was in a considerably different region of Mississippi from those I knew. The town had a long and exciting history, often regarded as romantic. Over the course of a century and a half, it had been all things to all men and had existed under four or five national flags. I traveled from Jackson aboard a "Little J" passenger train that gave the impression that it had been operating when the Spanish flag flew over the territory. The road was in fact a historic museum piece of railway in the Old Southwest. Its passenger trains were not noted for either speed or punctuality. The only promise they held out to passengers was that they would get them there eventually. That was agreeable with me because I was in no hurry to get to Natchez. On the day of my arrival the town was as silent as a Confederate mausoleum. There was very little traffic in the streets, but on all sides the crepe myrtle and magnolias were in bloom, even in the yards of the black shanties, and there were plenty of those.

I went aboard Quarterboat 12 at the upper end of the famous/infamous Natchez-Under-the-Hill. The quarterboat and barges had just been towed out of their winter anchorages and were being readied for a long summer's duty upstream. A work crew was being assembled, the pantry stocked with a fairly ample supply of staple groceries, and barges were being loaded with tools and lumber.

There was already aboard a florid-faced veteran of many a summer on the willow bars. "Cap'n" Frank Gross, like the quarterboat, had just come away from winter quarters in New Orleans. The old man had spent his entire mature life on or near the river; some said he had been born in a hollow log caught in a driftwood pile. Making up the flotilla were two quarterboats, several barges, and three tender towboats. The latter consisted of the small tugboat *Tunica* and the two sternwheelers *Teche* and *Lafourche,* vessels that bore the scars of past summers along the great willow bars.

We spent several days anchored beneath the Natchez loess bluff. The set of the river current had shifted until it bore directly against the headland of the notorious old underhill town where historically thousands of flatboats and steamboats had tied up on their downriver trips. When I saw this narrow shoulder of well-publicized earth in 1926 it was being gradually snatched away in great chunks by the river. We sat on the screened texas deck of the quarterboat at night and listened to the land caving into the river. It was as though the devil came nightly to foreclose on this ancient portion of sinful earth.

Although I had earlier spent two years on a dredgeboat, I had no firsthand knowledge of either a steamboat or a Mississippi River quarterboat. Too, I had not been told prior to my arrival in Natchez what my duties would be. I soon learned, however, that when we had stocked the boat and accompanying barges and assembled a work crew of black willow-cutters, we would be towed upstream to the willow and cottonwood bars to live for three and a half months virtually beyond the pale of civilization. One morning Captain Hornsby decided we were ready to depart for duty. There was considerable excitement as the tow was lashed together and the little sternwheeler *Teche* nosed up and attached lines to the stanchions of the barges and quarterboat. We were headed for Fairchild Island, upstream around the great sweeping Giles Bend.

Leon Joseph Toomey, the stumpy little captain of the *Teche*, had been married the day before, and he was much agitated at this sudden and unexpected turn of events. Cap'n Sam Hornsby, the "big" captain, was an unromantic soul who at that moment was concentrating on cutting willows and cottonwoods and weaving them into fascine mattresses, not on giving the nod to his steamboat captain's honeymoon. The *Teche* shivered and groaned as it exerted all its power to get us to our Fairchild Island anchorage. "Stumpy" Toomey swore vengeance against all unromantic rivermen who had ever negotiated Giles Bend. He was so short of stature that he could hardly see over the *Teche*'s oversized wheel. We moved against the river's powerful current at a snail's pace of between four and seven miles an hour. When we finally moved up alongside the island and lashed onto the forward "deadman,"* Stumpy unleashed the *Teche* and turned tail downriver at full throttle. The little sternwheeler had probably never kicked up such a high brushpile in its long life on the river. When the quarterboat and barges were securely anchored and all the deadmen were buried five or six feet in the sand, we were ready to invade the willow brake. We observed a shantyboat tied out only a hundred feet or so

---

* A log about eleven feet long that was buried deep in the bank to serve as an anchor

upstream, and its occupants became greatly agitated by our appearance. They rushed down to know if they should move their boat. They were uncertain whether, under the national and Engineers flags, we came as friends or foes. As a matter of fact we were not precisely either.

The following morning an old-time willow bar foreman and I led a contingent of a hundred or so black workers onto the island and began laying low the slender willow and cottonwood saplings that grew in such profusion. I certainly was no stranger to either the ax or black workmen, but never had I been thrown in company with so many human beings of uncertain background and experience. Many of our charges were alumni of the Parchman Penitentiary in Mississippi and the Angola Prison in Louisiana. Among them were individuals who seemed never to have swung an ax, and before I could get my three-man teams spaced and at work, one of the men swung an ax full force at a willow twig and split his shin. By noon some of the men had collected an assortment of head and shoulder bruises caused by falling willows. The men worked in threes, one to handle the ax and two to pile the willows in orderly windrows.

That first day on Fairchild Island we cleared several acres of ground, cutting the trees from around the shantyboaters' moonshine still, leaving it exposed for all to see. The next morning both the shantyboat and the still were gone, taken no doubt to a more secluded willow brake well out of reach of the "government men." In a few days we had cleared the island, and Stumpy Toomey and the *Teche* shoved us upstream to a much larger bar. At each anchorage, ways were built on which to fabricate fascine mattresses. These were woven similarly to coarse coco mats. The slender willow boles were laid in two-by-four frames, forty by seventy feet in dimension and approximately two feet thick. The willows and cottonwoods were laid in overlapping courses, and the completed mattress was battened together with a series of two-by-fours attached to upright stanchions. A foreman and crew worked each end of the mat, and the crews had to coordinate their movements to keep the weaving process even. The mattresses would eventually be towed to New Orleans and sunk beneath the harbor to stabilize the river channel.

Workmen laboring on the mattress ways were exposed to constant danger from the willows dropped in from overhead by a crane. A wayward bole could give a man a crippling swipe. Too, there was constant danger of a man stepping through the timbers into the swift river current. During the summer months the sun shone down on the sandbar in stifling fury. There was a constant roar from the noise of axes, falling trees, and laborers shouting, singing, swearing, or bantering. Occasionally a branch thrashed an overheated workman's face, causing a burst of temper. In that steamy river jungle the foreman of such a wild crew of virtually illiterate men, many of them ex-convicts, had to be work director, peacemaker, and stern disciplinarian. I was never threatened by any of the men, which was fortunate, since I was not armed to protect myself against a possible assault.

Added to the clatter of the workmen was that of anguished red-wing blackbirds and purple grackles. In the early summer months literally thousands of these birds nested in the willows and cottonwoods. It seemed that every other tree bore a nest. We splattered eggs and hatchling birds over the ground, and in late afternoon when we left the bar the windrows would swarm with screaming birds.

Wagon crews hauled the saplings to the mattress ways on long-coupled, mule-drawn wagons. This work was done by crews hired by a private contractor, and our captain had little or no control over them. They camped on the sandbars in shabby tents or with no tents at all. The mule skinners' sole objective in life seemed to be to live until sundown, when they could get into a crap game or go whoring with a camp follower. Our crews, of course, shared the same objectives, and frequent were the fights in those nightly carousals. There was, however, a vaguely defined social dividing line between the two crews, drawn largely by the fact that the quarterboat hirelings were better paid.

The United States Corps of Engineers, not noted for their humanitarian concerns, did at least not interfere with the workers' preferred vices. When we moved from one anchorage to another the men were allowed to load their crap boards and other recreational paraphernalia on board the lumber barges. I never knew how the whores traveled from one anchorage to another unless they followed the willow wagon trains. They seemed always to be on hand when we arrived.

We were cutting willows on the Louisiana side of the river on Buckridge Bar one morning when a worker came galloping up on a pony and said Cap'n Gross wanted me to come to the boat posthaste. I feared he was going to fire me or, maybe worse, throw me in the river. When I got to the mattress ways the old man's face was livid. He had just fired a mat foreman and been sassed by a laborer. He asked me if I had ever killed "a nigger." I assured him I was wholly innocent of that act. He told me to get up on the ways and to keep my end up with that of the old-time foreman on the other end. He further instructed me to see that his black nemesis was placed in a favorable position to be struck by falling willows or to drop through the mattress into the river. I had never seen a mat woven, but I had to learn the art almost instantly or lose my job. The crew generously helped me, and I found it unnecessary to commit assault and battery on a recalcitrant workman. Fortunately Cap'n Gross's temper cooled, and I was never placed in imminent danger of getting knocked into kingdom come by a willow or stumbling into the swift river current. After a few days I felt a reserved confidence that we could keep up our end of the mattress in the weaving process.

For me that first summer on the river was a season of frequent changes in assignment. Our boat was headquarters for the revetment operations above Natchez. It was equipped with an office, a fairly large fireproof vault, and an arsenal of firearms, including two or three Kelly machine guns, which I am certain no one on board knew how to load and fire. The steward of the boat was a general service man whose duties included bookkeeping, daily reporting, commissary, and other domestic chores. The old-timer who had that job was Sargeant Daly, a wily ex-soldier with a love of strong spirits in generous measure. By some means not known to Cap'n Hornsby, he was able to keep an ample stock of "red" liquor on board. One day the "big" cap'n uncovered Daly's precious stock and gave him unshirted hell for having it. Sargeant was ready with the answer—he was saving the liquor for the appropriate moment to present it to Cap'n Hornsby as a gift, expressing his high esteem. Apparently Sargeant had drunk his way through several lonely summer seasons on the quarter-boat and only some bureaucrat in New Orleans could say how many daily reports. He had tried Cap'n Hornsby's rather fragile patience many times over. One morning in mid-July 1926 his Irish luck played out. He was a week or ten days behind in preparing the daily work report, he had garbled a grocery order, he was hopelessly late in preparing the payroll, and he was tipsily drunk. Cap'n Sam fired him but required him to stay on the boat until he could instruct me as to procedures. Since I was the only person aboard who had been to college, Cap'n Hornsby assumed that I could bring order out of the confusion in the office. He took me off the mattress ways and put me in the office with stern orders that I was to bring the daily journal reports up to date almost instantly and get the next payroll ready.

In the midst of my consternation over the sudden turn of events (I knew as little about bookkeeping as I had known about mattress-weaving) the cook came up from the kitchen and said he was out of bay leaves, a necessary ingredient for his Cajun-style cooking. I was familiar with bay leaves growing on the trees around my home in Winston County, but that people ate them was bizarre news to me. I asked the drunken Sargeant how much bay leaves I should order, and he suggested that a hundred and fifty or two hundred pounds would be about right. When the order arrived aboard the decrepit old packet boat *Uncle Oliver*, the clerk enquired, "What in hell are you boys doing with these damned bay leaves? Eating them in place of turnip greens?" The bags containing the leaves were stacked up waist high and contained enough seasoning to supply every cajun cook all the way from St. Joseph to Avery Island.

When I was taken out of the unclassified work force and placed in the office, my conditions of employment technically were changed, but I was not a qualified civil servant. Because of this I was instructed to go into hiding if the district engineer should suddenly appear unannounced for an inspection of the operation. As predicted, the flagboat *John B. Newton* frequently anchored alongside one of our work barges with a spit-and-polish army colonel aboard. I went into hiding all right, but I found remarkably few places on the quarterboat to keep out of sight. Everywhere I turned I seemed to run into that nosy colonel. He must have thought the vanishing figure was an illegitimate son of Cap'n Gross. Fortunately he ignored my presence, but I have often wondered who he thought tended the office.

Being a steward on a Mississippi River quarterboat was a position that had few dull moments except for keeping that nagging daily journal current, a thing that no doubt was partly responsible for Sargeant Daly's taking to drink. The foremen, in the manner of college professors, checked their roll books twice a day and reported nightly the number of laborers at work and their hours. These reports were recorded in summary numbers in the daily journal report, along with the number of mattresses fabricated and under way, meals served, and all other pertinent operational data. The biweekly payroll was prepared from the foremen's reports, and requests for funds were made to the Engineers office in New Orleans. Paying the crew by check was out of the question. Probably many of them would have refused to accept a piece of paper in lieu of cash. Moreover, if many of them had legal names, they had forgotten them or wished to keep them well concealed. We carried some workers on the payroll as "Gold Tooth," "Broad Horn," "Brock Island," and other outlandish pseudonyms. The cash for the payroll was delivered by Railway Express to either Natchez or Vicksburg, depending on the location of the boats. The money then was delivered to the quarterboat aboard the *Teche* or the *Lafourche*. We would go the afternoon before and be ready to receive the money early next morning. It was delivered to us in two old-fashioned traveling-man valises. I carried the bags, and Cap'n Hornsby and Cap'n Toomey walked alongside, armed with revolvers. For some reason there was a rule against our riding in an automobile with the payroll money. On board the boat we stowed the bags in a chest underneath the seat in the pilot house, and the three of us sat on the box until we reached the quarterboat, where we placed the valises in the safety vault.

Paying off that sweaty, impatient crew of four or five hundred men was an impressive experience. The steward called each worker's name and the amount of wages due him, the man stepped forward and touched the point of a pencil to paper, and the steward entered his cross-mark in the "big" book. Cap'n Sam Hornsby counted out the correct amount of wages and handed the money to Cap'n Gross, who recounted it and handed it to the workman. No one, I think, knew how many of those laborers could actually write their names; the assumption was that none could. Anyway, the mode of paying off the workers was complicated enough, taking up almost three quarters of a day's time. To have secured written signatures would have made the task almost endless.

When payday was over, the boat and willow bar were largely deserted. The local members of the white crew hustled back to Natchez for the weekend, and the black workers went only God knew where. From that day in May when I went aboard the boat at Natchez until I left near Davis Island, just below Vicksburg, I never spent a night away from the river. Many weekends Cap'n Gross and I were the only whites left aboard. The first few weekends we ate our meals in tomblike silence, or we sat reading and napping on the texas deck without conversation. The old man had a habit of walking around with his galluses sliding down his arms until they finally drifted down to his knees.

Cap'n Gross obviously regarded me as a college upstart whom he had to tolerate along with aggravating workmen and sandbar heat waves. After several silent weekends he began to talk about his experiences on the great river, for which he had a passionate love and an abiding respect. He knew every bend from Vicksburg to New Orleans and had lived and worked in many of them. In his time he had known a host of old-time rivermen and the boats on which they worked. Cap'n Gross had witnessed devastating floods. He had seen the opening of earth-slashing crevasses that tore at the land as though some natural giant was wielding a mighty knife. He was fully aware that the willful Mississippi was constantly threatening to reopen its prehistoric path down the Atchafalaya to the Gulf. Like all old rivermen, Cap'n Gross was highly respectful of folk beliefs and superstitions. He was adamant: "Never cut a capstan"—that is, always pass it on the right. One night he awakened me saying that he had heard something fall off a shelf, a certain omen of death. His life was governed by the superstitions and taboos of the river. Sadly, I had no way of recording his reminiscences. They would have enriched even Mark Twain's *Life on the Mississippi*.

Contrary to popular belief, those old-timers were not boisterous and rowdy. There was not even a tinge of the legendary "half horse, half alligator" about them. They observed a rather strict code of civility, seldom using profanity or showing great anger. In many ways they were old-style southern Victorians. Sometime in the past there may have been an unpleasant incident concerning women aboard the quarterboats, for there was a strict rule against their coming aboard. In July 1926 our working fleet consisted of two quarterboats and an assortment of materials barges. Quarterboat 16 was anchored upstream about five miles above Buckridge Bar, and although it was part of our fleet, it was under the supervision of an overgrown, athletic engineer named Larson from the University of Minnesota. On one of those dull and humid Sunday afternoons the big Swede stripped off his clothes, jumped into the river, and headed for our boat in a marathon swim. At the same time two lady acquaintances of Cap'n Gross surprised him by coming aboard our quarterboat, rules or no rules against feminine visitors. They were hardly seated on the texas deck before Cap'n Gross looked upstream and spotted Larson plowing his way toward the boat in bold overhand strokes. Realizing the Minnesota engineer was buck naked, he went down to the lumber barge and refused to let him land. Larson was near exhaustion, but he made a final brave effort and landed on a sandbar downstream, out of sight of the ladies. I robed him in a bed sheet and headed him afoot back to his quarterboat.

Weekends were dull indeed. There was little to do except eat, read, and try to sleep. One of the foremen fought off boredom by close study of female anatomy as portrayed in the undergarment pages of the Sears and Roebuck catalog. Someone had left an outdated copy of it aboard, and the foreman had many vicarious romantic trysts. Somewhere he found a piece of red cedar and spent weeks carving a graceful Venus of the Sandbars. She was somewhat heavy in the loins, but graceful nevertheless. He cut out a pretty, youthful face and toasted his artistic production. When I left the quarterboat in September he presented me with his lady love, saying that he felt every college boy should have some intimate knowledge of the female figure. For sixty years this cedar lass has watched over me in college dormitory rooms, boardinghouses, and finally in my study, as much a relic of loneliness on a sandbar as a lesson in anatomy.

If only I had known some of the history of the Old Southwest during my summers on the Mississippi River, how much more exciting life could have been. Giles Bend and Fairchild Island were landmarks in the Aaron Burr–Harmon Blennerhassett debacle. A continuous flotilla of flatboats loaded with Ohio Valley produce and manned by self-proclaimed "half horse, half alligators" had passed that way en route to market at Natchez and New Orleans. After the advent of the steamboat came the hordes of emigrants and travelers who rode the packets to and from New Orleans. Once I stood on the spot and under the tree, not quite in Spanish territory, where it was said Andrew Jackson had married Rachel Donalson. The famous old boat landings at Grand Gulf and Rodney were now largely obliterated by hanging vines and lush riverbottom vegetation.

The only time I ever carried a pistol was on a trip across the tight driftwood pile at the mouth of the Big Black River on my way to Grand Gulf with a crew of black workers to assure that a shipment of groceries would wind up undiminished in our pantry instead of in those of shantyboat moonshiners, who had no scruples about laying hands on groceries wherever they could be found. On that occasion I was oblivious to the fact that I had made my way over the Big Black River at almost the precise spot where General Ulysses S. Grant's army had crossed on its campaign against Vicksburg. Buckridge Bar itself had clear claim to a historical footnote. That Louisiana riverbank wilderness had momentarily been opened to an eventful military maneuver, then was as quickly closed by a heavy growth of willows and cottonwoods. The jungle land had erased traces of civilization and history with bold strokes of natural concealment.

There was little of luxury aboard a working United States Engineers quarterboat, with two exceptions. The "texas boy" kept the rooms of the white crew spotless, and meals were served in old Natchez Hotel quality and style. The black waiter, Frank Hyles, was an ideal gourmet cook–waiter after the best Cajun dining tradition. There was not a Creole cook between St. Joseph and Avery Island who could prepare a more savory gumbo. Frank's other dishes were superb productions of Louisiana bayou country cuisine, including his dark roast coffee, which the rivermen gulped down by the gallon. Frank boasted of the fact that after three or four meals he knew what every man wanted to eat. Even later, after his return to the old Natchez Hotel restaurant, when a quarterboat man came in Frank would go into the kitchen and prepare an order to suit the visitor's particular taste.

Sometime in my early childhood I had heard people in the hill country say with disdain that Cajuns would eat anything that hopped, crawled, wiggled, or swam. There was much truth in this observation. The Mississippi River below Vicksburg swarmed with an abundance of small freshwater shrimp. Often the cook would lower a barrel baited with table scraps to just under the surface of the water, and after two or three days raise it to harvest a generous boiling of shrimp. These were placed in heavily permeated salt water, which caused them to ingest their maws. The boiled shrimp were then placed in the icebox, and in the evening the cook would bring these up to the texas deck where we would sit peeling, decapitating, and eating them until bedtime. I cultivated a taste for shrimp from those evening feasts. Once a bank caved into the river and dislodged a large ball of crawfish. The cook gathered these, and we ate them boiled-shrimp style. Occasionally someone would come aboard with a big bayou turtle, and the cooks would take several days preparing a soup that would please the palate of the most discriminating gourmet.

That quarterboat kitchen must have been one of the culinary wonders of the South. It was equipped with a large hotel-type coal-burning stove, a fairly large bake oven, and a couple of large stewing cauldrons in which most of the carcass of a steer, mixed with onions and potatoes, could be concocted into a stew. This stew, with huge pans of cornbread, was standard fare for the willow cutters. There was a room-sized icebox or refrigerator that could hold a couple of tons of ice along with beef carcasses, cases of eggs, crates of vegetables, and anything else that had to be kept cool. Behind the kitchen area was the cavernous workers' dining room, where ravenous men were packed in around long tables as tightly as sardines in a can.

The kitchen was one of the steward's thorny cares. There was eternal bickering between the cooks and the bakers. The cooks had to have a hot fire and the bakers a slow one, and they could never seem to agree to stagger their schedules. Aside from the heat and human irritation was the fact that the cooks worked with lethal butcher knives keen enough to play havoc with a human carcass. One sultry afternoon the texas boy ran up to the office to tell me that the head cook, Sol, was trying to make stew meat out of Aaron the baker. When I reached the scene of gore, Sol was hacking away at Aaron, who was crouched under a work table as far as he could crowd his body. When I got the knife away from the cook and made Aaron crawl out from under the table, I discovered that he had been cut to the bone across the skull, and his baker's cap had been cut in two. I resorted to the only first aid readily available on the boat—I filled the bleeding wound with tincture of iodine. We almost had to call out bloodhounds to catch that wounded baker. Miraculously he responded admirably to my treatment and in no time was back at his oven, fussing with his mortal enemy, Sol. These battles necessitated frequent pointed conversations that bore only temporary results.

Not only did we hold councils of war with the kitchen crew, we had to deal with the constant rowing among the laborers. As is always true in mass feeding, there was disgruntlement about the food. It was impossible to assemble that number of southern blacks without ensnaring several preachers among them, and they insisted on having grace in that inferno of a dining room before eating. A reverend would tap an iron triangle to announce the blessing, but getting an impatient horde of willow bar workers to observe such a formality was an adventure in utter futility. Yet Cap'n Sam Hornsby said I had to try. I armed myself with a hickory pick handle and demanded silence from the ungodly and brevity from the reverends. One evening following an unusually steamy ordeal of offering grace, I went out on the stern deck to recover my equilibrium. Two of the laborers lunged through the dining room door, and one of them brushed my back as he fell to the deck. When I turned around he lay at my feet writhing in the throes of death. A fight had started in the steaming dining room, and the dying man's assailant had hit him across the base of the skull with a capstan bar. A stream of furious diners pitched through the door and across the deck to the sandbar, ran the murderer down, and brought him back to the boat. Cap'n Hornsby was forced to take action. The prisoner was bound hand-and-foot, thrown across the back of a horse, and sent off under a select posse of his peers to the St. Joseph, Louisiana, jail. When the horse and posse had moved out of sight on the willow bar, I heard a bystander say, "When dey puts you in de St. Joe jail, dey ties de key to a swamp rabbit and you can't get out till you ketches dat rabbit and gets dat key."

Not all the rows that summer resulted in head cuttings and death. One morning a big, loose-jointed willow cutter named Broadhorn threatened to kill the mail boy. He said the boy had been carrying for several days a special delivery letter addressed to him. I got the fuming Broadhorn to delay his avowed assault long enough to open and read the letter. His family had written for him to come home at once—watermelons were ripe. I handed him the letter and told him to go ahead and decapitate the mail boy because he deserved the stern punishment for withholding such vital information. But by then no doubt the watermelons had already been eaten.

By no means was all of life on that boat a series of kitchen and sandbar rows, or even boring weekends. There were wonderful evenings on the texas deck when the old rivermen were in a reminiscent mood and talked of their experiences. They recalled distant summers they had spent in other bends and on other sandbars. They loved to recall the old steamboats that had once plied the lower Mississippi and the men who operated them. The pilots recited human tales of their cubbing days under old sternwheel captains who were even more colorful than Mark Twain's Captain Bixby. Every bend, cut-off, chute, and island had for them a history, often fraught with close calls and tragedy. Those men lived, loved, and respected the great river.

I can think of few more exhilarating experiences than breasting the powerful Mississippi River current in a sternwheel steamboat. Once we went on board the *Teche* to pick up the payroll in Vicksburg just at sunrise of a crystal clear day, and the wooded banks of the river seemed to part just to let us pass. That evening we went visiting aboard the steamer *Con-*

trol, the main sternwheeler of the Fifth Engineer Corps District. Its master, Bennie Bernstein, had "cubbed" under Stumpy Toomey, and Bennie had a score to settle. In a fit of anger on one occasion Stumpy had fired Bennie in midstream and made him jump off the *Teche.* Bennie was still smarting about this indignity, but also felt a sense of triumph because he was now master of a much bigger boat. After initially sparring over that old incident, the two captains began reminiscing about the fickle river and its way with steamboats.

The *Teche* drew an amount of water comparable to a heavy riverbottom dew. In fact Cap'n Toomey boasted he could run all the chutes and cut-offs between Natchez and Vicksburg. Nevertheless, his ego overpowered him. Even in midriver he would toot the whistle for a deckhand to take soundings. The man would toss the leadline as far ahead as possible and then feel the leather thong markers slip through his hands, and call out the marks. When he got tired of this charade he would call out, "N-o b-o-t-t-o-m-m-m, Cap," and wind up the line. In the morning after a night's carousal in the Vicksburg "quarter," the somnolent deckhand would be barely responsive on the downriver trip. When Stumpy tooted the whistle for the leadsman to take soundings, the man would drop the weight just over the prow and call out the markings in an almost inaudible murmur.

The sternwheeler *Teche* and its feisty master were soulmates. Both took the river in possessive strides. One afternoon when the little vessel was engaged in shifting barges and willow mats around out near midstream, the Standard Oil Company's "Big Momma," the *Sprague,* drifted silently out of the bend above Buckridge Bar in the sweeping slaunchwise, flanking movement of a long barge tow. The *Sprague's* pilot either did not see the *Teche* or out of pure devilment gave it a full spray of water from his boat's mighty forty-foot wheel. Cap'n Toomey was so infuriated at this insult that he ran out of his pilot house shouting eternal damnation to the Standard Oil Company, John D. Rockefeller, the *Sprague,* and its master of canine ancestry. I witnessed the incident, and when Stumpy came aboard the quarterboat I twitted him about stirring up a feud with the pilot of the river's famed leviathan sternwheeler, who could turn up a brushpile of water that would swamp Natchez. His reply was, "His boat may be bigger, but by God I'll cut him in two and whip half of him at a time!"

Our other tender boats, the *Tunica* and *Lafourche*, were absent most of the time, towing mattresses to New Orleans. Those boats stocked their pantries in either New Orleans or Natchez at government contract stores. The *Lafourche* carried a large enough crew to have a cook who acted as steward. Once the *Lafourche* came upriver and lashed to the quarterboat to await a tow. Her captain, a man named Pete, inquired about the condition of our stores. He said his drunken cook had stocked his boat with an overgenerous supply of maraschino cherries and little else. Cap'n Pete volunteered a generous exchange of cherries for some plain rib-tightening vittles. We added a limited surplus of maraschino cherries to our bulging store of bay leaves.

The flagboat of the Fourth Engineer District was the *John B. Newton*, which came up the river periodically on inspection trips. This boat was in a sense the commanding colonel's private vessel. Late one Saturday afternoon in August 1926, when our crews were away from the fleet for the weekend, the *Newton* glided in silently and lashed onto the downstream lumber barge. Already our fleet was putting all allowable pressure on the deadmen. The *Newton*'s crew intended to swab their flues and clean their boilers. Swinging out in the current, it threatened to yank us loose from our anchorage and set the whole fleet whirling off down the river out of control. Cap'n Gross spotted the *Newton* and headed across the lumber barges toward it. His galluses were easing off his shoulders and his face was becoming more flushed with every step. By the time he reached the *Newton*, his galluses swung down around his ankles and his temper soared into the stratosphere. He lashed the *Newton*'s master with an eloquent stream of vitriol that practically singed the boat's flag. Luckily, perhaps, the colonel was not aboard, but I doubt he would have intimidated Cap'n Gross in his state of rage. One thing was clear: Cap'n Gross did not intend to have us spend the weekend on a wild tow pitching down the Mississippi River. The *Newton*'s crew fired up and left us in search of a calmer anchorage in which to care for their boilers.

Those were transitional years on the Mississippi River. A new era in inland water transportation was dawning. The days of the grand old packets with their grand saloons had passed. Only two or three decrepit relics remained in service on the lower river. One of these, the *Betsey Ann* of Natchez, operated on an erratic schedule, hauling a few rural passengers and freight for moonshiners and picking up herds of cattle from swampland pastures. She was a shallow-draft craft that could poke her nose into almost any spot where there were passengers or freight.

Then there was the faithful old *Uncle Oliver* which, like a grand dame in her fading years, plied the river on a weekly schedule. On almost every trip she landed with us to unload freight and laborers. Once she arrived with a sizable shipment of six-inch bolts to be used in tying timber binders to mattress frame stanchions. On that occasion the pilot either misjudged the nearness to the quarterboat or was caught in a prodigal current and smashed three or four of the quarterboat's four-by-four fenders. Amidst the confusion one of our crew, waiting to unload the bolts, set off a second crisis. The *Uncle Oliver* had on board a mentally retarded, light-skinned deckhand whom our blacks teased by calling him "half-white." The dim-witted deckhand responded by throwing bolts at everything and everybody. Before he could be brought under control he had broken panes out of several windows and sent all of us scurrying for cover.

The *Uncle Oliver* had navigated in more glamorous days and under another name. Her architecture bore testimony to the times when Mississippi River packets were floating gingerbread palaces. She had a fairly large forward saloon and two rows of what must once have been comfortable staterooms. To complete her historical documentation she had a deep, mellow whistle and a large cracked bell that had once been aboard the famous *America*. Through the vicissitudes of storm and flood the bell had eventually been injured in a bridge accident and thereafter gave off a leaden clang. Nevertheless the *Oliver* bore an impressive pilot house and two tall smokestacks laced together by fancy bridgework. On several occasions the clerk invited me to be his guest on a round trip, but I was never able to go with him.

An interesting bit of folklore or superstition concerning the tramp dogs who traveled the river and were cared for by rivermen was associated with the riverboats and the older personnel of our fleet. The dogs would ride one of the government towboats or the *Uncle Oliver* and stop off with us and spend several days until the next boat came along, when they would be gone. I never learned whether or not they rode the big oil tows. Despite strict rules against bringing dogs on the quarterboat, these tramps were privileged animals. So long as the older rivermen could recall, there had been tramp dogs, and no one seemed to know their origin or their ultimate fate. To have mistreated one of them would have angered the gods of the Mississippi and maybe resulted in the fleet being torn from its anchorage in a storm.

There was the sternwheeler *Oleander*, which, almost like a wisp of river fog, made her scheduled runs to trim the navigation lights that stood lonely sentinel at the heads of the bends. Occasionally a strange boat from far upstream would slip by us, unnoticed and unidentified. Two new types of towboats had begun appearing on the river along with the three conventional Standard Oil Company boats. The latter delivered crude oil from the fields up the Red and Arkansas Rivers to the refineries at Baton Rouge. In the oil fleet were three large sternwheelers—the *Sprague*, the *Slack Barrett*, and the *D. R. Weller*. These boats pushed long tows of seven to nine barges, tows so long that it was necessary to mount white signal flags on their heads to give the pilots a notion of their positions in the navigational channels. The tows were too long to negotiate the river bends in straightforward thrusts, and it was necessary for them to make flanking movements. This was done by setting the wheels in slow reverse and positioning the rudder at an angle to drift the tow almost broadside to the current around the bend. The *Sprague* had been built in Pittsburgh to tow large numbers of coal barges, but she proved too large for the Ohio River channel. She was indeed a marvelous boat with her towering external skeletal superstructure, heavy low stacks, broad pilot house, deep mournful whistle, and, most of all, her forty-by-forty-foot wheel mounted with three- or four-foot-wide bucket planks. The big wheel was propelled by two massive rocker arms and kicked up a mighty brushpile that rocked everything afloat in its vicinity. The *Bar-*

rett and *Weller* were trimmer boats and less powerful than the *Sprague.* The "Big Momma" came the nearest to rivaling the river's power of any boat that had traveled it up to 1926.

In addition, there were two new diesel-fired, screw-driven, channel-type boats. These were operated by the newly organized Mississippi-Warrior Barge Line. The boats marked a radical departure in both mechanical and architectural design from the traditional Mississippi River steamboats. They were workhorses constructed for the utilitarian purpose of handling large volumes of grain and mineral ore out of the Midwest. There were both towboats and self-propelled barges, all painted a drab dark green, and all floating low in the water. They bore the names *Iowa, Illinois, Minnesota,* and other places in the Midwest. They had no traditional smokestacks, big bells, deep-throated whistles, or ornate pilot houses. The only remarkable thing about them was that they floated phenomenal tonnages of freight at better than average speed and earned for their owners rich dividends. They were forerunners of the modern channel-type, diesel-propelled towboats but retained some of the architectural features of the old sternwheelers.

Many nights I was awakened by the rocking of the quarterboat and the chugging of the engine and wheel sounds of a passing sternwheeler. It took two men on the long tows to make soundings, one to throw out the lead line and the other to shout the marks through a megaphone. Following a long-established tradition, the caller chanted the marks while turning the megaphone in a semicircle. I have never heard a lonelier sound than a lineman in the dead of night calling in a singsong voice: "Q-u-a-r-t-e-r l-e-s-s t-w-a-i-n, m-a-r-k t-w-a-i-n," and then, "N-o b-o-t-t-o-m-m-m-m!" Those days are gone. The leadlines with their leather thong markers are now museum pieces from the steamboat days, and it would be hard to find a deckhand who could call off the marks. Modern pilots have electronic devices at their fingertips that inform them about river depths and the condition of the channel generally.

During the summer there appeared in the Natchez and Vicksburg newspapers occasional accounts of human bodies being fished out of the river, some of them unidentified. I was still on the quarterboat when

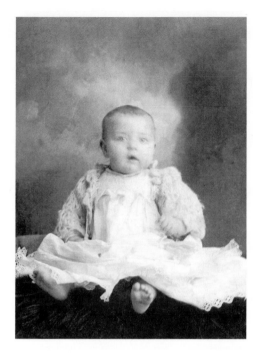

(Left) Thomas Dionysius Clark at age one. The first of seven children of John Collingsworth Clark and Sallie Jesse (Bennett) Clark, he was born July 14, 1903, in the homestead built by his great-grandfather Clark near Louisville, Mississippi, in the 1830s. "On this land the Clark family put down permanent roots," Clark wrote. "It would be occupied by several generations of the family to come."

Clark's father, John Collingsworth Clark, was a cotton farmer caught in hard times. "No hill country farmer ever exerted greater willpower and determination to survive adversity than my father," Clark wrote. His mother was a part-time schoolteacher, "a reader of books and magazines in a community where many people regarded such 'foolishness' as a waste of time." She instilled in him the love of learning that was to shape his life. (University of Kentucky Special Collections and Digital Programs)

Unless otherwise noted, photos are from the private collections of the Clark family.

(Above) A Cagle family reunion in 1904 brought together the descendants of German immigrants who had moved westward from South Carolina to Winston County, Mississippi. Janie Elvira (Cagle) Clark, daughter of a Louisville blacksmith, was Clark's paternal grandmother. One-year-old Tom is fourth from left in the back row, held by his father. His mother is to the right. (University of Kentucky Special Collections and Digital Programs)

(Below) This photo, taken about 1907, shows young Tom Clark standing with family members in front of his grandfather Clark's house, with its ample veranda. His parents are at left, his mother holding brother Marvin.

(Left) "My grandfather, Thomas Whitfield Clark, was representative of the traditional Virginia-Carolina social bearing," Clark noted. "His courtship notes to Janie Elvira Cagle are all in 'dripping' Victorian prose." After their marriage, Thomas W. Clark settled with his bride on land adjacent to his parents' farm. There they raised twelve offspring. (Right) "TD," as he was known in childhood, is seen here at about age nine (behind chair) with four of his siblings (from left), John Marvin, Walter Ervin, Wilma Effie, and Ernest Lester. One sister had died in infancy; another was born a year or two later.

(Below) Main Street in Louisville, Mississippi, in about 1903 boasted the county court-house, a bank, several stores, wooden sidewalks, and a public well in the middle of the street used by man and beast. Visible here are wagons laden with cotton crops. "Progress in Louisville mirrored the expansion in the life of the nation," Clark wrote. "It was an exciting time in which to be growing up."

(Above) Clark's maternal grandparents, Dyonicious Clark Bennett and Alice (McGee) Bennett, like his Clark grandparents, were farmers whose ancestors had migrated westward from the Carolinas. Their home (below) was a favorite visiting spot for young Tom and his siblings as they grew up. "My Bennett grandparents undertook to steer their grandchildren onto the road of success," Clark recalled.

Scotts Springs School, where Clark received some of his earliest education, was a typical rural one-room Mississippi schoolhouse of 1915. Clark's mother taught there and at other schools several months a year, earning about as much pay as a cotton picker. "Teachers, schools, and textbooks were working hard to prepare students to live by nineteenth-century standards as the twentieth pressed hard upon them."

(Right) On his sixteenth birthday Clark left home to take a job as cabin boy and deckhand on a dredgeboat carving a canal through Tallahega Swamp. He is barely visible here inside the dredge's giant dipper. "I lived perpetually smeared with grease and mud with little or no promise of future advancement," he recalled. "I was eighteen years old and becoming disillusioned." After more than two years of drudgery, he walked off the job and went in search of any school that would take him.

(Top left) Football proved to be Clark's passport to education. Although he had never heard of the game, he was immediately drafted for the Choctaw County Agricultural High School team. "Being a prospective player seemed to be far more important than being prepared to do high school work or even read and write." His junior-year photo (top right) shows a serious young man, perhaps still pondering his future life. The education he received in high school was meager, but it enabled him to enter the University of Mississippi ("Ole Miss") in 1925.

(Left) James Hopkins was Clark's roommate during most of his time at Ole Miss. "Hop" was to remain a lifelong friend, a longtime member of the University of Kentucky history department, a distinguished historian, and editor of *The Papers of Henry Clay*. His photo is inscribed "Your old Partner in Crime." (University of Kentucky Special Collections and Digital Programs)

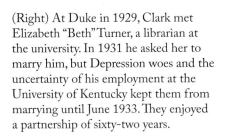

CHARLOTTESVILLE, VA. September 1 1931 DUE _____

On Demand _____ AFTER DATE, FOR VALUE RECEIVED I' PROMISE TO PAY TO

THE ORDER OF A. L. Bennett $ 1504,33

--------Fifteen Hundred and four and 33/100------------------ DOLLARS

NEGOTIABLE AND PAYABLE WITHOUT OFFSET AT THE NATIONAL BANK & TRUST CO., CHARLOTTESVILLE, VA.

THE MAKERS AND ENDORSERS OF THIS NOTE DO EACH HEREBY WAIVE THE PRESENTMENT OF AND DEMAND FOR PAYMENT OF SAID NOTE, AND ALSO WAIVE PROTEST, NOTICE OF PROTEST, AND NOTICE OF DISHONOR AND NON-PAYMENT THEREOF; AND DO HEREBY EXPRESSLY AGREE THAT SHOULD THE HOLDER OF THIS NOTE GIVE NOTICE OF PRESENTMENT, DEMAND FOR PAYMENT, PROTEST, NOTICE OF DISHONOR AND NON-PAYMENT THEREOF, THAT THE GIVING OF SUCH NOTICE SHALL NOT EFFECT THE VALIDITY OF THE ABOVE WAIVER; BUT SAID WAIVER SHALL BE AS VALID AND BINDING AS IF SUCH NOTICE HAD NOT BEEN GIVEN. THE SAID MAKERS AND ENDORSERS DO ALSO HEREBY WAIVE THE BENEFIT OF THEIR HOMESTEAD EXEMPTION AS TO THIS OBLIGATION, AND FURTHER AGREE TO PAY AN ATTORNEY'S FEE OF FIFTEEN (15) PER CENT. OF THE AMOUNT OF THIS NOTE FOR COLLECTION IN CASE PAYMENT SHALL NOT BE MADE AT MATURITY.

Money earned raising a cotton crop and work on the university golf course enabled Clark to graduate from Ole Miss in 1928. A loan from his uncle Albert Bennett then made it possible for him to pursue a master's degree in history at the University of Kentucky in 1928–1929. The toss of a nickel decided his choice of Kentucky for that degree.

(Left) In 1931, shortly before he received his doctorate in history from Duke, Clark sat for this portrait, a young man now sure of himself and ready to embark on his chosen career. "In spite of the Great Depression, 1931 was in many respects a fortunate time in which to begin a career as an American historian."

(Right) At Duke in 1929, Clark met Elizabeth "Beth" Turner, a librarian at the university. In 1931 he asked her to marry him, but Depression woes and the uncertainty of his employment at the University of Kentucky kept them from marrying until June 1933. They enjoyed a partnership of sixty-two years.

(Left) Frank LeRond McVey, president of the University of Kentucky from 1917 to 1940, was Clark's longtime mentor. He hired the young historian in 1931 to divide his time between teaching and developing the library's Special Collections department. "I owed my appointment largely to President McVey's vision for the university," Clark wrote. McVey acted, however, without consulting the head of the history department, Edward Tuthill (right), who never approved of Clark's collecting activities. The two were at loggerheads as long as Tuthill remained at the university. (University of Kentucky Special Collections and Digital Programs)

Clark was named head of the University of Kentucky history department in 1942, a post he held until 1965. In those years he built it into one of the premier history departments in the country, with special strength in southern history. He is shown here in his Frazee Hall office in 1955. (University of Kentucky Special Collections and Digital Programs)

In 1939, now with two young children, the Clarks were at last able to build a house of their own on Lexington's Tahoma Road that "became a true home base for my family." In its spacious office Tom Clark wrote many of his most successful books. (University of Kentucky Special Collections and Digital Programs)

(Below) A. B. "Bud" Guthrie was the Clarks' neighbor for several decades. Guthrie, then an editor of the *Lexington Leader* and later a Pulitzer Prize–winning novelist, shared many interests with Clark.

(Above) The two Clark children, seen here with their grandfather Clark, were enthusiastic about their new home. "The area around Tahoma Road was open country, and Bennett and Elizabeth grew up there as free spirits."

The Clark family developed many lifelong friendships in Lexington. This early 1940s photo shows them at the home of J. Winston Coleman Jr., a fellow historian and book collector.

In 1946 Clark, accompanied by his son, Bennett, the son of his colleague Clement Eaton, and a group of Boy Scouts, spent five happy days gliding down the Kentucky River. "We slept on mother earth wrapped in thin blankets and prepared our food in keeping with Boy Scout conceptions of cuisine," he recalled. Clark had explored the river earlier for his book in the Rivers of America series.

(Above) Collecting for the University of Kentucky library was one of Clark's major activities throughout his career. Here he examines materials he had gathered from country stores throughout the South in preparation for writing *Pills, Petticoats, and Plows,* published in 1944. "Collecting basic historical records is akin to drug addiction." (Below) *Pills, Petticoats, and Plows* was one of Clark's most successful books. Here he autographs copies at Morris Book Store in Lexington. Friend and neighbor Bud Guthrie is at left, Ethel Lobus at right.

The Book Thieves, less villainous than the name might suggest, were avid collectors of rare books and historical documents who met regularly to compare notes, talk about historical writing, and brag on their latest acquisitions. Clark was one of the founding members, and one of the youngest. Front row, left to right: Judge Samuel Wilson, Charles Staples, former University of Kentucky president Frank McVey, and William H. Townsend. Back row: Dr. John S. Chambers, Dr. Claude Trapp, J. Winston Coleman, and Clark. University of Kentucky president Herman Lee Donovan was a later member.

In 1948 Clark was invited to participate in the Salzburg Seminar in Austria, which brought together professors from several American universities and students from across war-torn Europe. The Leopoldskron castle, Clark recalled, "was haven to an international mixture of students who sought answers to their personal and national futures." This was the first of several overseas teaching assignments Clark undertook in subsequent years, including posts in Vienna, India, England, Greece, and Yugoslavia.

(Above) Clark's understanding of geopolitics was expanded by his overseas assignments. While teaching at the University of Vienna in 1950, he was frequently confronted with troop displays by the Russians, who shared postwar occupation of the city with the United States, France, and Great Britain. (University of Kentucky Special Collections and Digital Programs)(Below) Beth Clark stayed home to care for their children during her husband's early overseas teaching stints, but in 1961 she accompanied him on his assignment as NATO professor in the Universities of Athens and Thessalonica, Greece.

(Above) As chair of the UK history department, Clark encouraged faculty publication and himself produced a steady stream of books and articles. Here he and three colleagues (from left, Holman Hamilton, Clement Eaton, and James Hopkins) hold copies of their recently published books, which had been chosen for the White House Library. (University of Kentucky Special Collections and Digital Programs) (Below) For more than a decade Clark badgered University of Kentucky presidents to establish a university press as an outlet for faculty publication. In 1950, through his efforts, the University of Kentucky Press became a reality, and Bruce Denbo was hired as director. He would remain at the helm for twenty-eight years. Below, Denbo (left) and Clark examine a new book by historian Carl Cone (center). (University of Kentucky Special Collections and Digital Programs)

Clark's 1984 book *The Greening of the South* deplored the destruction of southern forests in the early decades of the century. Practicing what he preached, Clark nurtured several hundred acres of forest land in South Carolina and eastern Kentucky. Getting out in his woodlands was one of his greatest pleasures throughout his life. (University of Kentucky Special Collections and Digital Programs)

In no sense was his retirement from the University of Kentucky the end of Clark's teaching career. Other teaching posts would follow—six years at Indiana University and shorter stays at several other American universities. Here he lectures to a class of 350 at Indiana University in 1970. He would also continue to collect documents, lecture widely, and produce books and articles until the end of his life.

Besides teaching during his years in Bloomington, Indiana, Clark served as executive secretary of the Organization of American Historians and published a notable four-volume history of Indiana University. Here he and IU chancellor Herman B. Wells autograph copies of volume 3. (University of Kentucky Special Collections and Digital Programs)

preparations were made to desert Buckridge Bar. There was a lot of hard work and bustle to ready our expanded fleet for the move. Mattress ways had to be dismantled, tools and materials loaded on barges, and a crew sent ahead to bury willow and cottonwood log deadmen at the new anchorage. Just as the towboat eased us out into the channel I saw a dog stick his head out of a lumber pile. He belonged to a black willowbar gambler who had stowed away with his dog, a crap board, and an old-fashioned hand-wound graphophone. We could only give the man a strong warning and leave him on the barge until it landed. We moved at night, and when daylight came the dog, crap hoard, and graphophone were still with us, but their owner had disappeared. A week or so later a newspaper reported that his body had been fished out of the river, a victim no doubt of a willow cutter he had cheated in a crap game.

Cap'n Toomey suggested that I forget about going to college and become a steamboat pilot. I took the first stage of the examination toward becoming a cub pilot and passed it, but the pull of the university classroom was stronger. Perhaps as a pilot on a modern towboat I might have earned far more than as a professor of history, but life would have been far more hectic. At the end of the second week in September I went back to Ole Miss a far more mature sophomore because of my summer's brush with the rapidly vanishing history of the river. My "professors" on the quarterboat had been highly instructive, and far more interesting than many of those I had in the university.

WHEN I LEFT THE BOAT I WAS given assurances of a job the following summer. Nobody in that pleasant autumn, however, could have predicted that before the opening of another quarterboat season the Mississippi River would go on one of the wildest rampages in its history. Early in the spring of 1927 the whole lower river system was underwater, and the steamboats were engaged in rescuing victims caught in the flood. The flood not only forced thousands of people to flee their homes; it threatened a disastrous change in the course of the river itself. Once again the stream gnawed at the natural passway between the Mississippi and the Atchafalaya-Red River. Sometime in a far distant age this channel to the

Gulf of Mexico had been the main one, and the river has often threatened to reopen it, to the great injury of the Port of New Orleans. In addition the floodwaters slashed several deep crevasses across the loess riverbottoms and washed out deep holes in the channel while filling others with sand deposits washed down from much of mid-America. By the time the floodwaters had receded into the normal river channel, almost all navigational data had been altered. No one knew where a new sandbar might have raised its spine across what had once been an open channel.

In May 1927 Cap'n Sam Hornsby wired me to report to the United States Engineers at Morgan City, Louisiana, to work with an Atchafalaya River survey group. He changed his instructions, however, before I reached Natchez, and I was assigned to work on the survey Quarterboat 20 on the Mississippi between Vicksburg and Natchez. Before I arrived the boat had been towed upstream to an anchorage opposite Newellton, Louisiana, and I was sent overland in a Model T Ford with a driver to join the crew. The road was slimy with silt, and the devastated countryside was littered with debris dropped by the lowering floodwaters. Two deep crevasses had been sliced across the road, necessitating our leaving the car and walking along the levee for several miles to reach the boat. The embankment was strewn with the decaying carcasses of farm animals that had fallen victim to a deadly outbreak of charbon.* The poet Milton could hardly have depicted a more forlorn scene of death and defeat, heightened by the stifling stench of carrion and hovering flocks of vultures.

Quarterboat 20 was under the management of a good-natured engineer named W. I. Hooks. He too was an old-time riverman, but had a radically different personality from those with whom I had worked the preceding summer. The crew consisted of three white men, four black oarsmen, and a black nightwatchman and his wife, the cook. The boat was a single-deck affair with four white crew bedrooms, a bunk room for the oarsmen, and a bedroom for the cook and her husband. There were kitchen and dining areas and a large drafting room containing a broad

---

* Anthrax

drafting table. In addition, there was an oversized skiff with three sets of oarlocks and a sounding device mounted on a small platform. The sounding instrument resembled a bicycle turned upside down with grooved wheels containing strands of piano wire. One wheel was mounted with a sounding disc, and the other one had a linear disc for measuring distances out from the bank and between soundings. The sounder dropped the lead weight and called off the depths, and I, as recorder, noted the data in a platbook. I never had a more infuriating job than that of keeping the distance wire taut as the oarsmen maneuvered the boat into sounding position.

Located along the riverbank was a base line with metal markers every 300 feet. Some of these had become buried under several feet of silt deposited by the flood, and it was necessary to dig down and find them, a time-consuming task. The engineer would set his transit on the markers, and an anchor pin would be driven down to keep the boat swinging in a predetermined arc. This was indeed an archaic engineering procedure for channel survey, dating back to some foggy historical moment. Each day's soundings were recorded on an overlay map and placed over the preceding survey to determine what changes had occurred—some of which proved to be radical, necessitating major revisions in navigational charts.

The oarsmen who manned the survey skiff were powerful men acutely attuned to the ways of the river. They were much superior to the willow cutters I had known the summer before. Felix, operator of the sounding device, was intelligent enough to have run the outside survey without supervision. One of the oarsmen was a round-faced black giant we called "Forty-one Jack" or "Brock Island." He carried on a lot of chatter about a mythical place called Brock Island, where everything was done in gargantuan proportions. Jack had one of the heartiest laughs I had ever heard. To him everything was funny, even the muscle-straining tugs against the stubborn river current. That crew had worked together so long that they could stroke the oars in unison, rapping out a rhythmic beat in doing so. They were wise to the river and its moods and were prepared to deal with them.

The monotony of the survey work was broken by the occasional passing of towboats and the periodic visits of the *Uncle Oliver* to drop off ice
and groceries. There was no Cajun cook aboard to brew a superb gumbo,
no temperamental baker to fuss with the cook, no perceptive waiter to
size up each man's taste, no shrimp barrels to furnish evening feasts. The
food was ample but of a plain southern country variety prepared by a
cook directly out of the cotton field. I spent many weekends on board
that summer with only the cook and her lazy husband for company. To
pass the time I took two correspondence courses in the Bible from Ole
Miss, courses that revealed to me in that quiet setting the marvelous
literary qualities of the King James version of the scriptures, especially
the Psalms. In fulfilling the requirements for that course, I read and
underscored the scriptures. I still have that marked Bible.

An exciting moment occurred one hot day in August when we had
the sounding skiff out full-line in the river. There appeared two tall stacks
sending up billowing clouds of black smoke. This was something we had
not observed before. The oarsmen became emotional, yelling, "Great
God, yonder comes the *Kate Adams!*" They did not know that the moss-
covered ribs of the fourth *Kate Adams* were rotting away near Vidalia,
Louisiana. When the boat rounded the bend above us she indeed appeared to be a grand lady in the romantic style of the old packet days. But
when she blew her whistle, rang her bell, and swung around in a sidewise
flank, we saw that she was the *Tennessee Belle*. She had been brought to
the lower river to replace the decrepit old *Oliver*. That was a moment of
jubilee for our crew, all of them old-time rivermen who no doubt thought
that the *Belle* was but the head of a parade marking the return of the
packets to the Mississippi.

In mid-September 1927, I once again left the river at the opening of
the university. This time I went with a deep tinge of nostalgia because I
was almost certain I would not return for another summer. I took with
me an affection for the great and treacherous stream with its unbridled
force, its fickle ways, and the rich human culture it had spawned. Two
years later, when I entered Duke University, I undertook to persuade my
major professor to allow me to write my doctoral dissertation on some

phase of Mississippi River history. Probably he had never seen the river or a packet boat or had more than a classroom geographical knowledge of the stream. His perspective on American history was badly blurred by the Appalachian Highlands. He insisted that I write instead on the building of antebellum southern railroads.

In June 1934 I had a fleeting glimpse of the revolution that had come to river engineering. My wife and I were making our first trip to Mississippi together the year following our marriage. She had never met my family or visited the Lower South. After a visit in Louisville we drove to Natchez and went down to the government boat anchorage just as the bright new *Mississippi* was sidling in to land. Stumpy Toomey was at the wheel, shouting orders as usual. He saw me standing on the dock with my South Carolina bride and shouted loudly enough to be heard in New Orleans, "I'll be God-damned, look standing down there!" We went aboard the new boat and admired Stumpy's floating marvel of steamboat engineering. But times had changed. Quarterboats were no longer towed to the willow bars; in fact, few quarterboats survived. Concrete fascines, or rip-raps, had replaced the wooden mattresses. Gone too was the little survey boat with the infernal upside-down bicycle sounding machine. Soundings now were made inside a comfortable electronics room aboard the steamboat. There were no more unruly piano steel wires to jump track and threaten to amputate the hands of the operator. The *Teche*, the *Tunica*, and the *Lafourche* had met the fate of worn-out sternwheelers. In their place the elegant *Mississippi* performed efficiently a number of specialized services. Cap'n Toomey could at last look out from a lordly pilot house on a plane nearly equal to the *Sprague*'s arrogant master, Bennie Bernstein, and all the rest.

The day we went aboard, the baker had just iced a quarter-acre-square cake. For the moment I again experienced the pure joy of eating steamboat food and washing it down with a generous cup of Cajun-style dark-roast coffee—coffee stout enough to curl an alligator's tail.

7

WEST TO KENTUCKY

Two WEEKS BEFORE I COMPLETED MY COURSES AT THE
University of Virginia I received a highly unsettling letter from my cousin Howard Liddell in Louisville, Mississippi. Howard informed me,
without giving any reason, that the Louisville Home Bank was revoking
its commitment to loan me four hundred dollars on my personal note,
endorsed by my father. Losing the prospect of that money all but closed
the door on my future academic plans. I had no established source of
credit outside of Louisville, and it was exceedingly doubtful that I could
procure a loan from the conservative and stingy Bank of Louisville. I
showed Howard's letter to my uncle Albert Bennett, and he replied nonchalantly, "I never intended that you should borrow the money from the
Mississippi bank." What he did for me instead was to borrow the money
from the National Bank of Charlottesville.

The fact that my grades at Virginia were far higher than those at Ole
Miss boosted my confidence that I could successfully pursue graduate

work. Thus assured of funds to support me in the coming school year, and with the added assurance of better grades, I set out for Kentucky. On the evening of September 14, 1928, I boarded the Chesapeake and Ohio railway train the *George Washington* in search of an uncertain future.

My decision to seek a master's degree at Kentucky was actually a chance one. The previous spring I happened to meet the University of Mississippi chancellor while walking across the campus, and he mentioned that the president of the University of Kentucky was looking for a scholarship applicant. He suggested that I apply. I corresponded with William Delbert Funkhouser, the dean of graduate studies at Kentucky, who offered me a $200 scholarship in history. I had also applied to the University of Cincinnati and was offered a like amount there. I delayed making a decision because I was in a quandary as to whether I wanted to become a professional educationist or give in to my innermost yearning to pursue graduate studies in history. I received an impatient telegram from Dean Funkhouser asking for my decision. On a rainy morning I slipped away from the Ole Miss campus and went to the telegraph office at the Oxford courthouse square, still not fully certain which scholarship I should accept. I literally flipped a buffalo nickel, and it came down Kentucky.

Shamefully I had only the meagerest knowledge of either Kentucky or its university. I had read one or two books by James Lane Allen and John Fox Jr. I knew of the state's distilling industry because in my youth, prior to Prohibition, some of the few pieces of mail we received included the colorful advertisements for Kentucky whiskey. We knew too about the Owensboro Wagon Works, from which my family had purchased wagons. That was the extent of my knowledge of the state. The only Kentuckians I had known were H. L. Lewis, captain of the dredgeboat on which I had worked; an instructor in the department of English at Ole Miss named Kenneth Demaree from Frankfort; and Grady Roundtree, Ray Moore, and Rebecca Edward, students in the Virginia summer school. That summer I had heard another Kentuckian, Senator Alben W. Barkley, speak at the University of Virginia summer school convocation.

My extremely skimpy knowledge of the University of Kentucky was gleaned from its 1927–1928 catalogue. That document provided only limited information and made exceedingly shabby use of graphic arts in its presentation of the institution. Even I, an unsophisticated Mississippi country boy, recognized the typographical deficiencies of this publication. In time I learned that the catalogue was the product of a highly political state printer who gained his position by political manipulation rather than mastery of the printer's trade.

Once the *George Washington* got under way from Charlottesville there arose considerable excitement and bustle on the train. People were rushing up and down the aisle as if life itself depended on their getting to the rear. A chatty lady in the seat in front of me was accompanied by two young girls who were on their way to Louisville, Kentucky. She asked me if I knew who was on the train. I said that I did not but that whoever he or she was was creating a commotion. She informed me that Senator Charles Curtis, the Republican nominee for vice-president on the Hoover ticket, was aboard.

The next morning the porter awakened me at Ashland, Kentucky, so that I could get dressed preparatory to detraining in Lexington. Totally ignorant of Kentucky geography, I got shaved and dressed in double time. When I came back into the car from the lavatory the porter had made up only one seat, and it was occupied by a round-faced man with a cropped moustache. I recognized Senator Curtis from his pictures, which had appeared in the newspapers. He motioned to me to come and sit by him. He was the first Republican I ever met. As we traveled down through the rugged hills of eastern Kentucky we talked, though not about anything much. When the train stopped in Morehead the porter came in and informed Senator Curtis that a crowd had gathered at the station and wanted him to come out and make a speech. He patted me on the knee and said, "Keep your seat. This is a bad place." While the senator spoke to the crowd I stared out the window at the drab and shabby town, wondering what besides its appearance was bad about it. Years later, when I learned something of Morehead and its "troubles," I wondered if Senator Curtis really knew about the Tolliver-Martin feud or the Rowan County War. He surely had never read the frank and revealing Kentucky adjutant general's report on the troubles. This report had painted a grim picture of semibarbarians running wild in the hills. Later I was to learn something of the Rowan County feud from Dixon Shouse and "Tickey" Evans, Morehead natives who roomed with me at the Bender house. Shouse later became mayor of Morehead, and "Tickey" Evans inherited his father's lumber business there.

I was unprepared for the pandemonium that awaited the arrival of the *George Washington* in Lexington. When the train arrived before the old Central Station on time, at 8:05 A.M. on September 15, it was met by a howling mob, which the *Lexington Leader* later said numbered 25,000 Republicans. Many were crowded into the station, while others stood on the circle out front and along Main Street. One would have thought they were there to celebrate the Second Coming. As Curtis stepped from the train, the high school bands sent up a great crescendo of welcome that would have rivaled Gabriel and his horn on the Day of Judgment. With considerable effort, loaded down with my overstuffed suitcase and my set of golf clubs, I was able to stumble off the car. Happily the rest of my worldly belongings were stowed in my trunk and checked to the baggage room at the station, where they remained until the Republican storm simmered down. That would not be until Senator Curtis had tolled them away to Woodland Auditorium to describe the glorious new day that lay just ahead for America following the election of Hoover.

That afternoon I read in the *Lexington Leader* that a thousand-car cavalcade had stormed into Lexington from Louisville and that special trains and buses had brought Hoovercrats and high school bands to warm up the throng before it marched on Woodland Auditorium to listen to an unmemorable speech by the future vice-president. In the meantime a welcoming committee had rushed Senator Curtis away to the Phoenix Hotel, a block and a half from the station, to sit down to a breakfast with two hundred select supporters. The breakfast was sponsored by the Republican women of Kentucky. In the milling crowd that morning were former governor Edwin Morrow, Congressman John Robsion, Senator Frederic M. Sackett, Christine Bradley South, and the whole Woman's Republican League delegation. Also present was a Republican congressman of note, John Wesley Langley, who had been charged with accepting a bribe to get a sizable shipment of Belle of Anderson whiskey re-leased from a warehouse and onto the open market during Prohibition days.

Almost miraculously I was able to secure a taxicab and set off over South Limestone Street to the university campus. As I rode along that grim, cluttered street I thought it was the ugliest one I had ever seen. Not even the street that circled the Lafayette County Courthouse in Oxford, Mississippi, was as dismal in appearance. Every individual telephone pa-tron must have had his own private line strung along South Limestone. The Kentucky Utilities Company had added its adornment of sagging wires, and to cap off the scene the trolley company had a power line down the middle of the street suspended from cross wires. The tall red-brick houses along the street reflected the poor taste of a multiplicity of builders.

The taxi entered the university campus through the north gate and stopped on the top of a rise before a tall and somewhat grim administra-tion building. When I was out of the taxi and trying to find directions, I encountered a slender, lean-faced man coming toward me. He was, I later learned, Alfred Brauer, assistant professor of biology. He directed me to the office of Columbus Melcher, the dean of men, in the basement of the building. The dean was head of the German Department and wore an impressive array of organization keys strung across his vest front. From there I was directed to Mrs. Joe Bender's residence at 450 Rose Lane and told that it was a desirable rooming house. Her place was three blocks off the campus, and for the next three years, off and on, I was to make it my home.

After I had deposited my baggage in the room, I set out to find a boardinghouse that served meals. Walking down Euclid Avenue I over-took a dour-faced man who introduced himself as Russell Hocker, a watch repairman. He directed me to Mrs. Cooke's boardinghouse on South Limestone Street, just across the street from Boyd Hall, a women's dormitory. Mrs. Cooke was the veritable embodiment of all boarding-house ladies who had ever populated the North American continent. Her dining room was dark and gloomy, with a long table extending from one end to the other. At that board she fed a mixture of college boys and a few straggling citizens. I think surely she must have been a heavy stock-holder in the brown-bean trade because beans were the central item of her menu.

The other student boarders at Mrs. Cooke's were country and small-town boys who had fixed opinions on every subject, including the coming November election. I learned early that my erstwhile friend Russell Hocker was romantically interested in Mrs. Cooke's daughter "Tootsie." Tootsie had an upper front tooth missing, but that was no deterrent in her pursuit of a husband. I wondered what it would be like to kiss a girl with such a dark hole in her mouth.

On Sunday I set out up Euclid Avenue to see my new world. The Ashland Subdivision was new, and the houses, in contrast to the older Limestone section, were impressive and attractive. This was the first planned modern subdivision I had ever seen. I walked on to the university farm off Nicholasville Pike, where I was interested in the heavily laden apple trees until one of those neanderthal specimens of watchmen who prowl university campuses descended upon me as if I were the prince of apple snatchers. Thus it was that I came beneath the benevolent sky of James Lane Allen's domain.

My confusion in getting off the *George Washington* and getting dis-entangled from the Republican stampede was slight compared with the welcome I encountered in the Department of History and the registrar's office of the University of Kentucky. First I had to convince Mr. Ezra Gillis that I had indeed finished work for my A.B. degree at Ole Miss and the University of Virginia. He required me to sign an affidavit that I had done so. Since I had come straight from Virginia to Lexington, I had not yet received my Ole Miss diploma. Then came a period of beastly indecision in the Department of History. I met for the first time Edward Tuthill, head of the department, who was to be a thorn in my side for many years. I was the first holder of a scholarship in that department and was expected to prove myself in spades. I got the notion, however, that Dr. Tuthill looked upon me as some strange varmint that had crawled up out of the Pearl River bottoms, or that I was to become an academic

guinea pig in Clio's garden. Tuthill was one of the first two or three hold-
ers of the doctor of philosophy degree on the university faculty. He had
studied under some of the earlier, well-known historians, such as Frederick Jackson Turner, William Bennett Monroe, and Hermann Von Holst.
He was a Kansas Republican who daily paid fealty to Calvin Coolidge
and his financial acolyte, Andrew Mellon. Tuthill proclaimed loudly that
Mellon was the greatest secretary of the treasury since Alexander Hamilton. To him Calvin Coolidge's silence indicated profound wisdom. It appeared to me that every Kentuckian made a boastful point of supporting
Herbert Hoover in the coming election. There was one exception. My
roommate, who came from the backwoods of Garrard County at Paint
Lick, was an ardent Democrat. I also discovered that the *Lexington Herald*,
edited by Desha Breckinridge, a scion of the famous Breckinridge family
of Kentucky, was Democratic, as was the *Louisville Courier-Journal*.

To listen to the Hooverites, one gathered that the Republic was permanently on the high road to eternal prosperity. This was the age that
spouted forth the famous clichés "A chicken in every pot" and "Two cars
in every garage"—slogans that all too soon would ring hollow during the
Great Depression. For me the pre-Depression years were already a time
of biting financial stringency. I had to force the buffalo on every nickel to
do his utmost or I would fall through the gaping chasm of financial di-
saster. I was doggedly determined to secure a master's degree in one year
and be done with Kentucky. There was in the university community a
veritable babble about prosperity, with some professors playing the stock
market and bragging about their gains. I was certain Tuthill gave more
attention to the gymnastics of Merrill-Lynch than to his classes. He was
never available around the noon hour because of his habitual visits to the
Merrill-Lynch bucket shop in the Phoenix Hotel.

At this late date I turn back through the pages of the 1928 catalogue
and wonder how the University of Kentucky had the audacity to offer
work leading to the master's degree in history. It may well have been that
members of the department did not themselves aspire to do so but were
pressured by the university's president, Frank LeRond McVey. At that
time the department did not have sufficient faculty to offer even a broad

course of undergraduate study. Tuthill was the lone professor. Charles Merriam Knapp was an associate professor who had been employed through the Alberts Teachers Agency. I found him an interesting study in personality and intellectual qualities. He was one of William A. Dunning's last doctoral candidates in Columbia University and was also the son of a famous Teachers College professor of Latin, the author of Knapp's *Latin Grammar.* Not only had Dunning run short of students, he had practically exhausted the area of state Reconstruction studies. Knapp wrote on Reconstruction in New Jersey. He had further academic connections that exceeded his personal talents, for he had married the daughter of the famous entomologist professor Herbert Osborn of Ohio State University. Despite his brilliant academic connections, Knapp was fundamentally indecisive. He never seemed able to focus on a project long enough to see it developed, even though he had a burning ambition to be a major historian.

Besides Knapp there were two instructors in the department. Ellery Hall was a native son and a potentially brilliant student of British history. He was the ablest teacher in the department and, had his health permitted, would have become a productive scholar. The other instructor was Robert G. Lunde from Wisconsin, a graduate of St. Olaf College who looked upon Kentucky and the South as alien territory. He had played football at St. Olaf and took great pride in the fact that his team's picture had appeared in the *Spalding Book of Rules.* Lunde had begun graduate study in American history under the tutelage of William E. Dodd at the University of Chicago. President McVey had taught summer school there one summer, and Dodd had recommended Lunde to him. Lunde and I arrived in Lexington at the same time. Though Kentucky seemed strange to me, to Lunde it seemed as remote as the planet Mars.

That was the staff of the Department of History in the University of Kentucky in 1928. I entered the university in a state of vexing confusion. Tuthill and Knapp were indecisive as to which courses I should take. In the end I wound up in two of Tuthill's courses and two of Knapp's. I also enrolled in a course in political science taught by a young visiting instructor named Jasper B. Shannon. Soon it was decided that he had no business trying to teach graduate students, and I was transferred to a course in comparative government taught by Professor J. Catron Jones, head of the Political Science Department. Professor Jones had been a member of the Department of History until he and Tuthill had a parting of ways. I could not have imagined in 1928 how often my path in the future would cross that of J. C. Jones or under what peculiar circumstances. Jones was a tall, angular man with a somewhat brash personality. While a student in the Brookings Institute he had tutored the daughter of a wealthy man, then courted and married her. All this I was to learn later as a colleague. I never learned precisely what Jones's course in comparative government was all about, or which governments we were comparing. I did learn, however, that the professor was an ardent supporter of Al Smith, and my discovering a fellow Democrat helped matters considerably.

Comparative government aside, Professor Jones was both a realist philosopher and a crack spinner of yarns. Once he emphatically advised us that the way to rise in the world was to climb up on somebody else's shoulders. On one occasion he filled an entire class period telling a story about a Mississippi railroad company that set out to hire a chief engineer. A flood of applications was received, but only one promised to fill the bill. The applicant stated that he had an A.B. from the Essex. The directors sought to learn more about the University of Essex. When they inquired of the applicant, he informed them that he had able-body seaman papers from the freighter *Essex*.

One thing I did learn in Professor Jones's class—Kentucky had an antiquated constitution and a campaign was under way to revise it. At that date I had not even a meager interest in whether or not Kentucky had a constitution, effective or otherwise. I knew the governor was a Republican whom his detractors were calling "Flim Flam" Sampson. Maybe under that administration, I thought, the state did need a new constitution.

Tuthill was a dull, opinionated, eccentric professor. He brought into the classroom sheaves of yellowed and tattered notes that he surely must have taken as a graduate student at the Universities of Wisconsin and Chicago, and his lectures were equally tattered. Under his instruction I explored the mysteries of Europe as viewed from the perspective of those dog-eared college notes. In one of Tuthill's classes I encountered a rangy black-eyed and black-haired western Tennesseean named Bell Wiley, who was teaching speech in the conservative Methodist Asbury College at Wilmore, Kentucky, while pursuing a degree at Kentucky. On one of his tests Tuthill asked us to define Marxian socialism. Bell Wiley had never heard of either Karl Marx or his social and political theories, but that did not faze him. He proceeded to write a mini-essay on "marks in socialism" as understood in the Tradewater section of Tennessee. When Tuthill returned the test papers he delivered a sharply pointed philippic on the lack of knowledge and intelligence of the lout who had written so wide of the mark, even contending that he belonged in the confines of the eastern Kentucky insane asylum. I was so amused by that diatribe that I looked back through the class to see who the culprit was. I quickly spotted him. Bell's black eyes flashed the combined furies of Jove and Andrew Jackson. At that moment Tuthill could not have imagined that Bell would go on in the study of history to become a nationally respected scholar.

That year other members of the graduate group were Emily Ford of Georgetown; Ellen Scott of Paris, who later married the political scientist Jasper B. Shannon; and Hazel Kingham of Louisville, whose husband was connected with the famous old Owensboro Wagon Works. I could communicate with these people.

Under Knapp I explored both the westward movement and the Old South. Born and bred in New York City, Knapp had only an ephemeral notion about the westward movement and knew even less about the Old South. I suspect he had never ventured deeper into the hinterlands than Columbus, Ohio, and Lexington, Kentucky. Once he raised the weighty question of how the western pioneers produced boards to roof their cabins and palings to enclose their gardens and yards. Country boy that I was, I volunteered the information that they selected straight-grain oak, ash, chestnut, or cypress bolts and rived the boards and palings with a mallet and froe. He contended that there was no such a thing as a froe, which startled me. If he was right, then I had used a phantom tool to rive enough good Mississippi swamp cypress boards to cover a barn for my father. The professor's positive assertion about pioneer tools shattered my confidence in his knowledge of the sweaty details of pioneering.

Despite the froe problem, I did learn from Knapp something of the works of Frederick Jackson Turner, Frederick L. Paxson, and William E. Dodd, and of the existence of the great Draper and Durrett manuscript and book collections. More than that, I got a sense of the dynamics of the westward movement and the voluminous literature it had generated. At that moment there was in Kentucky and Tennessee a great weeping and gnashing of historical teeth over the "thievery" of Lyman Copeland Draper, whose collection of historic Kentucky and Tennessee documents resided in the Wisconsin Historical Society, and the villainy of the Durrett heirs in selling their father's collection to the University of Chicago. This furor was largely agitated by John Trotwood Moore of the Tennessee Historical Society and Library. He undertook to get the Wisconsin General Assembly to enact a law that would return the Draper materials to the states of their origin. No one explained that Colonel Durrett had generously offered to give his collection to the Commonwealth of Kentucky if the General Assembly would provide safe and suitable housing for it—something it failed to do.

In his course on the Old South, Knapp gave no clear notion of either the history of the region or the forces that had shaped it. The clearest recollection I have of that course is the fact that I purchased Dodd's *Cotton Kingdom* and Holland Thompson's *New South*, titles in the recently published Yale Chronicles series. Knapp probably also mentioned the writings of U. B. Phillips and the travels of Frederick Law Olmstead. Knapp knew Phillips partly because Phillips had been one of William A. Dunning's earliest students.

EARLY IN DECEMBER 1928 BOTH Tuthill and Knapp encouraged me to attend the forthcoming meeting of the American Historical Association, which was to take place in the Claypool Hotel in Indianapolis. Knowing that I was living on the slenderest financial shoestring, Tuthill suggested that I might go cheaply to Indianapolis by interurban cars. The difficulty was that there were two substantial gaps in the lines, one between Frankfort and Louisville, the other between Louisville and Columbus, Indiana. I wound up going in style by Pullman with Knapp on the Southern and Big Four railroads through Cincinnati. An upper berth cost only four dollars. Before we left Lexington I went down to the Thom McAn shoe store at the corner of Limestone and Main Streets and bought a three-dollar pair of shoes that turned out to be a size too small. I was tortured by aching feet throughout that meeting.

We landed in the gloomy old Indianapolis station on a cold, cloudy morning, and for the first time my feet touched soil outside the South. The attendance at that meeting was remarkably small compared with later years. Nevertheless, it was big enough to be strange and awe-inspiring to me. In the panel that discussed Ulrich B. Phillips's recently published article, "Slavery the Central Theme in Southern History," I sat almost beside the author. If ever there was a panel examining the contours of an elephant, this was it. Some members were critical of Phillips's research techniques, some of his thesis, and others of parts of his conclusions. Phillips responded with a cleverly arranged quotation from the Scriptures describing the dimensions of Noah's wife, which became inextricably intertwined with those of the ark, leaving confused the proportions of each.

One of the Phillips panelists was Richard H. Shryock of the newly organized Duke University. The following December I would be his graduate assistant, and eventually we would form a friendship that would endure throughout his lifetime. In the audience was Wendell Holmes Stephenson, one of Phillips's students, with whom I was in later years to develop a lasting friendship. Following the panel discussion, Professor Knapp introduced me to Professor Phillips, telling him that I was writing a thesis partly on the slave trade between Kentucky and the Lower South. Phillips sat down and discussed with me in the most cordial manner sources I might examine, among them *Debow's Review,* of which he said he owned two sets. I had tried to get access to this periodical through the Cincinnati Public Library, but their set had been loaned to a University of Cincinnati professor who contracted scarlet fever and was then under quarantine.

My classmate Bell Wiley was to study under Phillips's direction at Yale, and he later told me that he found Phillips to be a difficult, if not downright haughty, man with whom to communicate. This was out of character with Phillips's educational background. Dean Boyd of the University of Georgia told E. Merton Coulter that Phillips was the greenest freshman he had ever seen enter that university. Green or not, Phillips became a masterful researcher and writing stylist.

At that Indianapolis meeting of the American Historical Association I was to see many of the second generation of American historical scholars whose names had appeared on scores of books—who had "arrived." One of them was James H. Breasted, the famous Egyptologist and president of the association. I heard him deliver his presidential address describing the exciting discoveries of the Tutankhamen artifacts. Because of Breasted's work, the University of Chicago had become a major world center of Egyptological studies. In the *Dictionary of American Biography*, Edith Ware describes Breasted as not truly handsome, but exuding a certain elegance of appearance, with a magnetic personality that created the impression of good looks. Certainly he impressed me the night of his presidential address as a stately and elegant man with dignity to match his brilliance and the importance of his subject.

I am certain that my attendance at the Indianapolis meeting of the AHA had a profound influence on my personal commitment to become a trained historian. Not only was I privileged to be present at the discussion of Phillips's seminal essay, to hear James H. Breasted deliver his presidential address, and to meet many of the second generation of American historians, but I also heard the gossipy lobby chatter that was so much a part of professional meetings. I recall a group of professors discussing their favorite subject, low salaries. Professor Root of the University of Iowa said he lived in a house so small that he had to go outside to pull his britches on.

WHEN I RETURNED TO LEXINGTON just before New Year's Day, I brought back with me a clearer concept of what it meant to research and write history. More immediately I had before me the challenge of first-semester examinations. I was certain Professor Tuthill was not enamored with reading examination papers. He admonished his classes to send him telegrams, which meant he wanted the most highly skeletonized answers his students could devise. This was in itself a challenge because some of his questions about European history required rather complex answers. I have little recollection of the examinations except for the fact that Roy Owsley, a student in J. C. Jones's class in comparative government, was also a grader of the examination papers.

I wrote my master's thesis on the subject of trade between Kentucky and the Lower South in livestock, slaves, and hemp prior to 1860. The subject was determined by the fact that these were the topics on which I could locate the most source materials. The University of Kentucky Library contained almost no sources of value and no manuscript or documentary materials. The library was still operating as a minimal undergraduate reading center. The book collection was housed in the tiny Carnegie building in the middle of campus, and the reading room was located on the second floor of the administration building. Had it not been for the Lexington Public Library's book and newspaper collections, the Collins Collection housed in the Kentucky state capitol, the Kentucky Historical Society collection, and the records in the Fayette County Clerk's office, I would have been hard pressed to find documentary sources to support my thesis.

By mid-semester 1929 I knew I wanted to pursue graduate work leading to the doctorate in history. Earlier that semester Professor Knapp had encouraged me to make applications to several universities seeking a fellowship. My application to the University of Virginia was turned down. Years later I asked Dumas Malone about this, and he told me the university had no money for fellowships at that time. Ironically, somehow Dumas got fixed in his mind that I had studied under him, and on several occasions he introduced me as one of his "boys." I received offers of tuition grants from the Universities of Missouri and Wisconsin, but no sustaining grants. In the end I accepted a fellowship in the newly organized Duke University in Durham, North Carolina. At first Duke turned me down, but J. Fred Rippy, the Latin American specialist, came to the University of Kentucky to give a lecture and sent for me to come and be interviewed. He told me there was still a possibility of a fellowship appointment at Duke. He said that Professor William K. Boyd had decided to combine two scholarships and offer me a fellowship paying six hundred dollars.

While the Duke decision was pending I became involved in a bizarre bit of correspondence. I had applied also for a fellowship at Vanderbilt University, and belatedly I received a letter from Dean Walter Lynwood Fleming saying that Vanderbilt would grant me a $1,500 assistantship. This was like manna falling from the academic heavens, except that there seemed to be some kind of erratic overtone to the letter. Then I began receiving letters almost daily from Dean Fleming urging me to accept the assistantship. The letters seemed to indicate that their author was suffering from some kind of mental distress. Years later I learned that my intuition was correct. Had I accepted the Vanderbilt assistantship I might have arrived on the Vanderbilt campus in September without anyone in the Department of History having heard of me or the assistantship.

The year I spent in Lexington was a mixture of loneliness and happy adventure. Without being able to define the nuanced differences, I was thrust into a confusing rural-agrarian/snobbish-Bluegrass/more-humble-Appalachian-highland mix of social mores, all of which differed in subtle ways from those of my native Lower South. Too, the atmosphere on the University of Kentucky campus was entirely different from that at Ole Miss. I was aware in a vague way of the sharp differences between the brashness of the students who came from the Louisville-Lexington areas and those who came from the intensely rural areas of the state. Tuthill on occasion remarked that he never fathomed "the don't-give-a-damn look in a Kentuckian's eye." Despite forty years in the state he never fully appreciated its cultural and economic differences.

In later years I checked the catalogue listing of the names and places of origin of the 1928 students. A large number came from Lexington and its immediate Bluegrass surroundings. Most, however, came from such crossroads places as Waco, Wagersville, St. Helens, Utica, Fannin, Cadiz, Yosemite, and Poor Fork. In that year almost 95 percent of the stu-

dent body was made up of native Kentuckians and those from the immediately bordering states of West Virginia and Ohio. I was unaware
that these young people were also having difficulty adjusting to ways of
life on the campus and in the Bluegrass.

Among the University of Kentucky faculty at large there were more
professors with doctorates than at Ole Miss, and a good many of them
had published books and established solid reputations. There were the
older faculty, including W. S. Webb, a physicist but better known as an
archaeologist; Grant C. Knight, a productive scholar and sophisticated
teacher; Alvin E. Evans, who had a good reputation in the legal area of
wills and estates; W. D. Funkhouser, an extremely popular professor of
biology and, like Webb, an archaeologist; and Edwin S. Good, who had
a national reputation in the field of animal husbandry. Then there was a
group of younger professors who in time gave the institution scholarly
maturity. Among them were J. W. Martin in business, Amry Vandenbosch in political science, W. D. Valleau in plant genetics, E. Z. Palmer
in business, Arthur C. McFarlan in geology, and Morris Scherago in
bacteriology. The latter group would have been solid scholars on any university faculty. The general run of the faculty, however, was provincial
and pedestrian. There was no member of the Department of History
who measured up to the scholars just named, or to Charles S. Sydnor at
Ole Miss.

By far the most impressive personality on the University of Kentucky
faculty in 1928 was President Frank L. McVey, a native of Ohio and a
graduate of Ohio Wesleyan College and Yale University. He had studied
under the great William Graham Sumner at Yale and in the London
School of Economics. McVey had served as tax commissioner of Minnesota and as president of the University of North Dakota. Physically he
was tall, with an austere countenance and manner, but at heart he was a
somewhat shy man who found himself having to deal with Kentucky
politicians almost twenty-four hours a day. He had succeeded Henry
Stites Barker, a consummate politician who had been a less-than-
successful president. As a one-year student I was unaware of most of
what was happening in the university, but I was conscious of the leader-

ship of Dr. McVey. In Feburary, I think, the McVeys moved into Maxwell Place and held an open-house tea for students and faculty to view the renovated home of the president. Tuthill urged his students to go and eat everything in sight because the taxpayers were footing the bill.

Besides the score of promising faculty, there were some interesting students who were intellectually active and who in time established notable reputations. They included Richard Weaver, a campus rebel who actively supported Norman Thomas, the perpetual Socialist candidate for president; Clifford Amyx, who later became a professor of art and an able artist; David Jackson, who entered business; Roy Featherston, who became a successful New York lawyer; and Leland Howard, who boarded with me at Mrs. Ford's boardinghouse on Hagerman Court and became the chief operations officer of the U.S. Mint. The first Kentucky mountaineer I got to know was Roy Eversole of Hazard, who had a long career as superintendent of that town's schools and later became a banker.

Not all my time that year was devoted to the services of Clio. Harry Gamage and Bernie Shively had just come to the university as football coaches, and hopes for a winning football team were high. There buzzed about the boardinghouse dining tables the thought that the team might be headed for a bright place in the athletic sun. These hopes were subsequently doused by several losses. My interest in the football team was stirred by the fact that a round-faced Polish freshman football player lived at the Bender house. Cecil Urbanic had been recruited from Fairmont, West Virginia, and was a good natural athlete. He played both football and baseball. One afternoon he rushed into my room, grabbed me, and danced around excitedly as he told me he had just made a triple play unassisted in a baseball game. Two or three times I went downtown to Graves-Cox clothing store with Urbie to collect his "weekly wage"— though he performed absolutely no service for that store. That was also the year when a freshman wild horse from Springfield, Kentucky, was on the football team. John "Shipwreck" Kelly in time became one of the university's football heroes, but he created a greater sensation nationally with his marriage to Brenda Frazier in one of New York's most spectacular weddings.

During the Kentucky Derby I went to Louisville and roomed with some Ole Miss friends who were enrolled in the University of Louisville Medical School. Going to the Derby seemed a "must" before I could go back to Mississippi. At the Derby I managed to get a good position against the rail of the grandstand, but just before the running of the Derby there came a drowning downpour, and everybody sought shelter. I lost my rail position and did not see even an ear of little Clyde Van Dusen, the winning horse. That killed my desire to ever again attend the Derby.

I worked diligently and for long hours that year, keeping up with my class work and researching and writing my thesis. In the process I was exposed, timidly be it said, to the techniques for researching and writing history. No doubt my thesis was poor at best, and I am sure I would shudder if I now had to read it. But it served the purpose of such an exercise, and doing the research and writing was an essential experience for me on the path to becoming a historian. I had to do an extraordinary amount of digging, which introduced me to the possibilities for serious and more intensive research in Kentucky history in the future. All of this was tied up with the history of American pioneering and the spread of the westward movement.

I succeeded in completing my course work and thesis in one year. I had no difficulty in passing the oral examination and, with one exception, was finished with the technical requirements for the master's degree. To celebrate the completion of my work, I was taking a nap in my room when the landlady called me to say that Mr. Gillis, the registrar, wanted me to come to his office. I thought, "Here come those technicalities about my A.B. degree all over again." Instead Gillis handed me a slip of paper and asked me to write out my middle name. When I handed the slip back to him, he said, "Now you have spelled it three different ways." My grandfather spelled it "Dyonicious," the same way the Olivers of Georgia spelled it, no matter how the Greeks or I spelled it. Whatever the origin of that name and its spelling, it has been a nuisance to me over the years.

Commencement at the University of Kentucky was on the morning of June 4, 1929, and the one at Ole Miss was the next day. The Kentucky commencement was held in Alumni Gymnasium, hardly an inspiring place to end one's academic years. Carl Van Doren was the speaker, and as I recall a smooth and erudite one. Ellen Scott and J. Winston Coleman Jr. received master's degrees in that commencement as well. In time Winston and I would become close friends. Also in that commencement an elderly school administrator named James Anderson Yates received the first earned doctorate granted by the university. He was a native of London, Kentucky, but had spent his professional years in Kansas.

The afternoon following the commencement, McVey Hall was dedicated, making a substantial addition to the campus. After that ceremony, as I was walking around the corner of the Engineering Building, I met Dr. and Mrs. McVey, and they stopped to talk with me. This may indeed have been a meaningful chance meeting for me, possibly leading to my eventual employment by Dr. McVey. But my trunk was packed, and my heart was set on returning to Mississippi. At 3:00 P.M. I boarded the *Fast Flying Virginian* at the very spot where nine months before I had landed in that howling mob of Republicans. If all of the trains were on time I could reach Ole Miss just in time for commencement there. In Louisville I transferred to the Illinois Central to Milan, Tennessee, where I transferred to that company's branch line over which the famous Oxford special, the *Bilbo,* operated. With this many changes on roads that were not noted for keeping to schedule, my chances of getting to Oxford on time were minimal at best. In Louisville I also ran into a social problem. During my last year at Ole Miss I had persuaded my roommate, James F. Hopkins, to permit a boy named John Love to move in with us. John was the son of Mrs. Alma Love of Weir, and she had asked me to look out for her wild son. John was a pharmacy student and the previous summer had attended the University of Michigan summer school to make up some work. There he met a rather amorous lass from Buffalo, Kentucky. During one of the spring months I was surprised when John turned up at 450 Rose Lane for a visit, along with his Buffalo girlfriend. He introduced me to the girl, and I became aware that he meant to foist her off on me, a favor I neither relished nor accepted.

When the *Virginian* reached Louisville, however, there was John's girl to meet me, and she insisted that I take her to dinner. There went the money I had intended to pay for a berth. I had to sit up all night on a day coach. Miraculously the train from Louisville arrived in Milan, Tennessee, on time and three-quarters of an hour before the departure of the *Bilbo.* I found a nearby barbershop that was open, but no barber was around. The water was hot, so I proceeded to shave myself and walk out. Many times I have wondered what that barber's reactions were when he found a wet mug, a damp towel, and a dulled razor.

For once the *Bilbo,* honored by every Ole Miss student for its erratic schedule, was on time, and I had just enough time to catch a taxi and rush to Fulton Chapel. Just as I arrived the academic procession was disappearing through the door to the chapel. Dean Alfred Milden was holding my robe and cap, and I was the last man in line. I must have set some kind of a record for the briefest time spent at a commencement. By early that afternoon I was on my way home, over the same wandering railway system I had traveled in September 1925 when I entered the university. I had brought from Lexington a number of copies of *In Kentucky* magazine to show my mother and father what Kentucky was like. In looking at them I discovered that I had come to like Kentucky more than I had realized.

I had no immediate employment for the first months of the summer. Before I left Lexington I arranged with the Jaccard Jewelry Company of Kansas City to sell class rings, diplomas, and invitations to high schools in central eastern Mississippi that fall. But in June I had neither a job nor any money. Winston County seemed shabby in comparison with the Kentucky Bluegrass region, and I began to wish I were back in Lexington. Within ten days I received a telegram from Professor Knapp saying that President McVey had approved my application to make a survey of materials in easy reach of Lexington that would support research in Kentucky and frontier American history. The salary was minimal, but that job was perhaps the most important one I ever had. It gave me a golden opportunity to become acquainted with the nature and location of research materials in American history. It also deepened my growing interest in the westward movement.

Luckily my uncle Albert Bennett and his family were visiting in Mississippi at the time, and I was able to ride to Chattanooga with them. From Chattanooga I traveled to Lexington on the Southern Railway. In 1929 four interurban lines ran out from Lexington, connecting with Georgetown, Paris, Nicholasville, and Frankfort. I used them to bounce back and forth between Frankfort and Lexington, listing materials in the Collins Library at the state capitol and in the Historical Society at the Old Capitol. I not only listed titles of books and descriptions of documents, but I also recorded brief descriptions of them on a special mimeographed form. Aside from the two libraries in Frankfort, I surveyed materials in the Lexington Public Library, the Transylvania College Library, and the Georgetown College Library. I also visited the Centre College Library in Danville, where I discovered a very good serial set of United States documents. The Georgetown College Library contained some substantial files of early Kentucky newspapers and a modest, but significant, manuscript collection. Tragically these were destroyed by fire soon after I made the inventory.

I found that the public documents holdings of the Commonwealth were given next to no care and were more or less dumped helter-skelter into the basement of the state capitol and left wide open to pilferage. The state librarian was chiefly interested in the library of the Kentucky Court of Appeals and in serving the needs of the judges. So little attention was given the state archives that I could do little more than learn that both the original records and the Kentucky published documents existed but were in jeopardy.

Elizabeth S. Norton, the Transylvania librarian, went away to her home in Millersburg during the summer, but she gave me a key and permission to have free access to the marvelous old collection of that institution. One day a highly personable man turned up seeking access to the Transylvania College Library, in search of the record and thesis of the Georgia poet Thomas Holley Chivers. He was Lewis Chase, professor of English in Duke University. I asked him about Duke, and he told me something of William K. Boyd, the man who would direct my doctoral program there. In our search for Chivers materials we came across an early Trinity College annual in which Boyd's photograph appeared.

I got only partway through the cataloguing program during the months of June, July, and part of August before I had to return to Mississippi to begin my travels for the high school jewelry company. By that time, however, I had become well oriented in Kentucky and frontier history, topics that would become a significant part of my career as a historian.

8

~

THE WAY TO DURHAM

IN THE INTERLUDE BETWEEN KENTUCKY AND DUKE
University I tried my hand at being a traveling salesman for a high school
jewelry company. In order to travel I needed a car, but I had only a modest amount of capital. In Lexington I visited the Frazier Motor Company
on High Street. They had just taken in trade for a new car George Brady's
beloved Model T family touring chariot. It was for sale at the bargain
price of seventy-five dollars. Brady was a member of the Department of
English in the University of Kentucky. He had exchanged his old car for
the new Model A Ford. Glorying in the ownership of a sparkling new
state-of-the-art machine, he drove it to a concert held in the Alumni
Gymnasium on the university campus. When the concert was over the
professor discovered that thieves had stolen all four wheels from his black
beauty and the car lay flat on the ground.

I drove my "new" car around Lexington and made a trip to Danville
to make a final check of Centre College's library holdings. The vehicle

seemed roadworthy enough to make the trip over the winding gravel roads to Mississippi. In early August, together with a west Tennesseean named Ralph Parham, I set out on a long and venturesome journey south by way of Danville, Springfield, Scottsville, and Nashville. The roads were winding and rough, and three or four river and creek crossings were over toll bridges. We crossed the Tennessee River between Nashville and Memphis by ferry boat. As we waited in the line of cars to board the ferry, my seventy-five-dollar wonder went into apparent death throes. Ralph shoved it down the river bluff, and we landed at the head of the line for the ferry. On the other side of the river it took the entire ferry crew to push us up the landing bluff and out of the way, and they exhibited little cheerful charity in doing so. By some mysterious circumstance that Henry Ford himself could not have explained, the old engine then started and purred like a barnyard kitten. When we reached the railroad crossing village of Milan, Parham's destination, he got out of the car, stretched his arms, and proclaimed the special quality of Tennessee fresh air. My Mississippi destination still lay far ahead and over endless turns on dirt and gravel roads. I bumped my way home after two fifteen-hour days of driving and entered my sales territory.

I want to say without reservation that trying to sell class rings, commencement invitations, and diploma blanks would destroy the patience of Job and the psychological penetration of Sigmund Freud. I carried in my sample case superb and honest products manufactured by the Jaccard Jewelry Company of Kansas City, Missouri. The company was thoroughly ethical in its materials and workmanship. There were no big, rosy-red settings or oversized gold-washed rings. In the instructional session I had with the company's representative, he emphasized that jewelry of this quality would last a lifetime and more. With some schools the company had continuing contracts, and all I had to do was measure fingers for ring sizes and fill out orders. In other cases I faced aggressive competition. In several schools I would have the class sold when a slip of a girl would change her mind and lead the herd in a stampede of mind changing. Frankly, I was not a good salesman.

George Brady's beloved old family touring car groaned and strained going uphill. The radiator often generated enough steam to run a cotton gin. I drove over the dusty, nail-strewn dirt-and-gravel Mississippi roads from the patching of one tire to that of another. It seemed that I patched inner tubes every forty miles. Sometime the tubes would become so heated and worn that a cold patch would not adhere. Many times when I displayed my wares, my hands appeared to be those of a garage mechanic rather than a jewelry salesman.

Wherever I went in the Brady car I carried with me a bold advertisement for the Commonwealth of Kentucky. In 1929 the Flem D. Sampson administration was carrying on a vigorous campaign to proclaim the state's progress. The automobile license plate that year was oversize and carried, in bold blue and white lettering, the words "Kentucky for Progress." This must have been one of the most flamboyant tags ever to adorn the tail of an automobile. It looked like a billboard on the stern of my miniature car.

One night when I was driving into my sales territory I was greeted roughly by a head-on collision with another car. A boy and girl locked in a passionate embrace dashed around a sharp curve and into my car, which dived headlong into a deep ditch. Romantic passion that night shaded off into angry frustration when I insisted that the couple drive me forty miles to my father's home. A few days later I stopped in a country cafe and shared a table with a dry goods drummer who said he had just seen a comical sight near the backwoods town of McCool. There in the bend of the road was an old car with its rear end rared up in plain view and bearing a big blue and white tag that read "Kentucky for Progress."

Out among the high schools there were some earthy lessons to be learned, especially about school superintendents. One of the schools in my district was the Oktibbeha Agricultural High School, which was administered by my old Weir superintendent, T. A. Patterson. He virtually ordered the class to buy their rings and commencement invitations from me. I took the order and sent it to the Jaccard Company, but in about ten days I got a letter from one of the Jaccards scolding me for taking that order. They had received a letter from Patterson demanding a kickback. My order was canceled, and I was disillusioned that my old superintendent had done such a thing. In retrospect, I am reasonably certain the old rascal had also taken his pound of flesh from my own graduating class at Weir. I saw Patterson only once after that; by that time I had lost all respect for him.

For me the sale of high school jewelry and commencement paper bordered on the futility of selling left-handed monkey wrenches. The salesman put his fortune in the hands of flippant teenagers and a venal school superintendent. He also had ingenious competition from big fat rings and mounted marble-sized "rubies." I approached the termination of my contract with genuine relief. When I turned in my sample case I felt almost as if I had been let out of jail.

I FELT NO GREAT ENTHUSIASM about entering Duke University in mid-September 1929. Durham, North Carolina, was a long way from Mississippi. Once again I packed my worldly belongings into a trunk and set off into a vague future from the same depot from which I had departed for Ole Miss four years earlier. From Meridian, Mississippi, I traveled to the Carolinas, interestingly over the same general route my Clark and Bennett ancestors had followed in the mid-1830s. The Southern Railway train passed almost in sight of the old Clark homestead in Anderson County, South Carolina.

In Gastonia, North Carolina, the train was stopped for approximately an hour by a howling and angry group of people. I had not an inkling of what the mob was up to. Later I learned that I had been caught in a major incident in New South economic and social history. Textile workers throughout the southern industry were protesting the peonage in which they were being held in mills and company mill towns, with low wages, long hours, and grinding working conditions. The organized strikes and demonstrations resulted in revolutionary changes in the southern textile industry. Later George Tindall gave generous space to the subject in his book *The Emergence of the New South*, as did W. J. Cash in *The Mind of the South*. This movement occurred on the eve of the Great Depression and was especially meaningful because of the timing.

How complacently I sat in the train that night, weary from two days' travel. The furor in Gastonia finally calmed down, and the train moved on to Greensboro, arriving there just in time for me to make a connection with the somewhat primitive train that ran to Durham and Raleigh. I knew I was going to a brand-new university, but what I did not realize was that the Department of History at Duke had up until then bestowed only one doctorate degree.

Arriving in Durham on a pitch-dark evening was about as grim an experience as I could have imagined. Tobacco fumes swept over the town in almost stifling waves. I went to a plain if not uninviting restaurant near the depot and the Durham County courthouse. After taking a good swallow of the water the waiter served, I was almost ready to go back to selling high school jewelry. Next morning I read in the *Durham Herald* that workmen had dumped generous loads of grass clippings in the public reservoir.

Duke University in 1929 was actually a dream ready to become a reality. It had been in existence under the title "university" for only four years. There had been a major building and refurbishing of the old Trinity College campus, but the future West Campus was still in the early stages of construction. Seated in a bronze armchair was a statue of George Washington Duke, looking, so it was said, "for a freshman who could pass a course in English lit." Later I heard the version that he was looking for a virtuous coed. That night when the taxicab turned into the Trinity campus I spotted a mature-looking student and inquired of him directions to Jarvis Hall, where I had been preassigned a room. That student, as it happened, was to be my future roommate. E. Taylor Parks later occupied one of the major desks in the U.S. Department of State.

The Duke Department of History in 1929 consisted of two rather divergent layers of personnel, the old Trinity College professors and a group of young professors who had just been employed. William Kenneth Boyd and William Thomas Laprade were the senior members of the department. Despite the normal jealousies and other petty frictions inevitable between the two generations of professors, the department had the necessary talent to build a good graduate program.

Early on my first morning I went to the second floor of the East

Duke building to introduce myself to my future major professor. William Kenneth Boyd was not in his office, but there was a tall, slightly stooped man there who spoke in a sandy voice and assured me most positively that he was not William K. Boyd but rather William Thomas Laprade, professor of British history. I almost turned to leave when I recalled that I had seen the name Laprade somewhere in history department materials. When I explained who I was, he filled out my course schedule and had me registered in only a few minutes. I was to take seminars under Boyd and Laprade, North Carolina history under Boyd, and a course in Latin American history under J. Fred Rippy. Thus I was registered as a student in Duke University without ever having seen my major professor.

In many respects W. K. (Tubby) Boyd was from the start an enigma to me. At times I felt that both he and Laprade were overly judgmental. Nevertheless, Boyd, by his extraordinary energy, exuded a dedicated inner respect for the field of history. He had received his doctorate from Columbia University, where he wrote his dissertation, "The Ecclesiastical Edicts of the Theodocian Code," under the tutelage of James Harvey Robinson. He had succeeded John Spencer Bassett as head of the History Department in Trinity College. Unlike Laprade, he never became fully converted to the Von Ranke theories that, through the tutelage of Herbert Baxter Adams at the Johns Hopkins University, had been disseminated in North America. His sense of and dedication to history came from more provincial sources. He had been influenced by the teachings of William A. Dunning, Stephen B. Weeks, and Bassett. Weeks especially had fired Boyd's zeal for searching out documentary materials and building collections.

In time Boyd authored a volume in the multivolume history of North Carolina and edited William Byrd's *Secret History of the Dividing Line between Virginia and North Carolina*. In 1925 he published *The Story of Durham* and was founder and editor of the *South Atlantic Quarterly*. During the time I was at Duke, Boyd was engaged in gathering the great Flowers manuscript collection and serving as director of libraries, in addition to his duties in the Department of History.

During my two years at Duke I had no more than six hours' consultation with Professor Boyd. Professor Laprade planned my course program, and nearly all my dissertation direction was done by mail after I
left Durham. That was a challenge at times because Boyd wrote such a
scratchy hand that I spent a lot of time trying to decipher his comments.
I never got to know him well or enjoy the traditional affection between
professor and graduate student. Clearly "Tubby" Boyd's focus was on the
building of the library. The rapidly growing collection in that library far
exceeded anything I had seen in Kentucky, but there was a problem with
such rapid growth. The books and manuscripts arrived more rapidly and
in greater volume than the staff could catalogue and arrange them. In the
basement of the library were windrows of books awaiting processing.
Hunting for a title known to exist in that mass was a rare bibliographical
adventure.

As noted, there were two academic generations of professors in the
Department of History. Boyd and Laprade had come from the old Trinity College department and in many respects represented the small-col-
lege view. The younger professors had been employed to help usher Duke
University into a new era of advanced studies. Among them were Richard
H. Shryock, Ernest Nelson, E. Malcolm Carroll, Dorothy Mackey, J. Fred
Rippy, John Tate Lanning, and Paul Garber. All were bright and promising scholars who were capable of promoting a high degree of scholarship
and of bringing prestige to the department. I was assigned as a paper-grad-
ing assistant to Shryock and Nelson. Shryock was rather casual about giving tests. Nelson was meticulous with his and preferred grading his own
papers in order to gauge how well he was succeeding as a teacher.

That was a vibrant moment to be at Duke University. First, it was
exciting to be present at the inception of a really good university and to
be associated with a new faculty that was setting a fresh course to the
academic future. The Duke faculty was far superior to the one at Kentucky in background training, scholarly potential and motivation, and
understanding of the profession. Stephen B. Weeks and John Spencer
Bassett had worked diligently at building the library and manuscript collections and had laid a solid foundation for the new university to build

on. Bassett was a fascinating scholar who had been unusually productive in a small college that had not especially emphasized research and writing. At the Johns Hopkins University, in Herbert Baxter Adams's famous seminar, Bassett had received both the training and the motivation to become a prodigiously productive published scholar. Among his many titles were *A Short History of the United States* and a two-volume biography of Andrew Jackson. I had studied Bassett's *Short History* at Ole Miss and had heard my fellow students question the appropriateness of the word "short" in its title. In the pages of the *South Atlantic Quarterly* he had stirred the anger of Josephus Daniels, editor of the *Raleigh News and Observer,* and the entire racist populace of North Carolina by stating, "Booker T. Washington was the greatest southerner since Robert E. Lee." Daniels pressured the president of Trinity College to fire Bassett. The Trinity faculty united in his defense. Bassett eventually went on to Smith College, and he later died in Washington when struck by a car.

Although Duke University in the fall of 1929 was still very much in the chrysalis stage, it was on its way to becoming a good university. There was a contagious buoyancy about the place and bubbling expectations for the future. One became conscious almost immediately of the fact that a very determined effort was being made to shed the small Methodist-college image and to create the more glorious one of a major southern institution of higher learning. William Preston Few, a South Carolinian son of a Confederate surgeon and a graduate of Wofford College and of Harvard University, had had a long career as president of Trinity College and now of Duke University. He had helped persuade George Washington Duke to give financial support to Trinity College and had been instrumental in James B. Duke's creation of the Duke Endowment in 1924. President Few bore the marks of ill health. He was a tall, thin man with a scraggly beard that seemed to itch him constantly. He was eternally running his fingers through the beard. He had became president of Trinity College in 1910, but earlier, as dean of that college, he had gained stature in his stout defense of John Spencer Bassett in the racial incident.

Associated with President Few were several administrative officials whom some of the older faculty referred to as the "Wofford College brotherhood." Among them were William Wannamaker, William H. Glasson, Robert "Bobby" Flowers, and A. Carl Lee, a Duke Power Company engineer who was given oversight of building the West Campus. Few's dream for Duke University's future was possibly more ardent than were his actual plans for a full-blown teaching/research institution. On at least two occasions he assembled the graduate students and outlined his plans for the growth of the university. He was clear in his discussions and enthusiastic in expressing his vision for a great university. This was a highly exciting moment to witness as, spiritually and physically, a major university was rising from the ground. President Few made clear in his sessions with the graduate students his belief that the university's future reputation would depend in large degree on how well they turned out in their professions.

The spirit with which the university's president so fervently expressed his dream was very much apparent in the Department of History. There was emphasis on research and writing as well as teaching. The newer members of the department demonstrated their commitment to this philosophy by being highly visible in the library. As indicated above, William K. Boyd was a man who juggled many jobs at one time; he was, I felt, a somewhat detached director of graduate studies. Though not openly so declared, he was in competition with his old Columbia University colleague J. G. de Roulhac Hamilton of the University of North Carolina, who was traveling over the South gathering manuscripts and other materials with which to build the tremendously important Southern Collection in Chapel Hill. Boyd had more money and depended more upon dealers and "pickers" who came to Durham with almost tons of materials for the Flowers Collection.

Because of Boyd's involvement with the library collection, I was left virtually free to work out my own fate so far as my dissertation was concerned. In this instance my research and cataloguing experience in Kentucky proved golden. I went to Duke fully committed to major in the history of the South with special emphasis on the frontier aspects of the region, especially those of the Ohio and Mississippi Valleys. Vaguely, I suppose, I had planned to write a dissertation on the trade in agricultural and timber resources on the rivers during the flatboat and steamboat eras. Boyd, despite the facts that he had been born in Missouri and that his Presbyterian minister father was a native of Kentucky, could not penetrate the academic haze west of the Appalachian Highlands. He all but mandated that I write on the building of railroads in the Lower South prior to 1860. This subject had the virtue of being amply documented in newspapers, legislative statutes, company reports, and a specialized railroad journal, and there existed in Washington a transportation library. Boosting railroad construction in the United States prior to the Civil War had been no doubt the purest way to raise public expectations for a prosperous future. For almost three years I spent much of my time turning newspaper pages, reading company reports, and tracking corporate charter trails through the dry sands of state legislation. I lamented with bankrupt promoters and wound up with the story of a highly fragmented system of railroads scattered helter-skelter over the South with few or no major connections to vital centers of trade. I soon came to believe that railway history was a scholarly dead end.

Boyd was an effective classroom teacher, and he conducted a provocative seminar. He would enter the classroom lugging an overstuffed "Boston" bag that contained what seemed to be a hopeless jumble of notes crammed in without the slightest semblance of order. Nevertheless, by some guiding hand of Clio, Boyd could fish out a pertinent note with marked dexterity. Once he forgot this bag and asked me to go to his office and bring it to him. This gave me an opportunity to take at least a cursory glance at that mass of papers.

Though Boyd and Laprade acted in concert in their departmental relations, there was a distinct difference in their instructional approach. Laprade conducted a structured seminar in his private home study. His particular interest was the Queen Anne period. He often gave the designated reporter for a session a good workout with questions and biting criticism. This was fully demonstrated on one occasion when a poor, misguided victim ignored chronology and reported on William Pitt the Younger. Laprade allowed the luckless lad to go through his full report and then crucified him in a few sharp remarks on awareness. Either out of a quirk of scholarship or an attempt to be original, Laprade would often pursue an oblique line of reasoning. This was evident in his textbook, *British History for American Students.*

J. Fred Rippy presented a third dimension in classroom performance. He read aloud, literally word for word, the manuscript of his textbook on Latin America. He did it skillfully and with minimal effect.

There quickly developed a warm camaraderie among the graduate students, whether majoring in history or in one of the sciences. Almost all of us lived in the graduate dormitory and dined together at a long table in the university commons. That board became an informal seminar of sorts. Whatever the particular field of an individual scholar, there was the common cord of getting on with the task that bound us together. All of us were pursuing work leading to the doctorate in a university that still had to prove itself in the rarefied realm of ivy-covered academia.

When I arrived in Durham, Herbert Hoover was a fourth of his way through his term as president of the United States. Most people still held to the great delusion that prosperity was here to stay and that President Hoover could quickly seal any crack that might have developed in the national economy. But there was less political expression at Duke than in Kentucky. No doubt there was present on the campus a strong spirit of political and economic conservatism. In that booming stock market era I knew a graduate student who came to our room nightly to tell Taylor Parks and me how much money he had made that day. I suppose he was building his fortune on marginal capital. Some days he reported impressive gains in his growing portfolio. Despite rising labor unrest in the textile mills in the Carolinas and the ineffective attempts of the Hoover administration to stem the tide of recession, there prevailed an astronomical public unawareness of the impending financial and economic calamity. The stock market crash that shattered American complacency on that memorable October 24, 1929, reverberated even on the Duke campus. My friend of stock-market prosperity disappeared, no doubt with a staggering marginal debt to cover.

At the beginning of the Christmas vacation in 1929 I went to Charlottesville, Virginia, to visit my uncle Albert and aunt Katherine Bennett. To husband my slender funds I hitchhiked with my freshman roommate from Durham by way of Roxboro and South Boston to his home at Brookneal, Virginia. My stay in Charlottesville was brief, however, because I had to return to Durham to attend the meeting of the American Historical Association. I am certain the rather provincial Executive Council of that organization had been tempted to come South because they wanted to see what this *noveau riche* university was like. Four incidents that occurred at that meeting are stamped deeply upon my memory. First, the Department of History had assigned graduate students to do various chores, and, along with two or three other graduate students, I was detailed to sell banquet tickets. Somehow in all the confusion we mixed up the serial numbers so that it was almost impossible to tell how many people would attend the various meals. This caused Professor Laprade to go into a very unministerial shock.

Standing around in the lobby of the Washington Duke Hotel, feeling as awkward and out of place as I had done in the Claypool Hotel in Indianapolis the previous December, I was asked by an aged gentleman to find him a chair and help get him seated. He was Ephraim D. Adams of the Hoover Commission to Belgium and then of the Hoover Institute in Stanford University. Among his writings was his notable book *Great Britain and the Civil War*. In this capacity I was more useful than in selling banquet tickets. I did succeed in getting Professor Adams seated. I was impressed with the fact that he was to be the next president of the American Historical Association.

More important, on the program that year was a section dealing with a miscellany of topics, including slavery, free blacks, and Prohibition. Professor Chilton C. Pearson of Wake Forest College was scheduled to speak on Prohibition, and Monroe Work of Tuskegee Institute on slavery and black economic history. Pearson had a severe case of laryngitis and could hardly make himself heard in his long and boring discourse. In contrast, Monroe Work spoke in tones as clear as a bell and with pronounced assurance. I am almost certain that this was one of the first occasions, if not the first, when a black scholar appeared on the program of a professional association meeting in the South.

During a luncheon at that meeting I was seated beside Josephus Daniels and Kathleen Bruce, two confirmed southerners. Daniels appeared to be the veritable epitome of the Old South and was extremely attentive to Miss Bruce. On another occasion I guided Professors E. Merton Coulter, William O. Lynch, and John Oliver on a tour of the rising East Campus. In later years all three became my friends. The crowning event of the association meeting was Professor James Harvey Robinson's presidential address in East Campus chapel. A graduate student could have been little more fortunate than I to hear James H. Breasted one year and James Harvey Robinson the next. Later I read the proceedings of the meeting with regret that I had not sought out many of the prominent American historians present.

My first year at Duke was one of hard work. Fortunately I roomed with Taylor Parks the second semester. He was a disciplined scholar who set both a good example and a regular schedule for me. Taylor was an avid reader and clipper of the *New York Times*. I often wondered when, if ever, he referred to his great mass of clippings or what pertinence he saw in them to his writing about Colombia. I profited in another way from my association with Taylor. He was a Tennessean who had taught a summer session in the West Tennessee State Teachers College in Memphis. He suggested that I write the president of that institution and apply for a summer school teaching job there in 1930. I did so, and won an appointment that gave me my first experience with teaching.

THE PAY AT WEST TENNESSEE STATE was low and the workload heavy. Despite having never stood in a classroom as an instructor, I was scheduled to teach courses in American literature, political science, geography, and general European history. Almost in desperation I explained my challenges to Jay B. Hubbell, professor of American literature in Duke, who recommended a good textbook guide that would keep me fortified for five weeks. I had a good smattering of political science and considerable background in American physical geography. Fortunately I had also taken Tuthill's European history course at Kentucky and E. Malcolm Carroll's at Duke. Nevertheless, I labored under an unconscionable assignment as a first-time teacher. Surely it must have been the intense heat of that Memphis summer that addled my students so badly that they failed to detect how inexperienced I was as a classroom teacher.

That summer in Memphis brought me into association with two fascinating men whose personalities were as far apart as the magnetic poles. John Crowe Ransom, professor of English in Vanderbilt University, lived across the hall from me in the men's dormitory. At that time he was giving a last editorial reading to the manuscript for the seminal collaborative book *I'll Take My Stand*. He asked me to read some of it, but I was too unsophisticated to comprehend much of the Agrarians' arguments or their final objectives. Academically I was functioning in a far different approach to society and history. One afternoon I went with Ransom to mail the manuscript at the post office in Buntyn, Tennessee. I had no inkling of the debate this book would provoke or that the basic philosophies contained in it would have such lingering effects on much of the southern literary mind.

There was also on the summer staff a Wisconsin graduate student geographer named Staats. He introduced himself as "Mr. Staats" and would say in a piping midwestern accent, "You can spell it the same from both ends." Staats was the only one among the visiting faculty who had a car, and we often explored Memphis with him. One weekend John Crowe Ransom said he had never been to Ole Miss and would like to go there. This was at the time when William Faulkner was coming into focus as an important novelist through publication of two of his novels. Before we left for Oxford, we bought the Sunday edition of the *Memphis Commercial Appeal*, which contained an extensive story about the high-handed actions of Governor Bilbo and his henchmen on the university and college boards of trustees. They had dismissed Chancellor Alfred Hume and several professors of Ole Miss and had wrought equal havoc with the faculty at the Mississippi A&M College. When we arrived on the Ole Miss campus that Sunday morning, we parked the car alongside the old chapel building. At that moment Chancellor Hume came along and spotted the *Commercial Appeal* we were carrying and the Bilbo story. We gained the impression that this was the first he had heard of that highly dispiriting incident. Our meeting that day occurred within a hundred steps of the spot where two years before the chancellor had advised me to make application for a scholarship at the University of Kentucky. For Mississippi higher education the trustees' highly partisan and malicious actions proved devastating. They caused not only the loss of accreditation for the professional schools but the loss of trust in the integrity of the entire system of higher education in the state. It also resulted in the loss of Charles S. Sydnor in history and Arthur Palmer Hudson in English, plus the demoralization of those professors who remained.

That summer at West Tennessee State Teachers College was an important transitional time for me and for that college as well. West Tennessee State was one of those weak institutions begotten by politicians and sent out into the world of higher learning bearing the ephemeral mantle of a "teachers college." It suffered from a severe overdose of *in loco parentis*. The dean of women was Nellie Angel Smith. Hailing from Horse Cave, Kentucky, she nevertheless seemed to be the reincarnation of some blue-nosed, seventeenth-century Bay Colony Puritan. She ran a tight corral in which she dictated a strict code of social decorum and dress. Despite her title she drew no line between the sexes. She stoutly maintained that men students should be held to a strict dress code that required wearing coats at meals in the common dining room. A steamy Memphis college dining room was hardly the place to observe more than the essentials of a dress code. One noon the subjects of Dean Nellie's notion of proper attire lined up before the dining room door, placed their coats on the withering grass, and swore and bedamned if they would submit. I almost joined them until I realized that I had stepped over that imaginary line from being a student to becoming a "professor." My student protest days were over.

The tentacles of the Angel of Horse Cave ran deep throughout that college. One of her rules was that a member of the instructional staff had to be present in the library during its evening hours to thwart any attempted invasion by a frivolous Cupid into those sacred intellectual environs. When my time came to serve as monitor I went out in front of the building, sprawled out on the lawn, and went to sleep. I felt that a little hand holding and smooching might make Nellie Angel's Latin and Greek gods a little more welcome.

In 1930 there were some extraordinarily interesting people in Memphis. J. P. Alley was at the peak of his popularity as the "Hambone" cartoon artist. Daily he not only produced the figure of the lovable old black philosopher but also put words of folk wisdom into his mouth. In that region of the South, Hambone was quoted more often than the Scriptures. Ridley Wills was a *Commercial Appeal* columnist who enjoyed a wide readership. The editor of the paper was C. P. J. Mooney, a Chicago native who had come to the South and was a major crusader for agricultural diversification and social change. Beale Street was in its heyday, and the Chisca and Peabody Hotels were gathering places both for Delta cotton snobs and for those less affluent characters so eloquently portrayed in Faulkner's *The Reivers*. Spread over the city generally was a benevolent miasma of southern charm and folkways. Memphis, located in the river-pinched corner of western Tennessee, resembled Arkansas and Mississippi in character more than the other sections of Tennessee.

By MID-JULY 1930 THE SUMMER session had ended in Western Tennessee State Teachers College, and I hastened to Lexington to complete the cataloguing task I had begun the year before. I rode a bus on what seemed an interminable journey through Nashville, Bowling Green, Louisville, and Frankfort. Before I reached Lexington the devastating drought of that year had set in. This added to the deepening Depression and had sobering effects on the human spirit in Kentucky. I traveled daily from Lexington to Frankfort aboard the interurban cars and observed tobacco fields along the way being parched literally down to the ground. Lexington was falling victim to its ancient nemesis, the prospect that it would be without a water supply. The reservoirs south of town shrank daily. As a result of the impending crisis, construction of a water line to the Kentucky River was begun. Even the level of the river dropped to a frightening stage. We heard stories that people upstream could drive their wagons across the river. The drought that year was not really broken until September and October. In the meantime it had revealed how vulnerable the rich Bluegrass dome area was to drought and how dependent its towns were on the Kentucky River.

By mid-September I had completed, after a fashion, my listing of potential documentary materials in the area of the university. By the time that fretful summer ended I knew with certainty that my interest ran more to a study of the westward movement in American history than to the history of the Old South of Duke University vintage. Too, I now hoped I would have an opportunity to return to Kentucky to teach and do research. That possibility would confront me in the coming year. I had saved some money that summer, and with the Duke fellowship and modest loans from the Charlottesville banks with Uncle Albert Bennett's endorsement, I could complete my residential requirements for the doctorate.

That fall a lad named "Soup" Campbell came to Lexington in hope of being able to play football. Either he did not fit Coach Harry Gamage's needs, or Campbell was not pleased with the coaches and the team's prospects, so he decided to go to Duke to enroll as a freshman. He had an old Model T Ford touring car that he had driven from New Jersey. In mid-September he and I set out across the mountains and over difficult roads for Durham. At Bristol, Tennessee, we almost literally had to claw our way over the Unaka Mountains on a freshly machined road, taxing every ounce of the old car's power. At some places on that climb I ran along behind with a rock to chock the car while Campbell revved up the engine. Just past midnight the old car wheezed and snorted to a stop on the edge of the village of Trade, Tennessee. We piled up on the seats and went to sleep in the middle of the road. We were awakened at daylight to find a bunch of mountaineers staring at us. They proved to be both obliging and ingenious with a pair of pliers and a piece of wire. They conjured our car's weary engine to life, and we chugged along the long drive from Boone, North Carolina, by way of Yadkinsville, Wilkesboro, Winston-Salem, Greensboro, and Burlington to Durham. We arrived in Durham worn out after two days and a night traveling over less than modern highways. By that fall the Great Depression was upon the nation in dead earnest, and the future for a young historian was as heavily veiled as the fog-shrouded ridges had been back in the Unaka Mountains.

9

~

YEAR OF DECISION

IN MID-SUMMER 1930, WHILE THE GREAT DROUGHT scorched Kentucky and withered field crops to the ground, I am certain I did not comprehend the enormous pressure I would face in the coming academic year. I still had to complete a semester of course requirements at Duke and begin the perplexing preparation for the general doctoral examinations. Until I underwent that ordeal in the second semester, I would not be a full-status candidate for the doctorate. In addition to the field subject examinations, I had to satisfy the Duke requirement that I demonstrate a reading capability in French and German. There was also the nagging matter of finding a teaching position in the midst of a biting depression.

The Duke University I returned to in September 1930 had become a different institution from the one I had left in June. The West Campus was open for occupancy, though work was continuing on some of the buildings and in the landscaping of the grounds. In the midst of the sprawling Duke Foundation pine woods, impressive new stone buildings had arisen to give the complacent countryside a decidedly Gothic appearance. Gracing the end of the sweeping driveway, the overweening Gothic chapel-cathedral was rising stone by stone to tower over the entire Duke demesne. The impressive quadrangle was still littered in places with construction debris. All along the rows of buildings Italian sculptors were pecking away, creating bizarre allegorical faces and forms from blocks of North Carolina stone. On the east wing of the quadrangle the medical school structure spread its wing across the broad terminal way. In the heart of the transept of the quadrangle was the Gray Building, seat of the university's administrative authority, and facing it was the library. There in solid American collegiate Gothic stood the physical confirmation that a small Methodist college had given birth to a major southern university.

During the summer the library collection and classroom properties were transferred from the East Campus to the West. All summer long the library staff and movers boxed the tangled windrows of books and transferred them from the basement catacomb of the limited East Campus library to the spacious new building. Along with the books, the manuscript, newspaper, and documentary files were properly processed and made available. Figuratively the move to the new campus was as much an intellectual watershed as a physical one.

Not only were the new main buildings strange and sometimes confusing, but so were the library, the student center, the dormitories, and the dining halls. The room Taylor Parks and I shared on the new campus was in sharp contrast to the shabby, bedbug-infested Jarvis Hall room in which I had lived during my first semester on the East Campus. Gothic architecture has more external allure than internal convenience and comfort. The head of my bed was directly opposite the corners where a conscientious sculptor arrived at the crack of dawn all semester long to chisel a legendary apelike figure that has no doubt leered at every passerby during the past three quarters of a century.

Rivaling the noisy stone cutters was the contractor who roared up and down the quadrangle clearing its surface of mud and construction debris. A roaring bulldozer bulling its way back and forth between rows of dormitories created a kind of predawn paranoia. On one occasion a spunky, redheaded doctoral candidate named Charlie took direct action by going into town and buying a heavy-duty bolt cutter. Under cover of darkness he cut everything off the bulldozers that could be cut. That insured a week of sweet morning silence. After the machines were repaired they were driven away at quitting time to a secret parking place. Upon graduation Charlie became an assistant superintendent of the Pennsylvania public school system. I doubt those bulldozer machinations appeared on his academic record.

Reentering Duke University that fall was in fact comparable to matriculating in a different university. The professors in the Department of History were the same, but they functioned in an entirely new academic and physical environment. The library staff now operated with shelving and facilities that were entirely different from those in their cramped quarters on East Campus. This meant that, at a very strategic moment in my preparation for the general examination, I had to spend almost as much time locating books as I did in using them. The new library was more departmentally organized than in the older building. J. P. Breedlove, an old Trinity College holdover and brother-in-law to the famous American historian John Spencer Bassett, was librarian, in name at least. My major professor, William Kenneth Boyd, exercised a heavy hand in the library's management. He was still passionately involved in building a rich manuscript and documentary collection.

Obviously 1930–1931 was an exciting ceremonial year in the history of Duke University. During the Christmas holidays I remained on campus along with a Puerto Rican, Rodolfo Rivera, to prepare for the upcoming general examinations. That pile of gray stone during the vacation season was a cold and lonely place, but a quiet one. No stone sculptor or bulldozer operator broke the silence. Rivera and I broke the monastic silence with a comical caper. "Soup" Campbell had left his old topless Model T with me when he went home during the holidays, so Rivera and I resolved to snatch a touch of joy from the holidays. We invited two Durham resident girls of the library staff to go with us to Raleigh for dinner and a movie. I revved up Campbell's old wreck of a car, and we drove downtown to pick up the girls. They appeared dressed up as if to attend a wedding, complete with fur coats. When we arrived in Raleigh we parked well away from the Sir Walter Hotel and went on to dinner and the movie. When we got back to the old car a group of men and boys were standing around it looking at it as if it had wings. We walked away and strolled around the North Carolina state capitol, hoping our "admirers" would go away. They did not. Finally we resolved to brave our public and get out of town. When our fur-bearing guests were seated in the car and I got it started, I heard one of the bystanders say, "By God, they'll ride in anything these days."

There are folk linkages among graduate students. They share common interests, no matter the field. One generation passes down to the next a bundle of advice and folklore. Fortunately for my generation, enough candidates had gone through the "wringer" to describe the pitfalls. The ordeal of the preliminary or general examinations is potentially fatal. Specifically, we were told by our predecessors that among the requirements would be endless hours of intensive reading, a review of information about great movements in history, and a whole Dewey decimal system of bibliographical knowledge. Too, it was inferred that some knowledge of the philosophy of history might be relevant. On my execution week I was examined on the fields of British, modern European, and Latin American history. My two fields in American history were waived until I defended my dissertation.

Two of the examinations combined oral and written sections, but Laprade, of course, did things differently. He assigned five different, fairly broad-ranging topics in British history on which he instructed me to organize lectures accompanied by generous bibliographical references. The lectures were to be suitable for delivery to an undergraduate class in British history. He allowed five consecutive days in which to research, document, and type the lectures. This examination required a prodigious amount of time and searching. I spent every hour the library was open gathering the factual information and bibliographical entries, and then went to my room and typed the lectures. I never learned whether or not

Laprade thought well of the lectures. He only announced laconically that I had passed the examination.

Two things impressed me about Laprade's form of examination. First, it taxed my ability to gather and organize a body of factual information into an acceptable lecture form. Second, it demonstrated to me realistically the challenges I would face in preparing lectures to be delivered before a real live class of undergraduates. I could not have known in January 1931 that in the fall I would be confronted with a full schedule of freshman British history in the University of Kentucky.

The Duke Department of History held rigidly to the idea that doctoral candidates must demonstrate a reading knowledge in French and German. For most graduate students this was an awesome hurdle. Fortunately I had enough undergraduate preparation in French to pass that examination with little difficulty, provided it involved straightforward textual materials containing no colloquialisms. The morning I took my French reading test under the scrutiny of Professor Albert M. ("Rabbit") Webb, I was led deep down into the lower regions of the library where there were shelved, row on row, "prize" books that had been given to French schoolchildren and that Duke University had purchased from a foreign dealer. Professor Webb chose at random a volume of the correspondence of the historian-politician François Guizot. I got the impression that Webb had not fully familiarized himself with that collection, certainly not with Guizot's correspondence. He had me read up to and almost beyond my capability in the French language. Well after the noon hour he said casually that I had passed the examination but that he himself wanted to explore Guizot's writings further.

I had spent considerable time during my two years at Duke taking reading instruction in German, even employing a tutor out of my slender funds. On the examination in this language I was asked to read the famous German treatise on cotton culture in the South. This was somewhat akin to the predicament of Brer Rabbit and the tar baby. I was luckily thrust into a familiar and benign briar patch.

BY APRIL 1, 1931, I FOUND MYSELF in that academic purgatory from which many graduate students never return, that of being a faceless academic mortal with all but the dissertation status. This situation, which is much like traveling on a road that suddenly ends, nevertheless might be called the testing ground on which a graduate student demonstrates enough courage and energy to do the research for and writing of a dissertation. The Great Depression was bearing heavily upon the fortunes of young academics. While undergoing the stress of the general and language examinations, I was also looking frantically for a job. There could scarcely have been a more discouraging moment in American history for a young and inexperienced historian to find employment than the early 1930s. In those grim closing years of the Hoover administration, the chance of finding almost any kind of promising employment was slim at best.

One day I met Vice-President Robert Flowers just outside the Gray Administration Building. He told me that he and President Few had been requested to select a young man to go to China to teach history in the University of Shanghai, if I remember correctly. The assignment would be for an extended number of years. This request had come because Duke University, through its affiliation with the Methodist Church and its interest in the Oriental-American Tobacco Corporation, had a China connection. For many reasons the prospect of a teaching assignment in China held little attraction for me, but I asked my friend Lewis Chase in the Transylvania College Library for advice. He strongly advised me not to consider the job, saying that it would destroy my digestive system and intellectually would take me far away from my area of historical interest. Later Vice-President Flowers made a second suggestion, that I apply for an available job in the Naval Academy, of which he was a graduate. Although the latter position was more attractive than the one in China, I had not the slightest background in naval history and would have been a lost soul in the field.

Rodolfo Rivera, Elizabeth Davidson, and I were the only history graduate students at Duke seeking employment that spring. Elizabeth was hired by Coker College in Hartsville, South Carolina, and it seems that she had experienced no anxiety over finding the position. Rivera and I walked miles commiserating with each other over our grim futures. I perhaps had two distinct advantages over Rodolfo. I was Protestant and spoke English with a southern drawl, while he was Catholic and spoke with a Spanish accent. One day, however, he did get a nibble of a job at Limestone College in South Carolina and rushed to tell Dr. Boyd the news. Boyd's reply was, "I have told you boys to stay away from those South Carolina Baptist monasteries."

A ray of hope for me broke through the gloom in late March 1931. I had a letter from Professor J. Catron Jones, he of comparative government fame, offering me an instructorship in political science in the University of Kentucky. I accepted his offer, but a couple of weeks later he withdrew it when he learned that I did not yet have my doctorate. Surely a guardian angel was watching over me, but at that moment I attributed the guardianship to a less charitable imp. In my brief moment as a prospective political scientist I did some intensive soul searching. When I was "fired" I could only lament, with Sir Walter Scott, "Oh what a tangled web we weave / When first we practise to deceive!" I was no political scientist.

When I completed my general examinations and passed the French and German language reading tests, I was freed of further academic shackles, with the exception of my dissertation. I was now on my own, jobless and bankrupt. Luckily, and again through the good agency of Taylor Parks, I applied for and received temporary appointment to an instructorship in American history in the University of Tennessee. My job in that institution was to teach in the special spring quarter that was open to public school teachers seeking full accreditation of their teaching license. At the same time, Parks and I encouraged Joe Matthews to apply for the summer teaching job in Memphis, and he was hired. Joe was just finishing work for the master's degree and needed to earn some money to remain in school. He was the son of a Kentucky Methodist minister and a graduate of Kentucky Wesleyan College. Joe was a somewhat shy and retiring lad who had not impressed Laprade, and Laprade had not impressed Joe. He had decided to enter the University of Pennsylvania to pursue the doctorate in British history. Like me the summer before, he had not a moment of teaching experience. We arranged to travel together as far as Knoxville, where I would detrain. We pooled our meager funds and purchased a lower berth in the Pullman car. Our fellow graduate students came down to the grim old Southern Railway Station in Durham to see us off. In a moment of planned distraction, a practical joker pasted on the back of Joe's coat a placard reading, "Just married." As we boarded the car, we noticed that people were giving us quizzical stares. It was not until we undressed in the berth that we discovered the placard.

Being an old and experienced teacher of one term's service, I was in a position to give Joe some fatherly advice. Knowing his timidity, I advised him to prepare enough notes for at least four lectures prior to his first class meeting. I assured him that even then he would run out of "intellectual soap." When I left him on the train in Knoxville he looked like one of Father Abraham's lambs impaled on a burning bush, and perhaps he was. A couple of weeks later he wrote me saying that he had used up all his lecture notes in the first twenty minutes in class. Assuredly this was not to be so later, in his bright academic career as a professor at Ole Miss and then at Emory University. In both institutions he was to be a colleague of my old classmate at Kentucky, Bell Wiley.

I ARRIVED ON THE CAMPUS OF the University of Tennessee in April 1931, when both that institution and the city of Knoxville were in the throes of a calamitous financial situation. Knoxville was in an unusually depressed condition because of the failures of the Luke Lee and Rogers Caldwell empires. The Holston Bank was bankrupted, and Governor Henry Horton was under heavy fire because of fiscal irresponsibilities, if not criminal acts, in the management of highway matters. Up and down Gay Street, merchants were being forced to close their doors in the face of failure. The thoroughfare assumed the appearance of a ghost town. An air of impenetrable gloom settled upon the city in that pre-TVA era.

I was in no better condition than the city. My salary was just $125 a month. But in Depression-strapped Knoxville the cost of living was minimal. I rented a room with a private bath for $15 a month, and boardinghouse meals were cheaper than they had been in Lexington in 1928.

Whatever the local fiscal crisis, I felt far more comfortable in the classroom than I had the summer before in Memphis. My entire course load was in American history. My students were largely public school teachers and were mature and serious minded. This was challenging, but an improvement over the classes I had taught in the West Tennessee State Teachers College. Happily also, the situation in Knoxville enabled me to do some research on my dissertation. Both the university library and Lawson-Magee Library contained original documentary materials relating to the building of railroads in Tennessee prior to the Civil War. Tennessee before 1860 was virtually a keystone state in the construction of the southern railroads, north and south, east and west.

I enjoyed a pleasant teaching apprenticeship that spring in the University of Tennessee. Despite the thickening gloom of the Great Depression, there appeared on the horizon a thin gleam of hope. In time there would no doubt be a national decision on the development of the Tennessee River system. Senator George Norris of Nebraska was leading the crusade to nationalize such a project.

I was fortunate too in establishing warm personal rapport with my students, and they were graciously tolerant of a greenhorn instructor. My classes were on the top floor of the large central building, Ayres Hall, which was situated atop a steep ridge bordering on the Tennessee River. Walking up and down that hill and then climbing three flights of stairs was a leg-wearying exercise. On one occasion I caught the toe of a shoe under the rim of a stair riser and fell sprawling in the floor, splitting the seat out of my only decent pair of trousers. As I lay on the floor—unseen, thank goodness—I debated whether to get up and sidle down the stairs and go home with my rear end exposed to the winds of Appalachia. Instead I got up and backed along the wall to the classroom desk and took my seat, then waited until the room was deserted after class to sneak out of the building. Fortunately a pair of britches could be bought in bankrupt Knoxville at a giveaway price.

There were some eccentricities involved in affairs at Tennessee. One day Philip Hamer, acting head of the history department, told me that I was holding one of my classes too long. Dean Massey, titular head of the

Department of History, taught a class in the room the following hour, and he was accustomed to coming and sitting in the room twenty minutes ahead of the class hour. Thereafter I had to cut my class twenty minutes short in order to accommodate the popular old dean of men.

I also became a bystander in a withering romance. Before I left Durham, my roommate, Taylor Parks, had prevailed upon me to look up his girlfriend, who lived on the outskirts of Knoxville. When I met her I saw at once that she had too much vim and vigor for poor old pedantic Taylor. Then I received a letter from Taylor saying that he and the new Duke University Law School librarian were coming to Knoxville for a weekend to visit me—or, more likely, to visit that red-haired goddess. That weekend the librarian and I rode around in the back seat as we watched Taylor's romance unravel by the mile. I am sure Taylor never saw that lively redhead again.

During that brief period in the University of Tennessee I developed some lasting friendships. These included Lawrence Houchens of Bloomfield, Kentucky, later a professor of American literature in Miami University; Phil and Peg Hamer; Stanley Folmsbee; and Blue Kline, one of the lesser-known Agrarians of Vanderbilt. I carried nothing away from Knoxville more precious than a kind gesture by my students. On my final class meeting I was presented with a silvered watch chain as a token, they said, of appreciation. Never in all my teaching experience did a gesture of this sort touch me so deeply. I had striven to be conscientious in preparing for my classes, and I hope I did a passable job in the classroom. I have kept that chain all these years. The last vestiges of silver coating have disappeared, but it remains a reminder of the fact that I learned more than did my students that summer.

I approached the end of my appointment in Knoxville with no real promise of a job for that fall. During the previous academic year I had engaged in correspondence with various persons in Kentucky. Among them were Professor Charles M. Knapp and Miss Arti Lee Taylor, the reference librarian. Knapp, I was certain, wished to succeed Tuthill as head of the Department of History and might, I hoped, be casting around for future staff members. My correspondents were supportive of my desire to return to Kentucky, but they were uncertain as to whether there would actually be a job opening. In the course of time I was encouraged to write directly to President Frank L. McVey. My timing was fortunate. Within the fall semester 1931, the university would dedicate its new library building and was faced with the monumental task of developing an adequate collection of books and historical documents. I decided to visit President McVey.

Unexpectedly, however, I found myself caught up in an uncomfortable situation. Professor Philip Hamer proved reluctant to grant me a leave for the trip to Lexington. Had he not done so, I believe I would have resigned immediately. The prospect of being hired by the University of Kentucky was too important to me. Furthermore, the Mississippi Valley Historical Association was holding its annual meeting in Lexington, and I had a place on the program to read a brief paper dealing with my survey of original documentary materials still available in the central Ohio Valley region. I felt that perhaps Lyman Draper and Reuben Durrett after all had not made off with all the documentary materials in the area.

My association with Philip Hamer was otherwise amicable, and we grew closer as the years passed. Soon after I left the University of Tennessee, Hamer resigned to take an administrative position in the newly organized National Archives. Later he became director of the National Historical Publications Commission. In this position he had charge of the research and publication of the papers of major American political figures. In 1945 or 1946 I attended the annual meeting of the American Historical Association in New York, and there I met Phil in the lobby of the Pennsylvania Hotel. He asked me if I would organize a project to publish the voluminous papers of Henry Clay. In a naive moment I agreed to do so. I had no notion that the project would involve me in persuading James F. Hopkins to become editor of the papers, beginning a collective search for Clay's papers, and raising a major amount of money to sustain the project. The project ultimately resulted in eleven volumes published between 1959 and 1991.

My visit with President McVey was both pleasant and rewarding. He arranged for me to be interviewed by Dean A. E. Evans and Professor

Frank Randall of the Law School and James W. Martin of the College of Commerce. I must have impressed them enough, because they approved my appointment. McVey admonished me not to communicate with Edward Tuthill, head of the Department of History. Apparently the president had less than full confidence in Tuthill's management of his department. A week later I received a handwritten letter from the president telling me he was recommending my appointment to the Board of Trustees as an instructor in history. I would be required to teach a half schedule in the Department of History and spend half time helping to build up the library and its documentary collection. My ten-month salary would be $1,800. That blessed letter concluded for me a long and anxious period of wondering if I had gone through the travail of pursuing a doctorate to no avail.

Following my employment by the president of the university, there occurred over the spring and summer a chain of events that was both amusing and disturbing. Approximately two weeks after I received McVey's letter, I received one from Tuthill offering to employ me as an instructor of history. I had the unenviable task of writing my old professor and future department head that I had already been hired by the president for the post. For a decade this matter was to cause unpleasant moments. First, I was not informed about my teaching schedule until after the first of September. When I inquired of Tuthill, he told me that all future correspondence would be through Dean Paul P. Boyd of the College of Arts and Sciences. When I asked Dean Boyd about my courses, he expressed surprise that I had not been informed. Then, just before I left for Lexington, I received an angry letter from Tuthill scolding me for having written the dean. When I cited his instructions to me, he backed down, but not until he had burdened me with a fifteen-hour teaching schedule in British history. He never approved of my giving time to the library assignment.

As soon as the spring quarter ended in Tennessee, I hustled back to Durham for a very special reason. In October 1929 at Duke there had occurred one of those unexpected and decisive moments in my life that was to have lasting consequence. One noon break I was sitting on the entry steps to the library talking with several graduate colleagues when five or six library staff members returned from lunch, walking around the circular drive. Among them was a handsome blonde girl. I learned later that her name was Martha Elizabeth (Beth) Turner. She was a graduate of Furman University and the Simmons College Library School in Boston. She was the first library staff member hired for the new Duke University library.

Beth was born and grew up in Fairfield County, South Carolina. Her father was a cotton farmer, cattleman, and county superintendent of schools. The Turners' ancestors had immigrated from County Antrim in Ireland but were of Scotch origin. William Waugh Turner was a Presbyterian in religion and a loyal Jacksonian in politics. Beth's mother, Ruth Dorman Turner, a member of an Irish family that had immigrated to South Carolina's upper Piedmont, had taught school in Fairfield County. She was a dedicated Baptist.

Beth and I dated off and on during 1929–1930, but I had no glimmer of a future life with her. Not until my last year at Duke, after I had completed my preliminary examinations, did I beseech her to become my wife. Wisely, she was reluctant to marry me. I did not have a job, while she had a good one. At that time radios were blaring a song, its singer declaring in a Brooklyn accent, "Potatoes are cheaper, bananas are cheaper, now's the time to fall in love." If you were without a job, however, cheap potatoes and bananas had little meaning.

When I came from Knoxville to see Beth in Durham, her parents were there on a visit from South Carolina. That was the first time I met them. We visited for a couple of days, and when Beth and I, in our friend Clara Childress's car, guided the Turners out of Durham on the road to Chapel Hill and Charlotte, Mr. Turner said to me, "If you are ever in South Carolina, come to see us"—an invitation I was to take seriously.

Back in Knoxville I gathered up my belongings and headed for Washington to spend a hot summer doing research for my dissertation at the Library of Congress and the Transportation Library. Washington was not only hot but Depression-bound and fraught with anxiety over the great Bonus March and the cardboard city erected in the heart of the nation's capital. Life within the fold of the Library of Congress, however, was peaceful, and the environment was conducive to serious research.

Unlike many current-day graduate students, I had no scholarly resources to finance my research. All of it, including my stay in Washington, was financed from my slender cash resources. Fortunately, prices for meals and lodging in Washington were low. By word of mouth and mutual assistance, Duke graduate students had literally homesteaded a haven at 500 East Capitol Street, a two-story brick rooming house operated by a Mrs. Carleton. Her only boarders seemed to be from Duke. This residence was diagonally across the street from the Folger Shakespeare Library, which was in the final stages of completion. Stone sculptors were at work carving scenes from Shakespearean plays on the side panels of the building. Much of the summer I watched a sculptor chiseling out a scene from *A Midsummer Night's Dream*.

Mrs. Carleton's house was only a short distance from the Library of Congress, and there was a tiny neighborhood grocery on the way. This was a morning gathering place for researchers and library staff where for twenty cents they could purchase a breakfast of milk and sweet rolls. Other meals could be had for very reasonable prices at the Methodist Center, in the basement of the Supreme Court Building, and in neighborhood restaurants. However devastating the Great Depression may have been for the country, it had the saving grace of lowering the cost of doing research in Washington.

Although I spent day and night bent over newspapers and company reports, there were also moments of relaxation and pleasant associations with other historians. That summer some interesting and rising historian scholars were doing research in Washington. William B. and Katherine Hesseltine were doing research for his book on Confederate prisons. Fred Harrington, later to become president of the University of Wisconsin, was doing research for his dissertation. Culver H. Smith was plowing through the Jacksonian press. There was an almost constant stream of other scholars from Duke and elsewhere, among them Alex Mabry, Bill Simpson, and Robert Rankin, assistant dean of the graduate school, as well as my two of my colleagues from Tennessee, Peg Hamer and Stanley Folmsbee.

The Library of Congress possessed very good files of southern antebellum newspapers. These were indispensable to my study of the building of the southern railroads. Too, the library's holdings of company reports, pamphlets, and other contemporary sources were a veritable gold mine of information. I was, in fact, all but overwhelmed by the amount of data I discovered. Fortunately I had previously worked briefly at the library and was familiar with the routine.

Two work spaces were assigned to me. During the daytime I took possession of a spot in the newspaper section of the East Wing. In the evenings, when the newspaper wing was closed, I worked with special reports, local histories, and other published materials relating to the building of the antebellum southern railways at a desk on the balustrade of the magnificent central reading room. That great room symbolized both the Jeffersonian dream of a significant national library and the maturing literary culture of the Republic. It was within the wide circumference of that room that most people came to use the Library of Congress book collections. One night I witnessed a librarian's nightmare. A patron uninitiated into the rather demanding ways of librarians located the card entry for a book he wished to use. He ripped the card from the file case and presented it at the loan desk. The commotion that followed suggested that the patron had committed an error akin to presenting the decaying carcass of an elephant at the desk. The attendants went into a state of shock that promised to leave lifetime scars.

Regular researchers quickly learned that the easiest entry to the library was through a door beneath the main steps. Standing guard over this portal was a genial redheaded Irishman who greeted and joked with patrons. One evening I was at the desk in the reading room when the Irishman and another guard appeared and declared me under arrest. Some less than literary visitor had slipped past the guard carrying a quart jar of Appalachian-type moonshine into the men's room. In his jubilation to lift his literary spirits he dropped the jar, and in a few moments the whole library smelled like a fresh run up Greasy Creek. The guards maintained that since I was from Kentucky, it followed naturally that I was the culprit. They thought this was a great joke. I think it was at that moment that I felt I had become a Kentuckian, sharing in one of the state's dubious, if colorful, stereotypes.

One morning I saw Dean William H. Glasson of Duke reading the *Durham Herald* with great glee. He was chuckling over an article announcing the marriage of William Kenneth Boyd to a Georgia woman. I am sure both he and I felt that "Tubby" Boyd had about as much romance in him as one of the famous Duke University gargoyles. "Mink" Glasson jumped to the conclusion that Boyd had found some woman in Georgia who owned a big collection of family papers and the only way he could secure them was to marry her.

Beth came to Washington one weekend with Taylor Parks and his fiancée, Lois Fefry. We had an interesting weekend spent exploring the city, and Beth and I rented a canoe and paddled up the Potomac River. By then I had the satisfaction of a job waiting for me in the fall, but we still did not feel able to set a wedding date.

Sometime during the summer I received a letter from Dean Boyd at Kentucky asking me if I would go out to Georgetown and talk with a lady named Thian. He had been informed that she had in her possession a considerable collection of Confederate government papers. One afternoon I persuaded Culver Smith to go with me to call on Miss Thian. We located her big, old Georgian-style house. When we rang the doorbell we were immediately confronted by a very angry German police dog. When Miss Thian, the very embodiment of the late nineteenth-century woman, appeared, she told us she did have the papers and would be glad to see me at a later date.

Ten days later I called again at the Thian mansion. This time Miss Thian was dressed in a flowing black gown that could have come out of Woodward and Lothrop's 1890 stock. In the process of dressing she had inadvertently tucked the back hem of the dress into her panties. From the front she appeared normally dressed, but from the rear she presented full exposure. This created an awkward situation for me. I debated whether I should tell her or just let her discover her error. She showed me into a large parlor that was stacked with manuscripts. I sat the evening through examining them. Her father had been aboard the Confederate train that had departed from Richmond loaded with the records of the Confederate government. When the train was captured at Greensboro, North Carolina, he took possession of the records. This was an exciting collection. I reported my findings to Dr. Boyd, but I believe that the papers were later acquired by the Library of Congress.

That summer, down Pennsylvania Avenue in the neighborhood of the frowning old Post Office building, construction of the National Archives was under way, but the archives were not to be opened until 1934. The fact that prior to that date the federal records were stored in scattered depositories made their access and use almost impossible. In many areas, including that of my research, scholars had to depend in large measure on published documents and the great serial set of federal documents.

I left Washington early in September, still in the dark as to my teaching schedule at Kentucky. Nevertheless, I had been diligent in my research and was able to bring away with me almost enough notes to permit me to write my dissertation. I stopped in Durham to see Beth, and we set a wedding date for the following June. We so hoped the Great Depression would soon abate, with signs of better times to come. Then I began the bone-wearying journey back over the Southern Railway by way of Knoxville to Lexington to begin my career in Kentucky. When I arrived in Lexington early in the morning of September 12, 1931, I had only a buffalo nickel in my pocket—obviously not enough to hire a taxi. I left my trunk in the baggage room, gathered up my suitcase, my box of dissertation notes, and my portable typewriter, and walked down Scott Street and across the University of Kentucky campus to Rose Lane and my boardinghouse. That morning I entered into an entirely new relationship with the University of Kentucky from that of the past two years. I was now a member, be it said a highly tenuous one, of the faculty. I had come home to Lexington in a parlous economic time.

10

~

Depression Years

I BEGAN THE ACADEMIC YEAR 1931–1932 WITH CONSID-
erable trepidation. The Kentucky General Assembly was caught in a partisan deadlock I had not anticipated, and funding for higher education
was cut. In the immediate past the university's funds had been derived
largely from estate settlement taxes, and in the Great Depression this
source was greatly reduced. The Ruby Laffoon administration, following
the precedents of other southern states, attempted to secure passage of a
sales tax in 1932, but it failed to pass. In 1934 it passed, creating a glimmer
of hope that the university would reinstate full salaries. That glimmer
was short-lived, however. The tax was repealed in the following legislative session. In the meantime I felt that my appointment was in jeopardy.
I was single and, as the lowest ranking member in the Department of
History, I could be sacrificed with ease. For the time being I retained my
appointment, but my salary was reduced from the promised $1,800 to
$1,100. Beth and I reset our wedding date for the late fall of 1932.

In spite of the Great Depression, 1931 was in many respects a fortunate time in which to begin a career as an American historian. This was especially true in the South, where universities and colleges were expanding their social studies curriculums. There was a rising impetus to promote courses in regional history and a burgeoning interest in research, writing, and publication. Equally important, this was a period in which much of what had earlier been written about the Civil War, slavery, Reconstruction, and regional politics was being revised.

With the expansion of curriculums and the new emphases on research and publication, the collecting of source materials and the building of libraries became virtually mandatory. For the South, J. G. De Roulhac Hamilton of the University of North Carolina, William K. Boyd of Duke University, E. M. Coulter at the University of Georgia, and some of the historians in Louisiana State University ushered in a new era of collecting documentary materials. The nonacademic Filson Club in Louisville underwent a renascence following the loss of the famous Durrett Collection to the University of Chicago and began assembling a significant body of basic research materials.

At the same time as the stirring in the library field in the South, W. T. Couch was pioneering a regional university press at Chapel Hill. The University of North Carolina Press in the early 1930s published several seminal books: *Culture in the South,* largely as an answer to the Vanderbilt University Agrarians and their manifesto, *I'll Take My Stand;* Rupert Vance's *Human Geography of the South;* Howard Odum's *Southern Regions;* and various economic and sociological studies relating to the southern textile industry. Robert Woody and Francis Simkins published their revisionary study *Reconstruction in South Carolina,* and in the nonacademic area the novelists Thomas Stribling, Erskine Caldwell, and William Faulkner stirred southern emotions, if not the regional mind.

That September day in 1931 when I boarded a Southern Railway train in Durham for the long, wandering journey back to Kentucky, I could not have imagined that I was beginning my career in what might be considered one of the best scholarly historical eras. Measured by several criteria, I was that day headed toward a new frontier so far as the possibilities were concerned in teaching, collecting important bodies of source materials, and helping to develop a university library and a department of history.

WHEN I ARRIVED IN LEXINGTON, I learned that a second and major addition had been made to the staff of the Department of History. Edward Tuthill was crowing over the coup of having drawn Paul Hibbard Clyde away from the Ohio State University history department. Clyde's special field in both teaching and research was the Pacific, with special emphasis on Japan. Of Scotch descent and a native of Vancouver, Clyde had a bright personality. He had done his doctoral work under the direction of Payson J. Treat of Stanford University. It would have been hard to imagine two men with such distinctly different personalities as those of Tuthill and Clyde, or of Charles M. Knapp and Clyde.

I think Clyde became acquainted with Kentucky through teaching a summer session there. At the time there was considerable public discussion of the mandated islands under Japanese administration, but otherwise local interest in the Far East was limited, to say the least. I do know that Clyde, along with many other members of the Department of History in Ohio State University, became highly dissatisfied after the death of Dean Shepherd, a liberal-minded administrator in a politically administered university. The area of Clyde's academic specialty aside, he was the man of the hour in Kentucky, and some of his colleagues needed the bracing of his courage and brass.

Soon after I arrived in Lexington I heard that President McVey had tried to seduce E. Merton Coulter away from Georgia. I am of the opinion that he did not know Coulter personally but knew of his authorship of volume two of Kerr's *History of Kentucky*, a brief history of the building of the Cincinnati-Southern Railway, and his recently published book *The Civil War and Readjustment in Kentucky*. To my utmost gratefulness, Coulter chose to remain sequestered in Georgia, and Kentucky had to drop down many notches and hire an immature instructor whose only promise was a budding interest in the westward movement.

The Department of History had functioned in the past largely as a service department to agriculture, engineering, law, and education. So far as reliable records show, Tuthill had never done any serious research and only limited library building. Knapp talked an impressive line about scholarly activities but never seemed to accomplish anything. His reputation as a classroom teacher was evident in the phrase "Nap with Knapp," and it is unlikely that he covered any considerable scope of the prescribed courses he taught. The other professors, Ellery Hall and Robert Lunde, were burdened with rather heavy student enrollments in their undergraduate courses. Thus it was that Clyde almost immediately became the nemesis of both Tuthill and Knapp.

Like Lunde and Hall, I was derailed from teaching courses in my major field of interest by having to teach multiple sections in British history. The departmental curriculum was badly misaligned by the fact that at some time after 1929, Knapp had devised a basic course in American history that covered the entire western hemisphere. The fact that he never managed to get more than halfway through the more limited basic course in United States history only compounded the problem. In organizing this gargantuan feast of western hemispheric history, Knapp preempted a monopolistic claim on the American field. Later this led to a furious "shoot-out" in one of the few departmental meetings that Tuthill ever relented to hold. Knapp was gunned down, and so were his omnibus courses.

In the fall of 1931 the University of Kentucky registered slightly over 4,000 students. They came from all across the state, but not all of the 120 counties were represented. By this date the Great Depression was affecting every section of Kentucky except the Bluegrass area, which was in better economic condition to withstand a recession. Officially Kentucky was woefully unprepared to meet an economic crisis of any depth or duration. For the most part both the citizens and the politicians were attuned to the nineteenth century. This was dramatically true in the area of the Commonwealth's revenue system. There was a major dependence on the estate tax in financing public higher education, especially the University of Kentucky. This scheme reflected Kentucky's chronic efforts to avoid coming to grips with the fiscal realities of financing public education. It was, in many respects, reminiscent of the old, failed Virginia program of financing education by making limited land grants to counties. In 1931 the Kentucky programs for tax assessment and collection were about as defective as an imaginative political scientist could have devised. The university had been granted 50 percent of the inheritance tax by the General Assembly, and student fees were almost ridiculously low. The Great Depression quickly dried up a major portion of the estate tax resource, and at the same time tax assessments and collections declined.

In the years following 1926, the McVey administration undertook to improve the university's badly antiquated physical plant. By the fall of 1931 it had in operation the newly constructed McVey Hall, the new library, additions to the College of Engineering buildings, and a new girls' dormitory. In that year President McVey informed the Board of Trustees that if the student enrollment was sustained at the present rate of increase, the institution would be forced to resort to some form of selective admissions.

In the past, no division of the university had been more pressed for space than the library. If the institution had been proffered a gift of a half million volumes, it could not have housed them. Until 1931 library services had functioned in a quaint public-library-type building that had been financed largely from funds donated by Andrew Carnegie. The building was inadequate for serving its central purpose the day it was dedicated. In 1928 Dr. McVey persuaded the Board of Trustees to assign revenue from the estate tax and some other funds as bonding security for financing the construction of a new library building. The resulting modern building was a far cry from the Carnegie structure. Architects planned a facility that could be expanded in time to house a million books. This building was constructed at a cost of $430,000 and was ready for dedication early in October 1931.

The library dedication on that pleasant autumn day was far more significant than a mere perfunctory service for opening a new building. It symbolized the moment when the University of Kentucky at last shed its image as an agricultural and mechanical college and crossed over the intellectual dividing line to become a university in the most assertive manner. Dr. John Finley of the *New York Times* delivered a dedicatory address of high intellectual promise. Momentarily, at least, the future seemed bright and the new course of the university clear. But no one that day in October 1931 could have visualized the fiscal grief that building would cause. In the short interval between October 1931 and February 1932, the dark mist of the Depression became heavier. The rate of collection of the inheritance tax dropped dramatically, while the issue of debt service on the new library building remained demanding.

Not only was physical space all across the campus in short supply; for the most part the older buildings were shabby and decrepit. In the late summer of 1930, just before returning to Duke University, I assisted in moving some of the Department of History's property from the Administration Building to Frazee Hall. This rather small 1911 structure had been erected at an approximate cost of $15,000. It had been built to house the College of Education, a training school, and a laboratory for teaching domestic science. That summer the College of Education moved across Limestone and Upper Streets to its new building, which had been raised atop the city garbage dump. Behind them the educators and domestic scientists left a grimy and cluttered Frazee Hall. The four main classrooms were, nevertheless, well lighted and offered pleasant class surroundings. On the third floor there was a classroom and a fairly large auditorium. The rear end of the stage had been sealed off with the ubiquitous beaver board of the era to create a makeshift office. The partition, however, did not muffle the sounds emanating from the auditorium classes; one could take the courses held there without having to register for them.

Bob Lunde, Ellery Hall, and I shared the oblong communal office at the stage end of the auditorium. Knapp had a private office that had been sheared off one end of the domestic science kitchen laboratory, and downstairs Tuthill and Clyde occupied what had been the College of Education office. Looking back from the present day, when academic offices are largely private and electronically equipped, one can hardly believe that in 1931 a department thus housed could embark upon a program leading to the doctoral degree. The Department of History owned no typewriter, no duplicating machine, no dictionary, and only a few tattered out-of-date maps; it also employed no secretarial assistance. In our shabby old backstage office, the only assets were several large heat-leaking windows that let in an abundance of light. We had three rummage-sale desks, perhaps four or five different vintage chairs, a rickety stand for hats and coats, and a time-stained domestic science worktable. There were no bookshelves or filing cabinets. My desk was a hand-me-down from only God knew how many offices. It was an old-fashioned typewriter desk with a well in the middle to hold the typewriter and little else. Somewhere I rustled up a straight chair, and that was it. If the furnishings of the department had been piled up outside Frazee Hall that September and cried for sale by the popular local auctioneer, Dick Garland, it is doubtful they would have brought fifty dollars. This was the physical environment in which one department of an expanding university was attempting to begin a major program of graduate studies. It was little more than a cut above Mark Hopkins's famous "log."* Today I never pass Frazee Hall without looking up to the windows of that makeshift office on the third floor and recalling those troubled days when I stared out of the windows wondering if conditions would ever improve.

Compounding our austerity, Tuthill came with an administrative bustle and issued to each of us three sheets of departmental stationery, including envelopes. He said that it might transpire during the year that publishers would send us desk copies of textbooks and that we should thank them on university stationery. To have supplied stamps would have been a drain on the departmental budget. There was another Tuthillian burst of generosity that I did not, however, share in. One of the numerous downtown floods that year had swept through a grocery store, washing off the labels of canned goods. Tuthill bought up a supply of these nameless orphans and distributed some of them to Hall and Lunde. They could never tell whether they were going to open a can of tomatoes or sauerkraut for dinner. I never knew whether Tuthill was mean, penuri-

---

* Refers to a proverbial expression suggesting that the only thing needed for a good education was a log with a student at one end and Mark Hopkins (one-time president of Williams College) at the other end

ous, or dumb, but I suspected all three. He took great pride in the fact that annually he returned to the taxpayers surplus departmental funds.

I had been a member of the faculty scarcely a month when Tuthill came into my classroom bearing the mien of an undertaker and told me, in front of my students, that he and Dean Boyd had agreed to reduce my salary. In a fit of startled anger I turned to the class and asked the students to wait for me ten minutes, explaining that I had an errand to run, and that if I was not back in that time, perhaps I would never be back. I went straight to President McVey's office in the Administration Building and found him out in the hall. I explained to him what had happened. He asked me, "What in hell is Tuthill up to?" He told me to go back to my class and that he would take care of the matter. He must have done so because I never heard of it again. If any other job had been available I would have resigned instantly over that outrageous treatment.

Hall and Lunde were excellent office mates. Hall was a fine teacher and a thoroughgoing Kentucky gentleman from the tiny, poverty-stricken county of Robertson. He had taught in the Mount Olivet school. Bob Lunde, a tall former football player primarily interested in American history, was burdened with a heavy load of sections of European history. In fact, he was to spend his entire professional career teaching these introductory courses. Emotionally Bob Lunde never left Minnesota. Perhaps Kentuckians confused and intimidated him. Yet in years to come he was to create a rich legacy, having taught thousands of them.

Paul Clyde was a distinctly different personality. He was well trained and intellectually well motivated; he was ambitious but at times brash. Scholastically he was extremely well disciplined and orderly, and I am certain he made a deep impression on his students. Clyde quickly found himself at odds with Amry Vandenbosch in political science and with some of his other colleagues over the matter of Japanese policy concerning the Pacific mandated islands, as well as over Japan's aggressive actions in Asia. In time Clyde became impatient with Dean Boyd over some trivial administrative matter. In his household, too, he was constantly irritated with his wife, Mildred, over their different religious views. Clyde was of Methodist upbringing, and Mildred was an ardent northern Ohio Catholic. When a priest pressured him about his children's religious instruction, Paul would go into a Scotch rage. In time I more or less became a confidant to both Paul and Mildred.

I think one of the frustrating and nagging facts relating to the Department of History in those days was the lack of scholarly interest in and understanding of what was happening in the world of American academia. Tuthill perhaps never did so much as a concentrated month of serious research on any subject during his almost forty-year career. He was listed in *Who's Who in America* as the author of the sketch on Kentucky that appeared in the *Encyclopedia Britannica* and "other buls," whatever they were. Knapp's father had subsidized the publication of his dissertation on the subject of Reconstruction in New Jersey, perhaps William A. Dunning's last student study of Reconstruction. In 1931 Knapp had neither a writing nor a research project under way. Painfully, I came to realize that he might not be emotionally or physically capable of sustaining a long enough period of concentrated thought and energy to write a book. The scholarly stimulus that prevailed at Duke University was simply lacking in the University of Kentucky.

In all fairness to the faculty of the Department of History, it must be said that great scholarly zeal was not rampant anywhere in the university. On the one hand, the institution lacked funds to subsidize research programs, and on the other the professors were burdened with heavy teaching loads. Historically there had not been prevalent in the university a compelling interest in creative scholarship. Professors who did research and writing did so beyond their call of duty, on their own time and at their personal expense.

Aside from the niggardly support the Commonwealth gave its university, much of the prevailing scholarly attitude in the institution was chargeable to the college deans and their tunnel vision of the mission of the university. Though conservative in his administrative approaches, I am certain that President McVey would have chosen to broaden and enrich the scholarship of the institution. This position he documented eloquently in his published essays, speeches, and commentaries on education. In his book *A University Is a Place . . . A Spirit*, he revealed his sense

of the role the University of Kentucky should play, not only in the society
and culture of Kentucky but far beyond the bounds of the campus. In the
final analysis, perhaps McVey's most notable academic achievement was
goading some of the departments in the university to plan programs preparatory to granting the doctoral degree. In the case of the Department of
History, he not only advanced the idea of granting the doctorate, but also
gave substantial support and initiative to the collecting of basic documentary source materials to strengthen the university's library holdings. I owed
my appointment largely to President McVey's vision for the university.

IN PART BECAUSE OF MY obligation to collect for the library, I found that
owning a car was an absolute necessity. I went to the General Motors
dealer, Fred Bryant, to look for an automobile. He had just reclaimed a
Chevrolet coupe from an employee of the *Lexington Leader.* It was practically brand-new and was priced at four hundred dollars. I could have it
on an installment plan where I paid twenty-five dollars a month. I used
that car for more than collecting for the library. Early in the fall the
university's Department of Extension was seeking an instructor to go
once a week to the Paris High School building to give a course in American history for teachers. When I undertook this added assignment,
Tuthill commented that the people of Bourbon County would eat me
alive. My experience there proved quite the contrary. I developed a lifetime friendship with some of those students.

In spite of the many problems facing me in my apprentice year of
teaching, 1931 was in many respects one of the most exciting of my career
at the University of Kentucky. I strove never to go before a class for which
I had not made special preparation. One of the problems a young instructor has is having notes enough to fill up a fifty-minute class hour. To
run out of material before the bell rings produces a sinking feeling somewhat akin to stepping off a cliff. One thing I learned from the start—you
could not shortchange students.

Beginning a career in the classroom can often be a source of joy, but
it is not without its moments of uncertainty and unexpected incidents.
Realizing—or believing—that I had to keep control of the classroom, I

got into two rather trying situations in my early years of teaching. One day I looked back through the classroom and saw a boy sitting on a chair leaning back against the classroom wall country-store fashion. I asked him to let the chair down and sit up. When he did so there was a great clatter of something falling to the floor. I stepped back to see what had caused that thunderous noise, and there on the floor lay a big black .45 revolver. That was a tense moment. I quietly asked the boy to pick up the gun and leave the classroom—and to leave the class. Fortunately he went quietly.

Another time a boy came to class dressed in an Army Reserve Officers Training Corps uniform, with a sword buckled on and enough chains of some sort to fit a pair of mules. He would sit between two girls in the front row and drop off to sleep. One day I happened to see him wink at the girls and then pretend to go to sleep. That caused me to commit the rashest act of my career. I grabbed the boy by the collar and ran him—sword, chains, and all—backwards out of the classroom. Strangely, that act resulted in a friendship not only with the boy but with his brother and sister. They would return to visit me for several years after they graduated.

On the whole I found eager and responsive students in those early years. Among them was Elvis Stahr, later to be selected as a Rhodes scholar, secretary of the army, and president of both Indiana University and the National Audubon Society. David Weill, the son of a well-known Jewish Bluegrass landholder, would later become a top administrative official in the Long John Silver fast-food corporation and a civic-minded citizen. There was also Forest "Aggie" Sale, a star basketball player and a serious-minded student who later had a successful extended career as a legislator and Harrodsburg businessman.

There were laggards, of course. One was a boy from Allen County who wasted both his time and his father's money. His father wrote Dean Paul Boyd asking about the boy's work. Dean Boyd asked me to answer the letter. I told the father the truth, and when the dean later saw the letter, he said that I had stirred up a hornet's nest. Ten days later I received a letter from the father saying that I was the only person at the university who told him the truth. He added that he shared my opinion of his son, and he took the boy home.

By MID-DECEMBER THAT YEAR I was ready for a break. I was also anxious to go back to Duke to see Beth and to take some of the chapters of my dissertation to Dr. Boyd. We had planned for me to come to Durham so that Beth and I could drive to her home in Fairfield County, South Carolina. This was to be my first visit to her home. When I left Lexington there was a threat of snow, and before I reached Berea on the winding Highway 25 the ground was covered. Two women driving from Michigan to Florida bumped into the rear end of my car, breaking their windshield but doing little or no damage to my car. By the time I reached the saddle of Cumberland Gap, the running boards on the car were scooping up snow. At Morristown, Tennessee, I was told it would be impossible to cross the Unaka Mountain range to reach Boone, North Carolina. Foolishly, I kept driving, and just as I reached Boone a front tire blew out. Surely a guardian angel traveled with me that night. I think I never welcomed a safe, warm haven more than in the little backcountry Boone Hotel. I ate one of the most memorable meals of my life there that night.

The following day, with a new tire on the front wheel, I set off down the long eastern slope of the Yadkin Valley, past Yadkinville, North Wilkesboro, Winston-Salem, Greensboro, and on to Durham. The road was icy much of the way. After my brief conference with Dr. Boyd, Beth and I drove south to much drier roads and a more pleasant climate. We went by Southern Pines, Fayetteville, Cheraw, and Camden to Winnsboro. We spent a week with Beth's parents and once visited Columbia to see Maude Adams in a play. On that visit I saw for the first time the country from which my forebears, both maternal and paternal, had emigrated to Mississippi. Too, the Weir family had gone to Mississippi from Winnsboro and had founded the village where I went to high school. Some of Beth's family had also emigrated to Winston and Choctaw Counties.

Early in January I returned to Lexington, retracing the route I had followed in December, but on dry roads. By that time the Great Depression had virtually destroyed peaceful labor conditions in the Bell and Harlan County coalfield. Harlan County especially had been victimized by labor unrest. Theodore Dreiser had visited the area and created a great deal of press coverage. He had asked Governor Flem D. Sampson to provide National Guard protection during his visit. Dreiser and every other outside visitor was regarded as a communist. A group of New York women, no doubt dark pink if not red in their political affiliations and outlook, made Pineville their headquarters. On their heels came the president, faculty, and student body of Commonwealth College in Mena, Arkansas. This group was of an extreme, radical cast if not outright communist. At Middlesboro and Pineville they ran into violent vigilante resistance that turned them back on the road through Cumberland Gap. Just as I reached the saddle of that famous old frontier landmark, I met a veritable swarm of people being herded toward the Virginia border just down the hill. I was held up by this procession without knowing who the people were. In Middlesboro I learned that I had just experienced a minor chapter in eastern Kentucky coalfield history.

In the emotional storm stirred up by Theodore Dreiser, the New York women, and the Commonwealth College invaders, there occurred one comic incident. Henry Fuller, a serious-minded North Carolinian, traveled the Kentucky college circuit representing the Houghton-Mifflin textbook company. In physical appearance he no doubt gave the overwrought people around Cumberland Gap the impression that he was just another troublemaker. Henry traveled by Greyhound bus, hunkered down in a seat, reading a book or a textbook manuscript, a suspicious act in that section of Kentucky. When he got off the bus in Pineville with a portable typewriter in one hand and an overstuffed briefcase in the other and asked about the "troubles," he was arrested and put in jail. It took the intercession of Herndon Evans, editor of the *Pineville Sun*, to get him released. These incidents revealed how fragile were the Eastern Kentucky economy and the tempers of its citizens in that moment of biting depression. They also revealed the hold that outside vested interests had on both the regional economy and Kentucky politics.

I HAVE KNOWN FEW MOMENTS IN my life less cheering than returning to an academic office and a cold classroom after the Christmas holidays. I had a thin margin of time to finish up courses before giving examinations. Additionally, by January 1932 we had begun to wonder whether enough students would be enrolled in history to justify the retention of a full faculty. The situation worried me, as I was the low man on the departmental personnel roster.

Looking back to that apprenticeship year, 1931–1932, I marvel that I survived. I taught a full course load and an extension class in Paris, finished my dissertation, and collected for the library. When I got my dissertation far enough along to begin having it typed in final form, I had to find a typist who could prepare the manuscript along acceptable guidelines. I sought help from the staff of the university's communal stenographic bureau. They referred me to the secretary of the Department of Political Science. I learned that she was from up the far reaches of the Licking River astride the borders of Morgan and Magoffin Counties, and a good typist. She had typed a couple of chapters when I got a telephone call from another professor saying that the girl could do no more typing for me. I protested that she was typing on her own time, but he was adamant. Soon after that call I heard a whisper of campus gossip that Pierre Whiting, the revered and aged janitor in the Administration Building, had unlocked the professor's office door to sweep the floor and caught the professor and the secretary having intercourse. Soon, word was out that the girl was pregnant, and the professor found himself in hot water with President McVey, Dean of Women Sarah Blanding, and Dr. Alonzo Fortune, minister of the Central Christian Church and father confessor to the girl. The professor was relieved of his university position in a not too subtle face-saving move. Losing a typist during the preparation of my dissertation was frustrating because of my tight deadline at Duke, but eventually I found another.

Uncertainties about the fiscal condition of the university had simmered for some time. In February 1932 the university celebrated Washington's birthday with a good representation of the faculty present. Earlier that day, however, there had occurred an unhappy flare-up of tempers in Frankfort. Wellington Patrick, director of the university extension department and secretary of the Board of Trustees, had gone to Frankfort and irritated John Young Brown, Speaker of the House of Representatives, and Happy Chandler, the lieutenant governor. Rumors of that incident ran like wildfire through the crowd. Not even the eloquence of Senator Alben Barkley in praise of George Washington quietened the anxieties of the moment. Doleful financial news would continue to plague my life for several years to come.

By March 1932 the financial condition of the Commonwealth had grown progressively worse. Not only was the university's appropriation reduced again; the tax base on which it depended was rapidly disintegrating. (Kentucky's woes could be traced all the way back to the penurious delegates to the state's third Constitutional Convention of 1849.) Conditions had become so disturbing by March 1932 that President McVey called a special faculty convocation to assemble in Memorial Hall. That assembly was more funereal than academic. The president said that it had become necessary to reduce salaries, that in fact for some members of the faculty salaries would be reduced below the subsistence level. In my case it meant a hundred dollars a month, and in time not even that amount. I am certain that few of the faculty in that meeting were aware that the crisis had been created in good part by the university's inescapable obligation to meet payments on the bonded indebtedness incurred in building the new library. Three quarters of a century later I never pass that building without remembering the painful investment I made in its construction.

As soon as the spring semester was over, I went to Durham and remained there until after the Duke commencement. While I was there either Lunde or Hall sent me a copy of the *Lexington Herald* detailing the near calamitous financial condition of the University of Kentucky. In the same mail I received a letter from the General Motors Acceptance Corporation saying I was on the verge of being delinquent in meeting the monthly payments on my secondhand Chevrolet. I sent the copy of the *Herald* article to them, saying that I too was a victim of payment delinquency.

Beth and I still hoped to marry, but for the present my financial condition was too bleak even to consider assuming the responsibilities of maintaining a wife and a household. Beth's job as assistant director of the Woman's College library at Duke paid well. It would have been folly of the first order for her to give up that job at a time when I could not be certain I would continue to have employment in the University of Kentucky. The joy of having received my doctoral degree was badly clouded by the dark news from Kentucky.

When I drove away from Durham the first week in June 1932, I faced an uncertain future. The most pressing problem was to find some way to come up with payments on the car and to support myself through the summer. But the big question was whether I could ever earn enough salary to be able to marry Beth. I left her behind with a deep sadness in my heart. There was grave uncertainty as to whether I would have a job back in Lexington when the university opened its session in September. There seemed to be no teaching positions available anywhere. The Great Depression had settled down in earnest.

I I

~

Putting Down Roots

By the 1932–1933 academic year, I had begun to strengthen my position in the classroom, in acquiring material for the new library, and in laying the foundation for a special collection of rare books and manuscripts. In April that year I read a research paper at the Chicago meeting of the Mississippi Valley Historical Association, and my little book *The Beginning of the L&N*, based on my dissertation, was in publication. I was given administrative assurance that my employment was relatively safe. At last it seemed that marriage might be possible, even though Beth would be leaving a good and secure position at Duke: she had been promoted to assistant librarian of the Trinity College branch of the Duke library.

On June 8, 1933, I rented a house on Forest Park Road and furnished it with some pieces Paul Clyde had left for me to use while he was away doing research. I had also collected several pieces of antique furniture from Lexington junk stores and received from a craftsman in Mebane,

North Carolina, some solid walnut furniture that Beth had designed. To make certain we would have something to eat when we returned to Lexington, I planted a good-sized garden in fertile soil.

In scorchingly hot June weather I drove from Lexington to Columbia, South Carolina, in a car with no air conditioning except for the hot blast that flowed in through the open windows. I must have arrived in Columbia as one of the most dehydrated mortals in the parched South. I got as far as Winnsboro the following day. I think those fleshless creatures called "heat devils" singled me out for special persecution. But at last the two frustrating years were over, and on June 10, 1933, Beth and I were married in the parlor at Shady Grove Plantation. We spent four or five days drifting northward. We stopped in Knoxville for a visit with friends I had made in the university there, and then drove on to Lexington. For more than a hundred miles we drove through the mountains over winding Highway 25. Beth had never traveled through such a mountainous area and was almost ready to call the whole thing off and return to Durham. Today I never go through that narrow defile south of Berea called Boone's Gap, or past the spot where explorer Felix Walker described seeing a herd of buffalo and the Bluegrass plain to the north, that I do not recall Beth's hopes that we were finally out of the mountains. I also wondered as we approached Lexington how Beth would react to the house I had rented for thirty-five dollars a month. It was a nondescript structure set in the middle of a narrow, oblong lot, one of those red brick suburban houses that had been created solely to be rented. Its architect, if there was one, must have suffered from spasms of indecision. The house had two front doors, and neither our callers nor we could be certain which was the true entryway. Beneath the living room was an earthen pool that during most rains caught enough rainwater to float a horse. The most favorable asset of the house was the fact that it was owned by a gentle and generous landlady.

My backyard garden was producing abundantly, so potatoes and tomatoes were indeed cheaper. We lived near an A&P store that sold bacon for 15 to 20 cents a pound. Two pounds of coffee went for half a dollar for the best house brand, 35 cents for the lesser. A nearby gasoline station sold gasoline for 19 to 22 cents a gallon. We could buy a decent pair of shoes for $2.50 and a suit of clothes for $35.00. Luckily Beth had drawn a severance check from Duke University for $2,500. Depression woes or not, we were married at last and making our way.

Beth and I returned to South Carolina that August to attend the wedding of her sister, Dorothy, and as usual that state was caught in a scorching drought. I rigged up a contraption in the rear deck of the car and filled it with vegetables. Mrs. Turner pretended embarrassment when her son-in-law came driving up in what looked like a huckster's wagon, but my harvested vegetables were truly appreciated in drought-stricken South Carolina.

On Forest Park Road we lived on the periphery of the university community. Our neighbors were Paul P. Boyd, dean of the College of Arts and Sciences; Dr. John S. Chambers, university physician; Dr. Edward Ray, a urologist and Ole Miss graduate; and, two doors up the street, A. B. "Bud" and Harriett Guthrie. At that time Bud was writing his first novel, *Murders at Moon Dance.*

Unhappily the university's financial recovery did not come up to expectations. My body and mind still suffer at memories of the miles driven and the hours spent teaching off-campus extension classes just to make a modest living. During that stringent era I happened to visit the Lexington Public Library, and there Miss Florence Dillard, the librarian, introduced me to a young historian and his wife. They were Glyndon and Ruth Van Deusen. Glyndon was doing research preparatory to writing a biography of Henry Clay. In my conversation with them I discovered that they were about as strapped financially as we were. I went home and asked Beth if we could not allow them to use our spare bedroom and share grocery bills. They gladly accepted our invitation, and every night we listened to the saga of the Van Deusens' research at Ashland, the home of Henry Clay. We formed a warm lifetime friendship with Glyndon and Ruth.

During these early years of our marriage Beth and I formed many interesting, and some unexpected, friendships. In 1934 we had pleasant associations with Josiah K. Lilly, patriarch of the Lilly family of Indianapolis. I had recently published an article in the *Filson Club History*

Quarterly entitled "The Slavery Background of 'My Old Kentucky Home.'" I had been tempted to tread on this sacred turf by the debate over whether Stephen Collins Foster had ever been a guest at Federal Hill in Bardstown, Kentucky, where he was reputed to have composed the song, now Kentucky's official state anthem. Two good friends of ours, John and Silvia Manning, told us that the piano in Federal Hill that was presented to visitors as the one on which Foster had composed his famous song had belonged to John's family and had been sold to the Rowan Home Park, now My Old Kentucky Home State Park. In listening, reverently and admiringly, to the singing of the song, it had sounded to me mightily like the *Uncle Tom's Cabin* theme adapted to a popular southern melody, and I did extensive and careful examination of contemporary sources in tracing its background.

Almost instantly after the article appeared in print I received a letter from Mr. Lilly. I knew that he had gathered a marvelous collection of Foster manuscripts, but I had not examined them. I almost lacked courage to open the letter, feeling certain that, in all the debate about Foster, Mr. Lilly would be critical of my article. Quite the contrary; he approved of the article and invited Beth and me to come to Indianapolis for the weekend as his guests. After dinner on Saturday evening, Mr. Lilly drove us out to his Foster Library, which was housed in an impressive building in the middle of his apple orchard. It was in the charge of young Fletcher Hodges. They allowed me freely to examine Foster's workbook and other manuscripts so far as I had time. I never had a more exciting moment in doing historical research than when I sat with that aging workbook in my lap. I found that Foster had first entitled the song "Den Poor Ole Uncle Tome, Goodnight." At the bottom of the page, apparently as an afterthought, Foster had doodled a new title, "Den My Old Kentucky Home, Goodnight."

A week after Beth and I were in Indianapolis Mr. Lilly married the sister of the wife of his son Eli, placing him in the anomalous situation of being both father-in-law and brother-in-law to Eli's wife. Many years later we came to know Eli Lilly during our time at Indiana University.

In the summer of 1934 Professor Dexter Perkins asked me to teach a summer session in the University of Rochester. This was to be my first experience as a visiting professor in the "other fellow's" university, and rewarding it was. My colleagues at Rochester were hospitable, and the students were bright and responsive. Professor Ezra Gillis, registrar in the University of Kentucky, wrote a former student of his, the registrar at Rochester, that we were coming, and the registrar proved generously hospitable, inviting us to attend picnics and other gatherings. We met and became friendly with Howard Hanson, director of the renowned Eastman School of Music, and also with a creative engineer from the Folmer-Graflex Company and personnel from the Eastman Kodak Company. Folmer-Graflex was then in the final stages of developing a microfilm camera for production and sale, and I was invited to see the first one assembled. I later came back to Kentucky and persuaded Margaret King to order one for the University of Kentucky library.

Life in the Finger Lakes district of western New York was fascinating. Beth and I enjoyed our strolls along the Erie Canal and out into great cherry orchards burdened with ripening fruit. We formed an acquaintance with Ruth Webb Lee, an expert on antique American cut glass and author of an authoritative book on the subject. We also had a friend who lived in a house literally upon the water's edge of Lake Canandaigua. She invited me to swim in the lake, but one splash was enough for me. The water was colder than ice itself.

In 1937 I was again invited to teach in the University of Rochester. Our son, Thomas Bennett, known always as Bennett, was then a year and a half old. Some pleasant afternoons we would take him out to sit on the bank of picturesque old Genesee Canal. We never dreamed that in time he would return to Rochester as a college student. On this second trip to teach in Rochester, we took our beloved helper, Emma, with us. When we departed Lexington we had no inkling of the trouble we would have registering her in a hotel room. In Lebanon, Ohio, I was told harshly and directly that I could not register a black person in the famous old National Road Tavern (now the Golden Lamb). After a bit of irritated haggling, the clerk finally agreed that Emma could sleep on a cot in our room on the grounds that she was the baby's nurse.

Emma had a wonderfully good-natured personality. On one occasion we took her on a visit into Canada. Coming back into the States at the immigration gate, the officer passed Beth, Bennett, and me without much more than a nod of his head, then turned to Emma and in an authoritative manner asked her where she had been born. She replied, "Out in the country," meaning on the Georgetown Pike. About ten days after our return to Rochester from Canada I was awakened at one o'clock in the morning by a phone call. A Western Union telegrapher told me he had a telegram for Emma. He would not read it to me. I climbed up to the third floor and awakened Emma, fully expecting to learn that the telegram bore the bad news that some member of her family had died. Actually, she had written her family that she had visited Canada, and they had replied that she should go back to visit a relative who lived at some number on Maple Street.

In the mid-1930s, after almost two decades away from my childhood home, I found I had an urge to be a farmer and gave free rein to my dream of owning a Bluegrass farm. I became an avid reader of the "Farms for Sale" ads that appeared in the Lexington newspapers. I began a fairly generous viewing of land for sale, much of which had fallen victim to the Depression. My colleague W. R. "King" Sutherland, an instructor in debating in the Department of English, was also on the prowl for land. Neither of us had adequate cash resources, but we formed a loose partnership and bought a good small tobacco farm in Jessamine County. The farmer who owned it had been bankrupted both by the Depression and by the fact that he had borrowed money to construct two good tobacco curing barns. Sutherland and I grew three crops of tobacco, fattened a good number of hogs, and grew vegetables. He and his wife lived on the land. We suffered a slight setback when our tenant, between the end of cultivation and the harvest season, got drunk in Nicholasville and undertook to take possession of the town. He was locked in the county jail, and I advocated leaving him there until we were ready to harvest the tobacco.

Our daughter, Ruth Elizabeth, was born in April 1938. Her arrival brought an added dimension to our lives. First, her birth disrupted my plans to go to Indianapolis to present the manuscript of *The Rampaging*

Frontier to the Bobbs-Merrill Company for possible publication. More significant, the Forest Park Road house rather obviously had been built to accommodate a one-child family, and we had difficulty finding bedding space for both Bennett and Elizabeth.

Beth was afraid I would want to build a house on the farm and move in next door to the Sutherlands, who were experiencing some of the woes of farm life, aside from an incarcerated drunken tenant. She had escaped farm life in South Carolina and did not wish to go through that again. Under considerable pressure I sold my half of the farm to Sutherland and swore I would never again buy a piece of real estate.

How wrong I was. Soon after I sold the farm I came home late one afternoon to find that Beth had spent the day pondering the wisdom of buying a suburban building lot. Before I really understood what was happening I found myself on the side of a muddy clay streak of earth with a drooping homemade sign that said "Tahoma Terrace." We were shown a lot approximately an acre in size in the middle of a recently harvested tobacco patch. The developer strongly advised us to buy the lot because he hoped to turn his subdivision into a university professorial community. The price was surprisingly low. I was intrigued by the name "Tahoma," and I asked the developer about its Indian derivation. He told me the name had come to him in a dream. I thanked God he had not dreamed "Gitziguma," since I was almost certain we would eventually live there.

In fact, our living there occurred much sooner than I could have predicted. In mid-August 1939, after I taught my last class and turned in to the registrar my grade report, Beth and I planned to spend two or three weeks in Georgia and South Carolina. We drove from Lexington to Nashville, Georgia, with Bennett and one-year-old Elizabeth. I was exhausted by the trip and slept well into the next morning. I was awakened by a child coming into the bedroom with the *Atlanta Journal*. In a screaming headline the paper announced that Germany had invaded Poland. I read the news and was convinced there was grave danger of another world war occurring, and soon.

We cut our visit short and returned to Lexington to explore the possibility of building a house. At that moment we were short of cash, and I was not certain about our chances of borrowing money with a prospective house as chattel security. Stamped deep in my mind was the memory of building material shortages during World War I. Fortunately we were able to secure a mortgage that enabled us to proceed with the building. The Great Depression seemed to be tapering off a bit. Labor, building materials, and builders' contracts were at their lowest level since the spasmodic depression of 1921.

With the assistance of an amateur architect, Beth developed plans for a house that would suit our family's needs and taste. During the first week of November 1939 the builder cleared away the agricultural debris, leveled a square of ground, and poured a concrete base. I wanted no more swimming holes under my living room. The rising structure faced the muddy road on the north, with wide open farmlands on the south as far as the town of Nicholasville, several miles away. By late February 1940 the house was virtually fully constructed and ready for occupancy, even though the road in front was still a muddy path. When we moved in, our toddling daughter Elizabeth went from room to room expressing her approval. I was even more vocal in my appreciation. For the first time in my life I had a study, with built-in bookshelves and cabinets. I filled the shelves with books and had room for a writing desk. In time I was to complete in that room the manuscript for *The Kentucky* in the Rivers of America series. There also I wrote *Pills, Petticoats, and Plows; The Southern Country Editor; Kentucky: Land of Contrast; The Kentucky Cavalcade; Frontier America; The Emerging South;* and many other works.

The area around Tahoma Road was open country, and Bennett and Elizabeth grew up there as free spirits. Immediately behind the house was a broad sweep of pasture land that had once been a mule-breeding farm. By 1940 it had sunk to the modest estate of grazing two ancient horses. Those animals had great affection for children. They would come up to the fence and beckon the children to come out by shaking their heads up and down. The children could ride them and rub their noses. The only threat they offered was their broad, unshorn feet. There could not have been a finer open area in which children could range freely. The

"U" bend of the street formed a blackberry-overgrown haven between Tahoma Road and Shady Lane. It was there that Bennett's Turner ancestral strain turned him into a businessman: he "earned his living" by picking and selling blackberries to our neighbors.

Our lone frontier status in the abandoned tobacco field was short-lived. Our Forest Park Road neighbors Bud and Harriett Guthrie bought a lot alongside ours and built a good, large house that included ample room for Bud to research and write. In time he wrote there two highly popular novels on the West, *The Big Sky* and *The Way West*. It was in our living room that John Farrar, formerly of Farrar and Rinehart and publisher of the Rivers of America series, suggested the title "The Way West." The novel won the Pulitzer Prize.

Soon a number of other university professors bought lots and built homes nearby—so many, in fact, that we could have held faculty meetings there. The houses were in conventional urban Kentucky style, with one exception. Frank L. McVey, retired from the presidency of the university, and his wife, Frances Jewell McVey, broke the mold. They bought two big corner lots in the elbow of the university farm and built a modern square box house with a flat roof. That house attracted so much public attention that on Sunday good Kentucky traditionalists could not get away from church fast enough to view "McVey's Folly." The spectators choked both Tahoma Road and Shady Lane. One would have thought the McVeys were building a reincarnation of The House of Usher.

Our house on Tahoma Road became a true home base for my family, a place of pleasant neighborhood living, and a place of going away and of joyful returns. It was from that house that our children went away to college. Later still they returned with their spouses to live there until they could settle in their own homes. Two of our three grandchildren were brought there to spend the first months of their lives.

12

~

BUILDING THE
SPECIAL COLLECTIONS

WHEN I WAS HIRED IN APRIL 1931 BY PRESIDENT MCVEY,
my job description indicated that I would give half time to the classroom
and half time to collecting basic source materials for the library. The new
library had recently been named for its director, Miss Margaret I. King,
and was in an advanced stage of completion. For the foreseeable future it
would contain a maze of empty stacks with no books and no documentary materials. Almost anything in the way of books and documents,
original or published, would be a welcome addition.

In making my earlier survey of source materials held in regional libraries, I had discovered that the Kentucky state capitol contained a
hodgepodge of the Commonwealth's paper records as well as a mass of
printed and bound documentary materials. There was also a good run of
the United States serial set catching dust in the building's basement. I
spent almost a year moving these items to the University of Kentucky
library. In the process of transferring them from Frankfort to Lexington

I found that we might also secure some files of newspapers, the published state document series, files of Senate and House journals, and the *Acts of the General Assembly*. These items laid a solid foundation for building collections in both the university library and that of the Law School. I had no difficulty in procuring much of this material. As a matter of fact, I think the indifferent state librarian and the janitors were happy to part with it.

To be on safe ground, however, I prepared a bill authorizing the transfer of the neglected materials to the University of Kentucky Library and got Leer Buckley, a representative from Fayette County, to introduce the bill in the House of Representatives. Unfortunately, the presidents of Eastern Kentucky State Teachers College and of Western Kentucky State Teachers College spotted the bill and proceeded to amend it to assert the claims of their schools to the materials. They also made a change that altered the intent of the bill. When the bill was finally enacted into law it stated that "everything necessary to the operation of state government" was to be transferred. The original bill had provided only for those documents "not necessary." When the state finance officer read the new law, he virtually blew the dome off the capitol in proclaiming the person who drafted the bill to be an idiot and the legislators who passed it to be fit candidates for the Kentucky institute for the feeble-minded. I went to him to explain the unfortunate tampering with the bill by the college presidents. I found a veritable bull of a man smoking a huge pipe carved in the shape of a bull's head. He spouted streams of smoke like a logging locomotive and spoke in the expletives of the logging camp. I got nowhere with this roaring official. I then talked with Attorney General Bailey P. Wooton. In a much calmer fashion, he read the law with amusement. He assured me he would interpret it on its intent and not on the basis of its befuddled wording. Though mangled in form, the law threw open the door for the University of Kentucky to acquire an appreciable run of vitally needed state publications and newspaper files.

In time I was to haul a lot of books and newspaper files to the university library. In 1931 the university owned two motor vehicles. One was known as "the old Dodge." This truck was equipped with solid rubber tires and was hardly roadworthy. The other was "the new Dodge," a three-quarter-ton, stake-body, late model truck. Securing the use of these vehicles and the labor to load and unload them was almost as difficult as getting possession of the documents. On one occasion the old Dodge was too heavily loaded with books, and, coming down the hill just past Shannon Pike, it reared up, jumped over a fence, ran down into a pasture, and turned over, scattering books right and left. I got a phone call from Maury Crutcher, superintendent of buildings and grounds, pleading with me in the most forlorn voice that he be allowed to set the old truck upright and come home, leaving the books for the cows to read. I informed him that he should load the books—every last one of them— back on the truck and then come home.

There is a broad dividing line between a collector of books, documents, and manuscripts and a carefully groomed, library-school-trained librarian. I learned this in a comical way. I received word that a rather voluminous mass of documents from the old Kentucky Burley Association could be had just for the hauling away. I went with the driver of the University of Kentucky's new Dodge truck and rescued the records from a dusty tobacco auction floor. They were tousled and heavily coated with dust. When I got to the loading dock of the new library to unload them, I had to go to Margaret King's office to get a key to the basement. In doing so I passed two carefully manicured and coiffed women librarians looking out a window at the truck. One of them asked what was on the truck, and the other replied, "It's some dirty old trash Tom Clark is bringing into the new library!" In time I was to bring a lot of "dirty old trash" into the library.

In 1931–1932 I acquired a second collection of United States serial set documents that had been owned by Centre College. Over the years since 1819, that college had graduated many students who became senators and congressmen and who sent back to the college the published documents of the nation. In some way, I think in direct conversation with him, I learned that President Charles Turck would be happy to place that burdensome collection somewhere other than in his college's library. The Centre College library gave the casual visitor the impression that it had a very important collection, when in fact its actual basic book collection was small. There was some friction over the matter between President Turck and the Centre College Board of Trustees. Nevertheless the *Louisville Courier-Journal* commended him for making the transfer. Luckily the state's serial set holdings meshed wonderfully well with those from Centre College, and combined they formed one of the best sets in the country, including that in the Library of Congress.

The Centre College librarian was a quaint little man named Eddie Flagg. He was a cordial gentleman who seemed to have made the library his true love and his home. No matter how many times I wrote him that I was coming to Danville, he always greeted me with the words, "If I had known you were coming I could have had things arranged a little better." No doubt he later made that same excuse to St. Peter. Two years later, as we were removing the last truckload of documents, "Mr. Eddie" was still wringing his hands in lamentation that he had not known we were coming.

In 1936 Kentucky may not have been at the top of the list of states that had neglected their public records, but it certainly was near the top. The Commonwealth had no state archival authority and apparently no one directly responsible for preserving its documents. The first time I saw them they were piled, helter-skelter, in the capitol basement. They could be, and no doubt were, pilfered at will. Rogers Clark Ballard Thruston, a Louisville historian and a longtime leader of the Filson Club (now the Filson Historical Society), had visited the capitol in 1911 and picked up some documents just to indicate that he could do so.

In the second year of Governor A. B. "Happy" Chandler's first administration, he appointed a committee to review and rework the state's ancient revenue system. Professor James W. Martin of the College of Commerce in the University of Kentucky was in charge. Late one evening in 1936 he discovered that the state librarian, Ethel Gist Cantrill, had sold the records to a scrap paper dealer in Louisville and that two loads of papers had already been hauled away. He called me long before daylight one day in a frantic hurry to get to Frankfort to stop the loss. So anxious was Martin that he suggested I not take time to dress, just come in my pajamas. When we got to the capitol two trucks were almost fully loaded at the west entry of the basement. Martin went to the Governor's

Mansion and awakened Governor Chandler while I stood guard at the trucks to prevent their leaving. The paper dealer became excited and rushed to the librarian's office. I do not think Mrs. Cantrill had ever previously been awakened before daylight. I heard her coming down the corridor fuming that someone had interfered with her orders. When she saw me she all but screamed defiance. By that time Martin was back with the governor's instructions that the two trucks were to be unloaded and the two loads of papers already in Louisville were to be returned to Frankfort. Otherwise the dealer would be in the penitentiary by sundown. I was left to see that this order was carried out. Later we moved the records to the basement of Memorial Hall, where they were sorted and roughly arranged by WPA relief workers. When the state finally organized the State Archives, the records were returned to Frankfort.

IN COLLECTING PRIVATE RECORDS I found myself involved in no end of unexpected incidents. I do not intend to deal here with every collection I was able to acquire over the years, but some of them were as important as learning experiences as for the significance of the materials acquired. I received a letter from Mac Swinford Sr. of Cynthiana saying that he and his son were executors of the Simon estate in Cynthiana. Judge Simon had been a collector of Kentucky and early western frontier books and pamphlets. By that time I had my secondhand Chevrolet coupe and was mobile. I drove over to Cynthiana and called on the Swinfords. They instructed me to go to the Simon home, examine the judge's library, and report to them. At the large brick house Judge Simon's daughter took me to the second floor and left me. She apparently had little interest in the collection. The books, pamphlets, and other materials were housed in a large corner room. It took only a cursory look to see that there were rare and valuable materials in various forms.

The Swinfords said I could go through the collection and choose freely any materials I wished, but I needed help to dismantle the collection. On two or three occasions Margaret King went with me to the Simon house, and we came away with a treasure trove. On our last visit we spent what we believed was the necessary care and time to make certain we did not overlook some precious item. When we thought we had gathered up everything of importance, we left the room, but in attempting to close the door, we discovered that something was wedged under its base. It proved to be a rare and valuable compendium of Virginia official instructions to magistrates and constables. Many times I have wished that I had had the opportunity to go back to the Simon house and take a more relaxed look through the library. I learned from that incident always to take a third or fourth look to make certain nothing has been left behind.

At about the same time we were moving the Simon books, I read an account of and saw in published form the wilderness travel journal of William Calk and discovered that the original was still in existence at a Calk homestead in Montgomery County. I drove to the home on the Levee Pike and visited with Mrs. Price Calk. She was a collector of all sorts of papers and artifacts. For the first time I saw the original Calk journal. I also saw other papers and an impressive collection of artifacts, including the compass, jacob's staff, and chain used in surveying lands around Boonesborough and Mount Sterling. There were pots of several sizes that had been used for cooking along the trail into Kentucky in 1775 and a generous assortment of broadaxes. In addition there was a considerable collection of wedges, drills, spear points, and arrowheads, most of them dating back to the stone age in Kentucky. Mrs. Calk was anxious to show off the collection but would not consider putting it in a secure depository. I finally got her to allow me to copy a boxful of the papers on a Thermafax machine.

For nearly seventy-five years I kept track of the Calk papers and artifacts as they passed down through at least two or three generations. Recently I became acquainted with John Price Calk in Lexington, and in June 2003 he told me the papers and other historic materials were still in the Montgomery County farmhouse under the control of a cousin, Carolyn Niblett. Mrs. Niblett had spent much of her life in Washington, D.C., as a government employee but had returned to Montgomery County to live in the Calk homestead. Mrs. Niblett, I was warned, was a lady of strong will and unpredictable moods. Finally, in September 2003, through my former student Judge Caswell Lane, I was able to make an appointment for James Wallace, acting director of the Kentucky Historical Society, and myself to visit Mrs. Niblett. She had some kind of respiratory problem, so we had to move about the house tethered to her oxygen tank by approximately seventy-five feet of plastic tubing.

The afternoon of our first visit Mrs. Niblett agreed to make a gift of the diary, papers, and artifacts. My heart sank, however, when the woman caring for her could not locate the Calk diary. We looked through the rooms and even asked Judge Lane to see if the diary was in Mrs. Niblett's bank box. A week later James Wallace got a telephone call informing him that the diary had been found hanging on a wall. The second trip we made yielded not only the diary but still more papers and artifacts. On the third visit we acquired the Indian artifacts and more manuscripts, plus a turkey call said to have been sought by the Smithsonian Institution. The call bears some scrimshaw markings and is said to have been presented to a member of the Calk family as a mark of appreciation for kindnesses he had rendered a Shoshone or Sioux Indian who had been injured in either an accident or a skirmish of some sort. The turkey call is said to have been a passport of safety in travels through the territories of the western tribes. The fact that the Calk papers are now safely in the Kentucky History Center is a rich reward for three quarters of a century of patiently keeping them in mind.

On one occasion I was told that a woman living near Ruddells Mills in Bourbon County had a collection of old family papers. I drove there on a dark winter night to visit her. She readily consented to give the university the papers, but with the reservation that she wished to retain a muster roll to send to her son in Detroit. Six months later she wrote me, asking that I return the document. I spent far too much time searching frantically for it and suffered too much agony over the fear that I might have dropped it unknowingly in the dark that night. Fortunately I finally recalled her reservation and wrote the lady about it. She then remembered that she had already sent it to her son. I learned from that experience never to leave the premises without leaving behind a careful listing of papers and materials removed.

Early in 1935 or 1936 Ludie J. Kincaid of the Filson Club told me that

Reuben T. Durrett III had offered the club a miscellaneous collection of Durrett materials that had either been overlooked by the University of Chicago professors or had not caught their interest. Miss Kincaid suggested that I visit Mr. Durrett and inquire about the papers. I went to the big, gray Durrett home on Chestnut Street in Louisville. That visit was the beginning of a comical experience. When I rang the doorbell I was greeted by an angry dog who seemed to want to get at me. Inside a man and a woman were engaged in a heated quarrel. Finally the man, Reuben Durrett III, came to the door and invited me in. Clearly he was intoxicated. I explained my mission and was told I could remove the papers to the University of Kentucky. I suspected, however, that Reuben Durrett was not fully aware of what he was agreeing to. A few weeks later I made a second call and had almost exactly the same experience.

Taking a chance that the permission to remove the papers might be valid, I went to Louisville, loaded the documents on the university's "new" Dodge truck, and brought the first installment to Lexington. I made a second trip with the truck and two university workmen. We had practically finished loading the truck with the papers, which were stored overhead in a carriage house, when I saw Reuben Durrett III and a stranger come through a gate in the garden wall. Reuben came up and looked me over with a quizzical expression on his face. There I was, caught in the precise situation I had undertaken to avoid.

I explained to him that I had visited him twice previously and he had each time approved my removing the papers. The man with him was Mayor Joseph D. Scholtz of Louisville, who later in the great flood of 1937 was to prove himself a hero. Mayor Scholtz asked me if I would drive him to his office. On the way he asked me how long I had known Reuben Durrett III. I described my two visits. He told me that he had known Durrett since childhood. They had just come from the funeral of a mutual friend, and it was the first time he had seen him sober in years. Soon after that anxious meeting Reuben Durrett said to me, "Go ahead and take the papers." I was never fully aware of what was in the collection, though I spotted a few pamphlets of a historical nature that may have been unique.

I had a second collecting venture in Louisville. I received word that the famous old printery and publishing house J. P. Morton and Company had gone out of business and that the basement of their old building was filled with papers that we could have if we would remove them at once. Again I took a truck and two workmen to Louisville, this time on a Sunday, the last day on which we could have access to the building. I loaded a full truckload of papers and pamphlets. I have wondered many times about what might have been left behind. It would have taken at least two days of careful selection to save all of that collection.

We ransacked a lot of the county courthouses in search of state and local books, such as the acts and journals of the General Assembly and other stray materials. In the courthouse in Harrison County we found four or five volumes of the earliest *Acts of the General Assembly*, three of which had been printed by John Bradford in the *Kentucky Gazette* office. We also hauled a truckload of books out of the attic of the Hickman County Courthouse. In this case Ben Wall, my colleague in the Department of History, and I had the very helpful assistance of Judge Stahr. The books were stored in a tall turret and up a narrow stairway. We constructed a trough and slid the books down to the truck.

Once I went with Dean Alvin E. Evans of the College of Law to procure a good collection of state materials. We ran into a less than cordial reception from a fiery little county judge. He not only said, "No!" but also added, "Hell no!" At that I went to see the former county judge, who advised us to go home and be patient. Soon after that I received the most polite invitation from the judge inviting me to come back. He said he had not known what it was we wanted. He was the very soul of politeness and hospitality. In that instance I recalled a statement by George Reed that every Kentucky politician could be reached by somebody.

On many an occasion there turned up in my office an interesting specimen of that branch of the human race known as "secondhand book dealers." They usually turned up as if from the soil itself, almost always lugging a cardboard box full of books. On one occasion an "old rag picker" came along with a boxful of dime novels. His prices were low, and his books were in reasonably good condition. I took them to Miss Margaret

King, a lady of such social and cultural refinement that the mention of a dime novel sent her into total shock. To her, putting that trash into her library was akin to shelving a spadeful of horse manure. Though I crumpled her pride and conscience, she finally agreed to the purchase. She could not have made a better deal in Chase National Bank stock.

Then there was the lovable old hard-shell Baptist minister Mr. McArthur, who went abroad with his cardboard boxes of books when the Georgia watermelons were ripe and truckers were hauling them north to feed the Yankees. Brother McArthur would hitchhike into Kentucky with a watermelon trucker. He knew where all the good hard-shell Baptist "safe houses" were along the way, and he would spend the night with a fellow preacher and ransack his house for rare books. Brother McArthur had the true book collector's sense. He could smell an old book layered under a half century's patina of dust.

On one occasion McArthur appeared in the university library looking for me when I was attending a library committee meeting. At the moment he arrived, Margaret King had just told the committee that there were no more funds available for the purchase of books. There came my Baptist friend with his standard cardboard box. Somewhere in Garrard County he had enjoyed the hospitality of a brother and had come away with a full, matched set of the *Turf Register*, including the exceedingly rare volume eight. He offered us the set at a bargain price, but we had no money. I suggested that we trade him our set for his and pay his price for the eighth volume. He readily agreed to this, and somehow we scratched up the cash difference involved in the trade. Mr. McArthur went happily on his way— that is, until he told Will Smith of the Smith Book Company in Cincinnati about the trade. Will Smith was well informed about rare books relating to the Ohio Valley. He also was quick to express his opinions. He upbraided Mr. McArthur for not knowing more about books, especially the *Turf Register*. About three months later I went to Atlanta to attend a meeting of the Southern Historical Association. Just as I reached the Biltmore Hotel entrance, there was Mr. McArthur, cardboard box in arms. He set the box down and proclaimed me the greatest thief in Kentucky. I explained to him that we bought books and paid the dealers their prices.

We were not in the business of stealing, but we did try to keep well enough informed to know what we were buying, and we did not set prices or give advice to itinerant bookmen as to how they should conduct their business. At that, Mr. McArthur had no doubt reaped a rich profit because he had paid nothing for the *Turf Register.*

I developed a friendship with an interesting and highly intelligent book dealer, Richard E. Banta of Crawfordsville, Indiana. Dick Banta was well grounded in the nature of rare books, their contents, and the historical background of Kentucky, Pennsylvania, and Tennessee, along with the history of the Old Northwest. Every time he came to Lexington we bought scarce books and pamphlets from him. Banta had contributed sources and information to R. C. Buley when he was writing the Pulitzer Prize–winning book *The Old Northwest.* He was also the author of pamphlets and of *The Ohio* in the Rivers of America series. Later I wrote a brief introduction to a new printing of this book. *The Ohio* was perhaps one of the best-documented volumes in the series.

In 1934–1937 I taught extension classes in the Eastern High School in Louisville. In the meantime, through my friendship with Annie and Florence Dillard of the Lexington Public Library, I became acquainted with Mamie Pratt, and also with Professor Julia Dale and her brother William. Miss Pratt was related to all of them. She had been the librarian of the Louisville Free Public Library's Crescent Hill branch and had no doubt been urged to retire. She moved to Lexington to an apartment building at High and Rose Streets and came to one of my classes as an auditor. She often would visit me in my office. When she learned I was traveling to Louisville every week she asked to go along with me. On one of our early trips she told me she was reading the multivolume diary of her father, William Pratt, preparatory to having it bound. Later she showed it to me. I persuaded her to place it in the Special Collections at the University of Kentucky library. This diary is filled with insights into slavery, observations about Lexington and central Kentucky, and discussions of religious and church-related matters. In places it is hard to read because William Pratt wrote in such an illegible hand, but it contains an abundance of firsthand observations of time and place still waiting to be investigated.

In December 1936 I became ensnarled in one of the strangest and most vexing capers of my career. At a meeting of the American Historical Association in Chattanooga, Luther Evans, who had recently been appointed director of the Historical Records Survey, a New Deal agency under the Work Projects Administration, hired me to direct the survey in Kentucky on the condition that the University of Kentucky would allow me released time to do so. I was duly appointed and began unraveling the tangled web of WPA bureaucracy.

I discovered two things at the outset. Luther Evans and the mysterious powers in Washington had no firm notion of what the Historical Records Survey was to do or how it was to do its job. Almost weekly there would come through the mail instructions to alter plans and approaches for inventorying the public records. Additionally, the financial management of the project was placed under the Kentucky branch of the Federal Writers' Project, headed by a Disciples of Christ minister from Paducah, Urban R. Bell. Bell was a former minister of the Western Kentucky New Deal power broker George Goodman. This arrangement further confused the Records Survey issue.

My job was to set up three general districts in Kentucky, appoint a leader in each district, and find an assistant who could help keep up with personnel and the constantly changing instructions. All of this involved me in traveling around Kentucky, first to find workers, then to instruct them as to what they were expected to do. In a majority of cases the workers were willing but wholly incapable by education and experience to do the job. Many could not have differentiated a county court journal from a Sears Roebuck catalog in the garden back house. Then there were the strange characters who appeared on the personnel roll. In Ballard County we had on the roll of workers two women who seemed never to get around to turning in reports. With O. B. Wilder, my assistant, and Margaret McClain, who was in charge of the Western Kentucky district, we went in search of our employees. They were not at the courthouse, and everybody we asked about them gave us a quizzical look. Finally, at near noon we located their dwelling place. When we finally got the women out of bed, we discovered we had spent the morning in pursuit of the town's prostitutes. They were bleary-eyed from practicing their true profession the night before.

After a year of frustration I surrendered the honor of being the director of one of the most futile enterprises imaginable. I had accomplished little but came away with a generous education in the plight of simple, well-meaning, but nearly illiterate people struggling to earn a livelihood in a job in which the administrators in Washington were not sure what they wished to accomplish. I think only four or five counties completed the survey; the rest accumulated piles of disorganized paper. I did gain an intimate insight into the nature and volume of local official records, and into the gross deficiencies of much of Kentucky's system of public education.

During that year I was also necessarily associated with the Federal Writers' Project. Upon the request of the director I wrote a guide for writing about local history and other subjects. It was adopted to be used nationally. Too, I contributed the introductory history chapter to the Kentucky volume in the American Guide series, published as *Kentucky: A Guide to the Bluegrass State,* and I represented the University of Kentucky as reader of the final manuscript. The *Guide* entirely failed to sound the dynamics of change that were advancing upon the Commonwealth during the Great Depression and emerged as little more than a comprehensive highway guide and tourist handbook. The essays that appeared in the book were written by non-relief authors. Strangely, Kentucky, unlike Illinois, New York, Ohio, and Mississippi, spawned no creative authors among the WPA personnel.

With the WPA project behind me and out of mind, I set out in 1941–1942 to gather material relating to the southern rural furnishing mercantile establishment. During a year's sabbatical I collected a considerable volume of original and basic material, which I sent to the University of Kentucky library. If there is a better collection related to the old general merchandising system in the South, I am unaware of its location. I can say the same about holdings on the southern country newspaper press and the emerging post–World War II South.

Collecting basic historical records for safekeeping and proper preservation must be something akin to drug addiction. Not a year in my life passed after 1932 that I did not have an opportunity to collect a precious artifact or document for a public depository. For example, through my longtime friendship with William H. Townsend and his daughter Mary Genevieve and son-in-law Joseph Murphy, I was able to procure for the Kentucky Historical Society the watch Abraham Lincoln had on his body when he was assassinated. On another occasion there came a call from Mrs. Frank L. McVey, saying that she had a Robert E. Lee letter framed and hanging on a wall in her house. It was badly faded from too much exposure to light. She brought me the letter, seeking advice as to its preservation. It had been written by General Lee immediately after the surrender at Appomattox to explain to an Episcopal minister and his family why he had to surrender. The letter was so intimate that I felt in reading it as if I were riding away from Appomattox with the heavy-hearted general. Mrs. McVey was prevailed upon to present the letter to the Kentucky Historical Society.

The chronic shortage of money to acquire documents continued to plague me. William H. Townsend once procured for me a Daniel Boone manuscript. In my eagerness to acquire it, I failed to ask the price in advance. When he told me it would be twenty-five dollars, I could not have been more startled. I gulped and thanked him for his thoughtfulness but wondered where I could shave my board and lodging expenses enough to raise the money.

At about the same time, Dean "Little" Paul Anderson of the College of Engineering called to say that a New York gallery had a painting of Henry Clay by an artist named Hoffy. He suggested I bid on it. In my vast ignorance of the value of paintings, I bid $15 and got it. To say that I was in one hell of a mess would be a vast understatement. I raised the money by wringing arms for subscriptions. Today the painting hangs in the Peal Gallery in King Library North. It has appreciated many times over in monetary value.

As will be discussed in a later chapter, a major collection of books, pamphlets, manuscripts, and miscellaneous hand-inscribed documents had been gathered into an oversize private library by Judge Samuel Wilson, an insatiable collector of Kentucky and western American papers and documentary materials. On several occasions Judge Wilson told me that he was making me an executor of his literary estate, a statement I took to be one of his kind gestures but not really meaningful. I am sure he told William H. Townsend and J. Winston Coleman Jr. the same thing. Despite his frequent references to literary administrators, he never even vaguely hinted at his desire for the disposition of his library. After his death in 1946, when his will was probated, it was revealed for the first time that his entire collection was to be placed in the University of Kentucky library, with remarkably few restrictions as to housing and future use. And he had indeed made myself, Coleman, and Townsend executors, together with his law partner and overall executor, Clinton Harbison. Townsend, Coleman, and I met in the Wilson residence to begin the long and tedious process of locating and removing the collection. After that meeting, however, Townsend and Coleman were no longer involved in the process. Dr. Jacqueline Bull, director of Special Collections at the University of Kentucky Library, and I spent much of three years on the removal. First, we had to be exceedingly careful that we did nothing to upset Mrs. Mary Wilson; then, we had to locate caches of books on every floor, including the basement and attic, of the Wilsons' three-story residence, plus his law offices and basement storage rooms in the First Security Bank Building. Judge Wilson told me on one occasion that if I found duplicate copies of books and publications, I should consider them working copies. We found many duplicates. The judge, like every other successful collector, was too busy assembling his library to spend time cataloging it.

After the Wilson Collection was finally removed to the Special Collections and a brief dedicatory service was held with the judge's nephew, Dr. Keith Wilson of St. Louis, present, we had in place an exceedingly fine mother lode of rare and, in many cases, truly unique materials. On a Monday following church services in Christ Episcopal Church, we were informed that an unnamed but meddlesome woman was attempting to persuade Clinton Harbison to revoke the provision in Wilson's will and give his library to Transylvania College. We invited Harbison to have lunch with us and to inspect the care of the Wilson books and papers. He not only expressed satisfaction but did so with unusual feeling for so reserved a man. We never heard any more about the lady angel of Transylvania.

There was one concluding act in this drama. Through the intercession of Federal District Judge Church Ford, Judge Wilson had borrowed four or five volumes of the federal court's records. Judge Wilson no doubt looked upon the loan as an "extended" one. Judge Ford called me and, with a judicially imperative manner, ordered me to find the books. Luck favored me. I found them quickly and took them to Judge Ford's chambers in the federal court building. I discovered that he was agitated because by loaning out the books he had laid himself liable to censure by the director of the federal court depository in Illinois. He told me that, if Judge Wilson had been alive, he would have had him arrested and brought into court—a scene I would not have wanted to witness.

Looking back I wonder how in hell I taught classes, undertook to do research and writing, and still found time to collect for the library.

My COLLECTING CAREER ENDED ON two glorious notes. As mentioned earlier, in 2003, after seventy years, I was able to acquire the Calk Collection of artifacts and documents for the Kentucky History Center. While I was in the midst of the final Calk negotiations, Michael Courtney of Black Swan Books in Lexington told me that he was making an appraisal inventory of the library at Woodburn, home of the Alexander family in Woodford County. Michael said there was a considerable collection of manuscript and documentary materials that would not be considered in his appraisal. He told me someone should take a look at this material. I sought information from "Jo" Fisher of Midway, who had written a fine and detailed book about the longtime manager of the Woodburn livestock breeding establishment. She arranged a luncheon in Midway with Dr. Alex Alexander; Libby Jones, the wife of Governor Brereton Jones; my wife; and me. We had a brief "feeler" conversation with Dr. Alexander. After lunch we drove to Woodburn, where we sat in the library and discussed the possibility of his placing the collection in the Historical Society's care and depository. He responded favorably.

Libby Jones had told me that the collection included some kind of instrument that had been used in the survey that attempted to establish a permanent Kentucky-Tennessee border in 1820. We saw the instrument that afternoon. It was a handsome device that seemed to be a highly sophisticated form of sextant, a far technological cry from the compass and jacob's staff in the Calk Collection. Dr. Alexander seemed to have some desire to donate this instrument immediately. Later, James Wallace and members of the Historical Society staff went to Woodburn and made a preliminary examination of the papers and books. In consultation with Dr. Alexander's lawyer, Tommy Miller; his accountant, a Mr. Anderson; and his sister, Mrs. Robert Brewer, we were able to get the release documents signed and permission to remove the library papers and other artifacts on December 29, 2003.

I think I can say that over a period of more than seventy years I carried out the advice of Professor William K. Boyd, who admonished me to "collect everything, including the patches of your grandfather's britches." I think I can say that I darn near did. Long ago we made up for the loss to Kentucky of the Draper and Durrett Collections. In the new technological age we have even brought those collections home in the form of clear, usable prints. In 2004 important papers are still turning up in yard and flea market sales, and records are being discovered in abandoned attics and storage places. Modern businesses, institutions, and public organizations in Kentucky create records that in future may be destroyed or fall into the possession of unsophisticated collectors. I think the most mournful expression I ever heard is "I burnt them old papers a month ago."

13

YEARS OF PASSAGE

In 1941–1942 I TOOK SABBATICAL LEAVE TO COLLECT MA-
terial for the writing of what I hoped would be a trilogy devoted to the
institutions and way of life of the rural post–Civil War South. I spent
this time traveling, gathering source materials, and conversing with people of varied southern backgrounds and experiences. The first book was
to deal with the role of the furnishing merchant in the social and economic aspects of the region's agrarian life and with the sharp and bitter
criticisms lodged against those merchants. I published that book in 1944
under the title *Pills, Petticoats, and Plows.* The second study was *The
Southern Country Editor,* published in 1948. Unhappily for me, a historian
in Texas preempted the country school subject I had hoped to write as
the third volume in my planned trilogy.

Just before I returned to Lexington from the Lower South in September 1942, I was informed by Dean Paul P. Boyd and the new president, Herman Lee Donovan, that I had been appointed acting head of

the Department of History.* When I went to the department office—and literally before I could be seated—the phone rang. The call was from Colonel B. E. Brewer, head of the Reserve Officer Training Corps. He asked me to be ready immediately to receive something like two thousand soldiers in the Army Specialized Training Program (ASTP) over the next couple of years. He might as well have said twenty thousand because I did not have staff enough to handle two hundred soldiers. One member of the department had become vociferously involved in a conscientious objector incident, and the army ruled him unacceptable as an instructor; another was involved in a situation with a graduate student and the Dean of the Graduate School over a matter of neglect of duty; and an exceedingly fine classroom teacher was seriously ill. That left myself and another colleague to handle the military classes.

On Monday morning I went to what was called an orientation meeting with the troops and to hear the commandant harangue all of us about the strict rules of behavior and instruction. Memorial Hall was filled with the weariest and most disheveled corps of soldiers ever seen this side of Appomattox. The men had traveled two nights and the better part of two days in ramshackle day coaches on the Southern Railroad from Camp Polk in Louisiana. It would be difficult to describe the depth of anxiety I suffered at the thought of finding instructors to meet those tired souls in a classroom.

I managed to find a psychologist without classes, a football coach, a minister, a knowledgeable housewife or two, and the wife of a colonel who was at that time a prisoner of war in Bataan. I remain convinced that some officer somewhere behind a desk, with no definite assigned duties, had been ordered to dream up an innovative idea for preparing personnel for some imaginary informational service. Surely the selection process was governed by the loose rules of the children's game blindman's bluff. I had in class a bright young man with a Ph.D. in botany and others with advanced degrees in a wide variety of fields. I will never forget a big, brawny sergeant who had an unquenchable love affair with heavy artil-

---

* Clark's appointment as department head was made permanent as of July 2, 1945.

lery pieces and a legendary tongue to speak out, even in *Time* magazine. While the instructor droned on about the Whiskey Rebellion in late eighteenth-century Pennsylvania, he dreamed of firing a half ton of explosives into the heart of Berlin.

For three years I led a double academic life, caring for young women and 4-Fs in civilian classes and spending full days and many late nights with ASTP. By February 1944, when the program was ended, more than three thousand soldiers had passed through the university's classes. Every week we were required to administer a test that had been formulated by some unidentified specialist using that nonintellectual device called the multiple-choice test. So burdensome did this testing and grading become that I gave in to a form of academic prostitution. I went to a hardware store and purchased a hole punch the same diameter as the correct letter answer. In time we mastered the mechanical peddling of historical data. One day a soldier showed me a mimeographed verse that was being circulated among the "cadre." It was a lengthy soldier's lament with a "whip cracker" ending that went:

> When I grow old and take my grandson on my knee
> Won't it be hell to tell him I fought through the war in the ASTP.

Sadly, too many of our ASTP soldiers were thrown into the Battle of the Bulge with inadequate military training, with fearful results. One of the survivors came to my office after the war and told me he could take my rollbook and tell me where each soldier had fallen in that horrible encounter.

BY THE END OF WORLD WAR II I was on the verge of physical and mental exhaustion. The Department of History was caught in a three-way bind, having to expand the departmental offering of advanced courses, locate and hire competent staff, and get rid of the shabby tag ends of the military classes. But there was no time to relax between the disappearance of the last ASTP soldier and the in-rush of GIs anxious to get on with their lives. The veterans all but demanded the best-quality instruction. At this time the army sent us a unit they labeled Army Specialized

Reserve Program (ASRP). Apparently the army found itself stuck with the dregs of the human race and sent them to us, maybe in the hope that we would take them deep into the mountains and turn them loose. Again I had to provide some kind of instruction for the "guests." That meant hiring an instructor specifically for that purpose, which at the moment was difficult to do. I called a graduate dean of a well-regarded university and asked him if he could help me. He said that they had only one person but he was not recommending him. I think I asked him to feel of his man and, if the body was warm, send him to me. Later, almost overnight, the ASRP brigade simply evaporated, and so did the instructor. Where they went I never knew.

Reorganizing the department at the end of World War II proved to be a daunting challenge. It seemed that every other department of history was doing the same thing. In my case I had to scramble to get funds for a department whose former head boasted that his major accomplishment had been returning surplus funds to the university's general budget. We had to find adequate classrooms for the booming number of students, to secure as much library support as possible, and to be concerned about the physical stability of Frazee Hall. One morning the university engineer appeared in my office and handed me a floor plan of the building with suggested student limits in each room. I do not think there was another head of department in North America who had to be concerned lest a classroom floor give way and spill students onto the floor below in a scrambling mass of screaming scholars.

Reading a biography of Booker T. Washington, I came upon his admonition to "Let your bucket down where you are." The deepest well for us in 1945 was the combined local and regional areas; in other fields of study and research we could offer only selected courses. It was necessary to place emphasis on both undergraduate and graduate instruction. Accomplishing these objectives in the hectic years following World War II required an abundance of both energy and luck. Traditionally the history budget in the university was far from adequate, and competition for promising young professors was great. All the older professors of the department were gone, with the exception of Robert C. Lunde and

Charles M. Knapp. Among the staff members we recruited between 1945 and 1965, several were highly satisfactory teachers and publishing scholars. Among them were Carl B. Cone, W. Clement Eaton, James Merton England, Holman Hamilton, Mary Wilma Hargreaves, Wendell Holmes, James F. Hopkins, Albert D. Kirwan, Enno Kraehe, Shelby T. McCloy, Jill Nadell, Paul Nagel, Wendell H. Stephenson, Charles Talbert, Bennett H. Wall, and Ross A. Webb. Most of them made genuine scholarly contributions in their chosen fields of interest, including some in regional areas.

During these decades, members of the department published at least a score of books. Clement Eaton published at least four books on the South. Albert D. Kirwan published both *Revolt of the Rednecks* and a prizewinning biography of John J. Crittenden. James F. Hopkins and Mary Wilma Hargreaves set a high editorial standard in the editing of *The Papers of Henry Clay;* Hopkins also published a definitive book on the history of the hemp industry in Kentucky and a history of the early years of the University of Kentucky. Ross A. Webb published *Benjamin Helm Bristow* and *Kentucky in the Reconstruction Era.* Shelby T. McCloy produced three important books in French history. Carl Cone published a significant two-volume study of Edmund Burke and a biography of Richard Price. Charles Talbert produced a biography of Benjamin Logan.

Publication outlets for much of the University of Kentucky faculty prior to 1950 were limited. With considerable wisdom President McVey recognized this fact and sought to open a channel that would both provide a means of publication and stimulate faculty research. He had one or two conversations with William T. Couch, director of the University of North Carolina Press. Couch was pinched for lack of funding and discouraged the idea of establishing a new press in a university not yet known for faculty authorship of books. Nevertheless the spark of hope was timidly fanned, and by the grace of God the dream of creating a press survived. McVey set up a Press Committee to explore the possibilities further.

As was usual in that period, there was no money to hire a full-time editor or an editorial staff, to pay printers' bills, and to manage the review and sale of books. If ever there was an enterprise born of hope and sustained by luck, the University of Kentucky Press must rank high on the list. Although I had published a book with the University of North Carolina Press, I had almost no knowledge of the complexities of operating such an organization. At that point there occurred one of those fortuitous incidents that cannot be planned or explained. A personable young man appeared at my office door and introduced himself as P. J. Conkwright, a book designer who had recently moved from the University of Oklahoma Press to Princeton University Press. P. J. was a graduate of the University of Kentucky and had married into the Lexington Boone family. In our conversation he suggested that he and I prepare and reissue new editions of some rare eighteenth- and early nineteenth-century Kentucky classics. I agreed to write full introductions to each of them. The first was William Littell's humorous observations on men and their times, *Festoons of Fancy,* originally published in Louisville in 1814. I wheedled a grant of $500 from the frugal-minded guardian committee of the Margaret Voorhies Haggin Trust Fund, which allowed us to publish five hundred copies of the book in 1940. The second title was John Magill's *The Pioneer to the Kentucky Emigrant* (Frankfort, 1832), which we published in 1942, and the third was Harry Toulmin's classic *Description of Kentucky in North America* (1792), published in 1945. Somehow all three titles sold enough copies to repay the Haggin Fund. Each of them was handsomely designed by P. J. Conkwright, who in time would become a highly honored and internationally regarded book and type designer. Had his success come earlier, he might not have even considered designing the Kentucky books. All three won Graphic Arts awards, and the Magill book was a unanimous choice of the Graphic Arts jury. More important, all three appeared under the imprint of the University of Kentucky Press, even though no press yet existed. Their publication kept alive the idea of such a press.

During the decade 1940–1950 the idea of establishing a permanent university press almost went into eclipse, a fact documented by a letter the Press Committee received from an ornithologist. He ordered a copy of a bird book we had published that had been approved by the chairman of the Press Committee. The committee was assured that the professor wanted a copy of the book not because of its virtues but because it was the "worst bird book ever published." That bit of negativity spurred the decision to get into the business of publishing in a serious way by hiring an experienced director and editorial staff. In 1940 Frank McVey stepped down as president of the university, but he and I were able to persuade his successor, Herman L. Donovan, to recommend the establishment of a press, and on September 21, 1943, the Board of Trustees approved Donovan's recommendation. McVey was to be chairman of the new Press Committee. I was a member from that day until my retirement in 1968.

Even then, the University of Kentucky Press was slow in getting up a head of steam. Wendell H. Stephenson and J. Merton England of the Department of History both served brief tenures as part-time editors, though with little to show for their efforts. I finally persuaded the university administration to either fish or cut bait—either establish a genuine university press or give up the idea entirely—and in 1949 they at last adopted a comprehensive plan. Now it was time to hire a full-time professional director. I had earlier published a book with Louisiana State University Press, where I worked with an energetic young editor named Bruce Denbo. With the recommendation of Marcus Wilkerson, head of the LSU Press, Denbo was hired as director of the University of Kentucky Press in September 1950. In twenty-eight years as director, he would oversee the publication of hundreds of important scholarly and regional books.

The Press in time was to have a vital impact on the Commonwealth through its publications in Kentucky history and culture and on the world of scholarship at large in many fields. In particular, its impact on the scholarly production of members of the Department of History was notable. More subtle perhaps were the department's successes in the instruction of both undergraduate and graduate students. A highly encouraging number of our doctoral candidates gained national reputations as productive teaching and research scholars.

IN SPITE OF THE MANY accomplishments of the 1940s and 1950s, by 1965 the University of Kentucky had reached a troubled point in its history.

Over the years since my appointment as head of the Department of History in 1942, I had grown weary of trying to maintain a department of adequate quality. The university administration seemed to be stuck on a dead center of mediocrity. There was political dabbling of the country courthouse strain both within and without the institution. The faculty heard and spread rumors about the leadership. Many of the stories centered on Frank D. Peterson, long the university comptroller and now the vice-president in charge of business administration. I personally liked Peterson, but I was suspicious of his love of money and power—power well beyond his capability.

From 1960 to 1962 I served on the university's board of trustees, one of the first two faculty members to do so. This was long enough for me to get some notion of internal affairs. There was friction within the board over Peterson's purchase of lots along Columbia and Clifton Avenues near the campus. Clifford Smith, a Frankfort lawyer and consummate politician, was Peterson's nemesis. On one occasion he rode with me to a board luncheon at Spindletop Hall. On the way he told me what a scamp Peterson was. After the luncheon Peterson rode back with me and told me what a scamp Smith was.

Frank Dickey served as president of the university from 1956 to 1963. He was an honest and decent man who perhaps should never have been president. However that may be, he faced all but impossible challenges. He had to deal not only with internal problems but also with Smith, Peterson, A. B. "Happy" Chandler, who was governor from 1955 to 1959, and other power brokers. The more I learned about the administrative problems, the more I realized that matters academic were secondary to other concerns. This became clear at a meeting when the board ignored our immediate academic needs. The trustees were supposed to approve the university budget and professorial promotions, confirm student graduations, and deal with a special committee report concerning faculty pensions. The committee report recommended adopting the plan of the Teachers Insurance Annuity Association (TIAA) and its associated investment fund, the College Retirement Equities Fund (CREF). Up until that time the university had held its faculty in peonage with its nontransferable pension scheme. Clifford Smith made a bid for his client, a private pension firm in Cleveland. The trustees debated this issue for most of an afternoon without reaching agreement. A special committee of four members was instructed to meet in the evening and report a solution. The committee consisted of George Kavanaugh, Ralph Angelucci, Clifford Smith, and myself. We sat the night through listening to a dispute between Angelucci and Smith. By sunrise we had made no progress. I then suggested that I be allowed to ask the trustees for additional time to explore the TIAA-CREF plan. This was granted. Eventually Smith was bypassed and the TIAA-CREF plan was adopted. A half-century later I like to think that that traumatic night was not spent in vain.

On another occasion the trustees failed to follow the agenda for the meeting. A request had been made by the artificial-insemination cattle station in St. Matthews to use semen from the university's bulls. The trustees completely ignored academic matters and instead discussed this proposition. I found this incident demoralizing. Soon after that board meeting, President Dickey asked Aubrey Brown of the Department of Agricultural Economics, the other faculty trustee, and me to meet with him in his office on a Saturday afternoon. He outlined for us the pressing problems of the institution. At that point Frank Dickey was thoroughly frustrated. Without his saying so, it was obvious that he was troubled by Chandler's dabbling in university affairs, by the all but overwhelming problems of establishing a school of medicine and an associated hospital, and by low faculty morale. Unspoken but implied problems were Frank Peterson's reaching for power and campus gossip about a possible scandal in connection with the purchase of tires and the installation of soft drink machines in campus buildings.

The new governor, Bert T. Combs, was just coming into office in 1959, and several professorial groups may have talked with him about university affairs. Once Dickey announced his retirement, effective 1963, I went with several colleagues to discuss with Combs the importance of searching for the best possible presidential replacement to lead the university into the future. Combs assured us that he would in no way intervene in this process, and he admonished us to be diligent in our search.

A search committee was formed, and there began a gathering of names—in time more than a hundred—but only a corporal's guard of them seemed to have the combined academic and administrative qualities we sought. Three candidates were especially attractive: a private college president, a Cornell professor of English, and a Purdue University professor of agribusiness. At a special meeting to confirm the three, Stephen Diachun of the College of Agriculture presented the name of John W. Oswald of the University of California. No other member of the search committee had ever heard the name or knew anything about Oswald. I went to my office and searched *Who's Who in America,* but the name did not appear there. I wrote Dean John D. Hicks of the California Graduate School seeking information about Oswald. He knew nothing of Oswald, nor did John Caughey of UCLA. In the meantime I attended a meeting of the Organization of American Historians at which I saw Hunter Dupree, a history professor at the University of California–Berkeley. Hunter gave me a very critical estimate of Oswald. Though Oswald was a vice president of the University of California, Dupree said his service was largely to arrange meetings of the Board of Trustees. Dupree was direct in warning me that the University of Kentucky would not be well served if Oswald became its president. At the moment, I was hurrying to catch a plane home, and Hunter followed me to the taxi, repeating his warning.

I returned to Lexington anxious to convey Dupree's warning. When I arrived home Beth told me that Ralph Angelucci had called a meeting of the selection committee for that evening. I dropped my bag and rushed to the president's office. As I entered the room Angelucci was announcing that the search committee had unanimously chosen Jack Oswald. I had no opportunity to report my conversation with Hunter Dupree.

Shortly after this, along with other search committee members, I was invited to a dinner at Spindletop. Unknown to me, someone, I suppose Angelucci, had invited Jack Oswald to come to Lexington for an interview. When I arrived at Spindletop, the other committee members were huddled in a corner of the reception room discussing one of the university's chronic athletic vagaries. I had no interest in that subject and sat alone in another part of the room, waiting for something to happen. A stranger wandered into the reception room, obviously expecting to see someone. I introduced myself and discovered that he was the new presidential candidate. We sat and talked for an extended time while the huddle remained absorbed in its athletic discussion—an embarrassing moment. Governor Combs was there to accept the committee's recommendation, and Oswald was offered the appointment as president that evening.

Soon after that meeting I went to Berkeley to investigate manuscripts relating to the gold rush that were held by the Bancroft Library. One morning while there I went to have breakfast in a restaurant, and there I met Jack Oswald, who was bubbling over with plans for remaking the University of Kentucky. I got the impression that he wanted to clone a new institution from the loins of the University of California.

When Jack Oswald arrived officially on campus in September 1963, I think every disgruntled professor made tracks to his office to deliver an opinion on how to run the university—or how to run it their way. Jack asked me if I would do some public relations service out in the state by selecting a few central towns in which to hold meetings to answer questions and discover concerns about the university. It became clear at the outset that in organizing his administration Oswald was preaching the intellectual and management gospel according to "Saint" Clark Kerr. He took into his office young professors as acolytes, one of whom was Paul Nagel of the Department of History, a bright young scholar more endowed with learning than with good judgment. So it may have been with other appointees.

By some strange quirk of character, both Jack and Rose Oswald exhibited an almost frenetic anxiety about the past and about Kentuckians' love of antiquity, especially that relating to the university. No doubt much of this phobia was stimulated by the gossipy advice passed on to them by self-serving sycophants. But it would be grossly unfair to ignore the circumstances that justified some of their reservations. Oswald was assuming the administration of an institution whose programs had long languished for insufficient public funding. Kentucky politicians were shortsighted and in many instances no doubt venal. The Kentucky public school system was teetering on the brink of poverty. In so many areas Kentucky was desperately lacking imaginative leadership that could dream of a brighter future. The University of Kentucky was mired in the dog days of indecision at a time when there was a vibrant thrust forward by universities nationally.

At Oswald's request, I undertook to organize public forums in key areas of the state to discuss the University of Kentucky's mission. The first such meeting took place in Russellville, in Logan County. On the night of the meeting I met Oswald, Glenn Creech, and one or two other members of the administration in Bowling Green. They had flown there from Cumberland, where they had gone to dedicate the opening of a community college. We were driving by the village of Auburn when Glenn Creech pulled a flask of whiskey out of his pocket and offered Jack a drink. I advised Jack against drinking it, knowing that if the president of the university went into that meeting with the smell of liquor on his breath, there would be criticism. The discussion that night was a lively one. Later Glenn Creech was placed in charge of some of the future meetings, but the whole idea fizzled out, as did so many university projects. I took Jack to the office of the *Lexington Leader* and introduced him to its editor, Fred Wachs. I believe that that was one of the most bizarre situations I ever experienced. Wachs was not a college graduate and was ever conscious of the fact. Yet he knew all the answers to educational problems.

I suffered many disappointments in this era, not only from Jack Oswald's precipitate actions but also from the pettiness of some of my departmental colleagues who had more ambition than moral integrity. On one occasion, checking the history department budget and expenditures, I discovered that there was an ungodly high expenditure for long-distance phone calls, most of them to Stanley Zyzneskiy, a professor of Russian history who was on leave in Warsaw, supposedly doing research preparatory to writing a book on the German invasion of Poland. The calls had been made by Paul Nagel and Carl Cone and were facilitated by the departmental secretary, Neva Armstrong. I also uncovered the fact that Nagel and Cone had been talking with the provost, A. D. Albright, and directly with Jack Oswald, and were tinkering with the department's curriculum. I went immediately to discuss the matter with Jack, and I also had a session with Albright on the subject of administrative tampering with departmental curricula.

One morning soon after that, a stern-faced committee made up of two members of my own department and one from the Department of Geography marched into my office, saying they had come to investigate my professional conduct over the years I had served as head of the Department of History. An uninformed bystander would have thought I had stolen the Great Seal of the university and threatened to bomb the basketball court. I was both infuriated and insulted, and the investigation ended before it began. My three long-faced pallbearer colleagues retreated with about as much grace as a pot-licker hound caught sucking eggs. I never saw their report, if there was one.

These things troubled me, but I never experienced the trauma of some of my colleagues, who were knifed down by the Oswald administration. Nevertheless, I became so exasperated with all this business that I wrote out my resignation and sent it to Martin M. White, the dean of Arts and Sciences. Near midnight the following day I received a call from Jack Oswald asking me to withdraw my resignation, and after an extended conversation I consented to do so—a decision I regretted then and have ever since. I was notified that Carl Cone had been appointed head of the department. In the meantime I discovered that Cone had made some ethically questionable administrative decisions. I had a good "woodshed" conference with him in which he admitted his guilt. That night his wife, Mary Louise, called to thank me for my conversation with Carl.

The Cones celebrated his elevation to the departmental headship with a Sunday afternoon reception. At that party Beth and I were treated almost as coolly as if we had just escaped from a leper colony. There was considerable irony in all this. That year I won both the teaching and the research awards, and in the 1966 national survey of graduate departments, history and bacteriology were the only two University of Kentucky departments listed as adequate.

In time I came to feel that the gods had favored me in that chaotic moment. I was set free from a job that had become irksome. My only resentment was at the way in which the severance occurred, not the fact of change. I was nearing the age of voluntary retirement, and I could leave it all behind.

14

~

Indiana University

The telephone can be at once a blessing and a curse. Often it figures prominently in changing the course of one's life. In the spring of 1965 Beth and I were sitting at the dinner table when the phone rang. On the other end of the line was Oscar Winther of the Department of History in Indiana University. He asked me if I would accept an appointment as the Indiana Sesquicentennial Professor for the calendar year 1966. Indiana was celebrating the 150th anniversary of its statehood. The salary would be almost half again my Kentucky salary. I was not wholly unfamiliar with the Department of History at Indiana. I had served as chairman of the executive committee of the Organization of American Historians (formerly the Mississippi Valley Historical Association) when the decision was made to locate its journal at Indiana University. In fact, I had flown there from South Carolina on a scorching August day to complete the arrangements for the transfer of the journal to Bloomington.

This invitation came at a propitious time in my career. I had just been involved in the unsettling matter of transferring the headship of the University of Kentucky Department of History. I had no regrets at being relieved of my duties as chairman. The job had become a taxing one, physically, intellectually, and emotionally. I had little difficulty deciding to secure leave from Kentucky in order to spend a year in Bloomington.

My daughter, Elizabeth, was to be married right after Christmas 1965 to Richard G. Stone Jr. Thus my family was involved in the dual responsibilities of planning for her wedding and preparing to move to Bloomington for a year. We had to rush preparations for the wedding, pack for the move, and get the house ready for our son Bennett and his wife, Alice, to live in while he began his law practice with the firm of Stoll, Keenon, and Park.

Early in January I left Lexington ahead of Beth to take a carload of our belongings. That was a grim January morning in which it seemed the sun would never show its face again. In Louisville I became ensnarled in early morning traffic on the Watterson Expressway, which under the best of circumstances is among the most unpleasant stretches of road on this continent. By noon I was in Bloomington. Beth arrived in late afternoon. Traveling on the Watterson she made a wrong turn onto Interstate 65 and got almost to Elizabethtown before she discovered her mistake. I think both of us felt that day that we were temporarily severing our connections not only with our house and family but also with the South.

My responsibilities in Indiana University were of a dual nature. I was expected to teach a couple of classes and to travel about the state giving lectures on the westward movement in celebration of the state's 150th year. A special secretary in the Department of History arranged my itinerary for the year. She apparently had little notion of the geography of Indiana or the location of many of its towns. One of my first lectures, a challenging one, was at a luncheon gathering in Corydon. The Indiana state government had been organized in this village, and appropriately this was where the sesquicentennial celebration was to begin. Present at the luncheon was Governor Roger Branigin. Before I left Bloomington, Don Carmony, long known as "Mr. Indiana History," told me that the governor was a brash Irishman and that if he did not like my speech he would walk out. Before the luncheon I had a pleasant conversation with the governor. I learned that he had been born in Maysville, Kentucky, and had practiced law in Louisville. Later, at the rather trying moment when I was being introduced, I was conscious of the fact that I was going to be speaking in and about Branigin's "briar patch." When I was finished he got up and shook my hand warmly.

On several occasions Beth and I saw the Branigins, and I came to like him personally. Certainly I enjoyed the numerous stories about his direct way of dealing with people. A black woman on one occasion paraded along Senate Street in Indianapolis and in front of the governor's office carrying a sign saying that "Roger Branigin is a son of a bitch." Roger went out and told her that in some respects she had a point. One afternoon my phone rang, and a young woman said that Governor Branigin wanted to speak to me. He said, "Tom, your wife gave my wife a recipe for making pecan pie, and she has lost it. Will you get busy and send me another copy?" I felt that this was a matter of high state emergency, but more than that, it was a prime example of Hoosier folksiness.

Elvis Stahr, one of my first students in the University of Kentucky, had been appointed to succeed Herman B. Wells as president of Indiana University in 1962. Wells was now chancellor and remained a highly visible figure on the campus and in the affections of the university community. Elvis Stahr had grown up in the western Kentucky town of Hickman, also his birthplace. His mother was postmistress, and his father was the circuit judge for a two-county district. I knew Judge Stahr, a rugged rural Kentucky political character. Without knowing the precise facts, I suspect that Elvis's mother was the major parental influence in his life. He was exceedingly bright, earning an all-A record in my course in British history and in all the rest of his courses. I am certain that his aim from the beginning was to become a Rhodes scholar, and he succeeded in doing so. Elvis's interesting and varied career began with the practice of law in New York. He eventually was appointed dean of the University of Kentucky Law School, then went on to become vice-chancellor in the University of Pittsburgh, then president of the University of West Virginia, and secretary of the army in the Kennedy administration. In Bloomington I really saw more of Dorothy Stahr than of Elvis. Dorothy was not entirely happy in Bloomington and expressed to me her longing to return to Lexington.

I now have only a vague notion of the number of speeches I delivered or how many miles I drove in Indiana in 1966. It seemed to me that I went to half the towns in the state, all the way from Evansville and New Harmony to Hammond and South Bend, and made a speech to every kind of audience imaginable. When I spoke in Peru (pronounced "Pee-ru"), famous as winter quarters for the circus and as the hometown of Cole Porter, every member of the audience claimed some kind of kinship with the famous composer. Elsewhere there were some remarkable assemblies. I think I never saw a more polite and attentive group of students than those at Notre Dame University. I came away from that institution impressed with the discipline the Catholics instilled in their students. I found this also to be true when I spoke at St. Mary's College, just across the way from Notre Dame. But the morning I arrived there it was difficult to find a parking place, and when I did locate one, I saw no sign saying it was reserved. While I was giving my lecture one of those heavy snowfalls occurred. When I got back to my car I found a fiery note written by a priest whose parking space I had unknowingly taken. He implied that he was unforgiving of the Judas Iscariot who had cast him off into the snowstorm with no place to park.

In the fall of 1966 I was scheduled to speak at the St. Meinrad Arch Abbey. St. Meinrad is a quasi-baroque German village tucked away in a wooded area of southern Indiana near the Ohio River. When I arrived in that picturesque place I felt as if I had suddenly come upon a Bavarian village. That evening I had dinner with the monks of the monastery, and to my utter astonishment I found them to be a disgruntled lot and quite vocal in expressing their displeasure. In the evening assembly I spoke to a combined audience of monks and nuns. They were gathered in the beautiful chapel, with the monks on one side of the aisle and the nuns on the other. Standing behind the altar of that elaborate chamber, I puckishly thought, "What if my Methodist family could see me now!"

On occasion I went out to lecture accompanied by the famous Singing Hoosiers, a large group of lively young singers who took life on the first bounce. Among them was a peppy, petite blonde whose energy shone forth like a June moon. I got to know many of those talented students, and on one occasion when the Singing Hoosiers were performing before the "homefolks," the little blonde spotted me in the audience and gave me a wink, to Beth's astonishment.

At a campus gathering that year I met Eli Lilly. As mentioned earlier, in the 1930s I had met his father, J. K. Lilly Jr., who had given Indiana University an exceedingly fine library of rare books and documentary materials. When I went to Indiana University for the second time, in 1968, I was to become much better acquainted with Eli Lilly. He asked me to speak to a group in Indianapolis of which he was president. Beth and I were also guests in the Lillys' home. Before we retired for the evening Mr. Lilly told us to have no fear if we heard someone walking around in the hallway—it would only be the security guard. There was in that house an impressive collection of Americana, including prints, Indian arrow points, and other rare artifacts. He had a keen interest in the history of the Ohio Valley region and the westward movement in American history. We spent a day with the Lillys driving to the Connor Prairie restoration, for which Mr. Lilly had financed the reclamation of the farmhouse, outbuildings, and farmlands. We rode that day in his Mercedes, and Mr. Lilly asked me to do the driving. I have never touched the steering wheel of any automobile more gingerly. The unsettling thought went through my mind, "What if I wreck this expensive car?"

Soon after we arrived in Bloomington in January 1966, Dexter and Wilma Perkins of the University of Rochester came to the campus when Dexter delivered the Patten Lectures. These lectures took place over a period of approximately five weeks, and we were to see the Perkinses quite often. They were friends of ours extending back to the time when I taught at the University of Rochester. Dexter was a bit out of his element in Bloomington, but that did not dampen his curiosity for what went on in an "outback" university. One evening when we were having dinner with Wilma and Dexter, he revealed that in some way he had heard there was to be a screaming, head-breaking student riot in the great Indiana Auditorium. He rushed us through dinner, and we took off for the auditorium with Dexter leading the way. He was determined not to miss a yell, a thrown egg, or a fisticuff. When we arrived at the auditorium the students were as quiet and well mannered if they were attending a family funeral. The lecturer Dexter thought would touch off the conflagration delivered a mild speech, and everybody went home without so much as tossing a wad of paper. Dexter was immensely disappointed.

My office in Indiana University was located first in Lindley Hall and then up about six stories in the high-rise Ballantine Hall. One morning there appeared in the doorway a tall, rather handsome man, obviously a retired professor. He introduced himself as Stith Thompson. I knew him to be a world-famous folklorist. He was a native of Bloomfield, Kentucky, and still had a Kentuckian's bonding to place. He had a great fondness for reminiscing about his life and experiences in central Kentucky. At one time he had taught school with the novelist Elizabeth Madox Roberts in the village of Maud in Washington County. He had known her well and many times reminisced about that association. Little could I have imagined on that morning that for six years he would come to my office at precisely 10:00 A.M. each day and we would have coffee together. I think in those years we talked about everybody and everything in Kentucky. Thompson was suffering some pain over the fact that Richard Dorson had taken over as head of the folklore department where Stith himself had gained international fame.

The first semester we were in Bloomington we lived in the home of Robert Miller, the university librarian, who was away on sabbatical leave. That saved us from having to move much more than our clothing from Lexington. In the fall semester we lived in Oscar and Mary Winther's house, which was just across the road from the home of Tracy and Ruth Sonneborn, with whom we formed a lifelong friendship. At that time Tracy was deeply involved in research in the field of genetics and eugenics, which related to possible genetic engineering if not actual cloning. Both Tracy and Ruth were somewhat advanced freethinkers, which involved Beth and Tracy in arguments. Beth and I enjoyed the Sonneborns' liveliness and their rollicking views on life in general. We would go for walks with them in a nearby state park and would visit back and forth. We maintained a friendship with them until they were both gone.

Bob Miller's house was approximately a mile from the campus, and I drove back and forth in my little boxlike American family car. One morning I overtook a man walking toward the campus, obviously a professor, and stopped and offered him a ride. With some hesitancy he got into the car. He was Byron Carter, a professor of political science. That proved for me a costly act of samaritanism. About a month later I read in the *Indiana Daily Student* that my passenger had been appointed to a deanship. At a luncheon soon after that, at which Byron presided, I made a speech. I told the story about offering him a ride and said that if I had known he was going to become a dean I would not have done so. He retorted that he had had great hesitancy in getting into that motorized box I was driving. The car was a homely little American Motor Company Rambler. Except for the Model T Ford, the Rambler was the nearest thing to a Volkswagen an American carmaker ever produced. On hearing all that banter, Beth made me trade in the little car for a more stylish vehicle. Later I came to know and respect Byron Carter. For a time his office was downstairs from mine. By that time he had been appointed chancellor of the university. One afternoon when I was on my way home I found him standing on the steps of Wells Hall, and he told me he fervently wanted to return to classroom teaching.

I do not now recall when I first met R. Carlyle Buley, but it was sometime early in my teaching career. Buley all but worshipped his old professor, Logan Esary, who had first interested him in the history of the Old Northwest. His and my interest in the westward movement ran pretty nearly in the same channels, except that I never shared his narrow Republican concept of the way the world turns. In 1966 Buley had just won the Pulitzer Prize for his two-volume history, *The Old Northwest*. When he sent the manuscript to Alfred Knopf it was huge, enough for two volumes. There ensued an argument between Buley and Knopf over cutting the manuscript down to size. Knopf either refused to publish the book without deletions or Buley withdrew it, perhaps both. Mrs. Eli

Lilly then financed the publication of the book by the Indiana Historical Society and had it flown to New York for consideration by the Pulitzer committee. It won the prize. The irony was that, if his company had published the book in its full length, Knopf would have won the Pulitzer Prize, something he very much coveted.

R. C. retired from the Department of History in 1955 a less than happy man. Part of his unhappiness stemmed from his dislike of Robert Byrnes, the department's chairman. Bob Byrnes was much more liberal politically than Buley and, worse, he was not a Hoosier. R. C. still had an office in Lindley Hall, an office I would later occupy, and from there he carried on a feud with Indiana University and its press, which had also turned down publication of *The Old Northwest*. When I was settled in an office I called R. C. to tell him I was in Bloomington and would like to visit with him. I told the secretary that I was Tom Clark, and she turned and told Buley that it was Tom Clark calling. I could hear what went on at the other end of the line. Buley gave that poor young woman a tongue-lashing for calling me by my first name. When I got to his office that secretary looked like a whipped dog. I felt guilty at having caused her pain. I suppose I should have said that I was "Doctor-Professor" Clark, in good Austrian form. R. C. quizzed me about what was going on in the history department as if it was as far away as the West Coast. He even asked sarcastically whether the members of the department spoke English. This childish gesture was clearly coming from a man who, though still on the campus, felt left out of things.

I had another personal tie with Indiana in Elmer "Bromo" Sulzer. Elmer had been a bandleader and a public relations director before he established the University of Kentucky radio station and the eastern mountain listening centers. He was interested in abandoned railroads and women in about equal measure. There was also Bill Oliver, a professor in the Indiana University College of Law and a former student of mine. Bill, a poor but spunky boy, had worked his way through the University of Kentucky and went on to graduate in law from the University of Chicago. Every time I saw Bill he threatened me with mayhem because I had had the audacity to give him a B in a course.

Unlike Buley with his pettish attitude, the members of Indiana's Department of History were quite cordial and capable men and women, from Bob Byrnes, Leo Solt, Oscar Winther, John Wiltz, and Chase Mooney down to the last hired instructor. Solt had replaced Byrnes as chairman of the department. He was a fair and capable department head and a gentleman of the first order. I formed a special friendship with Robert Ferrell. I had served with him on a committee of the American Historical Association in which we had recommended that there be some kind of accreditation of departments of history that proposed to offer the doctor of philosophy degree. It seemed that everybody after World War II wanted to institute doctoral programs whether or not they had staff and library facilities strong enough to do so. Also in the department were Maurice Baxter and Arthur Hogue, good scholars. I had known Arthur Hogue when he was a dean in Hanover College. Irene Neu was the sole female member of the department, and I found her to be highly competent and hospitable. Too, I must mention Don Carmony, whom I had known in the past. He was a public historian before that term was invented. He was well informed about Indiana and able to give me some useful insights as to Hoosier audiences.

I shared an office with Robert Quirk and also came to know and like that colorful character John Lombardi. In later years John became president of the University of Florida. In Bloomington he had the unusual hobby of pawing through the city garbage dump in search of anything he could find. It was fascinating to hear John at the dinner table describing his exploits there. He also had a passion for watching the reconditioning of the huge diesel engines from semitrailer trucks. He and I once spent a day in the reconstruction plants near Huntingburg, Indiana, watching mechanics rebuild engines. They told me amazing stories of how far those engines could be operated without a major overhaul.

Beth and I both became acquainted with Professor Edward Cadys and his wife. Ed, a member of the Department of English, was a rather robust, free-swinging type of man. He had in his house a wide, breast-high table/desk on which he did his writing while standing up. Cadys left Indiana University at the end of that year to join the Duke University faculty.

During the spring semester Beth enjoyed the Indiana University musical and lecture programs, and she made some warm friends among the faculty wives. In April Ab and Betty Kirwan of the University of Kentucky history department came to Bloomington to visit us. We had a good visit, sampling some of the Indiana campus life and catching up on the troubled scene during the closing days of the Oswald administration in the University of Kentucky. I must say that I felt relieved to be away from Lexington in that troubled era.

WHEN THE SPRING SEMESTER ENDED, Beth and I returned to Lexington and prepared to go to Turnwell Plantation in Fairfield County, South Carolina, to spend the summer. Beth had inherited the land from her father in 1956. Bennett and Alice continued to live in our house on Tahoma Road, which made getting away easier than usual. Life in the pine woods of Turnwell contrasted sharply with life in Bloomington. I enjoyed being temporarily free of my grinding schedule of teaching classes, driving countless miles, much of the time at night, and lecturing. At Turnwell I spent a considerable amount of time marking land lines and purchasing additional tracts. Jack P. Coleman, who looked after the Turnwell house in our absence, asked me what it was like to live among the Yankees of Indiana. My answer was that they spoke with a somewhat different accent, but that the "southern Yankees" of that state thought, acted, and behaved like those South Carolinians sitting around in Reed Long's country store at the Salem Crossroads.

That summer at Turnwell I was struggling with the knotty problem of finding a pulpwood producer who had even a touch of honesty. Floyd Worthy, the son of Tom Worthy, who had bought from Mr. Turner sixty-five acres of Turnwell land, was our pulpwood cutter and head thief. He could have taught those at the Crucifixion some sophisticated lessons in the fine art of theft. I am sure he paid for the new Cadillac he drove with money he stole in the sale of our timber. I had to deal not only with an outright timber thief but also with a rascally consulting forester. Ernest Nutting of Camden was highly recommended to me but proved to be far less than trustworthy. He was generous in making promises but miserly in fulfilling them. I learned through my trusted worker Robert Hopkins that Nutting had instructed Floyd Worthy to tell me, if I asked, that he had been in the Turnwell woods when in fact he had never been closer to them than Camden. By 1966 I had a mature understanding of the fact that there is a vast sea of difference between being a tree farmer and being a university professor. There may have been rascals in the university, but they were amateurs compared with thieving pulpwood cutters and a faithless consulting forester.

Nevertheless, and in spite of all the anxieties and frustrations of trying to find honest timber harvesters, we experienced in the pine woods an exhilarating sense of freedom. That summer I walked miles along rows of newly planted pine seedlings to determine their rate of survival under the scorching South Carolina sun. I located heavily fruited muscadine vines and cherokee plum trees. There was pure joy at being in the woods, even if they did harbor ticks, chiggers, and copperhead snakes.

We broke the tedium of readjusting the management of Turnwell by renting a house in North Myrtle Beach, where we could relax by the oceanside for a week. Fortunately we were well outside the highly commercialized Myrtle Beach limits. The house we rented lacked the atmosphere and charm of those we had occupied on Pawleys Island in bygone summers. The strand at North Myrtle Beach was clear but unexciting. There were no creek marshes, no crabbing grounds, and none of the marsh hens whose chuckling we had enjoyed so much at Pawleys Island. But we paid pleasant visits to Pawleys and some of our other old haunts— Murrell's Inlet, Brookgreen Garden, Georgetown, and McClellanville. These quaint places seemed far removed from our usual worlds—Turnwell, Lexington, and Bloomington. Even within South Carolina there is a distinct dividing line, culturally and economically, between the low country and the Piedmont. When one reaches the fall line of the Saluda-Santee rivers opposite Columbia, the land and the culture are deeply influenced by the ridgeland and the loblolly pine woods, and especially by the drier soil. South Carolina has such radical sectional differences that the people of the two regions differ profoundly in the slant of their social and political views. I am certain that most of the older people of the

Piedmont would not feel entirely comfortable with those of the low country.

Back at Turnwell I spent the rest of the summer marking boundary lines and improving the house and lawn. A considerable amount of time was spent becoming informed about timberland management and the paper-making industry. This was when I became acquainted with the British-owned Bowater Paper Company or, more precisely, the Catawba Timber Company. The company had established its mill at Catawba and its offices in Lancaster, South Carolina.

EARLY IN SEPTEMBER BETH and I began the journey back to Blooming-ton by way of Lexington. This semester we would live in the home of Oscar and Mary Winther on Maxwell Street. This attractive modern house had a beautiful setting with an ample lawn and garden in the rear. Fortunately Oscar's interest in American history ran in nearly the same channel as mine, and his library was a godsend to me. At that time I was writing *Kentucky: Land of Contrast,* to be included in the Harper Ameri-can States series. I found the solitude I needed in Oscar's study.

Again I was heavily booked on the lecture circuit. I resumed the grinding task of teaching classes and delivering sesquicentennial lectures. Many times I spent the mornings in the classroom and the afternoons and evenings driving and lecturing. On occasion I would arrive back in Bloomington at one o'clock in the morning when all good Hoosiers were in bed sound asleep. There would boil up in me a bit of anger, but more self-condemnation for being so foolish as to agree to undergo such an experience.

So far as I knew I would return to the University of Kentucky and teach until 1968, when I would be able to retire and receive my pension. In the meantime I had to finish the punishing lecture schedule. I was booked for two lectures in Purdue University, and on one of those occa-sions Beth and I spent the night as guests of John Stover and his wife. John was a railroad historian, and in the past we had exchanged notes on the subject. Mrs. Stover was a highly successful children's book author and at that time was involved in writing a biography of Mary Cassatt.

One of the most exciting lecture assignments I had that fall was in Indiana State University at Terra Haute. I was eager to visit that legendary rough-and-tumble railroad town, in which law and order had once been more disregarded than in Dodge City. It was famous too as the boyhood home of Theodore Dreiser. The town had faded by 1966 and seemed to be just another complacent Hoosier community. I lectured to a very courteous and attentive audience and returned to the old-fashioned hotel for the night. I was awakened around midnight by loud shouting punctuated by gunfire. The next morning I learned that the students at Indiana State University had rioted in one of those senseless tirades of the 1960s. They were upset over some kind of administrative ruling that they conceived to be an encroachment on their rights. The gunfire was that of the police who attempted to quell the commotion. No doubt Theodore Dreiser would have been both interested and amused.

I also lectured that fall at Hanover College in Madison; twice in St. Joseph College; at Fort Wayne, South Bend, Hammond, New Harmony, and Indianapolis; at Earlham College, Anderson College, and Taylor University; and at a dozen other places. At Anderson College, I lectured to the woman's club. When I was through speaking, the chairwoman, with great enthusiasm, presented me with a redbud seedling. Anderson had to have something to enliven its drab condition, especially given the dour outlook of the Church of God. I had a few hundred redbud bushes on mountain lands and had the same use for another as for a seedling of ragweed. Nevertheless I was determined to preserve the bush as a symbol of downright folly. I took it to Bloomington and planted it in Oscar Winther's lawn until I could transplant it to Lexington. The tree lived to a ripe old age.

On one occasion I went to an out-of-the way public school located between Madison and Seymour. I am certain the principal had read the announcement that Indiana University was supplying a sesquicentennial lecturer without cost. When I arrived at the school, teachers and students were assembled in a dusty, drab little gymnasium. Present were children from grades one to nine. I was unprepared for such an audience, but I undertook to reduce my lecture to the most elementary level. About

midway through the program a bored little boy up in the bleachers mis-
behaved, and the principal climbed up and gave him a very sound series
of slaps, upsetting the whole audience. I had to go on speaking as though
nothing had happened. I am certain that Edward Eggleston's Hoosier
Schoolmaster would have been appalled at such an extreme disciplinary
act and that the professors in the Indiana University College of Education would have gone into shock.

During the fall Beth and I went out in the country to visit Bob and
Lila Farrell. They had bought a house in the middle of the Brown County woods, the arboreal region made famous by the Hoosier landscape
painter T. C. Steele. The house, designed by a Bauhaus disciple, was located on a ridge deep in the Brown County woods—as deep into a natural setting as a home could be built.

With a full classroom burden plus lecturing hither and yon, the fall
semester went quickly. One afternoon in November I received a telephone call asking me to come to President Stahr's office. When I arrived
he told me that in 1968 Indiana University would celebrate its own sesquicentennial. He asked me if I would consider returning to Bloomington to be the university's historian and write its history. If I would agree
to this, he would recommend to the Board of Trustees that I be appointed distinguished service professor at an academic year salary of
$25,000, an appreciable increase over what I was being paid at Kentucky.
I would be entitled to yearly increases, the university would pay the full
15 percent TIAA-CREF stipend, and I would be given sufficient research
assistance to gather information for the university history project. I had
no hesitation in agreeing to return to Bloomington if the appointment
should be approved. Stahr said it would take some time for him to get
confirmation from the trustees, but he assured me that the appointment
would be approved.

I returned to the University of Kentucky in the spring of 1967 determined to retire in 1968, contract or no contract with Indiana University.
In mid-July that year I would reach my sixty-fifth year and would be able
to retire with full pension. I was no longer tied to the university by the
old system of academic peonage. I could go where I pleased and still col-

lect my retirement pay. I came home to a year and a half of teaching and writing free of the worries of trying to maintain a respectable department of history.

Fortunately my rugged year of teaching and lecturing in Indiana had assuaged any anger I had regarding Jack Oswald's heavy-handed actions. By that time Oswald himself, rightly or wrongly, was in the first stages of conflict with Governor Louie Nunn and a growing number of Kentucky citizens. I resolved before I left Bloomington that when I returned to Lexington I would not become involved in the affairs of either Kentucky or the university. If the appointment at Indiana failed to materialize, then I would look elsewhere for a position. I still had some research and writing I wished to undertake.

One day in April I received a letter from President Stahr addressed to me as "Distinguished Service Professor." Thus I knew the news before I opened the envelope. That appointment made my remaining year at Kentucky much more comfortable. I was, however, placed in the very strange situation of sitting on the sideline and watching changes come to an institution I had served for many years. I felt almost like an alien in a strange land.

In spite of my resolve to remain uninvolved with university affairs, I was to have one more brush with Jack Oswald. I was chairman of the University Press Committee. One Sunday morning in 1967 I read in the *Lexington Leader* a review of a book published by the Morehead State College Press. This sounded a firebell in my mind. I reasoned that soon the Kentucky blight of competition between state institutions would spread and no institution would have a press worthy of the name. On the following Monday I had a conversation with Bruce F. Denbo, director of the University of Kentucky Press, in which we discussed the possibility of forming an institutional consortium that would include all of the state's colleges and universities and the two historical societies. Before this could be done, however, we had to gain the support of the other institutions and then gather as much information and advice as we could on the experiences of statewide presses.

This proposal required a good amount of discussion and selling and

involved me in my last battle with Jack Oswald. In one of his revolutionary spasms, Oswald almost defeated the program. We were just concluding the formation of the consortium that would turn the University of
Kentucky Press into the University Press of Kentucky. One morning on
my way to class, I met a professor of French history who informed me
that he had been appointed chairman of the Press Committee. I assumed
this meant that he would succeed me when my term as chairman ended.
When I got back to my office, Bruce Denbo called and said that the
change was to be made immediately. There could not have been a more
unfortunate time for this to happen. Bruce and I went directly to Jack
Oswald's office to discuss the matter. He called in A. D. Albright, and
they began to explain their actions. We interrupted them and explained
that we had come to do the talking and expected them to listen. We
demanded that they withdraw the appointment, and they backed down.

I retired from the University of Kentucky on the eve of the final approval of the press consortium, but I have lived to see it become one of
the most successful cooperative enterprises in Kentucky history.

Looking back on Oswald's administration of the University of Kentucky, I would have to say in all honesty that the institution needed revi-
talization, redirection, and the development of a new concept of its mission. Perhaps Oswald's greatest contribution was the disruption of the
old public school approach to guidance of the university. I suspect that
certain deans looked upon their responsibilities as a matter of maintaining departments on a level of stultifying mediocrity.

Jack Oswald had his supporters in Kentucky, chief of whom was the
Louisville Courier-Journal. At the same time, he created a strongly resis-
tant group of angry people. Philanthropist Earl Wallace told me that
Oswald lamented to him that he was leaving Kentucky without having a
friend in the state. My colleague in history, A. D. Kirwan, went to Maxwell Place to commiserate with the Oswalds, and Jack told him he was
leaving Lexington with the deep regret that he had not been able to have
Maxwell Place torn down. His wife, Rose, disliked the house, and they
had bought a residence in one of the Lexington suburbs. Nevertheless,
future presidents would continue to live at Maxwell Place, immediately

adjacent to the campus. Jack's fundamental weaknesses were his inability to accept past accomplishments and his desire to convert the University of Kentucky into the University of California, Lexington branch.

I had one last, and amusing, contact with Jack and Rose Oswald. In 1969 the Organization of American Historians met in New Orleans with its headquarters in the Jung Hotel on Canal Street. Attending that meeting was Professor George Pearson of Yale University. I knew George, and I also knew he had never before set foot in the South. He and I went for a stroll along Canal Street and through the French Quarter. When we returned I stopped for a moment in the Roosevelt Hotel, where he had a room. As I was leaving I met Jack and Rose Oswald. Jack was now president of Penn State, and they were there for the Penn State football team's game in the Sugar Bowl. They gathered me up with hugs and kisses. They could not have appeared more cordial if I were the prodigal son returning home.

15

BREAKING THE RACIAL BARRIER

RACIAL RELATIONS WERE CARDINAL FACTS IN MY
growing up in the Lower South. At the time of my birth in 1903 there
were more blacks than whites in Mississippi, and an almost unspoken
fear of race riots prevailed. This fear was shared by both races, and in my
childhood I heard expressions of the unknown crisis that might erupt at
any moment. There was an ambivalence in white-black relations in my
family and my youthful neighborhood. The two races had a close worka-
day relationship, but the line of demarcation was not clearly defined,
though it was clearly observed in social, economic, and political matters.
There were in fact two types of blacks—those who lived and worked in
close relation with whites, and those nameless black strangers who lived
and worked in other associations.

I worked on the farm with blacks, hoeing cotton, picking it, and
performing other tasks, and I developed a great affection for many blacks.
After a century I still carry memories of them deeply imprinted in my

psyche. I conformed to the prevailing code of not addressing elderly blacks by name but as "Uncle" or "Aunt." Never in my mind did these prefixes imply a sense of degradation. But in all my early relationships I was fearful of some unseen and undefined, but threatening, evil born in the distant past of the two races.

I think I had a sense of the unfair discrimination against blacks. When I entered the University of Mississippi I found myself stepping back into another age of southern history. That institution was deeply permeated with the aura of the antebellum past. Even the name "Ole Miss" may have had its roots in the era of southern slavery. The class annual for 1925–1926 was dedicated to Stark Young, author of the "moonlight and roses" novel *So Red the Rose,* and a sizable portion of the student body was made up of the sons and daughters of the Mississippi Delta plantation and cotton snob coterie. Some of the campus characters seemed to have stepped right out of the pages of *Uncle Remus.*

I experienced two incidents that were to influence my thinking on race. One rainy afternoon in the spring of 1926 I went alone to Oxford to see D. W. Griffith's film *Birth of a Nation.* I did not know at the time that the movie was based on Thomas W. Dixon Jr.'s novel *The Clansman.* I walked out of the theater that afternoon with a strange emotional reaction to the hatred, bigotry, and political violence portrayed by Dixon and Griffith. I had a feeling that the world of Mississippi and Ole Miss was turned upside down and irrelevant.

At approximately the same time, I witnessed a second event that revealed the inconsistency of racial discrimination. I stopped by the local greasy spoon and campus hangout, which was operated by two Greeks. That evening the place was crammed with blacks speaking Spanish. They were members of a Cuban track team that had come to compete with that of Ole Miss. Not a word of protest was uttered about their eating in a "white" restaurant and competing athletically with whites. There would have been an uproar if a group of young Oxford and Lafayette County blacks had stormed into Spiro's. It occurred to me that one way to improve racial relations in the South would be through athletics, and to a large extent this has proven true. In 2005 black players predominate on both college football and basketball teams, and black athletes speak for their teams to the press and on television. Racial turmoil in the South has been tempered in considerable measure by the zeal for winning games, especially basketball and football.

In September 1928 in Kentucky, I entered a far different world of white-black relationships. Blacks made up approximately 9 percent of the population and were concentrated in Louisville, Lexington, and some of the western counties. I was more conscious of the presence of eastern Kentucky mountaineers than of blacks. In the area of politics no Kentuckian office seeker I knew about was a blatant, ranting demagogic race baiter. No clone of James K. Vardaman, Theodore G. Bilbo, or Lee M. Russell stirred a cauldron's brew of racial hatred in Kentucky. Nevertheless, there were both reservation about the subject and outright discrimination, exemplified in the passage in 1904 of the so-called Day Law, which segregated both public and private schools in the state, and a kindred piece of nonsensical legislation containing bitter racial bias. The latter pertained to the distance black schools could be from white schools. The distance provision was later negated by the Kentucky Court of Appeals.

The Day Law was enforced for many years. It bore the name of Carl Day of Breathitt County, who was motivated by some personal conflict with biracial Berea College. The legislation was approved by both houses of the Kentucky General Assembly. Except for the two *Berea College v. Kentucky* cases in 1908, no effort was made to invalidate the law until 1948, when it was amended to allow black doctors and nurses to take postgraduate courses in public hospitals in Louisville. It was further amended in 1950 to permit blacks to attend an institution of higher learning if the institution approved and if no comparable courses were available at the state's only state-supported black college, Kentucky State College for Negroes in Frankfort. The law was used at times to head off desegregation of the public educational institutions.

The University of Kentucky, like its counterparts in the Lower South, was lily white until the late 1940s. This situation resulted more from a concern about public reaction to the admission of blacks than from the force of the Day Law. Occasionally black applicants sought admission to the university. In the late 1930s I heard President McVey say that a black man had applied for admission to the College of Engineering but was refused because he lacked high school training. Another sought admission on the grounds that he was a graduate of a barber-beauty school. I had no knowledge of how many blacks were turned away quietly by the registrar.

During the decades 1930–1960, there was a rash of federal court actions concerning discriminatory social, political, and educational issues. To my profound regret I do not now recall when I first heard of the judicial mandate that began unraveling past acts of segregation. Neither do I recall any conversation within the University of Kentucky administration or faculty of the landmark case before the U.S. Supreme Court in December 1938, *Missouri ex rel. Gaines v. Canada,* yet this case in large measure paralleled the situation in the University of Kentucky. The Court's majority decision, written by Chief Justice Charles Evans Hughes, found that denying blacks admission to a law school for whites would not be discriminatory if the institution paid the black student's tuition at a law school for blacks in a neighboring state. In a sense the Gaines case invoked the Fourteenth Amendment and began the review of the long-discussed case of *Plessy v. Ferguson,* which had established the principle of "separate but equal." There followed a succession of court cases that bore upon voters' rights, access to the polls, and educational institutions. The decisions in these cases swept away the last vestiges of *Plessy v. Ferguson.* They signaled the fact that the southern states were confronting political and social change, however reluctantly.

The most powerful of the court decisions, from a long-range historical view, may have been the most revolutionary. By the time the Supreme Court handed down the affirmative decision in the *Brown v. Board of Education of Topeka* case on May 17, 1954, I had become aware of what was occurring. When a reporter from the *New York Times* called and asked me to be prepared to comment, I wrote out a carefully worded statement, but I left it on my study desk; so when the *Times* reporter called on the afternoon of May 17, I found myself without my notes. I did, however, make this response:

It is the only decision the Supreme Court could make. Some of the southern states may become emotional over it but there will be a gradual mixture of the two races and it will work out in the long run. The young southerners are far ahead of their parents in thinking these things out. The decision will have a wholesome effect on the rest of the world, where we are always hammering out the race question. The decision comes at a good time.

Looking back a half century later I know I was wrong in my estimate of the emotions of southerners concerning the *Brown* decision. Remarkably, while some criticism of the Supreme Court decision may have been expressed privately in Kentucky, there was no great public outcry as there had been in several states of the Lower South. There was almost no activity by citizens councils, no mounting of "Impeach Earl Warren" billboards. Of far greater importance than my statement was Governor Lawrence Wetherby's direct answer that "Kentucky will do whatever it takes to obey the law." Possibly no one, including Chief Justice Earl Warren, could have guessed the violence the *Brown* decision would provoke.

As mentioned earlier, athletics became an active element in the history of the South and ultimately in race relations. I got a foretaste of this as a member of the University Athletic Council. The race issue seeped into the proceedings of that body when the question arose of desegregating the University of Kentucky football and basketball teams. Bernie Shively, director of athletics, in a near panic, said that if the teams were desegregated they could no longer meet Southeastern Conference teams. I sowed the seed of discord by suggesting that we drop the university's membership in the conference. I might as well have advocated removing the Henry Clay obelisk from the Lexington Cemetery.

In the desegregation upheaval there was a whisper at least that Adolph Rupp, the university's head basketball coach, was a racist. I did not have then, nor do I now, any hard facts concerning Rupp's views. He was a masterful quipmaker and was quoted as saying that a skilled black basketball player grew whiter as you looked at him. These things in 2005 are little more than an echo from the darkened cave of history. Black athletes now predominate on the university's football and basketball teams, and the very popular current head basketball coach is black.

I can only express an opinion that at heart Herman Lee Donovan, president of the University of Kentucky in 1954, was a segregationist not so much from the standpoint of race as from a fear of the rage of public opinion if black students were admitted to the university's classrooms. He may even have been uninformed about most of the desegregation court cases. I do know that in the instances of Edward Hatch and Lyman Johnson he did not fare well before the court. Edward Hatch was admitted to the University of Kentucky Law School in 1948, but President Donovan sought to have him taught alone in Frankfort. Law School professors held a single session there but refused to attend any more. President Donovan then attempted to set up a special instructional program using young Frankfort lawyers as professors, an act that threatened the Law School with disaccreditation. This angered lawyers who had graduated from the Law School. It also angered the federal judge, Church Ford, who later tried the Lyman Johnson case. The University of Oklahoma made the same blunder two years later. George W. McLaurin was admitted to the Oklahoma Law School in 1950 but was required to sit isolated in a narrow alcove off the classroom. I went out to Norman to make a Phi Beta Kappa address and saw him seated in what was little more than a broom closet.

I was aware of the Hatch incident but had no inkling of what was to come. Sometime in April 1948 I read a news story in the *Lexington Leader* that Lyman Johnson, a black Louisville schoolteacher backed by the National Association for the Advancement of Colored People, had made application to pursue work in the University of Kentucky Department of History leading to the doctoral degree. The news story indicated that he had come to the campus seeking admission accompanied by lawyers and photographers. Though I was both head of the history department and director of graduate work in history, I had no previous knowledge of the matter. In the following year my name was drawn for jury duty in Fayette County Circuit Court. In the trial of a traffic accident case I served as foreman of the jury. As we reentered the courtroom and I was trying to hand the clerk the written decision, I was confronted by a U.S. marshal who summoned me to a hearing in the case of *Lyman Johnson v. Univer-*

sity of Kentucky. My colleague, Professor Bennett H. Wall, also received a summons. On two occasions we spent a full day being quizzed by Thurgood Marshall, lawyer for the plaintiff, and an assistant attorney general of the Commonwealth, M. B. Holifield, for the defense.

General Holifield had a good and established reputation in the prosecution of discriminatory railway freight records involving the South. In the Johnson case, however, he was no match for Thurgood Marshall, who was well prepared and a tireless interrogator. Neither Professor Wall nor I offered any justification for Kentucky's discriminatory Day Law, nor for the position of the University of Kentucky. We did assert that we would not discriminate against black students in our classes. I stated positively that a graduate student in history could not receive comparable instruction and guidance in the Kentucky State College for Negroes in Frankfort, a point Thurgood Marshall dwelt on. This, in fact, was the one point on which the plaintiff could base his case.

In the following court trial an entire morning was spent in discussing the Hatch case, which was not on the docket. Nevertheless, Thurgood Marshall showed a deep interest in it, and so did Judge Church Ford. Young Edward Hatch sat well back in the courtroom and was only an observer of the proceedings. It was at once apparent that the Kentucky lawyers and Judge Ford had as great an interest in the case as did Marshall and Hatch. President Donovan took a humiliating drubbing in the questioning. Just as the court was adjourning for the lunch hour, Judge Ford asked him, "Who are your peripatetic professors you are sending around to teach law?" This angered the president, and he blurted out, "Put Tom Clark on the stand when we come back."

When the court resumed its session I was ordered to take the witness stand. Thurgood Marshall repeated his former question as to whether Lyman Johnson could receive the same quality training in graduate courses in history at Kentucky State College for Negroes as at the University of Kentucky. Before I could answer, General Holifield objected, and there followed a brief haggling between the lawyers. Thurgood Marshall turned to Judge Ford and requested a bench decision. Essentially his ruling opened graduate and specialized courses to all qualified applicants irrespective of race. This, however, was only a partial victory. The stultifying Day Law was left basically intact and on the Kentucky statute books.

At the end of the trial Lyman Johnson's position was changed from that of plaintiff with the support of the NAACP to that of our graduate student in history if he chose to seek entrance to the university. I took him to my office and had a long and frank conversation about his desire to become a doctoral candidate in history. Basically our discussion centered on the point that members of the department were color blind and that he could anticipate the most courteous treatment. I assured him that while most of the departmental staff favored the court decision, they expected good work from him. Later, when I saw his record from Michigan State, I wished it were more reassuring.

Lyman Johnson registered for summer school classes in courses taught by Professors James F. Hopkins and Albert D. Kirwan, both of whom expressed doubts about the quality of his work. In the fall Johnson did not return to the university, giving as his reason his responsibility as the executor of a relative's estate in Columbia, Tennessee. The following spring he wrote and offered me the excuse that because of personal business commitments he could not register for courses. He never came back. To me the Johnson case seemed timely and just, and I was disappointed that he failed to complete his studies and set a good precedent for other black students. It seemed to me that he was morally and intellectually obligated to carry through in order to fully prove the entire thrust of his court case and the judge's decision.

In following years I began to read newspaper articles in which Johnson implied that he had been discriminated against by professors in the Department of History. I confronted him personally about the matter, and he quickly denied that he had been slighted in any way.

In the University of Kentucky there were some aftershocks, as could be expected. These came from the administration, the Board of Trustees, some members of the faculty, and some students. President Donovan, fearing internal and external reaction, sent a memorandum to department heads, cafeteria managers, and other service individuals requesting them to practice a form of segregation in classrooms, in cafeteria seating, and perhaps in the assignment of dormitory rooms. I have no idea how widely this mandate was distributed. I threw my letter in the wastebasket, to my later regret, for now I am without the documentation. I do know that after desegregation was a fact, the attempt to segregate seating in the cafeteria was ignored by students, who were ahead of the administration on this issue.

When the Board of Trustees came to consider the implications of the Johnson case and a possible appeal of the Ford ruling, there arose a conflict among its members. Governor Earle Clements, soon to be a candidate for the U.S. Senate, vigorously opposed an appeal, and Judge Edward O'Rear, the dean of the Kentucky bar, strongly supported appeal. The two nearly came to fisticuffs over the matter. Clements was said to have invited the aged judge out into a hall to settle the issue with their fists. Amazingly no member of the board, including the lawyers, had read the decisions in related desegregation cases. The majority of the trustees supported the Clements position, the vote being 7 to 5. I am certain this was the feeling of nearly all the members of the Department of History and a majority of the university faculty. The Johnson case was not appealed, and the University of Kentucky escaped the notoriety of the Universities of Missouri and Oklahoma.

On May 17, 1954, in the case of *Brown v. Board of Education of Topeka*, the Supreme Court in effect invalidated Kentucky's ill-conceived and poorly enforced Day Law. The following year, in a basically pro forma procedure, the Kentucky Supreme Court ruled the Day Law invalid. In practice both the Kentucky public schools and the state's universities were thereby desegregated. The demise of the Day Law was followed by incidents in the Kentucky public school system that gained considerable notice. In the western part of the state, Citizen Council segregationists resisted the court ruling in the Clay and Sturgis school districts. Governor A. B. Chandler ordered out the state militia to put down the resistance. Almost two decades later in Louisville, the issue was more stringent, centering on student placement and transportation. This conflict proved to be damaging for Louisville, a city that had once enjoyed a reputation for peaceful desegregation.

In the University of Kentucky, with the removal of the Day Law and the charade of "special courses," the desegregation of undergraduate students proceeded quietly, on the surface at least. I was present at a Sunday afternoon reception when parents and first-year entering students were welcomed to the University of Kentucky. Four or five black students with their parents passed down the receiving line without creating any particular notice. It is too simple to say that this act marked the general desegregation of the institution, but I think the incident was a fitting farewell to the Day Law.

In the fall of 1965 I acted as chairman of the graduate school committee to recommend candidates for honorary degrees. We presented the name of Whitney Young Jr. He was the son of Whitney Young Sr., president of a segregated school at Simpsonville that had been created to serve blacks when they were denied access to Berea College by the Day Law. Whitney Young Jr. had applied for admission to the University of Kentucky in 1944 under the terms of the G.I. Bill but was denied admission. He then served with distinction in the United States armed services, attended the University of Minnesota, published books in the field of civil rights, and distinguished himself in the civil rights movement. When I read his name that afternoon to the graduate faculty, a newcomer to the university asked in a surly voice, "What has Whitney Young ever done for the university?" A quick-witted colleague answered that he had been "denied admission." Young was awarded an honorary doctorate in 1970.

Edward Hatch studied law in an eastern university and became a distinguished legalist in the field of domestic law. Years later the faculty of the University of Kentucky Law School invited him to Lexington to lecture. He was entertained hospitably in a manner that may have partially atoned for past misdeeds. Certainly there was a vast difference between the confused young man who sat in the federal courtroom during preliminary arguments prior to the Lyman Johnson hearing and the learned barrister who came years later to the University of Kentucky as an honored guest.

Looking back on the era 1935–1965 from the vantage of 2005, the whole rash of civil rights legislation and court decisions seems almost like a disturbing dream. In gathering information from oral and documentary sources preparatory to writing *The Emerging South*, published in 1961, I learned how deep feelings ran in the South at a time when a university, a state, and a region found themselves caught up in a veritable storm of cultural, social, and political change. I viewed with deep sorrow the turmoil created on the Ole Miss campus at the registration of James Meredith. That tragedy ended with his being escorted by armed federal marshals into the Lyceum Building, to the very room where I had registered as a freshman, up the hill from Spiro's, where I had seen the black Cuban track team dining in a "white" restaurant, and only a short distance from where I saw *The Birth of a Nation*. For me the passage of time and the court decisions that have erased so many of the old barriers, including that wrenching one of racial prejudice, have forced me to labor to clear my own soul in this area.

16

~

TEACHING AND
LECTURING ABROAD

AT THE CLOSE OF WORLD WAR II IN 1945, THE WORLD
was faced with the massive challenge of reknitting old cultural and intellectual bonds. As for me personally, I was glad the days of working almost day and night with the Army Specialized Training Program were ended. I knew that many professors were going abroad to teach or do some kind of national service, educational or informational. But I had no thought of doing so myself until 1948, when I unexpectedly received an invitation from the head of the recently organized Salzburg Seminar for American Studies in Austria. He inquired whether I would accept an invitation to become a member of the instructional staff at the second assembly of the seminar. The seminar had held its first meeting during the summer of 1947. One of the staff members that year was the famous anthropologist Margaret Mead.

Harvard students had negotiated some kind of lease arrangement for use of the historic Leopoldskron Castle, which was owned by Max Reinhardt, one of the original producers of the Salzburg Festival. The building was later a major part of the physical setting for the musical film *The Sound of Music*. Never at any time had I thought I would go abroad, certainly not to participate in an academic seminar enrolling a rather large assemblage of non-English-speaking students. But times had changed, and immediately after World War II American professors representing a wide variety of scholarly fields were going to Europe, Japan, and elsewhere to teach. I knew some professors who were sent to England to teach American soldiers in preparation for their return to civilian life and to enable them to take advantage of the G.I. Bill and enter colleges and universities. The Salzburg Seminar, however, had the goal of bringing together students of widely differing cultures, geographical origins, and educational backgrounds with an instructional staff from several American universities and other institutions. There were Wassily Leontief, a future Nobel Prize winner; William Rice, a well-known labor historian from the University of Wisconsin; Henry Nash Smith, author of the highly regarded book *Virgin Land* and a future professor in the University of California at Berkeley; Walter Johnson, professor in the University of Chicago; Robert Horn, a political scientist in Stanford University; and Randall Jarrell of the Woman's College of the University of North Carolina at Greensboro, later poet laureate of the United States. Each professorial staff member was allowed to take a student assistant with him. I took Will Frank Steely, who had a master's degree from the University of Kentucky and would soon become a candidate for a doctorate in history. He later served as president of Northern Kentucky University.

Early in the second week in July 1948 I drove Beth, Bennett, and Elizabeth to Fairfield County, South Carolina, to stay with the Turners. On July 14 I flew from Columbia to New York City. That was perhaps the most exciting airline trip I ever took. Between Columbia and Washington, the plane landed at the Durham-Raleigh Airport, and from the air I looked down on Duke University, where I had spent two years in graduate school. After flying over Washington and Baltimore it passed over Philadelphia at the historic moment when the Democratic Party was reeling from the conflict created by Strom Thurmond and Fielding

Wright over the issue of racial desegregation. The Dixiecrat rebels were causing considerable commotion in the convention. That night, in a New York hotel, I listened to the proceedings of the convention over the radio. I heard the account of the Dixiecrat Party's departure from the convention floor. I also heard the powerful speech by Senator Alben Barkley of Kentucky, which in fact saved the day for President Truman.

The next day I departed LaGuardia Airport aboard a Sabena Airlines plane headed for Zurich, Switzerland. I imagined that Christopher Columbus was no less excited nor more uncertain of what lay ahead than I was in approaching war-torn Europe. I was glued to the window of the plane, watching the coastline of the United States drift away until it joined that of Canada. We passed over Prince Edward Island and Nova Scotia, heading for the dark and isolated airfield at Gander, the port from which so many planes had flown during the war. Looking down, I thought I saw below me a wildly choppy sea, but the bright-eyed Belgian captain informed us that we were seeing a dense bank of cumulus clouds. The Newfoundland landscape still looked like a vital military point. Few lights were aglow, and the surrounding forest seemed amicably melded into shadows from the northern lights. It seemed like a very short time before we were over the northern tip of Ireland and then Scotland. I also saw below us a bit of the Rhine River, and then Zurich. In Zurich I had my first experience of walking on foreign soil. From there to Salzburg I crossed the Alpine frontier aboard the Arlberg Express.

Food and other household supplies for the seminar traveled the same route to the Leopoldskron, except that they were commandeered by the Russians, leaving the seminar on short rations. The Leopoldskron was located on a beautiful lakefront facing the Hohensalzburg range. A story afloat said that the baroque castle was built by a Catholic bishop or cardinal for his "nephew," or illegitimate son. During World War II it was occupied by German gauleiters. These tenants left behind considerable evidence of their occupancy. The castle was intricately wired with push buttons, and the stench of urine was everywhere, including in the bed I slept on. I was assigned to an upstairs room with Robert Horn of Stanford University. Next door, through a passage from our bedroom, was a long shed that was occupied by John Sweeney and his wife. John was curator of the Museum of Modern Art in New York City.

That summer, as war-torn Europe struggled to reknit society and governments, one incident followed another in quick succession in the Leopoldskron. For that brief time, while the quadripartite powers were in charge in Austria, the castle was haven to an international mixture of students who sought answers to their personal and national futures. Among them were the bright and the romantic. I think the mood was somewhat comparable to that portrayed in *The Sound of Music*. Uplifting moments were intermixed with postwar realities.

Generally the student participants in the seminar were serious minded, some of them almost deathly so. Like the Americans, they had to become acquainted with the various other nationalities present. This necessitated considerable attention and diplomacy plus an understanding of and tolerance for cultural and national differences. Though the purposes of the seminar were not clearly defined, we were generally directed to deal with cultural differences, to advance academic redemption following the war, to aid in physical and intellectual reconstruction, and to address economic and political matters. The American political, economic, and cultural recovery following the Civil War was highly pertinent to the situation in Western Europe at this moment, but many other phases of the American experience were discussed as well. I dealt with the sectional forces that had been significant in an expanding nation. At the time, one of the American books most widely read by Europeans was Margaret Mitchell's *Gone with the Wind*. European readers saw in this book reflections of their own plight.

The student directors of the seminar were surprisingly successful in drawing together a good, supportive library. At the moment there was appreciable interest in the American political system, especially the upcoming presidential election. Walter Johnson and Robert Horn were effective in this area. Both of them all but guaranteed that Dewey would defeat Truman. Henry Nash Smith stimulated interest with lectures drawn from his book *Virgin Land*. Rice, Leontief, and Talcott Parsons were also effective, despite Talcott's inborn dullness in discussing sociological matters. Shamefully, I had no knowledge of what Randall did or discussed.

Not all of our time was spent in the Leopoldskron. The trail across a field and up over the ridge to the Hohensalzburg was well padded by seminar members. Fortunately Salzburg had escaped the destructive bombardments of other cities, especially Vienna. The town remained an almost perfect print of a baroque town alongside the Salzach River. Store buildings stood undamaged and stocked with generous amounts of cheap merchandise, and the lifeblood tourist trade was reviving. That summer of 1948 the famous Salzburg Opera was revived, as was the Salzburg Volk und Musik Fest in the public square, and members of the seminar were able to secure tickets. I attended several of the performances, including one of Beethoven's *Fidelio*.

Certain incidents in the Leopoldskron lent a special flavor to life. A student from Czechoslovakia and three from Finland indicated that they did not wish to return to their homelands. This caused considerable concern on the part of the student managers of the seminar. They feared that if these students did not return home they would never again be able to recruit candidates from those countries. The faculty and student managers spent an entire night in the castle's grand dining room discussing the issue, but when the sun came up there was no answer. My personal attitude from eve to morn was, "Let the students go where they please and God speed them." There were other almost interminable faculty meetings that were equally futile and boring.

Two personal experiences stand out in my memory. Early on the morning of August 18, 1948, I went downstairs to join a party that was to visit one of the camps housing displaced Jews. At that time there were estimated to be 250,000 Jews who were homeless and had little hope of remedying their condition of life. The camps containing German and Austrian Jews were supported in large measure by the United States Army and the International Relief Organization. Before the visiting members of the Salzburg Seminar were admitted to the camp, we were briefed, poorly be it said, by some kind of official, until Mrs. J. D. Nichols of Texas took over and spoke with regional, down-to-earth frankness.

Once inside the camp we were overwhelmed by the refugees' reaching with outstretched arms in supplication for release. Never in my life have I encountered such a wave of human despair and hopelessness. There were children, adolescents, pregnant women, and ancient men and women who bore deeply incised lines on their faces from the horrors experienced as a result of Nazi inhumanity. Lined up in a virtual windrow were thousands of used shoes, articles of clothing, and other relief materials, contributed largely by American Jews.

I also visited a refugee camp containing Russian and Czechoslovakian Jews. This one was far more depressing than the German camp. So far as I was able to discern on a superficial visit, the pall of utter hopelessness lay much heavier on the victims here. Symbolically, the slightest ray of hope and self-expression lay in ornaments I saw that had been created by craftsmen from the most modest bits of material. That camp visit had such a heavy emotional impact on me that I had to leave before the official end of the visitation. In time this mass of derelict humanity was to move on to the newly created state of Israel and to become part of a new political world with great international significance.

For a reason not completely discernible, some friction arose between the student administration of the seminar and Dr. Samuel Williams, the educational coordinator for the United States Army. On one occasion Dr. Williams visited the Leopoldskron, and I think his suspicions were somewhat allayed. On August 13, 1948, as self-appointed goodwill ambassadors, Walter Johnson, Robert Horn, and I went to Vienna, partly to visit the city and partly to visit with Dr. Williams. Johnson was a bold if not brassy soul who believed in talking with the top people. Somehow he managed to communicate with the U.S. ambassador to Austria, Robert Orr Denny, and we were invited to have dinner with Ambassador Denny and Dr. Williams. Martin Herz, a Philadelphia newspaperman, was also present, along with other guests. We discussed the state of affairs in Austria, the coming U.S. presidential election, and quadripartite affairs. I think we pretty well ironed out the problems between Dr. Williams and the Salzburg Seminar, whatever they were.

In some now-forgotten way I became acquainted with Robert and

Tevis Armentrout in Salzburg. Robert was a captain in the United States Army of Occupation. Tevis was a member of the highly regarded Tevis family of Clark and Shelby Counties in Kentucky. They were most hospitably obliging to me that summer. Tevis came to the Leopoldskron and became acquainted with some of the other staff members. She had a Volkswagen in which she drove Walter Johnson to several places outside Salzburg, among them the salt mines at Hallein and Hitler's famous Eagle's Nest mountaintop hideout. She and Robert later helped Robert Horn, Walter Johnson, and me get tickets on the Occidental Express to London and assisted us in securing U.S. currency.

The final assembly of the Salzburg Seminar occurred on August 23, 1948. A majority of the students expressed enthusiasm at having been in free classrooms and satisfaction with the work of the professorial staff. There was only one fly in the ointment. Professor William Rice had invited an economics professor from the University of Leipzig to attend, and this visitor proceeded to deliver a Nazi harangue that ruffled a lot of feathers among the seminar participants. This last faculty meeting lasted until 1:00 A.M., getting nowhere in particular.

On August 25 Walter Johnson, Robert Horn, and I departed Salzburg aboard the bobtailed, two-car Occidental Express. Somewhere along the line the Russians had sheared the train of the rest of its cars. I think that night trip through Germany and France to Paris was one of the most anxious situations I ever endured. German officials were meticulous in examining passports, tickets, and other papers. For some reason they seemed to be seeking out individuals guilty of some unidentified crime. They awakened passengers all up and down the cars, shouting and even manhandling some individuals. Happily, aside from being unable to sleep, Walter and I escaped being involved in the melee.

Neither Walter nor I had ever been in Paris or any other part of France. In some fortuitous manner we found a hotel room opposite the famous Tuileries Gardens. Robert Horn was able to speak some French, enough that a patient Frenchman could catch the drift. Thus we were able to get around in Paris without too much trouble. Again Walter Johnson got in touch with some of the foreign service officials and arranged for us to have dinner with them. We were dressed in more or less casual work clothes and therefore were somewhat out of place. The student director of the Salzburg Seminar had instructed us not to dress up because of the financially depressed situation of the students. The main conversation at dinner with members of the American Embassy staff was the upcoming U.S. election in November. We again concluded that Dewey would defeat Truman. On Sunday, August 29, the three of us went by train to Versailles. This was a historic day for the French. The fountains were turned on before the palace for the first time since the end of the war, and the multitude of Frenchmen present reacted with deep emotion to the renewal of this symbol of peace. The palace was packed, and when we got into the Hall of Mirrors about all we saw were the ample hind ends of French patriots. I don't recall seeing a single mirror. In the crush of people on that historic day, I decided our khaki work clothes were ideally suited to the fray.

When Walter and I returned to our hotel, the desk attendant gave him the message that his wife, Catherine ("Tink"), had arrived in London. She had come to England as a member of the popular Chicago Radio Round Table group to discuss the coming presidential election. This was a surprise to Walter, and he became highly disturbed. Neither he nor I got much sleep that night. Early the next day we resumed our railway journey to Cherbourg. Along the way I saw both the ravages of war and the scattered debris left behind by the military forces. At Cherbourg we boarded a channel boat headed for a rail connection to London. By some kind of bureaucratic mix-up, I was not allowed to debark until I secured a landing pass. Walter got by the officials, boarded the train, and left me behind. When I finally was allowed to debark I caught the train for London and the Marble Arch Hotel, where I joined the Chicago party. Again the conversation centered on the election, with the roundtable pundits already inaugurating Thomas E. Dewey as president of the United States. I spent only a short time in London before going on to Devon to spend the three days before I was to board the troop ship *Washington* for the return to New York. I had been in Devon only a day when, to my surprise, Walter and Tink arrived. We wandered under the cliffs and along a trail across the moor. I almost immediately detected that not all was well with that marriage. When I left the Johnsons to go to Southampton and board ship for home, I was aware that I was leaving a troubled couple behind in Devon. Later they were divorced.

On the train trip to Southampton I gained at least one insight into the toll of war. Two women in the compartment with me asked me if I had nylon stockings in my baggage. One of them pulled up her skirt and revealed a major run in her stocking from heel to hip. Of course I could not help her out.

The docking building at Southampton was as gloomy as a locomotive repair shop. The *Washington* still contained bunk beds in its hold and on the upper decks. It seems that every G.I. who had sailed on her had carved his initials on the mahogany rails. The ship was fairly empty of passengers when it sailed, but it anchored off Cobb and took on a veritable multitude of New York and Boston Irish who had been home on a sentimental journey. They sang and danced twenty-four hours a day. I asked the burly Irishman who occupied the bunk just above mine if he was a New Yorker. He responded gruffly that he was from Boston and was not a cop. He added that his visit to Ireland had been so unpleasant that he never wanted to go there again.

ONCE I WAS BACK HOME IN Lexington preparing to begin a new semester in September 1948, I assumed my days of foreign travel and service were over. This proved to be a false assumption. In December 1949 I received a letter from Lieutenant W. Hodges, Office of the Under Secretary of War, Special Services, asking me to do some lecturing for the army in Austria and as a professor in the University of Vienna. I was granted a leave of absence from the University of Kentucky to accept the appointment. In the University of Vienna I would be assigned a general lecture course in American history and asked to conduct a seminar for graduate students. With only a vague understanding of what a European professor does or of the instructional system of the University of Vienna, Hodges asked me also to travel to cities in Austria to give public lectures.

On the afternoon of February 26, 1950, I left Lexington headed for

Washington. At the Pentagon I was sworn into the United States Army with some undefined simulated officer rank, briefed, given a typhoid shot, and sent to a Major King, who seemed to have about as much alertness and energy as an overweight retriever. His advice to me was to take it easy and have a good time. I am certain he was capable of doing both. I was presented a precious A.G.O. card and military orders. On the way to Washington I rode in the same seat as William Sloane, president of William Sloane Associates, publishers. That house had just published Bud Guthrie's Pulitzer Prize–winning novel *The Way West*. Bill was full of big talk about book publishing and his newly organized house. I am certain he believed that night that his company would become a major publisher, a dream never realized. I had in my briefcase a copy of *The Way West*, which I would read over the Atlantic Ocean.

Early in the dawn of February 28, I arrived at the Gravelley Point Air Base on the Potomac, headed for a night's layover in Massachusetts. The next morning I was loaded onto a C-14 transport plane headed for Frankfurt, Germany, by way of the Azores. The plane was crowded with wives, children, and baggage on the way to join servicemen in Germany. Aboard that flight was a baby who screamed endlessly. Despite the screaming I settled down to read Bud Guthrie's new book and dropped off to sleep. When I awoke and looked down I was startled to see the landscape covered with snow. The attendant informed me that we were over Mount Holyoke in Massachusetts, which at the moment was being showered with the release of overweight gasoline to permit a safe landing. The pilots had turned back because one of the plane's engines was firing weakly.

The following day we made a second start on the journey to Frankfurt. When I boarded the plane I was surprised to see Jay B. Hubbell of Duke University and his wife. They were headed for Vienna on a similar mission. Our plane arrived in Frankfurt to make connections to Vienna. The only choice the Hubbells and I had was to get passage on a military train controlled by the German occupational command. It took some boldness on my part to convince a sergeant that we wanted to move on, but he finally allowed us to board the train. Later I learned how jealous the separate commands were of their special trains. Professor Hubbell, a shy man, did the same thing for himself and Mrs. Hubbell, and we traveled together to Vienna.

I finally reached Vienna and the Bristol Hotel, where I was to reside during my period of duty. The afternoon after my arrival, Samuel Williams, director of cultural and educational affairs in Austria, came to the hotel to greet Dr. Hubbell and me. I had met Dr. Williams in the summer of 1948 and found him to be both an interesting and a somewhat strange character. He had been a member of the Rollins College staff in Winter Park, Florida, and was of a conservative stripe. Happily, just before my arrival in Vienna the administration of the city was transferred from Russian to British command. There was still ample evidence of the Russian presence—a red star was still attached to the front of a tall building on the Main Strasse, and Russian soldiers were everywhere. Evident also was a tenseness in relations between the Russians and the other three quadripartite members.

On March 6, 1950, Dr. Hubbell and I went to the U.S. headquarters building, where we were registered and granted access to the building and the post exchange. We were issued a cigarette ration card and turned loose on the Austrians. Provisions were made for us to have lunch with the Rektor, or headmaster, and Professor K. Kibbler, head of the English seminar. The same day I was to see the USIS library and introduce myself to the librarians. I met a Miss Abby, a career foreign service librarian, and a Miss Drew. They would be of tremendous assistance to me.

When I went to the office-study-library of the history seminar in the university, I met for the first time Professor Dr. Haunch, a Dominican priest. I quickly got the impression that he had not been properly informed about my coming. His academic environment—a leather-bound world of ancient books dealing with the Renaissance period—showed plainly where his interest lay. The tables in his seminar study were piled high with books and papers, and it was evident that he traveled academically along a far distant path from that of a twentieth-century university. Nevertheless, Professor Dr. Haunch enjoyed a considerable professorial reputation. He reviewed my class schedule with me and made arrangements to introduce me to the lecture section. Within the gloomy atmosphere of Professor Haunch's study and its ancient books, I felt as if I had stepped off the end of a plank into a fathomless pool of medievalism.

The University of Vienna that I came to know cursorily was housed in a block-wide structure that over the years had gathered a dark patina of time, emphasized by the ravages of usage and war. Its halls were dimly lit, and the only classroom I knew was stark and uninviting. At one end was a platform on which a raised lecture podium, reached by ladder-type steps, stood as a symbol of professorial authority—and maybe of dull lecturing.

The opening day of my lecture class was indeed, for me, an impressive one. I arrived at Professor Haunch's seminar with a briefcase in hand, stuffed with lecture notes. I found I was to be escorted to the classroom and introduced by both the Rektor and Professor Dr. Haunch. They gripped my arms as we began the long and winding march to the classroom door. I felt somewhat like a prisoner being marched to the gallows. Each of the officials addressed the students, then they beckoned to me to ascend the steps to the lectern. Once the Rektor and the seminar head departed, I came down out of that crow's nest and never went back. I invited students to be more relaxed and informal in our relationship. I also asked them to raise questions and express their views. I believe that the experience I fostered with the students in the lecture section was free and inquiring.

The advanced graduate seminar was made up largely of mature and serious-minded participants—with one exception. There was a middle-aged man who seemed to have no certain nationality and who spoke a language that no one in the seminar could identify, if in fact it was a language and not a lot of gibberish. He read a paper of which I understood not a single word, nor could I discover a hint of its origins. I watched the expressions of other students and sensed that they were as perplexed as I.

I developed a friendly relationship with several members of the seminar. One of the young men was in charge of caring for the young boys of the Vienna Boys' Choir. One day he invited me to go with him to their living quarters to have lunch with the boys and then to accompany them to the Hofburg chapel, where they were to sing in a wedding ceremony in which a rich Argentinian was to wed an Austrian baroness. The boys sang from the deep choir loft of the royal chapel. They behaved in the most impeccable manner, but when they were not onstage they were about the worst-behaved children I had ever seen.

Another bright student was the son of the official in charge of the royal wardrobe in the Hofburg Museum. One day he told me that the royal garments had been taken out for their annual airing and cleaning. He invited me to go with him to see and even feel of them, even lift some to get a sense of their weight and texture. Especially fascinating were the gold and silver strands woven into the royal robes. I was told by the curator that the women who created Charles X's and Marie Antionette's robes bled profusely in drawing the metallic strands through the fabric. There was a surprisingly large collection of royal garments, both elaborate and plain. Among them was a pair of lederhosen worn by Franz Joseph. The seat of the trousers had been ripped asunder by an alpine roebuck. To my surprise the lederhosen revealed that Franz Joseph was a relatively small man in stature.

A third student who stood out from other members of the seminar was a potentially handsome young woman who obviously was a child of depressed financial and domestic resources. She wore the same shabby dress to every meeting of the seminar. It had a round hole in the front that revealed her bare abdomen. Nevertheless she had a bright mind and a determination to earn a doctorate in history. I wanted to assist her in securing some kind of scholarship to enable her to do so, but I was unable to raise the money. There was, however, a happy ending for her. Three or four years later I went out to the University of Kansas to give a lecture. When I was finished with the lecture a beautiful young woman came up and asked me if I remembered her. She was the girl with the hole in her dress, her bright mind intact. She was in an advanced stage of earning her doctorate.

At the end of my session in the University of Vienna, Professor Haunch asked me to come to his study. There he invited me to become professor of American history in the seminar. This was flattering, but I could have earned no more than a bare living, to say nothing of the radical change that would be wrought in my family life and academic career.

The professorship and classes in the University of Vienna were only a part of my assignment. I was also obligated to deliver public lectures. Somebody in the military bureaucracy in Vienna insisted that I lecture on American Indian history, a subject for which I had no anthropological or archaeological preparation. I did not know at the time that an Austrian author, Karl May, had published several books on American Indians after the style of James Fenimore Cooper. I felt certain I would find myself lecturing to an Austrian ethnologist or archaeologist somewhere along the way and would embarrass myself and American historical scholarship. Every time I looked in a bookstore I saw May's Indian books. Fortunately the USIS library had some useful sources, enough to get me through a lecture on the subject, so reluctantly I agreed to organize such lectures on the condition that I give my first lecture in Salzburg, where I would feel slightly more comfortable, being on familiar ground.

At a late afternoon gathering in the Main Platz in Salzburg I faced an overflow audience. Happily no grizzled anthropologist or ethnologist rose up to dispute me. Outside the hall, however, I was taken to task by two handsome young Americans who said they approved of everything I said except for the origin of the North American tribes. One of them asked me if I would read a book they would give me. At that moment I would have read anything if it would have given me more information. When I was handed the Book of Mormon I was dismayed. I had not realized that my interrogators were young Mormons serving their missionary time abroad. In the end I was not persuaded to preach Joseph Smith's "Lost Tribe of Israel" theory to Karl May's fans, though in time I lectured to several overflow audiences on the subject of Indians.

One of my lecture assignments was in Linz, a U.S. military center. I had directions on how to reach the lecture hall. I deboarded the military train *Mozart* and got onto a trolley car. I was on the right line but mistakenly boarded a car going in the opposite direction from my destination. After a considerable ride I was landed in a cornfield in the dark. I noticed that another person was there too. He turned out to be an American soldier from Philadelphia, Mississippi. There we were, two Mississippi country boys stranded in an Austrian cornfield, far from home and a good distance from the center of Linz. Linz was the only place where I came into contact with U.S. personnel in my lectures.

My lecture schedule was synchronized with my class schedule. On four or five occasions I lectured in Vienna on Mariahilferstrasse in a dark and cavernous abandoned movie theater. The building was located directly across the street from the Russian headquarters. The first time I appeared there I landed in the midst of a crowd shouting at policemen. I thought something had happened with the Russians. When I learned there was an overflow audience crammed into the theater and no one else could be admitted, I basked for a moment in the street scuffle. The manager of the event said to me, "I must have overadvertised this event." I assured him that he had indeed.

One of my steadfast auditors was the Princess Bourbon-Parma, a fairly young and handsome lady of slender build who wore a hearing aid and sat in the front row, where she could hear. She asked questions, and once I had a conversation with her. On another occasion I was asked by the director of the USIS program to speak to a small, select group about Daniel Boone. Never could I have conceived of speaking about the old frontiersman in a sophisticated city like Vienna, but the life of Boone fitted in well with the Austrian interest in Indians. A member of that audience was a handsome white-haired man who had once been a head of the Vienna school system. He asked me if all Indians wore a long-tailed feathered war headdress. He told me that when he was head of the school system an Indian dressed in fringecloth and adorned with a long trailing headdress of feathers had come to advertise a traveling show, perhaps that of Buffalo Bill.

My professorial duties in the university brought me into association with a few docents and advanced students. For the most part they were bright and inquisitive. Their study of history often centered on the Medieval and Renaissance periods. I asked a docent I had come to know at the Leopoldskron Seminar why he did not turn his attention to modern

European history. He replied that such a study would prove too politically dangerous.

As a tentative member of the history seminar I was invited to attend some of the formal affairs in the university. One of them was centered on graduation exercises. Only a relatively small number of the professorial staff were dressed in academic robes and caps. Everybody stood throughout the ceremony. There was little speaking but much observance of academic ritual. In another area of the university I was surprised at the inadequacy of library materials. The library was located in a large lower-floor room and was freely open to users. Wondering if there were articles by Austrians who had traveled in the United States, I examined two segments of the holdings, American history and the journals. I found few of the first and absolutely none of the latter. The university library holdings were in sharp contrast to those in the Hofburg.

In a broader perspective, the city of Vienna was little short of a collective historical monument. On a rainy spring Sunday morning I went to the Capuchin mausoleum. I knocked at the door and was greeted by an elderly man, an almost perfect clone of my grandfather Bennett. He took me down a long flight of stairs into the mausoleum and left me alone. I spent the entire morning with the Hapsburgs, among them Charles X, Maria Theresa, Maximilian and his wife Carletta, Franz Joseph, and many others. Nearby also was the St. Stefan Kirche, which had been struck by an American bomb during the war, letting sunlight into the sarcophagus for the first time in its history. Left exposed were scores of human skulls and other body parts, which had been stacked neatly in rows.

Just across the street from the Bristol Hotel, and the centerpiece of the Platz, stood the bombed-out ruins of the Opera House. I often looked out the window of my room to see the piles of structural steel assembled there and the activities of the workmen restoring the world-famous seat of opera. The restorations of St. Stefan Kirche and the Opera House were symbolic of Austria's recovery from the political pit into which it had fallen and the rebuilding of national pride, both physically and spiritually.

The celebration of May Day brought tensions between the Russians and the American forces. The Russians had hauled in hundreds of people to celebrate the day with a parade through the Main Strasse. A rumor was spread that they would parade a man named Bear, who had been sprung by Russian soldiers from a prison in Salzburg. At a luncheon in the bank headquarters of the U.S. Army I heard discussion that if this occurred, sharpshooters would shoot him. On the great day Americans were instructed to stay inside and away from the Main Strasse. Not only had the Russians hauled in hordes of paraders but they also had positioned trucks at the end of the march waiting to haul them back to the beginning so they could parade all over again. I viewed the parade from a Bristol Hotel window, and it appeared to be interminable. In late afternoon I walked up the street and was interested to see strange-looking stubs of Russian cigarettes lying everywhere.

The concluding two weeks of my university-army assignment were filled with excitement and pressing duties. Spring had arrived, and the horse chestnut and other shrubs were in bloom. The Volksgarten at the Hofburg was bursting with roses. I experienced frustration because I was behind in my class schedule. Central Europe in 1950 was intensely interested in "Holy Year," and at times classes in the university were disrupted because of local celebrations or journeys to Rome. In the end I was pleased that the graduate seminar reports were surprisingly good and that lecture course examination papers were pleasingly satisfactory, considering the disruptive environment created by Holy Year celebrations.

As the end of my assignment approached I began the tedious process of securing passage home. I encountered a mix-up in securing passage on a military plane, and for a moment it seemed I would be stuck in Vienna indefinitely. Finally orders arrived from the Pentagon authorizing my travel aboard a commercial airliner. I flew to London and there boarded one of the double-decker Pan-American planes for New York. Early in the morning on this flight, just before arriving at LaGuardia Airport, I went into the lavatory to shave and comb my hair. While I was there two men came in. I recognized Edward R. Murrow; the other turned out to be Averell Harriman. I was intrigued at seeing this pair, whose names were household words. Murrow had gained fame in reporting on the removal of British troops from Dunkirk and the transport of British children to havens of safety. His voice on the airwaves had all but become that of Britain itself. Averill Harriman was well known because of his diplomatic activities. There I stood, in my undershirt and sagging trousers, my watch chain with my Phi Beta Kappa key having dropped out of a pants pocket. Harriman picked up the key and said, "I have one of those things."

Back in Washington and in the confusing passages of the Pentagon I once again found myself in the hands of Major King, who said he had been waiting for me. He relieved me of my orders and A.G.O. card and said, "Now you are out of the army." He also told me that that was my sole task for the day. I am certain I never felt freer in my life than at that moment. There were to be no more lectures on Indians, no more cigarette rations, no more rides on the *Mozart* or crossing Russian checkpoints with military orders in a coat pocket. Best of all, I was spared having to look once more at the huge red star on Vienna's Main Strasse.

I came away from Austria and its citizens and the University of Vienna knowing that I had acquired too little knowledge of their life, culture, and politics. In a broader sense, however, I had a fresh and much clearer perspective on world affairs following World War II.

17

AN ANCIENT LAND IN THE GRIP OF HISTORY

IN THE SPRING OF 1952 I READ AN ARTICLE IN THE *SATurday Review of Literature* written by J. Saunders Redding, a black author, in which he describes his adventures and misadventures in India. At that moment India was in the first stages of creating itself out of the crumbling British Empire. Figuratively the Raj was rapidly going home, and Gandhi's widely publicized crusade for independence and freedom was given considerable attention in the United States. Redding's article was published during the dark days when Senator Joseph McCarthy and his sleuths were looking for communists under every American cabbage leaf. I read Redding's article more out of curiosity than anything else. All I knew about India was its Kiplingesque image and the stories of Gandhi's crusade. I had no notion that I would ever get closer to that exotic land than Redding's article.

Soon after reading the article I received an unexpected inquiry from a United States Department of State official asking if I would go to India and follow much of Redding's journey, lecturing and making observations of the Indian attitude toward communism. I replied that I knew little about India, the social and political philosophies of Indians, or their history. I knew none of the Indian dialects. In retrospect, my decision to accept that assignment seems almost foolhardy. At the time, my colleague J. Merton England, editorial associate of the *Journal of Southern History,* asked me if I had the slightest glimmer about the turn of the Indian mind. I did not. Later I told an Indian university professor this story and he replied, "Does anybody know this?"

I taught my classes in the University of Kentucky on October 12, 1952; then Frank McVey drove me and my family to the Lexington airport. When the plane lifted into the air I looked down and saw him standing on the ground holding hands with my children, Bennett and Elizabeth.

I spent a week in Washington being briefed in the cultural affairs section of the State Department on what some officials believed to be true about India, its history, and its social and cultural customs. I was advised to take with me two tuxedos, one white, the other black. A female advisor instructed me to take along a generous supply of toilet paper, none of which I ever had need for.

After the briefing period in Washington I was ready to begin the long journey to Bombay. Before leaving the states, I traveled to Baltimore to have dinner with C. Vann Woodward, then president of the Southern Historical Association, and hand in my resignation as editor of the *Journal of Southern History.* At the end of dinner, Vann fumbled around for his billfold and then said he had left it in his apartment. I paid the bill, almost exhausting the amount of money I could take on to India.

In New York I had some time on my hands and called on John Farrar of Farrar and Rinehart, a firm that had published some of my books. I was startled to find his office and desk in more than their usual state of dishevelment. Too, his seemingly unsettled state of mind disturbed me. I did not know at the time that he and Mary Rinehart and her sons were about to take leave of the firm. I was saddened by the breakup of this venerable publishing house.

Finally, having made what I believed was a thorough preparation, I was ready to depart New York with my black and white tuxedos and my stock of toilet paper. I was to lecture in both India and Pakistan. Late in the afternoon, when I arrived at the boarding point for Trans World Airlines' *Star of Nevada,* the boarding officer refused me passage because I did not have landing visas for Teheran or Baghdad. After a couple of phone calls to the cultural affairs division of the State Department, I was instructed to go as far as Paris and there secure the necessary passes from the Iranian and Iraqi embassies. This I was able to do without great difficulty.

My layover in Paris was caused by the infrequency of flights to Bombay. When I was at last able to depart, I boarded a Trans World craft on a direct flight to India. En route I had the thrilling experience of looking down on Stromboli in slight eruption, on a portion of the North African desert littered with the debris of World War II, and on the upper end of the Suez Canal. When the plane landed at the Farouk Airport in Cairo, workers were chiseling the dictator's name off the side of the main building. From Cairo the plane followed part of the historic Mosaic flight from Egypt. Some of the ancient wilderness lay below, as did the mountainous spine of biblical fame. In time there drifted into view the Saudi Arabian desert, which was scored by oil pipelines and roads pushed out of the sands.

On board the plane were wives and children of employees of the Arabian American Oil Company. They deplaned in Bahrain and Kuwait, leaving the plane almost empty. Remaining on board were the president of the airline and his wife and maybe three or four other passengers. We flew across the Persian Gulf from Dubai to Bombay. There was a brief romantic moment as the plane passed over the Persian Gulf when the moon seemed extraordinarily large and bright. That struck me as a sign that I was indeed entering an ancient and unfathomable world.

At 9:00 P.M. the long journey ended as we landed in Bombay. On the drive in from the airport I saw for the first time cows crowding the streets and roadways and people sleeping under soiled sheets on the sidewalk. But I was too exhausted to be fully aware of the scene. I spent my first night in India in the famous old Taj Mahal Hotel, which exhibited all the stuffiness of the British Empire. The decor of the room I occupied was an Indian adaptation of Victorian decor.

Early the next morning I walked out to the Gateway of India and saw the impressive sculpture symbolizing the power and strength of the British Empire in the persons of Victoria and Albert. On the way I stepped around sleeping bodies on the pavement. I also saw for the first time blobs of what I thought was blood. It seemed to me the entire populace of Bombay was dying of lung infection. That was my first sight of "pom," or betel nut spittle. During the weeks to come it was a common sight, and often I was offered betel nuts, but I never accepted them because of their reputed narcotic effects.

I made the flight from Bombay to Delhi in a creaky DC-3 plane, called a "Dakota" in India. Along the way I noticed the plane's wings literally flapping in the draft. Like the Taj Mahal Hotel, the interior of the "Dakota" exhibited more than a touch of gaudy India. On board I was served a full breakfast of fruits, cereals, and bacon.

By the time of my arrival in Delhi I was almost exhausted from travel. I was met at the airport by Dr. Clifford Manschart, the director of American cultural affairs in India, who drove me directly to the Maiden Hotel in Old Delhi, another monument to the longtime British presence. I was informed that I had a speaking engagement at a men's club just outside of Delhi in approximately three hours. I was sound asleep in my hotel room when Dr. Manschart returned to drive me to the village. Never had I felt less prepared physically to make a speech. Somehow I mustered up the courage and wit to meet the challenge of the moment. I spoke to a group of local businessmen for three quarters of an hour and tried to answer a barrage of questions. That speech was the first of nearly a hundred I would make in India. Fatigued as I was, I learned something of the nature and responses of an Indian audience.

Soon after my arrival in Delhi I was surprised to learn that Hodding Carter, editor of the Greenville, Mississippi, newspaper, was there. Hodding was a liberal speaking out in Mississippi at a time when the issue of desegregation was at the boiling point. He arrived in Delhi loaded down with photographic equipment that his news photographer had selected for him. On a warm Sunday morning he and I tramped through the streets of Old Delhi to visit the thirty-foot red sandstone wall that surrounded the city, penetrated by seven gates. We wound our way through streets crowded with sleeping people, wandering cows and water buffalo, and horn-blowing cars to reach the Shah Jahan's masterwork, only to discover that Hodding had forgotten to put film in his camera. We had to make the journey all over again.

At the outset I found the Indian countryside even more exciting and romantic than Rudyard Kipling's descriptions of it. The land was sparsely dotted with trees, most of them strung along the roads. On the roads was a perpetual parade of carts drawn by water buffalo and plodding camels. Beside the roads I saw men and boys drawing water from streams using the balance-and-pole device that had come down from ancient times. In villages, edible foods and sweetstuffs were displayed in the open, with flies and insects swarming over them. Many of the houses were daubed with cow and buffalo dung patties, which created a nauseating odor. Nearly every country has developed its own food tastes, mode of food preparation and dining, and sanitary procedures, but it is doubtful that any country makes all these things as visible as India does.

Almost before I had sloughed off the lag of travel, I was on my way to Amritsar in the Punjab to begin my lecture tour and observations. The flight from Delhi to Amritsar was at a low enough level that I got a panoramic view of upper India. The sprawl of villages rolled out as if imprinted on a broad tapestry. I spotted farmers breaking the land with archaic implements drawn by buffalo and oxen. Occasionally a splotch of green would break the monotony of the arid gray landscape. When I landed in Amritsar on the morning of October 27, I was greeted with the sounds of gunfire in the conflict between Hindus and Pakistani Muslims.

I arrived in the Punjab with only the most minimal briefing about the region. From reading Kipling I knew vaguely about the Sikhs, but nothing of their religious and social mores. I had never heard of the ten gurus and their mythical history. I knew somewhat vaguely about the conflict between India and Pakistan over Kashmir. I was met at the plane by Mr. C. P. Chandari, city manager of Amritsar. We drove into the city and to his residential compound over a narrow single-lane road, with bicyclists dodging in and out of traffic, juccas* rattling along, stray cattle wandering about, plodding buffalo drawing carts, and flocks of people, all of them irritating to Mr. Chandari. His residential compound was a place of escape from all the normal irritations, and also from the threats from external forces.

I spoke to a club of businessmen in Amritsar on the subject of United States constitutional history. The audience was attentive and raised good and perceptive questions. I noticed during my lecture that there seemed to be a person behind a fabric room divider. Later I learned that it was Mr. Chandari's wife. She was obviously of a different cultural background and later told me she was a confirmed communist. She was passionate in describing the widely differing political views she held from those of her husband.

In Amritsar I lectured to several educational groups and became involved in some interesting social events. My greatest thrill, however, was a visit to the Golden Temple, the holiest shrine of Sikhdom. I removed my shoes and was led through the temple by an attendant of far less than guru status. Speaking to an assembly of young Sikhs was an exciting experience. They asked thoughtful questions and made bright and intelligent responses to my own queries. In one of the colleges I witnessed a game of soccer in which long strands of hair sailed out behind the players, who were dressed in traditional Sikh shorts. No doubt the players carried somewhere in their garments knives and combs. They played as they lived, aggressively.

The government college at Amritsar was largely focused on agriculture and animal husbandry. Late one afternoon I was accompanied by an attendant to the cattle stalls, which contained an impressive number of Brahman steers and water buffalo. The moment I entered the shed there went up a crescendo of snorting and bawling. I was told that my body scent was quite different from that of a Hindu herdsman.

The Punjab population was in an ambitious state of mind. They were

---

* Motorized tricycles

agitating for the establishment of an integrated, if not an independent, state. My audiences there revealed an active interest in the American experience of achieving independence. There seemed to be a growing movement to abandon the limited British curricula and teaching methods in the colleges. The British were said to have had as their educational objective in India the training of clerical personnel to serve in the imperial services.

After six revealing days in Amritsar I rode the Bombay Express to Ambala Cantonment. This was the first time I had ridden on an Indian train, and I did so in a state of complete confusion. First, I had difficulty determining whether I was on the right train and going in the right direction. In all the milling crowd in the station I could identify no one who seemed to be a railway official. When Indians travel they seem to take all their worldly goods along with them, including chickens, goats, and other livestock. To my relief I eventually spotted a sagging sign with the words "Ambala Cantonment."

On the train between Amritsar and Ambala I was able to see at fairly close range villages surrounded by patch agriculture. Again there were men drawing water from shallow wells with ancient cantilever-bucket devices. There were patches of sugar cane, peanuts, wheat, and assorted vegetables, and at many places men and women were flailing grain with a hooked tree limb. They winnowed it by tossing grain and chaff in the air.

When I arrived in Ambala, I came for the first time in direct contact with Indian culture. The town had a Presbyterian hospital and missionary station and a college and several schools. I was met at the train by Principal Joshi and his assistant. They came dressed in semiformal Indian-style garments consisting of tight-legged trousers and loose, unbuttoned shirts with white duster coats. I was conveyed in Principal Joshi's tiny car of undefinable make. We drove to an abandoned British officers' club for tea and a general conversation in which I was questioned about current affairs and lifestyles in the United States. I was astonished at the Indians' knowledge of my country and its national and international personalities. They knew about George Washington and Abraham Lincoln, the first because he had led the fight for national independence, the latter because of his actions concerning slavery. Fortunately I was then reading my friend Ben Thomas's *Life of Lincoln*. I carried an introductory card that contained a brief biographical note on the back in which the name Kentucky appeared, and in almost every case I was introduced as being from "Kentucky, home of Abraham Lincoln."

In Ambala Cantonment I spoke to three college groups, and in each case students were assembled and seated on uncomfortable wooden benches, similar to those I had sat on in Mississippi one-room schools at the opening of the twentieth century. By this time I was used to answering questions read from slips of mimeographed paper. So many of the questions were delivered this way that it caused me to wonder how much curiosity and imagination the students actually had.

The people in Ambala Cantonment had social, political, and emotional attitudes that I could not possibly fathom. But I did have conversations with them about the new government of India, as well as about poverty, the erasure of the ancient caste system, and the role of education. In one conversation I was told that the American religious efforts were fruitless but the contribution of the Presbyterian hospital was deeply appreciated. In informal conversations I heard favorable comments about social change, but remarkably there were denials that the untouchables, or *harijans*, still existed.

The girls' school in which I lectured had an enrollment of marriageable-age girls, but it was doubtful that a single one of them enjoyed enough personal independence to choose her own spouse. The ancient practice of arranged marriages was deeply ingrained in the social system. The girls were shy and asked few questions. I became convinced that few individuals in my audiences had any interest in communism. Questioners often spoke with what seemed to be deep-seated anger, but I soon learned that this was more an Indian style of address than an argumentative stance. I could see why J. Saunders Redding had been disturbed by this.

Late in the evening of November 7, after a full day of lecturing, a luncheon, and a tea, I became fatigued as I tried to answer questions ranging from the American diet to the role of women. I was therefore startled by the perfectly sincere query "Have the Americans published any books?" Of the literally hundreds of questions I was asked in India, this was one I could answer with unequivocal certainty.

On the early morning train ride back to Delhi I again saw villages at close range. Inhabitants were exercising their morning sanitary constitutional. Men and boys were lined up on one side of knolls, and girls and women were on the other side. The walls of many village structures were plastered with cow dung patties, and these were being used also as fuel for cooking.

India may have had an ancient culture, but one thing seemed evident. The great masses of its people were almost oblivious to what was happening in the rest of the world. For instance, I was able to get no information about Eisenhower's election as president until I got back to Delhi.

I registered once more at the Maiden Hotel in Delhi, feeling that never in my life had I experienced greater need for a bath and a change of clothing. Nevertheless the trip had disclosed what my life in India would be. On a visit to Dr. Clifford Manschart's office I received letters from my family and the news that my next lectures would be in Calcutta. I would be there for some time, but I was given almost no information about the cultural and commercial affairs of Calcutta. What I did know was something of the Sepoy rebellion and the Dum Dum conflict that had led to the creation of the legend about the "Black Hole of Calcutta."

I awakened early on the morning of November 10 for the flight to Calcutta. The itinerary for my extended tour of southern coastal India was an arduous one. I packed all my belongings, including a tuxedo, in a large suitcase and set forth on an adventure almost as extensive as that of Vasco da Gama. I could not imagine the experiences I would have before my return to Delhi.

Once in the air and somewhere over the neighborhood of Lucknow, I spotted outside the window of the plane what I at first believed to be a huge bank of cumulus clouds. It turned out to be a magnificent view of the Himalayas and the broad, muddy delta of the Ganges-Hooghly rivers. I ate lunch in the comfort of the plane's cabin and watched this geographical wonder unroll like a giant tapestry. Off in the distance I at least imagined I could see Nepal.

I was met at the Dum Dum airport by Hilene Aderton, a cultural affairs officer and a native of Newburgh, New York. Calcutta is an ancient polyglot city of commerce and political and social refuge, a city of many parts, encompassing every possible level of poverty, vice, chicanery, and culture. In Calcutta I was heavily scheduled for lectures in schools, colleges, and at the University of Calcutta. In addition I was instructed to dress in my tuxedo and attend a meeting of the English Speaking Union of Calcutta to hear a lecture by Sir Stanley Unwin, the great British publisher. Sir Stanley in his lecture followed the Shavian *My Fair Lady* theme. He paid warm tribute to the New Zealanders for their rendition of the King's English and a less warm one to the Canadians, but he came down hard on the Australians and the Americans. I was taken aback. I felt his criticism was unperceptive and unappreciative of the contributions made by all the English-speaking countries to the practical and vernacular use of the language. Perhaps in no part of the English-speaking world did English suffer more mangling than in England itself. It would be difficult to imagine a worse abuse of English than the Cockney speech heard in London. I let my nationalism fire me up, and after his speech I challenged Sir Stanley on the enormous contributions made by America to the language in both speech and written forms and in the wide world of nomenclature. His reply to me was, "My God, I did not know there was an American in the audience."

The staffs of the United States Information Service and the cultural affairs office were cordial and hospitable but, I thought, somewhat lackadaisical in making lecture arrangements. Two engagements, however, proved to be exciting. One was at an old college maintained by Hindus who had escaped Muslim ostracism in Bengal. When I arrived at the rather modest college building, I found myself in the midst of a student riot. The lecture hall was too small to seat all the students, so the professors had solved the problem by admitting the two upper classes and excluding the two lower ones. This had provoked the riot. Never before had I enjoyed the experience of seeing students rioting to hear me lecture.

I went to the university prior to my appearance there as a lecturer. The professors were cordial, but there seemed to be a nervous edginess about their relations with students. On the morning of my lecture I arrived in what seemed to be a thoroughly tranquil scene. The institution was housed in a fairly large compound of weather-beaten gray structures. I was warmly greeted by the professors, especially Professor Gupta, the senior member. He asked me to speak on the subject of research, historic publication, and major manuscript and public archives in the United States. His colleagues and students also showed an interest in these subjects. I was politely introduced to a crowded room of students and professors, I received good attention during the lecture, and questions came fast at the end. Many of the questions indicated a concern with national culture, the educational process, and national independence. There was, as I had detected elsewhere, a certain amount of aggressiveness on the part of the inquisitors. On the whole, though, I sensed a genuine desire to explore ideas in a calm and conducive academic environment.

At the end of the lecture I was accompanied out of the building by a cadre of professors. Around the entrance, a crowd of students were milling about, shouting angrily. The professors fled the scene, leaving me to face the angry mob. My driver had parked the Jeep in a most awkward and dangerous spot. At that moment I had to decide whether to flee with the professors or buck up my courage and wade through the crowd of rioting students to the Jeep. I tucked my briefcase under an arm and walked straight to the Jeep. The students parted ranks and politely allowed me to pass. Their anger apparently had been stirred by the failure of the professors to modernize the contents of their lectures and their teaching procedures. I think they had just cause for rebellion on the latter point. I was told that professors used ancient teaching notes without recognizing changes in modern educational methods.

The university was a large institution that placed major emphasis on scientific subjects. Its library was said to contain approximately 120,000 volumes and a respectable amount of manuscript material. So far as I could tell in a cursory view, the same concern existed here as I had detected in other parts of India, a desire to erase the last vestiges of the

British curriculum. Repeatedly I was either told or shown evidence of the inadequacy of teaching by rote. Many times I heard the story that a grandson could use his grandfather's notes and still be educationally current. I was constantly being presented personal cards with the individual's academic résumé inscribed on the back, occasionally with the notation "A.B. Degree, failed." I saw one that contained the legend "A.B. Degree, failed seven times." The subject had every reason to be proud; he must have set some kind of record.

It would be utter folly to claim that I learned much fundamentally about life in Calcutta and Old Bengal, or that I gathered much insight into the actual turn of mind in Calcutta or anywhere else in India. Calcutta, like London, New York, and Paris, could never be fully comprehended. Nevertheless, much of its history and individuality were revealed in its street scenes. I could stand in a lecture hall on Charinga Road and see a herd of Brahman cattle wander by, or come on a fierce-looking humped bull standing crosswise on the sidewalk chewing his cud as nonchalantly as if he were in a tree-shaded country lane. I also saw endless processions of corpses being borne to the burning vats, the social and economic condition of the departed's family being indicated by the amount of firewood used in burning the body. Many times there were only symbolic bundles of sticks for the ceremony. Then there were the ever-present pimps who offered the amicable attentions of every rank, from a high-born Hindu lady on down the scale.

Calcutta and its immediately surrounding region were populated by 3.5 million people. Perhaps the clearest testimonial to human desperation and abject poverty I saw in all of India was the throng of sleeping bodies in the streets of Calcutta and on every flat space on the bridge spanning the Hooghly River. Most of those people were fugitives from a devastating desert drought.

In many ways the time I spent in Calcutta and the mixture of audiences I addressed there proved enlightening, sometimes confusing, but always challenging. Certainly I discovered that one could have almost any experience imaginable in that city. While I was there I received a letter from Lawrence Thompson, the University of Kentucky librarian, asking me to procure some ancient manuscripts for the Special Collections division of the library. I visited the Royal Asian Society headquarters to seek advice as to where and how I might be able to purchase such materials. In the course of my conversation with the director I was invited to come and give a lecture on manuscript collections in the United States. Through this connection I was able to purchase an ancient document that had the physical earmarks of being genuine, wormholes and all. I had full confidence that the Royal Asian Society was not up to the accepted scalping practices of the public marketplace.

I think I can say with all modesty that in Calcutta I gave full measure of time and effort to my assignments. I lectured to a wide variety of audiences, talked to many people, and tried to be forthright and honest in answering literally hundreds of questions. In many instances, such as that at the University of Calcutta, I detected friction between teachers and students. I fielded questions about the future of India under the new political dispensation, religious divisions over class distinctions, and biting poverty. These questions cropped up in far greater measure than concern with communism. Sometimes I felt that my student audiences had more interest in the United States than in their homeland. I left Calcutta with a mixture of praise and criticism of the American personnel there. Many of them were hardworking and alert, but some with whom I had brief associations seemed to be taking life on the first bounce. In some instances I was forced to either make or complete details of my lecture schedule myself.

During my extensive briefing in Washington about the India tour, I had been given a multiplicity of warnings about everything from refraining from using humor in my lectures to being on guard about riding in taxicabs if there were two people in the driver's seat. I had one exciting moment in connection with the latter warning. Well before dawn on November 30, I got my baggage downstairs from my Grand Hotel room and out onto Charinga Road. There was a bearer for every piece of luggage, which exposed me to the possibility of theft. When I reached the curbside with my trail of chattering bearers, the waiting taxi had two men in the front seat. I refused to get into the car until one of them got out. There ensued a veritable babble among the bearers, the taxi drivers, and a third unidentified party waving a shotgun. It turned out that the man with the gun was the hotel doorman. Eventually he pointed the gun at the taxi occupants and the bearers, reestablishing order. He extracted the extra man from the taxi, and by the grace of God I got into the car with all my baggage accounted for. The ride in the dark to the Dum Dum Airport was both a silent and an anxious one. I had no idea whether we were on the right road or driving headlong into a den of robbers. On the way the taxi passed through Dalhousie Square and crossed the Hooghly Bridge with its great burden of refugees from the Rajasthan Desert drought. I got a bit of a thrill out of passing through the scene of the famous Sepoy Revolt of 1851–1859. I asked many people in Calcutta about the "Black Hole" growing out of the revolt and received almost universal denials that there had ever been such a thing.

That morning as I flew to Madras, I passed over country that I could discern from a fairly high altitude to be semitropical in nature. I did not realize at the time that as the plane approached the Madras area there was going on beneath me a great gathering agitating for the formation of a new state based on the local language boundaries.

My stay in Madras was too brief for me to gather more than a glimpse of the city. I was presented with a twenty-lecture schedule that was intended to take me down to the very tip of the subcontinent. I faced a rigorous test of mind and body. My first assignment was a lecture at the University in Annamalai. This town is located south of Pondicherry, a former French colony in the southeastern coastal region. The drive there led through an area of ancient temples. Shiva was very much in evidence on every hand, as were numerous other Hindu gods and mythological figures.

The winding road was bumpy in places, and there was no comfortable room for passing other vehicles. We wandered on for miles through groves of coconut and palm trees. Streams were unbridged and the driver plunged into the water nonchalantly. I cringed at every crossing out of fear that my non-English-speaking driver would have the notion that the car could part the waves at a high twain depth. Much of the country we drove through was laced with rice paddies. I was impressed with the primitive style of the farm implements being used in the rice paddies, and with the water buffalo employed as draft animals.

Annamalai University was located in a flat plain dotted with palm trees. The buildings of the university were of traditional Indian design, sturdy and adequate. I was greeted by the university vice president, a man with dignified manners. He was dressed in a white suit with a skirted coat. Deeply stamped on his forehead was a distinctive caste mark. I was received with an almost overpowering graciousness, and after a brief visit I was ushered out into the midst of the palm forest to what the English euphemistically called a guest house. The structure was a low, one-room affair with a deeply swaying bed in the front and a huge bathtub filled with algae-laden water in the back. Rudyard Kipling himself could not have imagined such a primitive room or one in a more romantic setting.

Promptly at 5:30 P.M. I went to the outdoor dining area of the university. The professors dined at a "high table," Oxford style. I was told that a special meal had been prepared for me with only a modest amount of "chilies" to add blowtorch piquancy. Even so, the food was hot enough to cauterize my entire digestive system. After the meal, which was eaten off palm leaves using fingers instead of tableware, I lectured to approximately two hundred students and faculty on a subject requested by the principal: life in twentieth-century United States. I received good attention. When I was through speaking there came a flood of questions. For more than two hours I stood on my feet answering them. Questioners always began their queries with "Don't you think . . ." Finally, at the point of near exhaustion, I violated the State Department's "briefer" and resorted to a bit of weary humor. A bowlegged student dressed in striped pajamas asked, "Don't you think there will be a war between the Great Britain and the United States?" I answered, "Yes sir, they will become embroiled over the issue of who can and who cannot make tea and scald themselves to death." That thunderclap of wisdom brought the session to a close.

When I was escorted back to my one-room palace standing alone among the palms, there hovered overhead one of the brightest full moons I had ever seen. That setting would no doubt have stirred the soul of Shiva herself. I locked my room door, undressed, and mounted the swayback bed as if I were mounting a double-humped camel. At the exact moment I got settled in that unforgettable bed, there came the most ungodly shriek I had ever heard. I literally broke out in a cold sweat. I was sure that an ancient temple god was angered at my intrusion and stood ready to behead me. Then there came a second scream, but that time I detected an animal overtone. A jackal had seated himself on the doorsill and was baying at that beautiful full moon.

On December 2, on my return trip from Chadalandrum to Madras, I had sufficient time to visit a couple of temples and got a much clearer view of many of the ancient landmarks. Soon after my return to Madras I went to the USIS office to get information about my future engagements. A change had been made in the agenda, which I regretted. Originally I had been scheduled to lecture in Cochin, almost at the tip of the Indian subcontinent, but a communist-provoked uprising in that area made it inadvisable to attempt to go there. All my other lectures were to go ahead as scheduled.

My next lecture was in Coimbatore. This center of agricultural experimental activities proved to be an exceptionally interesting place. The agricultural station was located in the midst of cotton and cane fields and rice paddies in a semitropical zone where traditional plants became perennials. Having been born and raised in the United States cotton belt, I was immediately struck by cotton stalks seven or eight feet tall, two or three growing seasons old. Ribbon or sugar cane bore blooms similar to cattails. On exhibit in the museum were samples of long-grain Louisiana and Arkansas rice. On inquiry I discovered that the cotton was one of the advanced Delta pineland varieties from Mississippi. The sugar cane was of Louisiana origin. There was also a fascinating exhibit of ancient Indian farm implements, simple types of uncertain age. Through my viewing of the seed and implement exhibits I gathered that at least a part of Indian agriculture was being lifted out of the dark ages.

I engaged in conversation with the curator of the farm exhibit, expressing my impression that India seemed to be entering an age of advanced scientific agriculture. He led me to a window that opened out onto a broad landscape of rice paddies. He said that every ounce of seed and improved chemical fertilizer and every new implement had to be transported on the backs of women treading rice paddy dikes. There were no roads, no canals, and no large or medium-sized farms. The rice paddies were too small to be managed with modern implements or to produce enough crops to be managed by modern methods of marketing.

In Coimbatore I lectured to a fairly large audience in the P.S.G. College. This struggling institution was housed in a shabby temporary building. The college derived most of its support from the P.S.G. family textile mills and from modest student fees. In that school I did get some communist party-line questions. There also for the first time a garland of heavily perfumed flowers was hung around my neck. In time there followed many other garland-hanging ceremonies.

The principal of the P.S.G. College introduced me to the school's librarian. The book collection was small, and as best I could determine contained no modern books. I was told they had no money with which to purchase current American books, and in many cases the librarian had to make abstracts of articles, especially those in scientific fields.

I lectured to a large audience in the auditorium of the Experiment Station. The audience was composed for the most part of young Indians, presumably interested in agriculture. In that gathering I discussed the process of electing a U.S. president, stimulated in part by interest in the fact that Dwight D. Eisenhower had just been elected. Questions came fast and furiously. One individual produced a clipping from a Russian newspaper describing Americans being herded to the polls to vote at the muzzle of a pistol. There were no doubt communist-leaning individuals in that south India audience. Essentially, however, I felt that Coimbatore, with its scientific and agricultural interests and the lingering influence of the coffee and tea plantations, teetered on the edge of major change in many phases of its life.

The English Club, where I was housed, was still the center of British presence in the region. I was there on a Saturday night when Englishmen came together to drink and sing the evening away. For me there was some nostalgia in listening to the old songs being sung with such gusto and in such sharp contrast to Indian music-making.

On December 7, I departed Coimbatore by early morning train to travel up the coast of the Arabian Sea to the ancient town of Calicut. This was to prove one of my most demanding assignments, and one of the most fascinating. Like so many cities and towns in India, Calicut had a distinctive character. It had once been a major port on the Arabian Sea. One of its claims to fame was the fact that Vasco da Gama had landed there in 1498, establishing the first trade route between Europe and India. Physically, Calicut was a semitropical center that produced coconuts, coir,* black pepper, cashew nuts, and some textiles. It was also a center for shipping both legal and illegal products abroad. Its harbor was filled with ancient single-masted sailing ships, a type that had sailed back and forth between Persia and India for centuries. Their masters set their sailing course unerringly by the moon and stars. This artery of trade had a tremendous impact on the art and culture of India. The sailors lived in a colony in Calicut and were surely some of the most agile humans on the globe. They climbed mastpoles as nimbly as seasoned athletes travel on land.

The area of Calicut where I was lodged in a coconut-thatched hotel was abustle with human movement around the clock. Fishermen cast their nets just off the strand, and men pushed two-wheeled carts loaded with coconuts, cashews, black pepper, tea, coffee, and coir through the streets. One night during my stay I heard a constant whine that seemed to come from some kind of winch. I went down to the strand to see what it was and found three men twisting hanks of coir fiber into strands, then twisting three strands into ropes. They told me they were making ropes for the British navy. I stood there in the bright moonlight in India witnessing a chapter of Kentucky's commercial history. The men were operating a rope walk, the same kind Kentuckians had operated in the early nineteenth century to make hemp rope and bagging. Partly because rope walks were so commonplace in Kentucky, no one had made a drawing of one. In Calicut I saw one in action.

By no means was my visit to Calicut a tourist holiday. I was well oc-

---

* A tough fiber made from the outer bark of coconuts

cupied lecturing and talking to groups of students and interested adults. As usual I was subjected to almost ceaseless questioning on every subject imaginable. One group was of particular interest. I was invited to lecture in a textile factory that had had a fatal brush with communist extremists. The audience were nearly all Parsees. The manager was a bright, dark-skinned Hindu who had miraculously survived a horrendous incident in which angry communists captured all the company officials save him and had them thrown into a roaring furnace. The rather arrogant Parsee women took me for a merry intellectual ride over the race problem in the United States. The Hindu manager finally broke into the discussion and went around asking the women if they would marry a Negro man. They answered unanimously in the negative. The manager then turned to the women and yelled, "Then shut up!" They did.

On another occasion, I fell captive to an unplanned and unexpected discussion. Bordering on physical and emotional exhaustion one day, I stripped to my shorts and took a nap. I had just fallen asleep when I was awakened by a noise in the room. When I sat up I discovered the room was filled with young people of both sexes. They came well supplied with questions about Indian-American political matters and social and cultural life in America. I was fascinated by the truly bizarre statements of some in that group. In one instance a lad spoke at length on the relevance of the writings of Jane Austen to current political conditions in the United States. I concluded that he knew little about either. This, I think, was an indication of how archaic were most of the Indian school and college curricula. This was the only occasion in my professional career when I conducted a lively philosophical discussion dressed only in my shorts. Maybe those intruding students assumed I was wearing some kind of modified dhoti, the long Hindu loincloth.

I departed Calicut on December 16 for Mangalore, traveling through interesting countryside with grand panoramas of the life of rural south India. I was met at the train in Mangalore by two young Indians who somewhat haltingly conducted me to the ubiquitous English Club. There I entered into conversation with a Scotsman who had spent several years in south India working for coffee and tea companies. At the moment there was considerable political unrest in the tip of India that bore on commerce in the region. Between swigs of beer, and before he became too intoxicated to talk, he expressed the opinion that India would never become a communist nation.

I delivered two lectures in Mangalore to alert and inquisitive audiences and was quizzed sharply about American activities in Korea, current American economic and political affairs, and the race problem. I visited one of the most revered Hindu shrines there right at the noon hour, and before I realized what was happening a Hindu acolyte sanitized me with a generous sprinkling of chopped green leaves. Mangalore was also a Catholic center in India, paying obeisance to Saint Thomas.

Three days later I made the rather long and tedious return to Coimbatore. There I was scheduled to deliver three more lectures, but even so I had time to visit a coffee-drying plant and a tea company, and once again to inspect cotton, sugar cane, and rice experimental plots.

After a few days I bade farewell to Coimbatore and began the long train ride to Bangalore. That city is well off the main line of travel and may well be considered an ancient backcountry place. I was met by Betty Winn of the USIS, who informed me that I had three lectures scheduled. The following day I met Ralph Purcell, a professor in the political science department of Emory University. His wife was from North Carolina, while Betty Winn was from Alabama. They were all hospitable, and we enjoyed a long, nostalgic conversation about the South. I delivered the three arranged lectures, each to a different type of audience. Perhaps fortunately, the last one was in a scientific college that specialized in mathematics, chemistry, and physics. My lecture was cheerfully received, the questions were well framed, and I felt capable of answering most of them. At that moment, however, my mind was beginning the long flight back to Delhi and escape from an arduous schedule of lectures and ceaseless questioning. There rang in my ears that crescendo of auditors who prefaced their questions universally with "Don't you think . . . ?"

Early on the morning of December 23 I went aboard an Air India plane to cross the length of India to Delhi. I arrived there late in the afternoon and found lodging in the Maiden Hotel, where I had begun my circuit. At that point I was physically and emotionally exhausted. Bucking up my strength and willpower that evening, I went to dinner in the hotel dining room. The management had decorated the room in what they conceived to be the appropriate Anglo-American holiday style. All around were strings of greenery and burning candles. Just after the waiter brought my meal, pandemonium broke out in the room. A candle had set the building on fire. I sat and ate my meal with the calmness of an Englishman in a country club. I discovered in that moment as the waiters leaped and screamed around me that, though Hindus and Zoroastrians expect to wind up on fire, they did not want that to happen to the Maiden Hotel.

Later I met an English lad at the hotel who was all set to take India in with a great gulp. He wore a new and freshly starched dhoti. After all my travels, I could have told him that Indians had disdain for tourists decked out in dhotis.

I discovered that Mildred McAfee Horton and her husband were registered in the Maiden Hotel. I did not know Mrs. Horton personally, but I knew of her Kentucky origins and her reputation as president of Smith College. The Hortons had just come from Ceylon, where they had made an extensive visit. Somehow they had managed to secure the services of a Jeep and a driver and invited me to accompany them to Agra to see the Taj Mahal. The drive on Christmas morning was a fascinating experience. The road was crowded in places with buffalo- and camel-drawn carts, and we got a ground-level view of life in the wayside villages. In one of them we were halted by a jam of carts and shouting Hindus. Women were plastering the walls with patties of fresh cow dung. Their smell was not exactly what we associated with Christmas.

The Taj Mahal is truly one of the most perfect architectural achievements to be found anywhere. Walking along one side of the reflecting pool leading to this breathtakingly beautiful white marble monument, I felt unreal. I could not fully grasp the beauty of the structure, much less the moving spirit of the place. It was difficult to reconcile this elegant expression of an ancient artistic culture with the binding poverty of the area in which it stood.

Almost unpublicized is nearby Fatehpur Sikri, Shah Akbar's six-teenth-century imperial capital, notable for the staggering number of horses, elephants, camels, and cattle the shah stabled there. Yet the num-bers do not obscure the beauty of marble screens and other examples of artistic craftsmanship that could turn a sheet of raw marble into a thing of enduring beauty. No wonder Sir Walter Scott found Elizabethan England's castles tawdry in comparison with Shah Akbar's palaces.

The visit to Agra and its palaces, as well as my very pleasant associa-tion with the Hortons, was a perfect winding down from my arduous exposure to India at the historic moment when it was reestablishing itself as an independent nation. In New Delhi I attended some of the New Year's Day celebrations with some of the USIS personnel and cleared all of my obligations, save one, with the office of cultural affairs. Already I had begun organizing my report for the State Department. I could not in any way claim that I had acquired deep insight into what was going on in India, nor could I be sure that I had fathomed public opinion or human reactions. What I did know were the themes and implications of the lit-erally thousands of questions asked me. No doubt there had been leading questions as to whether a totalitarian system of government was not more desirable than a democratic one. Many questions reflected a strong anti-British feeling. I looked back with a general feeling of gratefulness to those fascinating audiences I had lectured to and the individuals with whom I had had some association. On the whole the Indian and Ameri-can officials I met along the way impressed me for the diligence and ef-ficiency with which they performed their assignments. This was espe-cially true of Dr. Clifford Manschart, head of the cultural affairs program.

I left Delhi on January 3, 1953, making the return trip to Bombay. I had one more lecture before embarking for New York, Washington, and Lexington. That one was in Poona, north of Bombay, an old British sporting center as well as a base of Gandhi's activities. I went there by train from Bombay and was met by the school principal, who escorted me to the English Hotel, which had once been a center for gatherings of British sportsmen and society groups. I was taken up the river by boat, largely to see the elaborate residential structure that Gandhi had used as his headquarters. The riverside was lush and green, suggesting an extension of the English countryside. In Poona I delivered the last of at least a hundred lectures and once again was bombarded with questions. Before dawn the following morning I walked from the hotel to the railway station, most of the way stepping over sleeping bodies wrapped in the now-familiar dirty street blankets.

In Bombay I was at last on my own. Somehow—I was never certain how he located me—a wealthy businessman invited me to have lunch with him in his palatial home on Malabar Hill. His son was an engineering student in the University of Kentucky and had fallen in love with a young lady in Winchester. My host begged me to break up the affair when I returned home. He was certain that an American girl would find it impossible to adjust to the Indian marriage customs and the place of women in Indian society. I promised him I would at least look into the situation. I assured him, however, that I was not an expert at breaking up love affairs.

By January 4, 1953, I was clear of all duties for the State Department except one. The office of cultural affairs was sending two uninitiated village Hindus to the United States to make grand tours. The idea was that they would go home and spread word of their experiences. I was asked to look after them until I could deliver them in Washington.

At last I had my bags packed and found myself waiting in a room in the Taj Mahal Hotel for the departure of a Trans World Airlines flight to New York. The plane had not arrived in Bombay on time, and the pilots required twelve hours' sleeping time. The plane, however, had brought to Bombay copies of the *New York Times,* and almost the first thing I read was news of the death of Frank McVey. That was an emotional shock to me. I recalled the last time I had seen him, at the airport with my family as I departed Lexington.

As soon as I got my Hindu charges on the plane and strapped in place, I promptly went to sleep and was only partially awake when the plane landed in Geneva. I overheard a passenger ask the stewardess, "Is that man ill?" No, he was just a tired soul.

In New York, I steered my Hindu charges through immigration. Beth had come to meet me and was a bit surprised at seeing my clinging villagers. Having learned something of the Hindu way of life, I took the two young men to a cafeteria, gave each of them a spoon, and took them down the line, showing them foods they could eat that would not violate their religious principles. Neither of them had ever seen a spoon, and certainly they had seen none of the American foods or table settings. Their English was limited too. But at length I managed to get them onto a plane for Washington.

Upon my return to Lexington I completed my mission by finishing my report and mailing it to the Director of Cultural Affairs in the State Department. Sometime later I was surprised when a representative from the State Department appeared in my office and personally commended me for my service. I also received a letter from the Ford Foundation inviting me to return to India as a professor in the University of Delhi at a combined four-year salary of $81,000. I declined the invitation.

There was to be one final remarkable episode related to my India adventure. One of the village Hindus who had traveled with me to the states was a dark-skinned Caucasian. The people in Washington who arranged his tour sent him through the southern states, this in a time of high racial sensitivity. When he arrived in Lexington he literally fell into my arms with relief. He had been harshly mistreated in Mississippi and Tennessee. We took him home with us and tried to calm his anxieties. I took him to the university and introduced him to Professor Amry Vandenbosch, director of the Patterson School of Diplomacy. For some misguided reason Vandenbosch launched into a passionate denunciation of cow worship. Once again I had to pacify my abused charge, who had been brought to the United States to gain a good impression and spread the news at home.

In India I neither saw nor heard many of the things that had agitated J. Saunders Redding. I saw a lot of wrought-up people and had to answer many tough questions, but so far as I was sophisticated enough to observe, the Indians were simply living in a state of uncertainty as to what would happen after the Raj went home and a new government was in place. Too, there were internal anxieties that ranged from biting poverty and class demarcation to language partisanship. Obviously, being constantly on the move, I had no opportunity to make a capable assessment of what actually was happening. I heard a lot of talk, nevertheless. India was never again to be an unknown land for me, nor a land carrying a Kiplingesque image, or bearing the label stamped upon it so indelibly by the book detested by Indians, Katherine May's *Mother India*.

18

~

THE ROAD TO PROFESSIONALISM

As a young historian with my graduate work virtually finished in 1931, the road to becoming a professional historian was long and narrow, with many an unexpected turn. Aside from attending two meetings of the American Historical Association and one of the Mississippi Valley Historical Association during my years as a student, I had no professional attachments when I joined the faculty of the University of Kentucky in September 1931.

Joining with other historians was a vital step in the development of my career. One such organization was the Southern Historical Association, whose history paralleled my own. The SHA had rather nebulous beginnings in 1933 and held its first annual meeting in Nashville, Tennessee, in 1935. One of the sections of the program that year related to the collection and preservation of primary source materials relating to the South. Present at that meeting were James G. De Roulhac Hamilton of the University of North Carolina and William Kenneth Boyd of Duke

University, both of whom were building important southern collections in their institutions. By 1935 I had gained a good bit of experience in collecting materials for the University of Kentucky library. This meeting was the beginning of my close association with the SHA. Over the years I served on most of its committees, on its council, as president for a year beginning in 1947, and then as editor of the *Journal of Southern History* from 1948 to 1952.

My growing interest in the history of the westward frontier was also the central focus for much of the membership of the Mississippi Valley Historical Association, and I found its programs stimulating intellectually. The Association's 1931 meeting was held in Lexington in April of that year. I was then teaching in the spring quarter in the University of Tennessee. Philip Hamer, functional head of the Department of History there and an active member of the MVHA, reluctantly granted me a leave to attend the meeting. The visit to Lexington was vital to me because I was scheduled to read a paper during the meeting and, more important, to meet with President Frank L. McVey, a meeting that resulted in my being hired for the University of Kentucky history department. I read a paper again at the Association's meeting in 1933. In time I would become intimately involved in the affairs of the Association. I would serve as president for 1956–1957, then as chairman of the Executive Committee for six years, and finally as executive secretary from 1970 to 1973.

During the decade 1920–1930 the teaching and interpretation of American history underwent considerable revision, stimulated in part by the writings of Charles A. Beard and excursions into such fields as social, cultural, and economic history. These glimmers of hope for the future were dimmed by the onset of the Great Depression in 1929. Nevertheless, in good times and bad, the personal associations among historians survived. Each annual meeting brought into clear focus the human panorama of American history. Trusted benchmarks in the progress of American civilization were the faces, young and old, of scholars who had pioneered in special areas of interest. It was in the meetings of the MVHA that I came into close contact with the generation of historians preceding my own. I often found the lobby gossip more enlightening than the papers presented in the formal programs. Then there was the younger generation of laborers in the vineyard who, like stalwart second-growth trees of the forest, were advancing the discipline. In the background was the somewhat faceless crowd of young Depression-spawned waifs like myself, who stood humbly in the presence of such a gathering of elders.

Those were days when convivial clusters of members met in hotel rooms in delightful, if not always intellectually stimulating, sessions. Herbert Keller of the McCormick Historical Association was a master party-giver, and to be his guest was a memorable experience. Both humor and serious scholarly concern emerged. On occasion a full evening of the annual program was devoted to storytelling. In the Cincinnati meeting in 1935, for example, those master yarn-spinners Carl Wittke and E. E. Dale made their audience forget the serious concerns of American history for the moment.

There was an essence of both professorial dignity and social gaiety about the annual dinner that preceded each year's presidential address. Presiding officers repeated their recently filched after-dinner stories, and many presidential introductions rivaled the most eloquent country newspaper obituaries in their flowery commendations. The dinners gave those members able to rustle up two dollars for a ticket an opportunity to gossip, to bemoan, and to learn what was happening on the other fellow's campus. These were also occasions when the Association paid tribute to some of its elder statesmen.

Not all, however, was sweet professional fellowship where brothers and sisters met in harmony. Occasionally weeds of discord sprang up in the garden of common endeavor. There were thoroughly personal clashes that stemmed from such varied sources as rivalries for prestigious jobs, angular book reviews, jealousies over graduate students' idolatry, and just plain professional enmity. For those not directly involved, these clashes spiced lobby conversation. Departmental rows invariably erupted and spilled over into the public domain to become precious bits of gossip to be taken home and spread around as academic news. Probably no departmental row in the years 1930–1945 escaped attention at the annual meetings. In like manner, members noted when certain young scholars had mounted lightning rods of ambition.

In making a plea many years later for a change of the Association's name, Paul Wallace Gates said that under a more comprehensive title the organization could have greater political impact. In light of this statement I never look at the monumental and indispensable *Territorial Papers of the United States,* ably edited by Clarence E. Carter, without recalling the arduous struggle to get them prepared and published. Each year Milo M. Quaife of the Detroit Public Library lashed his yeomen correspondents into extracting commitments from their congressmen to support the Carter project. I kept Congressman Virgil Chapman of the old Ashland District constantly nettled for the cause. Quaife spurred his troops onward with one boot and used the other to keep the editor spurred on to accomplish his work. The fact that Congress supported the *Territorial Papers* project was a tribute to both the former editor of the *Mississippi Valley Historical Review* and the Association. Other historical causes were morally supported by the Association and its tireless Committee on Historic Sites.

A cardinal moment in the Association's history came as the nation was being drawn into World War II. Some people wondered how much American history their fellow citizens knew. The *New York Times* published a shattering answer to this query in the results of its polls; most Americans, it found, knew far too little to wander safely out on Main Street alone. As usual in a moment of national humiliation, there was a search for a scapegoat; this time it was the teachers of history. A special committee was named to work jointly with a committee from the American Historical Association to explain the disastrous results of the *Times* findings and to seek remedies. The findings of the joint committee were published in a slender book, and at the annual meeting in St. Louis in 1944 the report was discussed in a plenary session and in the Executive Committee meeting. Most persons present were aware that several prominent newspaper reporters were in attendance, and they realized their remarks might receive wide publicity. Never before had reporters found the sessions of the Association so newsworthy. No one was more

After his retirement from teaching, Clark undertook a second and equally significant career as an unofficial but much honored "public historian," lecturing widely, advising Kentucky's legislators and governors, and serving as advocate for a host of progressive causes, in addition to writing a continuous stream of books. In 2004 the American Historical Association lauded him as a "model historian, leader, advocate, teacher, and person [who] continues to remind us what historians should be, and what they should do." In appreciation of his many contributions to Kentucky, the General Assembly in 1990 named Clark the Commonwealth's first and only Historian Laureate for Life.

(Above) Honors of many sorts were showered on Clark in his post-retirement years. In October 1984 Governor Martha Layne Collins presented Clark with the Governor's Medal for Distinguished Service, the highest honor the Commonwealth bestows. She lauded him for his dedication to preserving Kentucky's public records, for his contributions as teacher and historian, and for enabling Kentucky's citizens to better understand their heritage. (Kentucky Department for Libraries and Archives) (Below) Clark's accomplishments as teacher and scholar were recognized with honorary doctorates, nine in all. He is seen here at Indiana University in 1978 with IU president John Ryan (center) and fellow honorees (from left) Tracy Sonneborn, John Edward Horner, and Henry Radford Hope.

(Above) Clark instilled in his students a sense of the importance of history as a guide to the future. Many went on to achieve notable careers in public life. Here Clark discusses educational issues with former student Robert Sexton, executive director of the Prichard Committee for Academic Excellence. The committee's efforts, strongly aided by Clark, played an important role in bringing about the Kentucky Education Reform Act of 1990. (Below) Clark's close ties with former student Edward "Ned" Breathitt Jr., a 1948 UK graduate, were especially long lived. Clark sparked Breathitt's interest in politics while Breathitt was a student and lived to see him serve as one of Kentucky's most progressive governors, 1963–1967.

(Above) From his earliest years in Kentucky, Clark personally rescued neglected records of state and county governments from destruction or decay. The 1982 completion of a modern home for those records in Frankfort was the culmination of his efforts. Here Clark and Edna M. Milliken of the State Archives staff celebrate the Archives' move into their new quarters. (Kentucky Department for Libraries and Archives) (Below) Bobby Falwell's striking sculpture, made of wood from Clark's eastern Kentucky woodlands, served as backdrop as members of the State Archives and Records Commission, Friends of Kentucky Public Archives, and other officials celebrated the tenth anniversary of the State Archives building in 1992. Left to right are state archivist Richard Belding, John Duncan, Clark, Elizabeth "Libby" Jones (wife of Governor Brereton Jones), Jack Ellis, Paul Coates, Porter Harned, and Ken Colebank.

(Above) In 1992 Clark addressed the assembled dignitaries at the Archives' tenth anniversary celebration. He had been the prime mover behind enactment of the State Archives and Records Act of 1958 and a member of the Archives and Records Commission from that time until his death in 2005. In 1993 he was honored with the J. Franklin Jameson Award for Archival Advocacy from the Society of American Archivists. (Below) Not content with construction of the Archives building, Clark continued to work tirelessly on behalf of Kentucky's public records. In 1996, he led Governor Paul Patton, his wife, Judi Patton, and leaders of the state legislature on a tour of the Archives building to demonstrate the need for additional storage space.

Clark's long nurturing of the University of Kentucky Press culminated in 1968–1969, when he oversaw its transformation into a statewide consortium, the University Press of Kentucky. In November 1988, the Press's new home was named for Clark. Beth Clark cut the official ribbon. At left is Press director Kenneth Cherry. (*Lexington Herald-Leader*)

As the first recipient of the Henry Clay Medallion in 1993, Clark thereafter made the annual presentation to other recipients, including Supreme Court Associate Justice Sandra Day O'Connor in 1996. The medallion, presented by the Henry Clay Memorial Foundation, is awarded to "an individual whose life and work reflect many of the admirable characteristics of its namesake, Henry Clay." Clark was also instrumental in obtaining funding for publication of Clay's papers, a thirty-three-year project.

(Above) Beth Clark's death in July 1995, after sixty-two years of marriage, left her husband "mired in almost overpowering loneliness." In November 1996, at age ninety-three, Clark remarried. His new wife was Loretta Gilliam Brock, a talented musician and watercolorist who had also lost her spouse in 1995. Their marriage, Clark wrote, was "one of those turns of fortune that give fundamental meaning and spice to life." (Photo by Joe Murphy) (Below) In the fall of 1997, Clark took his new wife to meet his remaining siblings in Mississippi: left to right, Ethel, Ernest, Wilma, Tom, and Marvin. The family's longevity has attracted the attention of medical scientists at Harvard and Boston Universities. (Photo by Loretta Clark)

(Above) On June 1, 1992, Kentucky celebrated the bicentennial of statehood. Most significant of the events held across the state was publication of *The Kentucky Encyclopedia,* for which Clark was an associate editor and the author of many entries. The first printing sold out in less than a day. At the Kentucky Book Fair in November 1992, a long line of admirers sought Clark's autograph. (*Lexington Herald-Leader*)

(Below) Over the course of his life as historian and writer, Clark's papers grew to enormous proportions. During his later decades he presented more than four hundred boxes filled with his notes, photographs, and a variety of other items to the University of Kentucky library. At a dedicatory ceremony in October 1992, Clark shakes hands with UK president Charles Wethington, as William Marshall, director of Special Collections, looks on. (University of Kentucky Special Collections and Digital Programs)

Throughout his seventy-five years in the state, Clark was one of the staunchest supporters of the University of Kentucky library, most significantly through his lifelong quest for materials for the Special Collections Department. His energy and prestige were significant also in the campaign for the William T. Young Library and later, as at left, in the library development campaign of 1997.

Clark's 1937 *History of Kentucky* remained the benchmark study of the Commonwealth for six decades. In 1997 he was pleased to pass the torch to leading historians of a younger generation, state historian James C. Klotter (center) and Lowell Harrison (right), professor emeritus of history at Western Kentucky University. Their *New History of Kentucky* became the new standard, taking advantage of many documentary materials that Clark himself had rescued from oblivion.

(Above) As the 1990s advanced, another of Clark's dreams approached reality, a fitting home in Frankfort for the collections of the Kentucky Historical Society. Brereton Jones, governor 1991–1995, and his wife, Libby Jones, worked closely with Clark to win the support of the state senate for construction of the Kentucky History Center. (Below) In the as-yet-uncompleted History Center, Clark looks over the beginnings of the terrazzo map that would adorn the Center's lobby, showing Kentucky's 120 counties. (*Lexington Herald-Leader*)

(Above) After years of planning, the Kentucky History Center was dedicated on April 10, 1999. Gathered for the ribbon-cutting were, front row, left to right: Kevin Graffagnino, director of the Historical Society; Lieutenant Governor Steve Henry; Clark; Kentucky First Lady Judi Patton; Libby Jones, wife of former governor Brereton Jones; former governor Jones; and Governor Paul Patton. The History Center now serves as the setting for a wide variety of events centering on Kentucky's past and present and looking toward its future. (Below) Clark sits with other members of the Kentucky Historical Society Foundation Board in 2002 in front of the bust of Abraham Lincoln at the History Center. Clark rejoiced that, within the Center's collections, "future generations . . . will have in place a rich documentation of the past."

History enthusiasts of all ages gathered in downtown Lexington in August 2002 to salute the promise of another historical center. A plaque in the museum characterizes Clark as the "father" of the institution, "a man of the soil . . . of the mind . . . of action . . . of words," but "most of all . . . a man of the people." (Photo by David Cronen; courtesy of the Lexington History Museum)

Clark's popularity as a public speaker kept him on the road for decades. His mastery of Kentucky history enabled him to speak extemporaneously on almost any occasion. In 2004 he spoke at the reopening of the historic Cumberland Gap trail, newly rebuilt to the contours of the ancient Indian and buffalo path through which thousands of early settlers had crossed into Kentucky. That speech, he recalled, "reached deep into my emotions. . . . I felt I was taking part in the opening of a new chapter in American frontier history." (Cumberland Gap National Historic Park)

(Above) Clark's one hundredth birthday on July 14, 2003, was celebrated with several gatherings of dignitaries, former students, and hosts of admirers. At a gala party at the University of Kentucky's William T. Young Library, the Clarks, flanked by UK President and Mrs. Lee Todd, cut the cake. (*Lexington Herald-Leader*) (Below) Four generations of the Clark family sat for a portrait on Clark's hundredth birthday. From left to right, front row, are son Bennett Clark; his wife, Alice; Loretta and Tom Clark; daughter Elizabeth Clark Stone; and her husband, Richard Stone. In the back row are grandchildren, their spouses, and great-grandchildren.

To the end of his life, Clark remained the productive scholar. He is seen here tapping out his final book on the manual typewriter with which he often declared himself to be "simpatico." He never made the shift to computers. (*Lexington Herald-Leader*)

In 2002, at the age of ninety-nine, Clark coauthored with Margaret Lane *The People's House,* a book exploring the history of the Kentucky governors' mansions and the lives of those who had lived in them. It was to be the last book published in his lifetime. By then he had long since become the beloved "people's historian." (*Lexington Herald-Leader*)

Even as he approached the century mark, Clark never lost his curiosity, his enthusiasm for life, his infectious smile, or the twinkle in his eye. (Photo by Ed Houlihan)

After his remarriage, Clark moved to his new wife's home on Lexington's Kentucky Avenue. In spite of continuing writing projects and speaking requests, he found quiet moments in the garden to reflect on the accomplishments of his long career. "I have found both intellectual and spiritual satisfaction in the profession of historian," he wrote. (Photo by Loretta Clark)

On July 9, 2005, five days short of what would have been Clark's 102nd birthday, dignitaries and hundreds of admirers gathered in Frankfort to celebrate the renaming of the Kentucky History Center for the man who had so long dreamed of and fought for its creation. As the new name was unveiled, staff members of the Kentucky Historical Society tossed their hats into the air and a band played "My Old Kentucky Home." Thomas D. Clark died on June 28, less than two weeks before, but his spirit lives on in the hearts of his fellow Kentuckians.

concerned about the possible publicity than Clara S. Paine, secretary-treasurer of the Association, who for some reason feared that an interloper might get into the meetings of the Executive Committee. In the subsequent discussions, although they were provocative and at times convincing, little more was resolved than the obvious fact that large segments of the American people lacked formal knowledge of their history.

Clara Paine was as devoted as a human being could be to the welfare of the Association. She helped run decorous meetings and had the personal bearing to lift the most commonplace affair to one of gentility. Long and hard experience enabled her to act at all times in the best interest of the organization. This I learned positively on one occasion. I was sitting in my office on a hot afternoon in the late summer of 1943, trying to unravel some of the insufferable problems of the Army Specialized Training Program in history, when my phone rang. A highly exercised Charles Ambler, president of the Association, asked, "What in hell if anything have you done about the program?"—meaning our planned joint meeting in December with the American Historical Association. I had done nothing; that was the first time I had been told that I had any such responsibility. Ambler gave me a peremptory order to begin at once to find the best speaker possible, adding that money for an honorarium was no problem. He jolted me so hard that I forgot the ASTP and the war. I had to find a top-flight speaker, and at once. In my moment of shock, I called the British Embassy and asked if it might be possible that Lord Halifax, British ambassador to the United States, would accept an invitation to address a gathering of American historians. His Lordship accepted so readily that I wondered if I had in fact reached the British Embassy. Aglow with instant success, I called Ambler to tell him I had a blue-ribbon speaker and asked how much the Association would be able to present as an honorarium. I had read the financial reports of the organization, and I knew the money could not come from the accounts that were published. I thought perhaps some gracious donor had established a separate account of which I knew nothing.

Ambler told me that he would have to speak with Clara Paine about the money. Within a half hour she was on the phone, setting me straight about the hard economic facts. We would not pay even King George V an honorarium, and I had better get busy and undo my arrangements. If ever there was a benighted former program chairman on whom the gods smiled, it was I. First, the annual meeting was canceled because of restrictions on wartime travel; then the Churchill government called Lord Halifax back to London. I regretted that it took an international crisis to pull me out of a hole, but I was relieved that the problem was so amicably resolved.

As chairman of the program committee for the Cedar Rapids meeting in 1943, I found it difficult to organize even a curtailed program. By April of that year wartime travel had become both difficult and uncertain. In peacetime the largest hotel in Cedar Rapids could not have accommodated the members of the Association, but in this year it could by straining its facilities to the utmost. The Association was deeply indebted to Torch Press of Cedar Rapids, which printed the *Mississippi Valley Historical Review,* and to its generous manager, Ed Misack, who was instrumental in bringing the convention to Cedar Rapids. Many times the Press had waited for payment of the Association's printing bills, and Misack proved to be a genuinely devoted friend. For years he had been a fixture at the meetings, always in the hotel lobbies greeting members. Loyalty and gratitude to Misack apparently kept convention officials from investigating local hotel accommodations. It made little difference anyway because the membership that attended could probably have bedded down in a half dozen large rooms. In fact, we knew so little about the headquarters hotel that I could print only a general location for many of the sessions. Program in hand, I endeavored to extract from a harassed hotel manager information about rooms where sessions might be held. Misack was of no immediate help. His notion of a successful meeting was that it be "well-watered," but Iowa was dry. When we arrived in Cedar Rapids, he was in St. Louis rustling up a supply of liquor to be run contraband over the dry sands of the Corn Belt.

That annual meeting was one of the best I ever attended. Good academic neighbors made up for the shortcomings, and the sessions were enlivened by Misack's generous hospitality. Not all was jollity, however, in those serious wartime days. There I heard Dwight Dumond, in his deepest sepulchral Methodist-circuit-rider intonation, predict that the Association would never hold another meeting. In fact, he was positive that civilization itself was tottering toward its certain end.

Resolutions at the business meetings each year were as vital as bridal bouquets at weddings. If Milo Quaife was not ready with one, then Jeannette Nichols would offer one designed to spur congressmen, the Librarian of Congress, and the Archivist of the United States on to greater and nobler efforts in history's behalf. With some regularity Grace Lee Nute, longtime chairman of the Alvord Memorial Commission, would ask the Association to help free records vital to her fur-trade research. Everett Dick, a longtime and diligent chairman of the Historic Sites Committee, was ever ready with resolutions soliciting public responsibility in this area. Prior to 1950 nothing much more vigorous was passed than votes of thanks to local arrangement committees. Times changed, however, and business meetings, like the content of the programs, began to reflect historians' deeper public concerns. In the postwar years controversial subjects such as the excesses of the House Un-American Activities Committee and the vicious antics of the McCarthy investigations inspired resolutions.

An issue of fundamental social readjustment came before the Association in the early 1950s—racial desegregation. Almost from the beginning of the Association, slavery and abolition, Reconstruction policies, and lynching had been subjects of sectional programs. Individual members entertained pronounced feelings on the subject of race. Scholars such as Dwight Dumond, Avery O. Craven, Howard K. Beale, and Frank L. Owsley were often poles apart in their views. Annual meetings often featured fiery statements and equally fiery rejoinders on the subject of race.

Following World War II, the race issue assumed new dimensions. The Truman policy of desegregating the armed forces, various court cases that gave blacks access to the polls in the Lower South, and the landmark decisions in college admission cases made changes more deep-seated than some members of the Executive Committee seemed to realize. States, cities, and hotels became targets of racial crusaders. Tulane University had been exceedingly generous in support of the *Review*. In 1950 Wendell H. Stephenson, chairman of the Tulane University history department and editor of the *Mississippi Valley Historical Review*, invited the MVHA to hold its annual meeting in New Orleans sometime in the future. Doubtless few of the Executive Committee members were aware of the near fanatical segregationist attitude that prevailed in parts of Louisiana. After Stephenson's invitation had been accepted, there occurred considerable comment in the public press about racial discrimination in the South, and as a result some members raised the issue of the Association's meeting in an atmosphere of flagrant discrimination. Almost immediately it became urgent that a racial policy be promulgated in keeping with the changing times.

In its meeting in Cincinnati in 1951, the Executive Committee all but paralyzed itself in a discussion of the prospects of meeting in New Orleans. To solve its dilemma a special committee was appointed with Carl Wittke, dean of liberal arts at Oberlin College, as chairman. The committee was charged with devising a policy that would satisfy a majority of the members. Wittke was liberal-minded and capable of forthright action and blunt expression of his personal views. Sometime early in the spring he became disgusted by an apparent lack of intellectual courage on the part of some members of the Executive Committee. He waited until just before the annual meeting in Chicago in April 1952 to prepare his straightforward report. He either could not or would not attend the annual meeting. He sent me the report with instructions to read it to the Executive Committee in the dullest singsong voice.

The Wittke report recommended that the Association accept no invitation to meet in a city or hotel that discriminated against any member. When I appeared before the Executive Committee, I was startled to learn that it had anticipated Wittke's report and had already approved a less positive racial policy—a serious blunder, in my opinion. Nothing was settled by this precipitate action, and the dissension continued. It was resolved, somewhat apologetically, that the issue be studied further, and a small committee was asked to undertake once again the task of resolving the issue and reporting to the Executive Committee the following April. The committee consisted of Dumond, the chairman of the Executive Committee, and myself.

That summer a meticulously worded proposition was prepared and sent to members in the form of a postcard ballot. It asked for a "yes" or "no" response to a policy desegregating all of the Association's activities, including places and facilities for future meetings. A few bitter-enders wrote caustic comments on their ballots, and there was an outcry from some reincarnated William Lloyd Garrison in a Wisconsin state college who wept in anguish, largely because the card bore a Lexington, Kentucky, postmark. In the end, the vote stood at 673 "yes" and 567 "no."

I had submitted my report at an earlier meeting of the Executive Committee, and it had been approved for circulation with the ballot. I reported the final vote to the general business meeting in Madison, Wisconsin, on April 23, 1954, less than a month before the United States Supreme Court rendered its historic *Brown v. Board of Education* decision. There was little discussion of the new policy from the floor, and it was ratified without a show of emotion.

The new policy was largely the one outlined in the Wittke report. At the meeting there was a mild remonstrance against the Executive Committee for having allowed the discussion of future meeting places to become disputatious. The general membership appeared to be more advanced in its racial attitudes than were the members of the Executive Committee. There was a plea for renewed solidarity and cordiality within the Association and for an end to internal wrangling.

The wounds inflicted over the New Orleans rejection remained somewhat raw and painful. It became necessary to placate some members as well as Tulane University. Stephenson, a conscientious Hoosier Quaker, was placed in a difficult situation. Personally and philosophically, he no doubt favored desegregation, but at that time he was a realist living in militantly segregationist Louisiana.

Actually, racial desegregation of the annual meetings had occurred before the Madison, Wisconsin, action. The Executive Committee felt that an attempt should be made to meet south of the Ohio River. It asked me, as the working member of the second racial policy committee, to determine if the 1953 meeting could be held in a Kentucky city. The Southern Political Science Association and the Southern Sociological Association had already held limited desegregated meetings in Atlanta under heavily insulated social conditions. These experiments, however, did not exercise so full a policy as that proposed by the Association for its 1953 meeting. I opened conversations with the managers of the two major hotels in Lexington, one privately owned, the other controlled by a northern chain. The manager of the chain hotel was adamant—no blacks would be entertained either as lodgers or as dining room guests. But Len Shouse and his son, owners of the Lafayette Hotel, thought the idea over and concluded that inevitably they would soon have to desegregate, and this seemed to be a safely controlled occasion for them to start. During the Association's meeting the Shouses were hospitable but anxious. A few crusty old permanent residents growled, but the managers received many letters commending them for their courage and foresight, and that quieted the growling. The Shouses told me later that they were happy they had made the decision to desegregate their hotel, really a pioneering move in the South. I am not aware that there was ever again an objection to the Association's meeting in the South because of racial discrimination. I actually had more difficulty over a conflict with racing dates in Lexington than with segregation.

I wish I could write that all parts of the meeting in Lexington went off as smoothly as the desegregation experiment. Out of this meeting came one of the most embarrassing and ticklish incidents in the Association's history. The acting secretary-treasurer asked me to make a financial settlement before I had an opportunity to balance my accounts. The burden of registration and local arrangements had fallen largely upon Mary Elizabeth Billington and me. She almost single-handedly collected the money, issued meal tickets,. and gave out information. Our cash receipts and canceled tickets were locked away in the hotel's safety vault. In order to relieve the unseemly anxiety of the secretary-treasurer, I gave him my personal check in the amount of $650 with the understanding that it was a sort of bond to be held in escrow until I could render a full accounting of the funds in my hands. He took my check and literally dived into his car and roared away to Oklahoma City. Within a week my bank called me to say I had an overdraft. The same day I received a hand-written and interminable letter from Dwight Dumond in which the an-gry chairman of the Executive Committee asked me to give him an im-mediate rendering of my account and to hold on to all funds because he had discovered that the acting secretary-treasurer was in default in his management of Association funds. For the next year I was involved fi-nancially in this unhappy mess, which soon became a matter of whis-pered gossip. The accounts of the Association were audited by Philip G. Johnson, CPA, of Lincoln, Nebraska, and the chairman made a veiled report to the Executive Committee at its December meeting in 1954. There were innumerable complaints about subscriptions to the *Review* and other matters pertaining to its distribution. This was a sad case of a single prodigal act casting an unwarranted shadow on the noble prede-cessors whose very names were synonymous with that of the Association. Eventually the incident was resolved in full honor, but not without leav-ing a scar.

Just as expansion and change characterized the colleges and universi-ties represented in the membership list, the Association itself was sub-jected to impulses of change that it could not ignore. There now hangs in the office of the Executive Secretary in Bloomington a panel of portraits of former presidents of the Association and of the Organization of American Historians, the successor to the MVHA. Portraits of editors and secretaries adorn the walls of the board room, and along with these there is a group picture of the 1909 meeting in St. Louis. These photo-graphs portray nearly a century of common professional interest and fra-ternal association by a significant body of American historians. They also reflect a tremendous advancement on a major intellectual frontier. Among those portrayed are the authors of major studies in varied fields of special interest and some truly fine scholarly statesmen.

The small coterie of founders of the Mississippi Valley Historical As-sociation believed their fledgling organization to be a rib from the side of the American Historical Association. A feeling nevertheless prevailed that at least some of the Valley historians were not as cordially received by the older organization as their scholarly attainments merited. Too, there lay about them rich, unexplored areas of regional and national history. There were documentary collections to be gathered into libraries, and libraries themselves to be organized. Universities and colleges were to be stimulated in the organization of departments of history and in devising history curricula. The name "Mississippi Valley Historical Association" had fitted aptly the needs of both the region and its historians in the first decades of the twentieth century.

The Association's most distinctive contribution was its impact on the organization and enlargement of departments of history, on the teaching of history, and on the creation of a widespread awareness of the subject among laymen. The expansion of libraries and archives, the writing and publication of hundreds of articles and monographs, and the success of the *Review* were tangible evidence of the Association's achievements. By 1940 the *Mississippi Valley Historical Review* had achieved a secure reputation as a scholarly journal under the editorship of innovative and dedicated historians.

Yet with all these accomplishments, the Association and the *Review* seemed to be handicapped by their regional designation. Moreover, phenomenal changes and expansion had occurred in the fields of historical research and writing. The name of the Association, said some younger historians, had become too restrictive in its implications. The prospect of changing the name of the Association had surfaced on several occasions in the latter years of the Great Depression and during the war, and with the suggestions came outbursts of sentiment and resistance. After 1945 it became clear to perceptive scholars that although the Association had served magnificently as a broad regional body of scholars, there was a compelling need for a fundamental realignment of scope and purpose.

At the annual meeting in St. Louis in 1944, Paul Angle, chairman of the Committee on Policy, discussed the change of names with the Executive Committee, but his report was filed away. Six years later Paul Wallace Gates was appointed chairman of a special committee to consider changing the names of both the Association and the *Review*. Gates made a preliminary report on the subject at the Cincinnati meeting in April 1951. Discussion of this question was given considerable publicity in the September issue of the *Review* that year. John D. Barnhart argued strongly against any change, concluding that if some members wanted a national association, let them organize one. Harold Bradley of the Claremont Graduate School said that both names were respected by historians everywhere, and he doubted that a break with tradition would be wise. He appealed to sentiment, saying it was appropriate that the Association that had become the major body of American historians had originated in the Great Valley. Gates agreed that the Association enjoyed national status, but argued that agencies such as the accrediting associations, the newly formed Council of American Learned Societies, the foundations, and others still seemed to regard it as a regional society. He believed a change in title for the *Review* would attract articles of higher quality and that a broader national name would give the organization a more secure base from which to solicit national political support for projects from Congress and the foundations. He suggested substituting the subtitle *Journal of American History* for the *Review*.

The Gates committee plodded through the mire of sentimentality and semantics, searching for a new name for the organization. Its difficulty was revealed in the six proposals that I submitted: "The Mississippi Valley Historical Association," "The Society for American History," "The Association for American History," "The National Historical Society," and the "Association of American Historians." To compound their dilemma the committee prepared, largely under the dictates of the Executive Committee, a complicated ballot that promised almost instant confusion and defeat. Although I never saw the final count, I am certain that no proposed new title received a major preferment.

The name-change issue was still hanging fire when I completed my six-year term as chairman of the Executive Committee in 1963. I was given the onerous task of serving as chairman of the newly formed Committee on the Future of the Association. At the time, three or four things seemed urgent if the Association was to fulfill its larger scholarly commitments. The title of the *Review* had to imply broader national emphasis. The perennial issue of pleasing the national accrediting bodies remained unresolved. Many librarians seemed not to be attracted by the *Review,* there were few international subscribers, and revenue from advertising was meager. At the midwinter meeting with the American Historical Association in Philadelphia in December 1963, the Committee on the Future met and, at the urging of Oscar Winther, adopted the *Review*'s subtitle, *Journal of American History,* as its main title—the name Gates had proposed in 1951. This time the popular vote favored the change.

The change of the *Review*'s title was in fact the concluding one in a series of changes. There was a certain timeliness connected with the beginning of the new era. The Torch Press had earlier reported that it could no longer produce a journal of top graphic quality. An emergency meeting of the Executive Committee took place in June 1962 to select a new printer for the *Review* and to discuss further the search for a new editor and sponsoring institution. A printing contract was entered into with the George Banta Company at this meeting, and on December 28, 1962, arrangements were confirmed with Indiana University to sponsor the *Review,* with Oscar Winther as editor and Chase C. Mooney as associate editor. In June 1963 the new group published its first issue.

The year 1963 and the early months of 1964 passed with no one having solved the nagging riddle of the organization's title. We had to come up with a national name distinctive enough to avoid confusion with those of the American Historical Association and the Society of American Historians. On April 29, 1964, I drove through a dreary, cold Ohio Valley predawn morning over the frightful old Highway 25 from Lexington, Kentucky, to board a plane at the Cincinnati airport, en route to the annual meeting of the Association in Cleveland. Twin worries nagged me that morning—poor driving conditions on narrow winding roads crowded with semitrailer trucks, and the fact that I had no name to propose to the Executive Committee. By the time I reached Florence on the outskirts of the Cincinnati airport my duodenal ulcer had me in tears. I stopped in a greasy-spoon restaurant for milk and realized the time had come to make a desperate effort to come up with some kind of a name, acceptable or rotten; I had to take something to Cleveland. By the time I reached the meeting, I had settled on "The Organization of American Historians." If nothing else could be said for it, there was no confusion of titles, even if it lacked something in euphony.

Before appearing at the Executive Committee, I once more had to placate my ulcer. I went into a coffee shop near the entrance to the Statler-Hilton Hotel, where I overheard a waitress ask her co-worker, "What is the Mississippi Historical Society doing meeting in Cleveland?" This at the moment when Mississippi and Governor Ross Barnett, in particular, were all but making the name of that state anathema in the desegregation fight. Before I presented my suggested new name to the Executive Committee, I repeated what the waitress had said. When I did offer the new name, Gates, chairman of the earlier committee, rolled this one on his tongue and came out with the abbreviation "OAH." He moved its adoption, and Joe B. Frantz, a new member of the Executive Committee, seconded the motion. Craven, the oldest member of the Association present, seemed to want to debate the motion, but good-humoredly acceded to the change.

Within an hour after its adoption by the Executive Committee, everybody knew about the name change. The Committee on the Future of the Association was instructed to prepare a postcard ballot. The vote was favorable, and Billington presided over a plenary corporate session in April 1965. On that occasion I sat beside James L. Sellers of the University of Nebraska, the unofficial historian of the MVHA, knowing that he was under genuine emotional stress. When we left the meeting, he said, "What a shock it would have been to Mrs. Paine." She had died in Florida the previous month. I shared some of Sellers's nostalgia and reservation, for the MVHA had been a part of my own "growing up," and for hundreds of its members it symbolized rich professional experiences.

By 1965 the location of a national headquarters had become a matter of some urgency. The Nebraska Historical Society had been exceedingly generous in support of the Association for more than a half century. From its offices in Lincoln, Clarence and Clara Paine, James Olson, and William D. Aeschbacher had served most effectively as secretary-treasurers. But by now the OAH had definitely outgrown its dependence on such a generous cooperative affiliation. Aeschbacher had accepted the directorship of the Dwight D. Eisenhower Library in the summer of 1963 and moved from Lincoln to Abilene, Kansas, leaving behind some of the Organization's files, and later he moved to the University of Utah, where he gave up the office of secretary after many years of devoted and meticulous service. He was succeeded by Charles Peterson, then by David E. Miller and Dorothy Mortensen, each of whom did yeoman service in keeping the Organization functioning. In his annual report for 1969–1970, Miller gave ample proof that some decisive action had to be taken to consolidate the affairs of the Organization in a unified headquarters.

I had been completely separated from the administration of the Organization since 1965 when, in the fall of 1969, Martin Ridge came to my office (I was then teaching in Indiana University) and asked if I would consider accepting appointment as executive secretary of the OAH. Leo Solt, chairman of the Indiana University history department, also urged me to accept the appointment. I could hardly refuse, since as chairman of the Executive Committee and then of the Committee on the Future, I had argued the need to establish a permanent and independent national headquarters. Since the name change, this seemed to be even more imperative. Indiana University agreed to support the establishment of a national headquarters near the *Journal*'s editorial offices, and in January 1970 I began the arduous task of organizing the headquarters. I operated for a time from the corner of an already overloaded work table in Lindley Hall. In the meantime Indiana University was negotiating for the purchase of an 1840s Georgian residence on North Bryan Street. Chancellor Herman B. Wells had expressed to me his keen desire for us to have the house. Fortunately the sale was completed and we moved the office late in the spring of 1970. The house was still cluttered with family belongings, and we were under a near mandate not to disturb an attic lined with "pet" bats, a request we quickly ignored when one of the staff members looked down and saw a bat clinging to her skirt. We immediately had the house fumigated.

Chancellor Wells gave further support to the Organization by purchasing several pieces of early American furniture, using his personal funds. We were able to furnish the downstairs in the period of the house by ransacking university warehouses for odds and ends of office furniture. Among the treasures given us were "Daddy" James A. Woodburn's oaken rolltop desk, a symbol of a half century of the Indiana history department; a stately leather-upholstered Victorian desk chair used by John Foster when he was secretary of state and then by his grandson John Foster Dulles; and an overstuffed swivel chair used by R. Carlyle Buley when he wrote his Pulitzer Prize–winning *Old Northwest*. Salvaged from the recesses of a warehouse was a handsome Victorian whatnot to grace the entry hall. With the house we inherited a legend that later became a nuisance. Sometime in the dark past a rumor had been set afloat that the house had been a station on the Underground Railroad. As a result, the house constantly attracted visitors who insisted on seeing the dungeon and secret doors. If there ever was a runaway slave or a secret passage in the house, evidence of their presence had long been obliterated.

Thus in April 1970, with a stately house, a legend, and physical disorganization, we began a new chapter in the history of the Organization of American Historians. I was blessed in being able to employ a loyal and industrious staff, most of whom had never heard of the OAH. Ingrid Winther Scobie, however, had just completed work for her doctorate in history at the University of Wisconsin, and I employed her as associate secretary. She proved to be an excellent organizer who deserves great credit for solving a multitude of problems. Jane Wines, previously employed by Dow Jones in its Washington office, contributed valuable accounting experience. She and Jeanette Chafin organized the books, billing procedures, and monthly reports. One of the luckiest personnel finds was Patricia Dyszkiewicz, who tackled the addressograph jungle of membership lists with the bloodthirstiness of a big-game hunter. In a reasonably short time she reduced the number of protests that came with each day's mail. In the late spring of 1970, Scobie and Wines went to Salt Lake City and shipped a considerable volume of the Organization's records to Bloomington. Other cases of records were shipped from the Eisenhower Library.

Confronting us in the spring of 1971 was our first meeting. At last we were going to New Orleans, a city that had been central to the bitter racial controversy in the early 1950s. At the outset the Organization suffered a double tragedy. On the eve of his death, Richard Hofstadter resigned the presidency, and David Potter, the vice-president, was seriously ill and confined to a hospital. I communicated with Potter almost to the day of his death. The annual business meeting that year was a somber one indeed, with five or six sets of resolutions for departed members—not a good omen for the future. Despite a somewhat arduous start, we began to operate and think like a complex organization of American historians—the realization of a dream that had been so long in its conception and so troubled in its unfolding.

In 1973 the Council of American Learned Societies sent a query to me and to Dr. Paul Ward of the American Historical Association asking us to suggest one or two projects to stimulate research. Dr. Ward and I met in a New York hotel and discussed the challenge. He agreed to put forward studies of the then-burgeoning interest in women's history and exploration of the WPA Federal Writers Project archival collection. I proposed too that the Winifred Gregory *Guide to American Newspapers* be extended and brought up to date. This project received a grant from the National Endowment for the Humanities and got off well under the direction of an able young historian. The scope of the guide was extended to include some international newspapers, and finally it was placed on a continuing basis in the Library of Congress.

In short, at the end of three foundation years, we successfully established a headquarters of some permanence in the stately brick farmhouse at 112 North Bryan Street within the physical pale of Indiana University.

Throughout the years of my secretaryship I tried to persuade the Executive Board to agree to publish a periodic newsletter. For some unfathomable reason the suggestion was tabled. I had in mind an informational organ that could be produced more economically than a section of the *Journal of American History*. Finally, as a going-away favor—or perhaps a good riddance gesture—the executive council approved such a publication. More than a quarter of a century later I look back with pride that the *OAH Newsletter* has become an integral part of the Organization's publication activities.

At the time I retired from the executive secretaryship of the Organization of American Historians it was well on its way to shedding the last vestiges of its regional past. Looking back, however, I have often wondered why I accepted the position at a time when there was general unrest and change in so many areas of American social, cultural, and political affairs. The answer lies in the fact that I had campaigned for changing the title of the *Journal* and then of the organization itself, and then served as chairman of the long-range planning committee; I simply could not refuse to accept the appointment. In a final look back, it must be recognized that the nationalization of the organization justified those decisions.

In March 2004, the Organization of American Historians made a change of some sentimental importance. An architect drafted an attractive logo that remembers the Mississippi Valley Historical Association, preserves the often battered but much revered steamboat, and presents "OAH" in bold but dignified prominence. The Boston meeting marked the opening celebration of the Organization's centennial anniversary. Almost with tears in my eyes and memories bubbling up from the innermost folds of my soul, it dawned on me that I had been four years of age when that small coterie of imaginative historians organized a regional scholarly association that gave much broader implication to American history. I glory in the fact that I have lived to see the Organization mature into a major national and international body. Four times a year the *OAH Newsletter* is dropped through my door. It has become an indispensable organ of professional communication. The great newspaper project is now an electronic resource of enormous proportions. Winifred Gregory and E. G. Swem might have dreamed of such a resource, but could never have conceived of its reach and significance in documenting the unfolding tapestry of this republic and its people.

19

~

SPEAKING KENTUCKY
(AND A LOT OF OTHER PLACES)

DURING THE PAST THREE-QUARTERS OF A CENTURY, I have often left Lexington to fulfill a lecture engagement and wondered what bizarre incident would befall me. I knew the possibilities were many. Just as often I wondered if I had left my common sense at home. It was long ago in rural Mississippi when I first heard the "old folks" bragging on some public speaker or another. I soon learned that the art of public speaking—if it is an art—had its own particular mores.

I arrived in this world at a moment when oratory was in full flush and orators were as plentiful and hardy as sweet-gum sprouts. Aside from the never-ending chorus of windy politicians, there were lawyers, school-teachers, preachers, and Sunday school teachers who plucked the eagle's tail feathers, and there were ample public occasions on which to trap willing audiences. None, however, stroked the chords of eloquence so mightily as the Confederate reunions. On these occasions orators felt no restraint as to fact and time. Spirits soared, and so did the orators. No

Johnny Reb was ever portrayed as less than a full battlefield hero, even though all he ever did was hold a cavalryman's horses.

Between reunions there were plenty of occasions to keep the home-grown Demosthenes in tune. The quarterly sessions of the circuit court offered dockets crammed with cases that called for great outbursts of oratory in place of familiarity with the statutes. Traditionally court days in Winston County were as much festive as judicial, and the courtroom was as much an amusement chamber as a legal one. It was there that the local wheelhorse barrister thundered in Vesuvian roars. Among the power front benchers was "Aus" Brantley, he of the high stiff collar and butterfly bow tie. One-armed Lee Hopkins could be heard defending a chicken thief from one end of Main Street to the other. Leonine Judge Henry Rogers added dignity to the chamber, while Whittle Boystun made the plea of heaven in the defense of his murderous brother.

As a country boy, I was often among those anxious to sip a free drink of ice water on court day and read the county clerk's eloquent spencerian declaration that "the pen is mightier than the sword." A boy could hardly grow up in rural Mississippi in the early twentieth century without being aware of the demagogues who prowled the state. I have tucked away in my memory the fact that I once saw the great "White Chief," James Kimball Vardaman. My earliest memory of political jousting, however, was of that between two sons of nature who sought election to the "high" office of constable in a district that had never made law and order a primary objective. The honorable Elihu Mayo opposed the right honorable Modest Passons. The two candidates looked as if they had stepped directly out of the pages of Augustus Baldwin's classic *Georgia Scenes* without having been touched by pen or brush. Neither could have identified his name in print if it had been dragged before him in boxcar-sized letters. Both men were deeply committed to the theory of free enterprise so long as it could be lodged near a field of corn on the edge of a canebrake with a freshwater spring. Their views of the law began and ended at the barrel of a .38 Special Smith and Wesson revolver. Election to the office of constable mandated its carriage as a symbol of office. This bit of well-advertised absurdity appealed to my grandfather Bennett's sense of humor. He saddled three of his best horses and took my brother Marvin and me to hear the lions of creek-bank democracy mangle history, the English language, and each other. That was my first experience with freestanding debating.

I also vividly recall hearing Mississippi's "The Man," Theodore Gilmore Bilbo, sweep snuff-stained, rednecked constituents into Neverland. By no means was Bilbo an orator in the ancient southern mold; he was a master mesmerizer. I heard his famous brick-road litany delivered to a completely transfixed audience. He promised that when elected he would line Mississippi with red-brick roads. He said that when the bricks wore out on one side, they would turn them over and wear them out on the other side, and then they would stand the bricks on edge. I cast my last vote in Mississippi in the 1931 general election. I voted gleefully against the great wizard of the red-brick roads that never got built.

In the summer of 1946 I heard Bilbo deliver his last speech, in a tiny movie house in Fayette, Mississippi. At the time I was doing research for *The Southern Country Editor.* In that speech Bilbo drew and quartered "Old Man" Roosevelt, "Old Lady" Roosevelt, "Old Man" Henry Luce, and "Old Lady" Claire Booth Luce. He came loaded down with copies of *Time Magazine,* the *Washington Post,* the *New York Times,* and the *Chicago Tribune.* These publications gave him a merry ride. His main devil, however, was the "inside" columnist Drew Pearson, who had labeled him "pastemaster general" because he had once been employed as a newspaper clipper by the United States Department of Agriculture.

In addition to the demagogues, big and little, whom I heard orate in my youth, there were the hellfire-and-damnation preachers, especially the revivalists who appeared with seasonal regularity to cleanse our souls. In the thunderous tones of Gabriel's trumpet these "Brothers" proclaimed over and over the verities of the Scriptures and the wages of sin. Early in my childhood I became captive to the annual Methodist Children's Day recitals. A thwarted elocutionist undertook to direct a gaggle of us to recite some of the sweet pablum that flowed so fervently out of the Methodist Publishing House in Nashville, Tennessee. On those occasions I had acute strokes of tonal paralysis caused by having to face an audience whose horns seemed to grow by the minute.

I became enamored at an early age of the reputation of the great Mississippi orator Senator Sargent Smith Prentice. I may have read something about him in the ancient Lowery and McCardle history of the state. Whatever the source, I discovered the eloquent Prentician peroration, which stated that "the musical name of Mississippi links us to the aboriginal past." This line lingered in my mind and taught me that a good peroration made up for a mediocre speech. Later I attempted oratorical flights inspired by the "Old Master."

Unfortunately, I think, my crippled-wing oratorical outpourings in high school attracted the attention of a young, starry-eyed speech teacher. Miss Ruby O'Quinn of the Choctaw County Agricultural High School faculty ensnared me and undertook to peel off several layers of Mississippi vernacular. She had been hired by the penurious old school principal from the dropout list of junior class members in the Mississippi State College for Women. Miss O'Quinn was hardly the stern type to undertake such a monumental task as revising Mississippi ingrown vernacular and southern abuse of the King's English. Whatever Miss O'Quinn's true destiny in life may have been, she placed on my shoulders the charge to try and learn to speak with a hint of grace.

At the University of Mississippi I found in the curriculum only a vague suggestion of public speaking, this in spite of the fact that oratory was considered a major native art. There I avoided joining the debate program, although I discovered later that I would have been given academic credit for participating. I redeemed myself slightly by actively participating in the lofty discussion sessions of an ancient literary-oratorical society. The campus Young Men's Christian Association, being an active outreach body with missionary tendencies, was another source of training. The campus secretary of the YMCA dabbled in student affairs and local religious activities. He organized us into stock units and sent us into the hill country of Bill Faulkner's Yoknapatawpha County to stir the souls of the Compsons and the Snopeses. Later I wondered what we might have said in those speeches that could have stirred anything.

At the time I joined the faculty of the University of Kentucky in 1931 I had gone through a dormant public-speaking period. The nature of my job, however, required me to speak in public as a way to make the acquaintance of possessors of historical materials or of persons who could give me leads to persons with collections. Many of the early audiences I addressed were patriotic societies, male and female, such as the Daughters of the American Revolution and the Society of the Cincinnati. Long ago it became a hard and fixed fact in American organizational history that every meeting of a group of people, from chicken farmers to the Sons of Kingdom Come, had to have a speaker as part of its ritual. Members of these societies expressed a passionate love of the past, whether or not they had read an up-to-date book in American history. Figuratively they were armed and at the ready to shoot Shawnees along the Licking River and Cherokees in Cumberland Gap. The white crosses on the chest of British Regulars were dead-set targets. Kentucky audiences seemed never to grow weary of listening to tales of frontier adventures and wars.

It would be unforgivably self-serving if I failed to admit that I got a thrill out of the challenges and excitement of speaking to a wide diversity of audiences. I could never imagine what unusual thing might happen, but I always tried to be prepared for any unexpected occurrence. I recall occasions when a program chairman would get things mixed up and two speakers would appear. When that happened, I would eat the proffered meal and leave my fellow speaker to carry on.

One could write an extensive essay on those creatures who roam at large as introducers, or on those intrusive expert raptors who glide down to grab the microphone in their talons and throw the whole system awry. There must have been a time far back in history when the microphone was used as an amplifying device. Not so anymore. It has become a plaything for the self-appointed, diploma-mill electrical engineer in every audience. I shall never be able to reconcile the facts that we can put human beings on the surface of the moon but we can never place a workable microphone at a speaker's podium.

Introducers range from those oratorical florists who scatter sweetness and errors of fact with lavish hands, to the cryptic introducers who simply turn to a speaker and say, "Now it's time for you to say your piece." Many times I was baffled about who was being introduced, myself or the introducer. One thing was clear: in most cases, neither my mother nor Saint Peter could find grounds for objection.

I learned early that persons designated as "introducers" could draw together an egregious number of misstatements of fact and that it was a mistake to attempt to correct them. Other antsy introducers were concerned less with what speakers said than with the requirement that they sat down at the end of twenty minutes precisely. There were even occasions when the introducer could not recall my name, if in fact he or she had ever known it. I had a startling experience of this sort in 1947. I had been invited to deliver the Fleming Lectures in Louisiana State University. Professor James Silver of the University of Mississippi invited me to come to Oxford and spend the night there. He would drive me to Baton Rouge the next day, since he had been asked to introduce me. When the moment came for him to do so, he could not recall my name, and I had to tell the audience who I was.

There were nearly always present in these ritualistic gatherings one or more self-glorifiers who had to say their bit, relevant or not. Impressed deeply in my memory was the performance of a lady in Frankfort who had taken on the ominous duty of introducing me at a meeting held in one of the stately old mansions of that city. She came stocked with data wholly unrelated to the objective of the assembly. She had bundles of newspaper clippings, a rack of old clothing, charts, and family photographs. After she had recited a listing of family breeding records reaching all the way back to Father Abraham, the timid chairman gave the lady a gentle nudge. She called out my name and sat down to catch her breath for another go at the audience in an after-speech commentary on her version of social history.

Then there was an occasion when I spoke to a group of women's club members. The bosomy lady who presided was the type who had to make certain every napkin was folded correctly, the flowers were perfectly arranged, and everybody was seated properly. When it came time to introduce me, she took a flight of eloquence into the blue yonder and introduced me as a professor "EM-U-Ritis." I pinched myself to see if I was still alive.

Many times I tried to decipher the dynamics of patriotic societies whose members adorned themselves with ribbons, buttons, and badges. Many of these organizations, especially the Daughters of the American Revolution, showered their members with red, white, and blue ribbons and adorned their blouses and coats with enough symbolic trinkets to stock George Washington's troops in Valley Forge. Some of the officers of these groups wore more decorations than George III, Lord Howe, and Johnny Burgoyne combined. There were always rituals involving the flag, the swearing of loyalties, and salutations. But I wondered how much members of the sons and daughters societies actually knew about the bills of rights in their state and national constitutions, and even about the American Revolutionary War.

The Daughters of the Confederacy were a little less lavish than the DAR in the splash of symbols. They took a pledge to the Stars and Bars while looking over their shoulders at the Stars and Stripes. This organization early on involved itself in a battle of semantics by referring to the Civil War as "The War Between the States." Not even the most committed Johnny Reb in my home county would have gloried in this title. But in speaking to the Confederate societies one had to be prepared for a lecture from a Confederate political-correctness member. I spoke on several occasions to the Daughters of the Confederacy. Coming from the Lower South, I think I had some understanding of and feeling for their sentiments. As a matter of fact, my tenuous relationship with this organization yielded a rich dividend for the Department of History in the University of Kentucky. A member of that society had painted a full-length portrait of General John Hunt Morgan and had no place to hang it. I let her hang the portrait in one of the grim hallways in Frazee Hall. Later the building caught fire, and the first thing to go was the oil portrait of General Morgan. I had no idea of its artistic virtue or monetary value, but when an insurance inspector asked me, I set the value high enough to finance the construction of a walnut-lined seminar room for the department.

On another occasion I was asked to speak to the national convention of the Daughters of the Confederacy in Detroit. I spoke at the convention early in the evening, flew to Atlanta overnight, and the next morning read a paper in a sectional meeting of the Southern Historical Association on the subject of logging in Appalachian Kentucky. That was about as strange a mixture of audiences, places, and subjects as one can imagine.

Kentucky seems always to have been a happy hunting ground for organizations and clubs interested in using free speakers as freely as they did land and firewood. Among the masculine clubs were the Rotarians, Optimists, Lions, Kiwanis, and—lower on the totem pole—the Civitans. All were on the prowl for so-called free and inspirational speakers who in twenty minutes could analyze and solve sticky local and national problems—or, better still, could predict how well the local football and basketball teams would do next season. On at least two occasions I spoke to the large Louisville Rotary Club, paying my own travel expenses. On one of these occasions I had the unusual experience of being accompanied by Wilson Wyatt, former mayor of Louisville, lieutenant governor, and federal housing administrator, as I searched for my lost car in the cavernous parking area under the Galt House Hotel.

There were moments when I was both amused and dismayed in speaking to men's clubs. Once I spoke to a small, unaffiliated men's civic club in Hustonville. For several years I had bought chickens, eggs, country hams, chestnuts, and black walnut meats from a country produce dealer named Ralph Hovious. One day he asked me if I would speak to his club. This casually organized group consisted of country merchants, farmers, schoolteachers, and a preacher or two. The club met in an abandoned country store. Members drifted in, paying little if any attention to the stated time of the meeting. Finally Ralph introduced me, and just as I began to speak a highly excited man rushed through the door of the room and announced that a tobacco worker had fallen from a high-level tier rail in a nearby tobacco barn. In less than a minute I was left standing alone in the old storeroom. I never learned what happened to the man in the barn.

I could not guess how many women's clubs I spoke to over the years. Some were little more than local fashion shows. On one occasion I addressed a women's club in Elizabethtown. Many of the women in that group were wives of employees of the military base at Fort Knox. The ladies were as dressed up as if they were on their way to a wedding. One lass sitting in the front row exposed ample leg, with her feet encased in bright green high-fashion shoes. It struck me in the middle of that speech that one of those shoes probably cost about four times the so-called honorarium they were paying me.

I came almost to believe that the miscued or unexpected incidents that occurred in public speaking engagements were more exciting than the speeches. I still recall with humor an incident in 1946 or 1947 in Newport, Kentucky. A conservationist group asked me to speak at the dedication of an original log house somewhere near the Ohio River. I was instructed to come to the famous/infamous Smidt's Playtorium for lunch. This place of "sin" was a haven for "tired" Cincinnati businessmen and their neighbors. At the luncheon, the usually noisy Playtorium was as quiet as a tomb—the gamblers, bartenders, and ladies of the night were enjoying a siesta. After lunch we drove some distance to the far humbler log house. The structure appeared to be of indeterminate age and architectural style. It may have had some kind of historical bonding with the conquest of the western frontier. The building contained one central room of modest dimensions. Tucked in beneath the sloping rafters was a gallery, or perhaps an early sleeping space. When we arrived, the main room and the gallery were jammed with a high school brass band and guests. The band, equipped with bass horns and drums, created a thunderous roar that shook the rafters. Amidst the roar the presiding gentleman darted through the crowd like Ariel himself, making last-minute arrangements and giving instructions. In one of his spidery dashes he bumped his head on a rafter and was knocked out cold. He was carried out of the room, a victim not of a Shawnee raid but of a spiteful log cabin. At that moment I wondered whether it would have been more appropriate to speak on the last ferocious act of western pioneering.

In the years after 1930 I spent much time "out there" in the great

Neverland of organizations and public speakers. At the outset I learned that the art of speaking involved generous expenditures of patience, humanity, and good humor as well as time to season understanding. I was called on to exercise all of these when I visited the settlement school at Hazel Green in Wolfe County. The principal sent me precise directions to the school, but just as I reached the door of my office to start the trip, my phone rang. The call was from Goebel Ratliff, a banker in West Liberty. He asked me to come to West Liberty and have dinner with him. I knew Goebel, and it turned out that his invitation was also to a meeting of the local Kiwanis Club. We wasted what I thought was precious time, but Goebel assured me that he was chairman of the Hazel Green board of trustees, and nothing was going to happen until he arrived there. Finally we set out from West Liberty to wind our way through the Wolfe County backcountry. It seemed to me that Goebel and I drove over enough winding narrow roads to reach Paducah before we finally arrived at the Hazel Green school.

We found the place in pandemonium. The heavily perspiring boys were busy cutting a pine log into blocks on which to place pine seating. The scene must have been comparable to the building of Noah's ark. The principal told Goebel and me to go ahead and seat ourselves on the platform at one end of the room, and he would join us when he had seated the crowd. Occupying the entire front section were young women, each of whom had a baby at breast. When the infants were not sucking away, they were crying. I sat there amid that commotion wondering how I could say anything worthwhile to that audience. I resorted to giving a simple description of the discovery and settlement of Kentucky. When I concluded my speech the ancient school patriarch jumped up and grabbed my hand, saying, "Son, you rung the bell!" I think that was the most heartening thing I ever heard at the end of a speech.

High school graduation programs were always colored by some unusual incident. I was invited once to deliver a commencement speech in Virgie, deep in the highlands of Pike County. So far as I could discover, in those days there was no restaurant on the road between Winchester and Pikeville. I assumed I would be invited to dinner in Virgie. When I

arrived at the school, the building was deserted. I finally located a somewhat addled local son who told me where the school's principal lived, up
a creek. Somebody that evening was frying country ham, and its aroma
filled the air and whetted my appetite.

I had to cross a footbridge to reach the principal's house. He greeted
me bare to his waist and instructed me to return to the school building
and await his arrival. He made no mention of a meal. I doubt that any
other Kentucky commencement speaker ever sent a graduating class out
to face the world while on the verge of starvation. I drove back to Lexington that night after every country store in Eastern Kentucky was
closed. I must have been the hungriest commencement speaker in the
history of Kentucky. Years later the secretary of the Kentucky Education
Cabinet asked me to go to Virgie to represent her and the state library
and archives at the dedication of the town's new public library. This time
I was royally received and well fed.

Soon after the Virgie commencement caper I was invited to deliver a
commencement address in Tompkinsville High School in Monroe
County, in south-central Kentucky. That morning I taught two classes
and attended to some departmental problems before I began the long
drive south across the waist of Kentucky to the Tennessee border. I arrived in Tompkinsville almost exhausted, but fortunately I had some
time on my hands. I went to the local hotel and sought a room in which
to take a nap. The clerk did not ask my name, and I was too weary to give
him any information. I fell sound asleep, but before long there was a
pounding at the door. The clerk asked my name and said the school principal was looking for me.

That night I spoke in an impressive rural Kentucky adaptation of a
Gothic chapel. The graduating class was small, but the chapel was
crowded with parents and well-wishers. When I finished my speech
there was not a single hand clap or any other sound, and not the slightest
show of emotion. As I watched the seniors receive their diplomas I wondered if I was not still lying in a comatose state on a hotel bed. Later
other speakers told me they had had the same experience. Audiences in
that area of Kentucky, they said, never applauded a speaker.

Kentuckians are so enamored of festivals that some counties have difficulty finding something unique to celebrate. There are hound dog days, tater days, morel mushroom observances, sorghum molasses stir-offs, and so on down to wild onions. I have spoken to audiences at some of these festive gatherings, and I believe that it is not a true festival if the program does not get fouled up in some way. On one occasion I was asked to speak in a festival in Perryville (the central theme of which I have forgotten, if I ever knew it). There was the usual milling around of a full battalion of hot dog munchers. The arrangers of the festival had scheduled at least twice too many events, among which were my speech and a flyover by a squadron of the 101st Airborne Command from Fort Campbell, followed by the sale of a pig at auction. The pig sat in a cage directly in front of the speaker's stand. The flyover was late in arriving, and I was left to sit facing the pig. I think that poor animal had the most forlorn expression I ever saw on man or beast. By the time the planes finally arrived, most of the allotted time had been lost. In fact, the pig and I had only three minutes left. I hardly had time to say, "Mr. Chairman." After giving a short speech about nothing, I left the platform to the sad-faced pig, who would meet his foreordained fate as best he could.

I got trapped in an almost identical situation in Barbourville. Some ingenious souls dreamed up a scheme to breathe life and excitement into that flood-ravaged town. They came up with the idea of negotiating a "treaty" with the North Carolina Indians. The citizens of Knox County would allow the Cherokees to sell an assortment of goods along the main highway and to trim cane along the banks of local creeks in exchange for a guaranteed year of freedom for the whites from warriors of the Cherokee tribe. I think I can say with assurance that the Cherokees had no plans to raid Knox County—ever. The festival intended to amuse tourists with the firing of muzzle-loaded guns and a grand display of baskets, colorful blankets, and plaster casts of animal and human figures. On top of all the pow-wowing there were to be a speech and a basketball game. I was invited to speak, and after the usual loss of time on such occasions, the chairman announced that the audience could choose to stay and hear my speech or go and see two high school basketball teams fight it out.

Hardly had the chairman finished his announcement than there was a rush to the basketball court. I was left with only the halt and lame as an audience. This was one of the few times in my life when I lost my sense of humor and my temper in public. As I was stepping into my car to return to Lexington, the chairman came running up, begging me to come back and speak to the token audience. As I drove home that night I was convinced that only a damned idiot would ever agree to speak to anyone, anywhere. I hoped the Cherokees would abrogate their treaty and scalp the entire festival committee.

I never ceased to be amused at individuals who would invite me to speak and then, when asked what they wanted me to speak about, would answer, "Oh, anything." I often thought it would be amusing to respond that I would speak on the removal of the dome from the Kentucky capitol, the removal of 120 counties, or the outlawing of basketball. Those subjects might keep audiences in place and away from flyovers, pig auctions, and basketball games.

The appeal of subjects changed over the years. When I began my career there was an ear for humorous stories of frontier origin. In the early 1930s Franklin Meine and Walter Blair published excellent books in this field. I was involved during those years in the research and writing of *The Rampaging Frontier*. On occasions when a slightly humorous subject seemed appropriate, I could recite the proceedings of a greenhorn Wisconsin Debating Society or quote a chandelier-shaking Kentucky legislator pounding a minuscule subject to a pulp in the local vernacular. There was never a better way to end a speech than to recite that bit of Hardshell Baptist oratory "Whar the Lion roareth and the Wangdoodle Mourneth for His First Born, ah."

The publication of one of my books almost always resulted in an invitation to speak about it. This was especially true of *The History of Kentucky*, *The Rampaging Frontier*, *The Kentucky* in the Rivers of America series, *The Emerging South*, and *Pills, Petticoats, and Plows*. As a result of the last, which dealt with the role of the southern furnishing or country store, I was invited to participate in a panel in Princeton University to discuss the role of small businesses in American economic history. A member of the panel was from the Dennison paper products company. At the time the name Dennison was almost as well known as that of Santa Claus. The company's famous crepe paper adorned every elementary schoolroom in the land. Women's clubs designed crepe paper rosettes and all sorts of decorative things to hang in homes, churches, and banquet rooms. Mr. Dennison was a down-to-earth speaker, and I was as excited to see him in the flesh as if he had been a character out of the Grimm Brothers' fairy tales.

Through three score and ten years of public speaking, I received a lot of flattering and earnest attention and generous showers of cordiality and good humor, seasoned with a few irritations. I have found it difficult to forgive a smart-alec *Memphis Commercial Appeal* reporter who flagrantly fabricated a story about me. In 1954, I was invited to participate in a loosely organized forum in Memphis State University. Preceding me was William B. Hesseltine of the University of Wisconsin, formerly a professor of history in the University of Chattanooga. Hesseltine no doubt arrived in Memphis fully intending to stir up the animals. The *Commercial Appeal* reporter said that Hesseltine had told a Memphis audience that Nashville was a more cultivated city. By the time I arrived in Memphis and read about the furor he had touched off, Hesseltine was back in Madison, no doubt chuckling to himself. I resolved that I would avoid anything that would further enrage the local citizenry. I spoke about the changes that had come to the New South in industry, forestry, and agriculture, with all their social and economic implications. I spoke of the revolution wrought by plant breeders. I made no mention of the culture of Memphis or Nashville. Sometime after I returned to Lexington, my son, Bennett, came into my wood shop with a clipping from the *Denver Post* saying that in Memphis I had advocated that southerners quit singing "Dixie." That story touched off a firestorm. The *Jackson Daily News* in Mississippi ran a full-page tirade reading me even out of my birthplace. The *Winston County Journal* in Louisville chimed in with an angry diatribe, which upset my mother. I quickly had enough of this southern insanity. I went to Paul Flowers, a member of the *Commercial Appeal*'s editorial staff whom I knew, and raised a protest. The reporter, a recent arrival in Memphis and an escapee from the *Chicago Tribune* menagerie, was dismissed, and the "Dixie" defenders found comfortable bedding with the Citizens Council.

Never did my ego receive such a boost as when I saw in the *Miami Herald* that I had addressed the Florida Bar Association. There was my picture in the paper to prove it. By some mix-up known only to newspaper morgue keepers, my picture had been run with the Bar Association story instead of that of Associate Justice of the Supreme Court Tom Clark. I have always tried to imagine what Justice Clark's reactions were.

There are many audiences and speeches that I recall with genuine joy. I remember the deep satisfaction I derived from addressing the annual meetings of the Kentucky rural electric cooperatives. I could bond spiritually with that assemblage. The introduction of electrical energy had meant a new way of life to rural Kentuckians. I could address that audience conscious of the fact that the Rural Electrification Administration had improved the lives of my own parents.

There was a truly exciting moment when I spoke at the dedication of the great Durrett Collection in the safekeeping of the new University of Chicago library. Almost the first thing I heard when I arrived in Kentucky in 1928 was that the state had lost the Durrett Collection of books, papers, documents, and other basic historical materials. Making the dedicatory speech on that occasion was truly memorable. I had similar feelings about a speech I was invited to make to Daniel Boone's descendants in the Northwest. A Mrs. Buchanan had come to Athens, Kentucky, to attend a Boone dedicatory occasion. She asked me if I would speak at the Boone assembly when I came to Seattle to teach in the University of Washington. I had supposed there would be fewer than a dozen persons present. When Beth and I arrived at the church, situated literally on the shore of Puget Sound, the building was overflowing with Boone descendants. Presiding over the meeting was a Boone descendant who was president of the Boeing Airplane Company. At that date the mammoth 747 was under construction. Facing that impressive assembly of Boones and their guests was a unique experience. I concluded that Daniel Boone had sowed his seed all the way across the continent.

There were at least two other speaking engagements that reached deep into my emotions. One was the dedication of the $39 million tunnel under Cumberland Gap. On hand that cool, rainy morning in October 1996 were three or four governors, a gaggle of congressmen, state officials from Virginia, Kentucky, and Tennessee, and a large assemblage of ordinary citizens, all standing in the rain at the mouth of the tunnel. In that seminal moment, with a sense of the historic changes the tunnel would bring about, I felt I was taking part in the opening of a new chapter in American frontier history. Almost simultaneously with the opening of the tunnel, barriers went up across both ends of the ancient road over the saddle of the gap to permit its reconversion to the contours of the ancient Indian-buffalo path. I had the privilege also of making the dedicatory speech at the reopening of the historic trail in October 2002.

As I look back from the perspective of 2005, I have no idea how many speeches I have made or where I made many of them. One thing I have learned is that the word *gratuity* has stringent limitations. If I had framed all the certificates I received in lieu of cash, I would have to build a tobacco barn to find wall space for them. I received ballpoint pens by the handful and enough mugs to drink a good portion of Colombia's production of coffee beans. Many times I have driven home at night along a winding country road after making a speech, wondering if I was not, after all, the victim of an incurable cranial deficiency called "emuritis." I only wish to have had the opportunity to say to Senator Sargent Smith Prentice and Miss Ruby O'Quinn, "Look what a hell of a mess you got me into!"

20

~

THE BOOK THIEVES

THE YEARS BEFORE THE GREAT DEPRESSION WERE AN
exciting time to be in Kentucky. A modest literary renascence was under
way. Tucked away in seclusion in Springfield, Elizabeth Madox Roberts
achieved critical acclaim with her poetic offerings and her novels *The
Great Meadow* and *The Time of Man*. Elizabeth Chevalier of Maysville
published her novel *Drivin' Woman*. Irvin S. Cobb of Paducah and New
York was easing into the sunset years of his newspaper and writing career. In Lexington, William H. Townsend enjoyed a burst of popularity
on the publication of *Lincoln and His Wife's Home Town*. At the same
time, Elizabeth M. Simpson captivated a generous readership with her
romantic *Bluegrass Houses and Their Traditions* and *The Enchanted Bluegrass*. Working a somewhat more modest literary vein, Charles Richard
Staples was deeply involved in writing his *Pioneer Lexington*. In Louisville, Alice Hegan Rice and Eleanor Mercein Kelly were still writing. A
group of rejuvenators brought to life the 1880s Filson Club, and that or-

ganization began the publication of a high-quality historical quarterly. E. Merton Coulter published his seminal study *The Civil War and Readjustment in Kentucky*. He was also coauthor, with William E. Connelley, of the first two volumes of the so-called Kerr's *History of Kentucky*. John Wilson Townsend had published his two-volume *Kentucky in American Letters*.

Along with the writers were the librarians of the Louisville Free Public Library, the Lexington Public Library, and the historic Transylvania College Library. Mrs. Charles Norton was the veritable epitome of Transylvania College's era of glory. She had single-handedly resurrected the college's rich collection of rare books and manuscripts, which had been in storage since the Civil War. Florence Dillard, Lexington Public Library's longtime director, was not only a chronicler and bibliographer but also a teacher. Two of her charges were David Cliff, who became president of the American Library Association, and bibliophile James Cogar, who established a national reputation in his restorative work at Williamsburg and Pleasant Hill. Charles Staples, an almost full-time patron of the Lexington Public Library, became a human encyclopedia of local history.

In October 1931 Charles Staples asked me if I would like to go with him to call on a young civil engineer who was showing signs of becoming a book collector. On a Saturday afternoon in October we drove out to Dudley Road to visit J. Winston Coleman Jr. An aunt had just made him a present of the two-volume *Collins' History of Kentucky*. He treasured the book so highly that he had bought a combination desk/bookshelf to house it. That balmy Saturday afternoon we feasted on sardines, cheese, and crackers and washed it all down with guarded gulps of Winston's ungodly home brew. We spent the afternoon talking about books, the search for materials, and the writing of history as youth are wont to do in the eye of the tunnel.

After that first Saturday afternoon, the three of us began meeting with some regularity, still feasting on sardines, cheese, and crackers washed down with Winston's bathtub brew. Our main delight, however, was the talk about books and manuscripts. Charlie Staples knew all there was to know about Lexington and Fayette County history. To him the rest of Kentucky was no more than a matrix that held the central jewels in place. He was more familiar with the characters who had once paraded before Postlethwait's Tavern than with those who passed the Phoenix Hotel in the 1930s. He had instant recall of places and incidents, the contents of ancient newspapers, scraps of eighteenth-century gossip, and the eternal scandals: he knew whose wayward feet showed under the beds of almost every prominent family in the central Bluegrass.

After several sessions we were joined by William Henry Townsend and Dr. John Sharpe Chambers. Townsend was a popular local attorney, and Chambers was the university physician. At that time Bill Townsend was riding the crest of local literary fame. Immediately after its publication in 1929, his *Lincoln and His Wife's Home Town* had made him one of Lexington's most successful authors. He was assembling a remarkably valuable collection of books and artifacts relating to Abraham Lincoln and his age. Bill almost rivaled Charlie Staples in his knowledge of the mores and social patterns of central Kentucky. His yarns about the antics of members of the local bar would have made a fascinating book.

"Brick" Chambers also had some claim to literary stature. He had just published the results of his survey of the medical needs of eastern Kentucky. Aside from the abject medical needs of the Commonwealth, the Chambers survey revealed the high incidence of parasitic infestation among students from the hills. In many ways his booklet may be considered the first very modest stone in the edifice that later came to be the University of Kentucky College of Medicine.

Sometime in the early months of our group Charlie Staples brought along his lifetime friend, Dr. Claude Wilkes Trapp, a highly respected eye specialist whose practice covered central and eastern Kentucky and beyond. He was an erudite collector of first editions and a discriminating literary scholar. I do not believe he ever visited England, but he had developed a familiarity with both British authors and British book dealers. In addition to his interest in books he was an amateur musician and had a fondness for vintage violins.

By the time the membership of the Book Thieves, as we came to call ourselves, had thus doubled to six, the group became too urbane to munch the viands of the founders. There began a rotation of somewhat formal luncheons and dinners followed by marvelous afternoon and evening discussions of libraries, book collecting, research, and writing. All the members except Claude Trapp had a book under way, which meant we were forever searching far and wide for original materials and ideas. Yet by no means were the conversations solely about the refined art of writing books. These men were good storytellers, and they found in the circle of Book Thieves an attentive audience.

Our membership became much more imposing when Frank LeRond McVey, president of the University of Kentucky, and Judge Samuel Mackay Wilson, dean of the Fayette bar, joined us. I am convinced that McVey came to the meetings of the Book Thieves because he was willing to make any prudent effort to further the process of building the university's library collection. I introduced him to the Book Thieves because he owned a far better library than the average university president. I believe, too, that he readily welcomed the chance to get away from the nagging problems of his office during the Depression years and to seek relief from the complaints of the hard-pressed faculty for whom he could offer so little promise.

Judge Samuel M. Wilson was a bulldog of a man who had fought many a fierce courtroom battle and who never undertook a project halfway. Once a fiery redhead, he was now a square-jawed, white-haired, cigar-chewing, granite-like elder statesman, always eloquent of speech, who enlivened any group to which he belonged. He was founder and host of the prestigious Cakes and Ale Club, of which I'll speak later. Judge Wilson was dean of Kentucky historians and an insatiable collector of rare books and manuscripts of local and broad sectional interest. After serving in World War I as a major in the Major General's field services, he came home with enough souvenir German military artifacts to fill a basement. His reverence for the military extended back to the American Revolution. He was also the author of several books, pamphlets, and articles. The judge's home in Fayette Park, his law offices, and the basement of the Security Trust Building at Short and Mill Streets were crammed to their ceilings with his books and papers.

This completed the membership of the Book Thieves, with the exception of late joiner Herman Lee Donovan, who became president of the University of Kentucky in 1941. At the time, Donovan was self-conscious about being elevated to this position from the presidency of Eastern Kentucky State Teachers College (now Eastern Kentucky University). Largely because of this he began building an impressive library of biographical materials relating to American university presidents. Later, in a far more self-assured moment, he wrote a highly revealing book, *Keeping the University Free and Growing* (1959), in which he discussed his experiences in dealing with the ever-present and stifling political hand that sought to throttle academic affairs in the state.

Few Kentuckians ever derived more pleasure and intellectual stimulation from an association of kindred souls. Collectively the Book Thieves possessed an astonishing amount of information, not only about Kentucky but also about national issues and institutions. These were stirring years in America: the Depression, global war, the postwar era. There were important issues that faced all American education and the University of Kentucky in particular. One of them was lifting the level of scholarship in the institution. Frequently Dr. McVey talked of his dream of someday organizing a university press comparable to the one at the University of North Carolina. The Book Thieves gave him hearty encouragement to keep the idea alive and, at the proper moment in the university's development, to begin an academic publishing program.

Judge Wilson was a strong personal force behind the preservation of historical sites, especially Boonesborough and the Blue Licks battlefield. He gloried in the celebration of historical anniversaries, and woe betide the upstart who cast aspersions upon the reputations and prestige of Kentucky's forefathers. He had married Mary Shelby, and throughout his life with her he militantly defended Isaac Shelby, Kentucky's first governor, and his rightful place in the history of the American Revolution, the founding of the Commonwealth, and the War of 1812. He was president of the Daniel Boone Memorial Association and of the Blue Licks group, both of which promoted the formation of state parks on historic sites. Every August 19, Wilson gathered up a huge sheaf of notes and strode onto the Blue Licks Battlefield to flail the British and Shawnees who had waylaid the Kentucky pioneers with such devastating results.

Judge Wilson was also an inveterate letter writer. He carried on an extensive correspondence with historians, librarians, booksellers, and members of pioneering families. Writing in a bold, angular hand, he discussed books and research with a broad spectrum of authors and scholars. Occasionally he became involved in controversies with those who had failed to do their homework and with any craven soul who dared defame Isaac Shelby, John Bradford (Kentucky's first printer), or Daniel Boone. He was an aggressive and stubborn adversary in a historical argument. In many of the books in his library he had written extensive marginal notes, and in many of these he quarreled with the author. The judge had a major hearing problem and often could not follow with certainty the course of the Saturday afternoon discussions. Sometimes he voiced comical and irrelevant responses to what he thought was being said; sometimes he made emotional responses that went wide of the mark.

Until 1934 it is doubtful that there was a more ardent Democrat in all Kentucky than Judge Wilson. He wore lapel buttons of his favorite candidates; he decorated the mantel in his library with brass roosters, donkeys, gavels, and other political mementos. He had a near worshipful loyalty to Woodrow Wilson, believing that possibly they had sprung from the same sturdy Scottish ancestral stem; at least they were both Presbyterians. By 1934, however, the judge's Democratic ardor underwent a massive cooling off. He came to loathe Franklin D. Roosevelt, believing that he was on the verge of destroying the nation. Later, mention of the president's court-packing attempt sent him into a purple fury. This came to be true of the WPA and the PWA as well. One afternoon a whimsical conversation turned to the restoration of Belle Brezing's beloved shrine to Venus on Megowan Street in Lexington. Through his static-laden hearing aid the judge got the notion that someone had said the PWA was doing the repair. He was eloquent in his denunciation of every letter in the alphabet that implied the New Deal—so eloquent in fact that we piled into automobiles to accompany him on an inspection of the Brezing place. I think he never realized that neither President Roosevelt nor the PWA was aware that the old house of ill repute existed.

Charlie Staples was an extrovert and a lovable character of parts. He was a safety inspector for the Southern Railway System, a job that made only modest demands on his time. In his extended spare moments he came to know every book dealer on the railroad, from New Orleans to Washington and Cincinnati. He had an elephantine memory and an even more expansive imagination. He was never willing to admit that he was unfamiliar with a book. Often he turned up with "sleepers" for which he had paid almost nothing, and in some cases he excoriated the dealer for not taking better care of his stock. When someone asked Staples about a book, his stock answer was that he had seen a copy but that it was in very poor condition. On one occasion Winston Coleman and Bill Townsend tested Charlie's literary integrity. They began a discussion about a "very famous" Kentucky book entitled *The Grey Cowl,* by lay brother O'Shaughnessy of the Trappist monastery in Nelson County. This book was so rare, in fact, that it existed only in the minds of Coleman and Townsend. They asked Charlie if he had ever seen the book. He replied yes, but the copy he had examined was in horribly poor condition. Nevertheless, Staples gave all of us many a valuable lead on books and manuscripts that could be acquired by the University of Kentucky library. We had always to be aware that we too might turn up a *Grey Cowl* sleeper.

Bill Townsend was an aggressive collector. Through his law practice and his knowledge of family relationships he was able to get access to Todd, Helm, and Cassius M. Clay papers that was denied others. The popularity of his book on Lexington brought people to his office, and in the depth of the Great Depression, many came with papers, books, and relics for sale. Once he called me to say that a Mrs. Curd from Curd's Ferry on the Kentucky River near High Bridge was in his office and had a Daniel Boone letter that she wished to sell. He asked me if I wanted to buy it. I was so taken by surprise that I impulsively said yes without asking the price. He bought the letter for twenty-five dollars, a sum that at that time nearly equaled the national debt. I almost had to resort to the use of a pistol and mask to raise the money.

Townsend was without a doubt one of the most charming raconteurs ever to enliven a party in the Bluegrass. He could adorn even the most commonplace yarn and make it seem classic. His oft-repeated philosophy was never to let mere facts stand in the way of telling a good story. He knew all the Lincoln scholars: Senator Albert J. Beveridge, William Barton, James G. Randall, Ida Tarbell, Edgar Lee Masters, Oliver Barrett, Paul Angle, Roy Basler, Benjamin Thomas, Carl Sandburg, and Otto Eisenschiml. Bill talked about the personalities of the Lincoln era as if he had been a confidant to Abe and Mary and their families. He had a phenomenally well-trained trial lawyer's memory and could recall the places, dates, and surrounding circumstances of most Lincoln incidents.

Once Bill told a story about an experience he had with Carl Sandburg. One morning he was sitting in his office working on a brief when Sandburg walked in with a valise in one hand and a guitar in the other. He explained casually that he was on his way to make a speech in Owensboro that afternoon and had decided to run by Lexington and chat with Bill about Lincoln. Despite the consternation Sandburg's ignorance of Kentucky geography caused him, Bill listened. Sandburg had been a volunteer in the Spanish-American War and had been stationed at Fort Clay. On one occasion a soldier had gotten a bit overseas in one of the famous West Main Street saloons. Staggering back toward camp, he went out Main Street and wound up in the Lexington Cemetery. Addled by drink and darkness, he stumbled over the tombstone of "King" Solomon, the grave-digging hero of the 1833 cholera epidemic in Lexington. Back in camp he said that he had seen King Solomon's grave, and his buddies bet five dollars apiece that the burial place was not in Kentucky but where it had always been. The skeptics went to the cemetery to prove the drunken wanderer wrong and wound up losing their money.

My wife and I were hosts to the Book Thieves at our home on Forest Park Road when we had as a special guest George Fort Milton, editor and owner of the *Chattanooga News*. He had just completed a draft of his voluminous biography of Stephen A. Douglas, later published under the title *The Eve of Conflict: Stephen A. Douglas and the Needless War* (1934). Almost from the instant he was introduced to Bill Townsend, the two became embroiled in a debate that became almost as ardent, if not as acrimonious, as the famous Lincoln-Douglas confrontations in Illinois in 1858. Milton was a chain smoker, and the kitchen bowl he used as an ash tray was full of butts when the argument ended and the Book Thieves departed. The meeting, however, did not end the contentions between the Lincoln partisans and George Fort Milton. He asked me to act as his go-between and get Ben Thomas, Paul Angle, and Roy Basler to read his manuscript. Sometime later I delivered to him letters that were as vigorous with argument as was the heated discussion with Bill Townsend.

Townsend's memory was almost infallible. He boasted frequently that he could recognize Lincoln's handwriting style almost instantly. Out of his hearing, Claude Trapp once said he could forge any signature with his left hand. Later, at a Book Thieves meeting in his home on East Main Street, Trapp brought out a book of proper vintage, wrote "Abraham Lincoln" on the flyleaf, and placed it on a table where Bill Townsend would be certain to see it. Townsend came in chattering away and, as usual, chose the most comfortable chair in the room. He picked up the doctored book, glanced at the signature, and almost instantly declared it a forgery. Trapp put the book back on the shelf in his library and no doubt forgot the joke. After his death, representatives of a New York auction house came to Lexington to prepare the library for public sale. Mrs. Trapp called me to ask if I knew anything about "Dock" owning one of Abraham Lincoln's books. I have wondered many times since then if there might be some unknowing collector of Lincolniana who boasts to envious friends that he owns one of the martyred president's very own books when what he actually has is a relic of Claude Trapp's horseplay.

Trapp was a man who had had many fascinating moments in his longtime practice of medicine in Lexington. As a young graduate physician just returned to the town, he was called upon to minister to the fatally wounded William Cassius Goodloe, who had fallen victim in the murderous Swope-Goodloe encounter. The two men were at outs politically when they engaged in a duel in the old post office on Main Street. Two days later Trapp and a colleague struggled to save Goodloe's life while the hearse bearing Swope's body rolled past the Phoenix Hotel.

Trapp knew a host of people in central Kentucky, and no doubt had most of them as patients. One of them was Louis Lee Haggin of Mount Brilliant Farm on the Russell Cave Pike. Haggin, a wealthy man, had collected a magnificent library of sporting books, paintings of animals, and original prints. Among his treasures was a full file of William T. Porter's *The Spirit of the Times*. On several occasions he had been a guest of the Book Thieves, but the sensational moment in this casual association was in either 1935 or 1936, when he had the group as guests at Mount Brilliant to meet the famous American rare-book dealer A. S. W. Rosenbach of Philadelphia. Dr. Rosenbach had brought along some of his choicest treasures, one of which was an elaborately bound leather case that he said contained a mummified part of Napoleon's torso.

Through the years there were many other guests of the Book Thieves. Among them were the lovable old Pickwickian character Otto A. Rothert, secretary of the Filson Club; Governor Simeon Willis; John Vance of the Legal Division of the Library of Congress; Richard E. Banta, the Crawfordsville, Indiana, author and book dealer; Dr. W. T. H. Howe, president of the American Book Company; W. Clement Eaton of Lafayette College, later professor of history in the University of Kentucky; A. B. Guthrie of the *Lexington Leader;* Joe Jordan, author of the column "Four Bits" in the *Leader;* Holman Hamilton, biographer of Zachary Taylor and later a member of the university's history department; John Wilson Townsend, author and book dealer; Willard Rouse Jillson, geologist and prolific bibliographer-historian; and John Tasker Howard, the biographer of Stephen Collins Foster. In 1938 that bright American author Constance Rourke was a guest. So far as I can recall she was the only woman to attend a Saturday afternoon meeting. Miss Rourke had a notable literary reputation as the biographer of John James Audubon. She had come to Lexington ostensibly to speak to women students at the university on choosing careers, but she was especially interested in consulting local historical sources on the maturing of American culture. Tragically, she died before she could finish that manuscript.

Following commencement in 1938, and at the end of an unusually trying year for President McVey, he invited the Book Thieves to go with him on a roving literary jaunt. We went first to be luncheon guests of Dr. W. T. H. Howe at his country place, Freelands, near Alexandria on the Ohio River. There we met the well-known book dealer Walter Hill. I am of the opinion that at the time Hill had only Howe as a client. I knew Dr. Howe as a crusty publisher, but as a host and away from his office he was the soul of hospitality. He had in his simple frame house at Freelands many unopened boxes that he said contained books and manuscripts of famous New England authors and poets. He showed us one of the most dramatic historical documents I have ever read; it was the lengthy unpublished statement of John Brown written while he awaited the completion of the scaffold on which he was to be hanged in Charlestown, Virginia. No one, not even Dr. Howe or Walter Hill, knew precisely what precious first editions and manuscripts were in those boxes, packed away from scholarly eyes. Soon after our visit, Dr. Howe was fatally stricken in a Pullman berth on one of his weekly commuter trips between Cincinnati and New York. His collection was bought at auction by a donor to the New York Public Library.

From Alexandria we went across Indiana to Crawfordsville to visit with Dick Banta and to examine his fine collection of books and newspapers relating to the Mississippi and Ohio Valleys. At that time the university library was purchasing from him as many rare books as it could afford. He had furnished most of the travel books now in the Special Collections Department, books that are easily identifiable by his distinctive price coding. During our visit there was a considerable amount of chuckling over the fact that our host said he had once found Dr. McVey propped up in bed with an old-fashioned in one hand and a volume of the Bobbsey Twins in the other. This was not exactly the kind of university library material we had set out to examine.

We retraced our way to a place just south of Indianapolis to visit what turned out to be one of the most extensive non-book collections I have ever heard about. Dr. McVey had corresponded over the years with an old lecture-bureau agent named Stout, who had boasted about his collection. Stout's books were stacked in shelves, on tables, on and under beds, on window sills—everywhere. He had been forced out of his house into a humbler abode in the backyard. By no means did we go through all of his bizarre collection, but I did not see any title more significant than a dog-eared copy of a novel from the Rover Boys series. Later, as a professor at Indiana University, I shuddered every time I had to drive past the Stout mansion and recall the monumental and ungodly caricature of a book collection it contained.

From Mr. Stout's literary junk pile we went to Ann Arbor to be guests of Randolph G. Adams. He permitted us the utmost freedom in examining the stunning manuscripts and other basic source materials in the William Clements Library. Adams brought out for us to see some tremendously exciting documents, among them letters of Martha Washington to George during the harsh Valley Forge winter, letters intercepted by the British. These letters, however, were only rich historical tidbits compared with the voluminous caches of official papers and correspondence of British military and administrative officers during the American Revolution. This great library, then as now, contained rich documentary materials awaiting skilled editing and annotation. One of our objectives in visiting Adams was to explore with him the possibility of the McGregor Library Fund Committee including the university library as one of the beneficiaries in its program for the purchase of rare books in the field of regional Americana.

At this juncture I wish to set the record clear for all time to come on Lexington's infatuation with Belle Brezing, the Megowan Street madam. One day in August 1933 that joker Bill Townsend drove into my driveway, blew his horn loudly enough to wake up Rip Van Winkle, and, in a voice clear enough for all my neighbors to hear, asked me if I would like to go to a whorehouse. He then told me that Dr. Charles A. Nevitt had called him and said that he believed Belle Brezing was near death and wanted someone from the university to come out and go through her library with the possibility of accepting it as a gift. Bill and I drove to Megowan Street, but in the meantime the old lady had suffered another sinking spell, and we saw neither her nor her library. Later I went with Bill and Winston Coleman, and we did have a chance to examine her small collection of miscellaneous books, none of which I thought was of any consequence. Belle Brezing gave me a haphazardly collected scrapbook of random news stories that she had torn from the *Herald* and the *Leader.* The first clipping in the book was a story about Bishop Lewis W. Burton of Christ Episcopal Church. On this second visit Bill Townsend gave "literary asylum" to a small and sketchy account book that contained a few personal entries, one of them referring to the father of one of his law partners. We saw no diary or any other documentary material except some pictures of courtesans who had lived in the Todd House on West Main Street and later on Megowan. Afterward I acquired a copy of *Housekeeping in the Blue Grass* from John Wilson Townsend and later discovered that the book had belonged to Belle Brezing. This book is now in the Special Collections Department of the Margaret I. King Library.

No doubt there are still people in Lexington who believe the unfounded gossip that we swiped Belle Brezing's diary by throwing it out a window and then running around the house to recover it. Not so. With equal emphasis I affirm that President McVey never sent a letter of appreciation and an elaborately engraved certificate out to Megowan Street. This is a classic case in which dull facts have not been allowed to cloud a good folk story.

Once, when the Book Thieves were guests of President Donovan at Maxwell Place, Mrs. Donovan was inspired to do something original to cheer the old boys. She asked each wife to bring one of her husband's prized books or other literary possession. After lunch that day Claude Trapp spotted a familiar copy of a rare first edition and remarked, "I have a book identical to this one." When he opened the book, he exclaimed, "Hell, this *is* my book!" When each fellow had recovered his precious little gem, it turned out that Frances Jewell McVey had sent along a volume of Dr. McVey's current diary. I rode home with the McVeys after that meeting and heard the president deliver an eloquent Scottish lecture on the sanctity of personal privacy. I have always wondered if the Donovans restrained their curiosity enough to honor the confidentiality of that diary by not reading it. I was fascinated also to see what the wives believed to be their husbands' choicest treasures.

One more McVey anecdote. While he was president, McVey often lamented that the university's students were oblivious to what went on around them. He thought a majority of them would be unable to tell a visitor the name of the president of the university. I wondered if he was right and undertook to determine the truth. In a test in early American history I listed the names of individuals to be identified. Among them I included Frank L. McVey. The president was right: they did not know who he was. He was thought variously to be a great traitor in the American Revolution, on General Washington's staff, a member of Jefferson's cabinet, or a British officer. One honest scholar answered, "I'll be damned if I know who he was!" Joe "Jay Jay" Jordan, the *Leader* columnist, was present when I showed the Book Thieves these comical responses. Dr. McVey enjoyed the humor most of all. We forgot, however, that this was grist for Joe's mill. The story appeared in his column "Four Bits," and was picked up by the Associated Press and distributed widely. Astonishingly, this whimsical story appeared as far afield as the London *Times*. Later Dr. McVey asked me to leave his name out of future test questions, and we heard no more complaints about student unawareness.

Many events gave rich human dimension to the gatherings of the Book Thieves. When Charlie Staples completed his manuscript on pioneer Lexington, he celebrated by carelessly mislaying it. After a frantic search he concluded that it must have been sent away with the household garbage. He rushed out to the Lexington garbage dump and spent an afternoon digging through heaps of vile-smelling refuse. At a Book Thieves luncheon he described with realistic olfactory details the stench of the place. Bill Townsend ended that discussion in short order by saying, "General, you should be ashamed of yourself for writing such vile-smelling stuff."

It would be impossible to fully assess the impact the Book Thieves had in laying the foundation for the Special Collections in the University of Kentucky Library, whether by giving vital information and advice about available collections of books and papers, or by directly donating materials. On several occasions some of the Book Thieves accompanied us to solicit owners of collections to place their materials in the library.

The truly significant Wilson Collection went far in restoring to Kentuckians the serious loss of the Durrett Collection, which was sold out of the state in the early years of the twentieth century. I am positive that the judge never would have made this gift to the university had it not been for his congenial association with the Book Thieves.

By any criteria of literary measurement, Bill Townsend's collection of Lincolniana was one of the most important ones remaining in private possession. Tragically, most of it was sold outside Kentucky. David Turnham's copy of *The Revised Laws of Indiana,* the first law book read by Lincoln, was acquired by Townsend in 1923 and sold to the Lilly Library at Indiana University in 1967. Most of the rest of the collection was sold to Justin Turner, a southern California collector, who in turn sold it to the New York Public Library for several times more than the original purchase price.

The Claude Trapp collection of first editions was sold at public auction by a New York firm. Charlie Staples's books and papers were dispersed, the university acquiring many of them. I am not sure what disposition was made of John Sharpe Chambers's books and papers. I do know that his papers once contained a considerable body of research notes on early Kentucky medical history.

As mentioned earlier, both McVey and Donovan had assembled rather good libraries. Dr. McVey was an avid reader in many areas of interest and, like Judge Wilson, made generous marginal notations. Besides his library, the beginnings of which dated back to the days when he was a graduate student in economics at Yale University, he had a considerable collection of personal correspondence, also dating back to his college days. For years he kept a day-by-day diary, making cryptic observations on the life about him. This multivolume personal record is now in the Special Collections Department. Library personnel went through his books and selected those that were not duplicated in the library's holdings. I shipped the duplicates to an economics and business library in Bangalore, India. The president of that institution had made a direct plea to me for books when I visited that city as a State Department lecturer in 1952. Donovan's books were also given to the university library.

None of the Book Thieves' personal libraries contained as complete a collection of books relating specifically to Kentucky as did that of J. Winston Coleman Jr. By the time of his death in May 1983, Winston had collected several thousand books and hundreds of precious manuscripts. The latter he had arranged meticulously in forty or fifty scrapbooks. At an earlier date he had willed this collection to the university, but for some reason he became offended at the institution during the presidency of John W. Oswald. He did, however, give the university a sizable body of his correspondence and copies of all of the books and pamphlets he had written.

THE LIBRARIES COLLECTED BY THE individual Book Thieves were important, and three or four of them were of major significance, but the collections by no means overshadowed the literary contributions of the members. William H. Townsend achieved broad recognition with his *Lincoln and His Wife's Home Town* (1929) and later published a considerably revised edition that contained two fresh chapters. In these years Townsend also published *Lincoln and Liquor* (1934) and revised Dr. William Barton's two-volume biography, *President Lincoln* (1933). Possibly he gained even wider recognition with the recording of the speech on Cassius Marcellus Clay that he delivered to the Chicago Civil War Round Table in 1952. His last book, *Hundred Proof* (1964), was comprised largely of the anecdotes he told the Book Thieves over the years with such great joy. For years Townsend and Chambers were bosom friends. Their families went on summer vacations together, and they visited back and forth with regularity. Bill greatly encouraged Dr. Chambers not only with his medical survey but also in the research and writing of his landmark book *The Conquest of Cholera* (1938).

Early in his academic career Dr. McVey published a slender book on populism, and for several decades it appeared as a standard entry in post–Civil War historical bibliographies. While a member of the Book Thieves, he wrote and assembled a tremendously interesting presidential documentary under the title *A University Is a Place . . . a Spirit* (1944). Then he wrote the provocative book *The Gates Open Slowly* (1949), in which he dealt with the history of public education in Kentucky.

Charles Staples published only one book, *The History of Pioneer Lexington* (1939), which he originally thought to entitle *The Little Town of Lexington*. No man ever held his hometown in greater affection, a place he called "Lexin'un." Charlie's literary memorial must be one with twin columns. Not even he could say how many authors, young and old, he encouraged and assisted in their research and writing. Among his debtors were John Bakeless, Niels Sonne, Bernard Mayo, Glyndon Van Deusen, James F. Hopkins, Holman Hamilton, all of the Book Thieves, and a host of others. Occasionally, when I walk down Lexington's bleak Main Street, my thoughts turn to what General Staples would think of the sterile piles of plastic and glass, and the debris-strewn parking lots where once familiar old buildings stood. They have torn down and robbed the general's "little town of Lexin'un" of its once charming individuality.

Judge Samuel M. Wilson published many books and essays, including *The First Land Court in Kentucky* (1923), *The Battle of the Blue Licks* (1927), the second volume of *A History of Kentucky* (1928), and a much-disputed essay on the first printer in Kentucky that appeared in the *Filson Club History Quarterly* and immediately provoked a heated exchange of views with Willard Rouse Jillson. Tragically, the judge died before he could locate all the numbers of John Bradford's "Notes on Kentucky." The three or four missing installments turned up later in the McCalla Collection, which was transferred from the Library of Congress to the West Virginia Library. The judge nevertheless left an appreciable body of editorial and annotative notes that remain unpublished.

Claude Trapp never wrote anything more extensive than a prescription, yet he was widely read and a stimulating conversationalist. He no doubt possessed as good a critical judgment of earlier British writers and poets and their works as a sophisticated professor of English literature. Because of his broad interests he could have joined a British literary club and felt quite at home. In his medical practice he had many loyal patients, but his practice could always be deferred in favor of chats with book-collecting friends.

A. B. "Bud" Guthrie was never a regular member of the Book Thieves, but he attended a good many meetings over the years, and during this time he was reading everything he could lay his hands on about the West. His first novel, and one he has all but disclaimed, was the bastard offspring of that reading, *Murders at Moon Dance* (1943). His two monumental books, *The Big Sky* (1947) and the Pulitzer Prize–winning *The Way West* (1949), were written in Lexington. Bud gave his papers to the University of Kentucky Library.

None of the Book Thieves made a greater contribution than Winston Coleman. He proved to be a literary marvel. I doubt that before 1931 he had even remotely thought of collecting books and essays, nor had he written anything more ambitious than a check on the Second National Bank. His first effort at writing, a history of the Masonic Lodge in Kentucky, was somewhat burdened with detail, like almost every other author's first effort, but by 1935 he was rapidly becoming a dedicated collector and researcher. His *Stage-Coach Days in the Bluegrass* of that year is not only a good piece of local American transportation history but also a lively bit of reading. There followed in 1940 his *Slavery Times in Kentucky*.

In 1946 Bill Townsend, Winston Coleman, and I went as invited guests to Lincoln Memorial University in Harrogate, Tennessee. We ran into a blinding rainstorm opposite Barbourville, Kentucky, and had to pull off the road to await its abatement. In that interval we convinced Winston, considerably against his will, to undertake the compilation of a bibliography of nonfictional writings about Kentucky. The result was the enormously useful *Bibliography of Kentucky History* (1949). There is neither space nor necessity at this point to list Winston's other publications, except to note *Kentucky: A Pictorial History* (1971), which has perhaps outsold any other non-textbook title about the Commonwealth. The last thing he published before his death in 1983 was a brief account of the Book Thieves.

Most of the Book Thieves were older men, and in the late 1940s the grim reaper began to thin their ranks. Judge Wilson died in 1946, Claude Trapp in 1947, Dr. McVey in 1953, Charlie Staples in 1954, Dr. Donovan and Bill Townsend in 1964, Brick Chambers in 1971, and Winston Coleman in 1983, leaving the author of this reminiscence as the sole survivor. After 1960 the remaining members gradually stopped meeting, and the organization became only a pleasant memory. But the years of its existence were profitable ones for the University of Kentucky, Transylvania University, the Lexington Public Library, and Berea College, as well as for the bibliographic and literary history of Kentucky.

THERE WAS A SECOND, AND OLDER, rare-book-oriented club. It was organized, planned, and hosted by Judge Samuel M. Wilson. Judge Wilson owned a large gray brick house in the somewhat exclusive cul-de-sac neighborhood known as Fayette Park. He named his "castle" Landover Lodge, dreaming, no doubt, of a secluded estate nestled in the hills of the Cotswolds during the reign of Queen Elizabeth I. In the winter of 1925–1926 he conceived a plan to celebrate George Washington's birthday by entertaining a company of book lovers and would-be book lovers with a lavish dinner and much book talk. He spent an inordinate amount of time composing his invitation in what he conceived to be sixteenth-century English, then spent hours inscribing the elaborate invitation to be imprinted on dignified fawn-colored paper. He drew charts of his dining and sitting rooms, indicating the seating of each guest, and worked out many other details.

Some of the recipients of the quaint invitation undertook to respond in kind. No respondent, however, expended as much time saying "Yes" as did "Farmer" Frank Jones. Frank said he lived at Muir Station, Fayette County, near Bourbon—"The county, not the likker." He spent a good part of the winter composing a reply in quaint Kentucky English as it was "spoke and writ." A sample:

Well sir, jedge, hit looks like you git worse rightin the english langwage instid of gittin better, whin i opens yore letter an you starts out say my der friendes, i thought it was a letter from the president but whin I got to that Hi ho, hi ho, i thout hit wuz frum rudy valley. why don't you go out to doctor frank mcvays school and git him to give you some lessons, but i gess he aint much time for that since he tuk up paintin. he showed me one of his paintins and I says, what a pretti sunset. "sunset yore eye," he says, "that's a cow." hit might a been a cow's big brother, hit shore weren't no female cow. if it wuz a cow, thin i am going to stop drinkin milk.

There were others who also wandered deep into the bogs of the English language.

Unlike the informal Book Thieves gatherings, Judge Wilson's Cakes and Ale Club was a noble, stately affair. Selected guests were asked to come dressed formally, and they could expect a hearty welcome inside the portals of "Ye Landover." Judge Wilson's guests were a mixture of judges, lawyers, bankers, authors, professors, and selected yeomen. Reception of one of those easily identifiable invitations in February signaled that you were still in good standing at Landover lodgement.

Though "Farmer" Frank Jones accepted the judge's invitation in the Kentucky vernacular, he was in fact a polished gentleman who came dressed as formally as if he had just stepped out of a gentlemen's parlor on Bond Street. Frank Jones was the manager of the Whitney Green Tree Horse Farm on the old Maysville Road. He was a masterful toastmaster, in much popular demand. With a combination of wit and polished style he added much color to the meetings of the Cakes and Ale Club. On one occasion I overheard an aged court judge say to a friend that Columbus came to America because he had heard Frank Jones was acting as toastmaster on the corner of Main and Limestone Streets in Lexington.

Oratory and wit, however, had serious competition from the banquets prepared by the famous Mrs. Quarles. At one of the Friday evening meetings I entered the dining room between two good Irish Catholics, Dr. Louis Mulligan and Colonel James Roche. Dr. Mulligan was the son of James H. Mulligan, who wrote popular pieces of poetic doggerel, including the oft-reprinted "In Kentucky." Colonel Jim Roche had the appearance of the "emerald isle" stamped on his face and personality. He held social court daily in his quarters in the old North Bank building on Short Street. When that pair got a glimpse of Mrs. Quarles's glorious feast and a whiff of her prime, two-year-old Kentucky ham, Dr. Mulligan turned to Colonel Roche and said, "Jim, if you won't tell on me, I won't tell on you."

At the conclusion of the dinner, after the cigars had been passed around and lit, the judge would place at least two cardboard boxes on a table and for an hour and a half would display and describe some of the rare books and pamphlets he had acquired during the past year. Almost always he would invite a guest to display his treasures or to make a bibliographical speech. I recall vividly when that impassioned Winchester Pike literary critic, John Edward Madden, fortified with a considerable quantity of bourbon, delivered an inspiring lecture on the uplifting literary virtues of the *Police Gazette,* a wrinkled copy of which he happened to have in hand.

Judge Wilson was not only a talented bibliographer, researcher, and writer of local history; he was also a shrewd horse trader when it came to books. He encouraged his guests to bring along their own rare possessions, and it was not unusual in the rarefied environment of those meetings for a book to change ownership. I got stuck in such a situation on one occasion. Somewhere I had bought from a dealer the historical half of the rare book *The Indigo Merchant's Daughter.* I had no idea what had happened to the other half. It turned out that Judge Wilson had it. I suggested to him that we put the two halves together and then flip a coin to determine who would get the full book. He refused to go along with that proposition. Before I knew it I held a nicely autographed photograph of the judge, and he walked off with the *Indigo Merchant's Daughter* intact.

Judge Wilson died in 1946 in St. Louis. Unhappily, no member of the Cakes and Ale Club had a "manor house" large enough to accommodate the annual meetings, or a library collection of such completeness and worth. Perhaps most important of all, there was nobody who could exhibit so many truly rare and important books as the judge owned. They were tucked away in many rooms at Landover and in other places. Dr. Jacqueline Bull and I spent three years removing the Wilson collection of books, pamphlets, manuscripts, and memorabilia to the Special Collections library in the University of Kentucky. The big house in Fayette Park was crammed tight with books, the basement was filled to the gunwales, and so was the attic. Judge Wilson's office in the Security Trust Building was lined with nonlegal books, as was a storage room in the bank's basement. We found the cardboard boxes of materials the judge had assembled for the meetings of the Cakes and Ale Club. We recovered his detailed plans for the annual meetings, and other related materials.

The Cakes and Ale Club faded into history, but not before it met for one more time in memory of its founder. A final meeting was held in the ballroom of the Lafayette Hotel. Absent that night were a host of men who had played prominent roles in Kentucky life and affairs, including the Cakes and Ale Club. "Farmer" Frank Jones had gone on to be toast-master at a bigger gathering in Valhalla, Judge Andrew McConnell January Cochran had adjourned his last court session, Rogers Clark Ballard Thruston had long since presided over his last meeting of the Filson Club, Bishop H. P. Almon Abbott had blessed his last pack of fox hounds, and Douglas C. McMurtrie had passed his last stilted judgment on a piece of Americana. Over two decades the list of departed guests would grow longer, and with their passing Kentucky and Lexington lost some of their best leaders. That night in the hotel ballroom, an era in Kentucky history ended. No living or departed guest, however, had created such an enduring monument as Judge Wilson. In attendance were of course Americana and Kentuckiana collectors and bibliographers, but not one breathed so much soul into the acquisition of a rare book as did Judge Sam Wilson.

I frequently turn through one of what he called his "working copies" of a book and see his generous marginal notations. I picture him sitting by the ever-burning fireplace and hearth of Landover of an evening, in-tellectually and almost literally devouring that book.

21

~

FAMILY

Robust health and longevity were not common attributes in the Lower South at the opening of the twentieth century. The course of life in that era was beset with as many hazards as was Odysseus's journey in the roiling waters between Scylla and Charybdis. Somewhere in an earlier age, some members of my ancestral chain latched onto some good genes, good enough to attract the attention of longevity researchers. A team of life scientists in the Harvard University Medical School and Boston University School of Medicine discovered my family and asked us to participate in their longevity study. We did so and responded to their queries, submitting blood samples. I have seen no report of the group's findings.

There were six of us, four boys and two girls. As I write this in 2005, four of us are still living—my brother Ernest, my sisters Wilma and Ethel, and myself, all of us in our nineties or beyond. If there is a secret to our longevity, we have never discovered it. Miraculously we did not contract the life-threatening menaces so common in the South during our early years. We tested negatively in the famous Styles-Page-Rockefeller crusade to eradicate the hookworm. I was the only one who contracted the regional devitalizer, malaria. At the time I was living amid swarms of mosquitoes along the Tallahega Canal.

Growing up on a combination general subsistence/cotton farm surrounded by virgin forest, we lacked neither exercise nor appetite. We thrived on homegrown, home-canned vegetables and fruits. Year-round there was served on our dining table a hearty countryman's diet of all these viands plus syrup of our own growing and processing. We never had any dietary analysis of the nutrients contained in sweet potatoes and black-eyed peas. We ate them without question.

The immediate post–World War I years were an era of near impoverishment for my family. Like our neighbors, we were almost completely dependent on cotton production. By mid-summer 1919 the crisis was clearly evident. Boll weevils had destroyed 80 percent of our cotton crop. It was then, as I explained earlier, that I became partially separated from my family. As a growing sixteen-year-old boy I got a man's job with a dredgeboat crew. Never again was I to be intimately associated with my family for any extended length of time. In 1921 I went away to a boarding high school, and for almost all of the following decade I was a dormitory dweller. Nevertheless, my mother wrote every week and scolded me for not writing back promptly. Over half a century, until her death in 1977, I received her traditional two-page letters. Only once did I receive a letter from my father.

True to the American family tradition, my siblings and I went our individual ways, but in a more or less desultory way I did keep in touch with them. Only now, in reading my brother Ernest's rich memoirs, do I realize how little I knew about my siblings and their activities. Ernest graduated from Mississippi State University and became a Smith-Hughes teacher in high schools in Tennessee. He was an airplane pilot and during World War II was a staff member of a contract company that trained pilots for the Allied Powers. Later he was an employee of the United States Aeronautics Authority in Oklahoma City.

My brother Marvin briefly attended Mississippi State University, then dropped out to get married and manage a fairly large timber stand for a local company. Later he went to Oregon to represent a Louisville, Mississippi, company that manufactured logging machinery; eventually he became a staff member of a federally supported technical school and spent the remainder of his life in Denver, Colorado.

My youngest brother, Ervin, partly handicapped by strabismus, a muscular dysfunction of the eyes, graduated from the Mississippi State Blind Institute in Jackson. Ironically, his problem could have been corrected by a simple outpatient operation had it been available. In life he succeeded in several crafts for which he had been trained in Jackson. Later, Mississippi mounted an active campaign to attract industries to the state with promises of tax concessions, factory sites, buildings, and roads. Contained in the concessionary agreements was a clause that reserved the right for handicapped Mississippians to be awarded contracts to operate company cafeterias. Ervin was awarded the contract to operate one at the Spartus Clock plant in Louisville. In time he became better off financially than any of his brothers and sisters.

My sisters, Wilma and Ethel, married local men. Wilma's husband was a successful cotton farmer and public official. Ethel's husband was a member of an old and established family in Houston, Mississippi. He did some farming but was also an employee of the Mississippi Highway Commission.

A PROBLEM THAT ALL PROFESSORS face is that of dividing their time between their professional duties—the classroom, research, and writing—and the time they can devote to their families. I faced this problem in full measure. One of the most precious joys in life is the opportunity, for almost a score of years, to have warm and eventful associations with your growing children. One such golden moment for me was the occasion when I accompanied my son and a group of Boy Scouts on a canoe-paddling adventure down the main stream of the Kentucky River. Early in 1946 I made plans for such a journey with Bennett and Bill Eaton, son of my colleague Clement Eaton. But I forgot I was living next door to a nosy newspaperman, Bud Guthrie. I told him about the proposed "voyage," and the next thing I knew a reporter showed up to ask me about the trip. After a story appeared in the *Lexington Leader,* I received a telephone call from a group of Boy Scouts who wanted to go along. Our party immediately expanded.

I was familiar with the river basin, having traveled up and down it many times gathering data for the writing of my book *The Kentucky.* On a late August afternoon our canoe flotilla set out at the confluence of the North and Middle Forks that form the headstreams of the Kentucky. On our first lap we paddled past the confluence of the South Fork and past Beattyville. At that point the broadening river looks like a channel bored through an overarching forest. Our canoes glided along as easily as if they were pieces of mountain flotsam in search of a resting place. So peaceful was it that I almost forgot about the possibility of danger. Some of the denizens of Heidelberg, an abandoned lumber village, were reputed to be rather unbridled spirits, so I was on guard as we approached the bridge there. When we appeared in the pool between the lock and the bridge, a group of young boys ran onto the bridge yelling, "Yonder comes a lot of Indian boats!" I felt uneasy lest they might start throwing rocks at us. We glided past the danger zone without incident, however.

The vista of the forest and the rugged rocky banks of the Kentucky is startlingly beautiful. The quiet towns, villages, and farmsteads, in the context of their place and time, are as appealing as those of the Hudson River. We spent five days and nights on the river, paddling through rapids and "sucks" without trouble. We slept on mother earth wrapped in thin blankets and prepared our food in keeping with Boy Scout conceptions of cuisine. When at last the bridge pilasters at Valley View hove into sight, I felt the same delight returning sailors must experience when coming home. Physically we must have looked like a huddle of groundhogs whose hibernation had been disrupted. But stamped on my heart and in my memory is this adventure I shared with my son.

From the children's early years, we spent time almost every summer at Pawleys Island, South Carolina, where we would rent a ramshackle beach house. We enjoyed the beach, the nearby creek, and the broad marshes. Crabbing was a favorite occupation. We especially enjoyed the chuckling of the marsh hens, who noted the changing of the tide with such hysteria that one would almost believe they had never experienced it before.

In the summer of 1946 I was invited to teach a summer session in graduate work in history in the University of Chicago. We rented the home of a law professor, a somewhat gloomy house on Fullerton Avenue just off the Midway and backing up to the university's International House. Outside and inside, the house was a sharp contrast to our house on Tahoma Road. When we drove up to it for the first time, both children got out of the car and fell on the steps sobbing and saying they wanted to go home. There were no broad fields in which to play. Almost immediately, however, we discovered how hospitable Chicago could be for children. The museums, the zoo, the Planetarium, the Aquarium, the Art Institute, and the Museum of Science and Industry were wonder worlds for young visitors. Elizabeth loved the Art Institute, the Planetarium, and the aquatic exhibits. Bennett almost lived in the Museum of Science and Industry, which was only a short distance from our house.

In the summer of 1948 I was invited to teach in the Salzburg Seminar in Austria, and two years later I again visited Austria, this time as a professor of American history in the University of Vienna. In 1952 I was again invited to lecture abroad, this time in India. With the children still in school during these years, we decided it would be best if my family remained at home.

My family's first European visit occurred in the summer of 1953, when I was invited to be a member of the professorial staff of the British-American Seminar at Oxford. This time Bennett and Elizabeth accompanied Beth and me. We sailed on the *Queen Elizabeth* and returned on the *Queen Mary*. That summer the children got a good taste of life in an English country village. Bennett explored the area around Oxford by bicycle. After the Oxford session ended we had a lengthy interval before the *Queen Mary* was to sail, so we took a wide, sweeping journey through England, Scotland, Belgium, Holland, Germany, Austria, Italy, and France. We wanted the children to get some notion of Western Europe.

The following summer found the whole family in Cambridge, Massachusetts, where I taught at Harvard University. Cambridge and Boston proved as appealing to our children as Chicago had been. Bennett, who had just graduated from high school and would enter the University of Rochester in the fall, took a course in English at Tufts College that summer. The night we went to the Southern Railway Station back in Lexington to send Bennett to the University of Rochester was a heartrending moment in our lives. I realized we had moved into a new stage in our relationship. Four years later, in 1958, he had a bachelor of arts degree and a naval commission as ensign, and was wandering about the Pacific Ocean aboard a naval destroyer, the USS *Maddox*—a far cry from paddling a canoe on the Kentucky River.

Elizabeth was two years younger than Bennett and still had two more years in high school. She rode with me daily to the University High School. That was a period when I had a close association with my daughter. She too graduated from high school all too soon. When Beth and I drove her to Lynchburg, Virginia, to enroll her in Randolph-Macon College, I was emotionally unprepared for the parting. Beth and I had assumed we would have dinner with her and bid her an affectionate goodbye. Instead, we deposited her luggage at the entrance to her dormitory, and with a wave of farewell, she was gone. I never in my life felt so desolate.

Beth and I now entered a new phase of our lives, alone, as we had been when we started our married life in 1933. In 1961 I received an invitation to become a NATO professor in the Universities of Athens and Thessalonica, Greece. This appointment was similar to my professorship in the University of Vienna. I was a member of the law schools and lectured throughout Greece. Beth traveled with me to all the lecture engagements. She thoroughly enjoyed living in Athens and visiting other parts of the country and the Greek islands. A memorable visit was to Pieria, near Mount Olympus. After my lecture Beth went to see the classical treasures and the remains of ancient athletic fields, while I strolled through the Sea of Olives. We met at the Pierian Spring, birthplace of the Muses of classic mythology, and sat beside it, dipping our hands in the water and looking up to the towering rocky cliff that sheltered the eternal spring on two sides.

By the time of our visit to Thessalonica, our departure from Greece was drawing close. Beth left me and flew back to Athens, then to Rome and Florence. I knew the USIS librarian in Florence and asked her to look out for Beth. She did, in full measure. I never saw Beth so happy and jubilant as when I met her there. She almost skipped along the landing chute with joy over her week in Florence.

We continued to enjoy many rewarding moments with our children. Bennett came home from the navy and spent a year in business before entering the Duke University law school. Later he became a partner in the firm of Stoll, Keenon and Park in Lexington. In June 1963 I served as best man in his marriage to Alice Hemphill, the daughter of Edwin and Susan Hemphill. Ed was editor of the John C. Calhoun Papers in the University of South Carolina.

Elizabeth graduated from Duke University in 1960 and went on to do graduate work in the University of Michigan. She majored in medical social work and later became a staff member of the medical school at Chapel Hill, North Carolina. She vowed early in life that she would not marry a professor, but she did, and I performed the fatherly duty of giving her as a bride to Richard Gabriel Stone, the son of Marye and Richard Stone of Raleigh, North Carolina. Dr. Stone was president of the Episcopal St. Mary's College. Richard and Elizabeth lived in our Tahoma Road house in 1968–1969 while Beth and I were living in Bloomington, Indiana. The following year Richard joined the Department of History at Western Kentucky University and has spent the remainder of his career there.

After 1965 Beth and I spent many long summer vacations at Turnwell Plantation in Fairfield County, South Carolina. Beth had inherited the place, approximately seven hundred acres, from her parents after her father's death in 1956. Those were rewarding years for us. I was deeply involved in the management of our pinelands there, and Beth was able to visit often with members of her family. I spent many nights at Turnwell working on *The Emerging South*, published in 1961, and drawing together materials for *The Greening of the South,* which would be published in 1984.

One particularly stirring historic moment occurred while we were at Turnwell. On July 16, 1969, a clear summer evening with a full moon hanging overhead, I had the television set on and sat in the moonlight watching Neil Armstrong take his monumental first steps on the moon's rock-strewn surface. I remember going outside and looking up at the great ball of light to see if I could spot even a shadow of movement.

ONE SUNDAY IN THE SPRING OF 1966, while Beth and I were in Bloomington, Indiana, the phone rang, bringing us news of the birth of our first grandchild, Thomas Bennett Clark, always called Tom. Bennett and Alice's second son, Edwin, was born in 1968. In time our two grandsons were to take wives and bring us three great-granddaughters and one great-grandson. Elizabeth and Richard presented us with our only granddaughter, who is married and soon to be a mother herself. Beth and I rejoiced in each new addition to our family. Sadly, she did not live to know our great-grandchildren.

At the end of July 1995, Beth died quietly in her sleep at the age of eighty-eight. We had been married sixty-two years. Her passing left me mired in almost overpowering loneliness. There raced through my mind memories of our lives together and of the children she had loved and molded into decent human beings.

At the time I was left alone, Loretta Gilliam Brock was having a kindred experience following the death of her husband, Walter Brock, a Lexington attorney. I had had only a brief, passing acquaintance with Loretta. Harriett Van Meter on an earlier occasion had asked me if I would read Loretta's manuscript history of the Woman's Club of Central Kentucky. I did so and found it well researched and well written, as well as an interesting contribution to local history. I wrote a brief introduction for her book, which was handsomely published. Beth had often mentioned Loretta to me in connection with the Monday Club, to which both belonged. Loretta is one of five children of the Reverend Adolphus Gilliam. Her father served Methodist churches in Estill County, Clark

County, Paris, Danville, and Lexington. She is a graduate of Sayre College (now Sayre School), attended Transylvania College, and was graduated from Centre College. She is a talented musician and a watercolorist whose paintings have provoked much favorable appraisal.

After Beth's death I became better acquainted with Loretta, and in 1996, in my ninety-third year, I asked her to be my wife. I had some concern that a marriage at our ages might provoke idle chatter. Not so. Our marriage was greeted with the kindest expressions of well-wishing. I recall one humorous incident related to the event. A radio station in rural southern Illinois reported our marriage and that we were on our way to Mississippi. Earlier I had participated in a two-day conference ostensibly concerned with the danger of quail extinction. I had read there and later published an article about the history of hunting in Mississippi, and I wanted to go back to the fine natural history museum in Jackson. A Mississippi Fish and Game official traveling in Illinois heard on the radio of our marriage and phoned his office that we were heading to Mississippi. Somewhere between Louisville and Jackson somebody spotted our car and reported that to the museum. Subsequently the museum received a report that we were in Jackson and stopping for gas. As a result of all these calls, when we walked through the entry door of the museum, the young receptionist, without a word, rushed out of sight and immediately reappeared with the museum director. They practically offered us the museum as a wedding present. Back home, when Loretta's son Walter heard about the radio chatter, he told her that we were the reincarnation of Bonnie and Clyde roving through the South. There was, however, the difference that no reward was posted for our capture.

Loretta's sons, Walter and Robert Brock, their wives, and their three children have brought unexpected blessings to my old age. Walter is a teacher and filmmaker in Louisville, Kentucky, and Robert is artistic director of the Kentucky Repertory Theatre of Horse Cave. After eight and a half years, I can say with joyous certainty that my marriage to gentle, talented Loretta has been one of those turns of fortune that give fundamental meaning and spice to life.

DURING NEARLY FOURSCORE YEARS OF living in Kentucky, I have often had to plead guilty to the fact that I was born on alien soil. I cannot recall a single occasion when I have been introduced to speak that this fact has not been mentioned. I suppose my mother should have chosen to give birth to me someplace between Mills Point and the Breaks of Sandy. In self-defense, however, I submit that I share this affliction with Simon Kenton, Daniel Boone, Dr. Ephraim McDowell, Henry Clay, William "King" Solomon (hero of the great cholera epidemic of the 1830s), a whole passel of Kentucky's governors, and many others who have made significant contributions to the Commonwealth. I would point also to the fact that, with two children, two grandchildren, and four great-grandchildren all now living in Kentucky, I have at least planted firm family roots in this land.

22

~

A Time of Reckoning

An academic career necessarily involves joys, humilities, and serious introspection. This is especially true when such a career spans almost fourscore years. I derive some pleasure from memories spread over all but three years of the twentieth century. The turnings and changes of life over such a broad span have obviously involved a generous dose of reality. At the end of the first quarter of the century, I stood in the middle of a field of cotton in full bloom that constituted for me the promise of a college education. Day after day in that field I tried silently to unravel the mystery of higher education. I tried to imagine where the bending of that road might lead me. In the expressive words of Robert Frost, would I ever regret "the road not taken"? From that agrarian setting the future seemed almost as sealed in as a road across Tallahega Swamp after a foggy summer rain. Perhaps I had a vague interest in history other than the folk kind, but if so it was a latent one.

Growing up in the Lower South, I was from childhood immersed in

Civil War reminiscences, in Indian lore, and even in the homeboy stories of the Spanish American War. But I did not sense the breadth and depth of universal history. Two lessons I learned at the outset of my career as a college student: the strangling death hold of pedanticism on learning, and the academic sin of foisting on the beginning student a textbook written by a matter-of-fact author whose organization and writing style would take second-place honors to the writers of patent medicine almanacs. My own early academic experience included some fortunate encounters with good teaching. As a graduating senior in the University of Virginia I was enrolled in two summer school courses in Shakespeare taught by well-prepared and able teachers. Through those courses I came to realize how important a sound historical background was to understanding the deeper and more subtle meanings embodied in Shakespeare's plays. This knowledge was confirmed later when I taught British history.

I brought away from my undergraduate years some comprehension of how intellectually stimulating serious reading and research in history could be. Yet, although I graduated with a major in history, I still had not matured a fixed plan of concentration on any regional or national area of study. But that fickle quality known as luck stepped in. In January 1928, although I had never heard of the University of Kentucky, not even its basketball team, I was awarded a modest scholarship by the institution, and on a gambler's choice I accepted it. I did not even know if the university had a department of history. It did, but that department was largely viewed as a service to prospective public schoolteachers so they could show on their records a competence to teach the subject.

The University of Kentucky's Department of History in that era was probably similar to other history departments in the South. In many of them history was a one-man operation supported by part-time assistants. I can assert positively that the department had about as much drawing power as a wilted ironweed. One of the courses finally included in my prescribed academic plan related, though only tangentially, to the westward movement in American history. The professor was New York born and bred and Columbia University trained. The only frontier he had ever laid eyes on was the New Jersey marshes across the Hudson River. To his credit, and my profit, he exhibited an interest in the subject. He also taught a course in southern history from the perspective of his major professor, William A. Dunning, leaning heavily on the contributions to Yale University Press's Chronicles of America series by William E. Dodd and Holland Thompson. Those professors' South bore little resemblance to the one I grew up in.

The decade 1920–1930 was a good time to be a neophyte historian. A renascence of historical research and writing was under way, along with a good measure of revisionism. In the wake of World War I there began an almost psychopathic search for war blame and for a formula for lasting peace. The era saw also the reorganization of European geography and a somewhat timid American expansion into the Far East. Throughout the nation, historians busied themselves with exploring neglected areas in the broader social fields, while the revisionists were bringing some of the old writings under critical scrutiny. Charles A. Beard and Mary Beard made decided departures from the traditional treatment of the Constitution of the United States and the motivations of its framers. I heard Dr. Beard deliver his address as president of the American Historical Association, and I heard the rumble of resentment that followed. There gradually crept into the teaching and writing of national and regional history a greater emphasis on social and cultural aspects of American society, breaking in appreciable measure the traditional stronghold of political and military history.

In my college years and at the beginning of my professional career, I found myself by coincidence enrolled in three universities caught up in transitional stages. I entered the University of Mississippi at the moment when that institution was creeping out of the cesspool of neanderthal politics. The University of Kentucky I first knew was struggling to shake off its parochial branding as an agricultural and mechanical college. And Duke University was in the process of converting a denominational college into a major institution of higher education. Just as these institutions were passing through their chrysalis stages, so too were subject disciplines. In perhaps most public universities the parameters of fields offered in history were too constricted to call for in-depth exploration of documentary sources or expanded searches for truth. There were some genuine academic advantages in being present during those years of change, no matter the limited decisions of administrations, the public, and boards of trustees. The transformation of these institutions involved a considerable degree of intellectual drama.

On the eve of the Great Depression, Kentucky's political life was paralyzed by the virus known as partisanship. This was especially true following the adoption of the Eighteenth Amendment to the United States Constitution, when most Kentucky counties experienced an extended "dry" spell. From that pleasant day in mid-April 1750 at Cumberland Gap when one of Dr. Thomas Walker's exploring party surely must have hoisted a flagon of home-distilled spirits to properly consecrate the occasion, much of Kentucky's public image has been drenched in alcohol or drugs. As in most of the nation, "moonshining" became a subterranean industry during the Prohibition years, when nearly every free-flowing spring branch had its still. Although few, if any, illicit distillers kept records, that chore was often performed in their behalf by revenue officers, the courts, and the newsmen.

Many of the Kentuckians I knew in those early years bragged, almost by rote, about southern hospitality, and I personally was a beneficiary of their generosity. I shared also their boast of beautiful women, but I never mounted one of their horses or had a paunchy colonel for a grandfather. I did discover quickly, though, that Judge James Hilary Mulligan spoke with scriptural verity when he wrote his immortal dictum that "In Kentucky, politics [are] the damndest." This pronouncement went forth on thousands of souvenir postal cards and was proclaimed endlessly by public speakers who found themselves with nothing else witty to say. Conversely, in all my years in Kentucky, I have heard few people boast about the Commonwealth's superior secondary schools or colleges.

Among the failures in Kentucky, both institutional and governmental, was a plain lack of vision and of will on the part of much of the public to accept the new findings in nearly every area of advanced learning. In a state where a discouragingly small proportion of the population got beyond the restrictive boundaries of the "three R's," improvements in education became one of the Commonwealth's greatest challenges.

I arrived in Kentucky just as the smoke was clearing away in the great controversy over evolution, a subject that neither legislators nor fundamentalist religious leaders were prepared to discuss objectively. The theory of evolution was of far less importance than raising the abysmally low level of learning in many areas of the Commonwealth. I listened to much rage from the pulpit and elsewhere against accepting, as the fundamentalists said, the "theory of monkeyish ancestry." But even in this moment of darkest anti-intellectualism, there were a few Kentuckians who felt that the simian tribe had been libeled. The University of Kentucky and some of the liberal religious bodies in the state actually profited in a tangential way from the sound and fury of the evolution controversy. In the end, the freedom of intellectual search for truth was established. The university faculty I joined had been strengthened by the "great crusade for righteousness." The anti-intellectual forces were driven into a state of quietude. No doubt the Great Depression that followed so soon was another factor.

In the broader fields of applied government, Kentucky was surely affected most basically by the dynamic development of new and modernized highways and bridges after 1930. No phase in the breaking of land barriers was more immediately effective than the pioneering work of the Civilian Conservation Corps. Their work removed barriers that had held many areas locked in place and time, opening them to new social, economic, and cultural influences that helped draw Kentucky humanity into a tighter common bond, if a not shared mind-set. Similarly, no one at the turn of the twentieth century could possibly have visualized a rural society with access to cheap electrical energy, or of a veritable lacing of fiber piping that would give country dwellers deep in the swamplands of western Kentucky or on the dry, rock-ribbed eastern highlands a constant flow of spring water from the innermost bowels of the land. In the scope of a half century, most of the arduous burdens of life on the land were wiped away.

Like a once flourishing plant shriveling in a drought, two centers in the Kentucky way of life were passing into oblivion, leaving behind only a soulful moaning of nostalgia. "Main Street," with all that the term implies, has faded into and almost out of memory. Highway "string towns" now line the roads with fast-food franchises and chain stores huddling under the spreading bosom of something called an "anchor store," all of them almost as impersonal as old-line patent medicine barkers.

Equally, the political campaign activism of the courthouse square has been quelled by television, with its name calling, its cute tricksters, and its character assassins. It seems at times that would-be servitors of the people have lost every vestige of civility. More and more with each passing session of the General Assembly, there appear summary articles in the press reporting the staggering expenditure of self-interest in governmental affairs. If, in fact, they ever existed in the political experience, the old ideals of simple Jeffersonian democracy are going the way of Main Street and burley tobacco.

Being a faculty member in a public university almost necessitates a concern with public affairs. This was especially true in my career. Aside from my active involvement in building a special collection of text and documentary materials for the university library, I became involved in one way or another with other public issues. For a brief time in 1947 I served as chairman of the campaign to bring about a modernization of the Kentucky constitution, then as vice-chairman with Paul C. Blazer of Ashland Oil Incorporated. We failed in that effort, largely because the electorate lacked understanding of the issues involved, but also because of Kentuckians' inborn resistance to change.

The Kentucky I first knew in the late 1920s was, in most of its areas, almost as devoid of libraries and books as were the remote villages of China. When I directed the WPA Historical Records Survey in 1936–1937, I had access to no local libraries. Occasionally educational missionaries would pack limited numbers of books on "book mules" to be ridden into intellectual wastelands. The mid-twentieth-century crusade to organize public libraries throughout Kentucky was a masterful movement. Many times I have rejoiced at the privilege of being present at a meeting in Louisville's famous Seelbach Hotel, organized and promoted by a group of intelligent and imaginative women, from which "seed corn" planting there emerged the procession from traveling bookmobiles to the organizing of sustaining local libraries. The movement was spurred in part by a local yearning for books and organized information that would make communities more attractive to new businesses and industries. In 2005, 117 of Kentucky's 120 counties have public libraries. I can think of no gauge of social and cultural advancement that more accurately reflects the quality of community life. I glory in the fact that I had the good fortune to be present when the highly literate "Granny Women" delivered the bawling and screaming idea of making public libraries a fixed part of Kentucky's public institutional life.

Interrelated by parallel interests are librarians and authors. During the post-1930 decades there appeared important books by a new generation of authors. Their writings marked a distinct cleavage with those of the past, fathoming the innermost spirit of Kentucky and expressing new insights into the people, their land, their deep sense of place, and the impact of the changes that had erased so many of the old ways. The contrasts were sharp between the writings of Robert Penn Warren and those of James Lane Allen, between Jesse Stuart and John Fox Jr., and between Harriett Arnow and Alice Hegan Rice. Kentucky thus reaped a rich harvest of intangible literary value. I feel both assured and comfortable in asserting such a judgment.

Along the way I personally became aware of the limitations Kentuckians faced in buying books. When I presented the manuscript of *The Rampaging Frontier*, the publisher accepted it without delay but told me, "You come from a state where people do not buy books." This was confirmed for me in my first book-signing experience. In the famous old W. K. Stewart Book Store on Fourth Street in Louisville, I sat at a table alongside Dr. William Lyons Phelps, the popular journalist and theologian. Streams of women came in to fawn over Dr. Phelps, while not one looked my way. At the end of the session Dr. Phelps came over to comfort me as if I were an expiring parishioner. *The Rampaging Frontier* did encouragingly well, but not in Louisville on that day.

Happily, the last quarter of the twentieth century has seen what may be called another literary renascence in the organization of the Kentucky Book Fair under the leadership of Carl West of the *Kentucky State Journal*. Over a quarter of a century this festive literary occasion has grown in cultural significance and as a refutation of my publisher's derogatory statement. The success of the Book Fair reflects not only an increase in the sale of books and an upgrading of Kentucky's cultural level, but also heartening benefits for school libraries. Indicative of the increased interest in books is the fact that on June 1, 1992, the first printing of the voluminous and model *Kentucky Encyclopedia* sold out its first printing in a single afternoon.

When I began my search for materials to be deposited in the newly created special collections in the University of Kentucky library, I learned that Kentuckians had come to consider Lyman Draper and Reuben T. Durrett as thieves of the night who had made off with the Commonwealth's documentary heritage even as the state did little or nothing to preserve the documentary materials that remained. Yet I discovered that by no means were all the historical records of the state in Madison, Wisconsin, or Chicago, Illinois. Groping in the dark recesses of the cellar of the Kentucky state capitol on several occasions, I found the Commonwealth's public records tossed into windrows of neglect, an experience comparable to viewing the Louisville city trash dump. I had difficulty reconciling the horrendous wails against the Draper-Durrett "larceny" with those piles of shamefully neglected and deteriorating public documents. It took a generous amount of persuasion seasoned with shame and anger to stir administrators and legislators to action. The resulting change, wrought by intelligent record management and the construction of a dignified depository for archival materials, was almost as important to the state and university as being one of the "final four" in a national basketball competition.

Caught up in the flurry of change in the preservation of Kentucky's historical heritage was the effort to breathe life into the drowsy, quasi-private, quasi-public Kentucky Historical Society. Often over a half century I wondered if in fact the organization would ever join the ranks of the better historical societies across the nation. In recent years, however,

I have often used both the Kentucky Archives and the new Kentucky History Center with an almost passionate gratefulness that future generations of Kentuckians will have in place a rich documentation of the past. Kentucky has ceased to be the "happy hunting ground" for aggressive thieves of historical documents. Young historians will be able to use these materials to write a more comprehensive account of the progress of the nation's heartland.

ADVANCES IN SO MANY AREAS OF human endeavor have come so rapidly in the twentieth century as to constitute a revolution in the American way of life. How challenging it has been to be alive and to experience these transformations. The latter three quarters of the twentieth century were a seminal era in which to launch a career in the field of history. During those decades I read perhaps hundreds of books and turned countless pages of primary documents, but none made such a deep impression on me as the slender primary reader of 127 pages that I first encountered as a child. The very first thing I learned from it was that a hand-drawn circle was a B A L L, or so the inscription said in both type and script. Nearly a hundred years later, I can observe that my simple little circle has been expanded to become a W O R L D—marked, and often abused, by its human occupants, actions that will challenge generations of historians to explain.

Over the broad scope of years I have frequently pondered the wisdom of decisions I made and roads not taken. Often I have wondered whether, had I expended as much time and energy in practicing another profession or engaging in some business, my life would have been richer and more materially rewarding. Yet, after all, those are idle questions. I have accumulated precious riches that thieves cannot steal nor moths destroy. No human can earn a sweeter reward than when, after the passing of years, a former student, well away from the grade book, says, "You touched my life."

Through a half century of standing before rooms full of students, I never lost sight of how easy it is to snuff out a student's interest in history. Figuratively, I sat beside my students and endeavored to instill in them both interest in and comprehension of the vital meaning of history to them personally. I held steadfastly to the conviction that every human being, no matter his or her social or intellectual level, has a warranty claim on at least a microscopic stone in the arch of history and the scroll of mankind's experiences.

If, at this confusing moment in the first decade of the twenty-first century, I were asked if I would again choose an academic career, the answer would be yes, without reservation. My forty-nine years in the classroom have been the most wonderful experience any human could hope for. I do, however, reserve the privilege to wish that I had been a better teacher, written a better book, or done other things more effectively. But those surely must be the essential quandaries of life itself. In a more positive vein, I owe a heavy debt of gratitude that I had the privilege of standing before classes in free classrooms.

I humbly offer a benediction by once more standing, vicariously, in a classroom facing an assembly of youthful students from whose ranks would come governors, physicians, lawyers, judges, authors, and good and productive historians and archivists. Just as rewarding, however, was that wide-eyed young woman whom I saw years later bearing the marks of a lifetime in a schoolroom. She glorified her fellow man when she faced a classroom full of primary scholars and drew a chalk circle and proclaimed it a B A L L. For the first time in their lives her charges received a glimpse of learning. For them the naked circle would in time be converted into the W O R L D, a greater symbol. Deeply etched within the circle would be the historical accounts of civilized man's successive triumphs and defeats as recorded by historians throughout the ages, ever challenges to new historians searching for truth.

From my own modest and limited pinnacle, I look back into the opening decades of the twentieth century with considerable wonder. It was near the end of the first quarter of the century that research, writing, and the teaching of history underwent a process of expansion. Greater emphasis was placed upon the collection and utilization of documentary sources and the development of better techniques for reentering these basic source materials. The phenomenal advances made and promised in the latter part of the century have lifted historical research onto a new plane. The introduction of ever-expanding electronic and technological devices has placed historical research in a new time frame. Even so, there linger the basic and essential questions of how much historical information is needed for the populace to make informed decisions in matters political, economic, and cultural.

I have found both intellectual and spiritual satisfaction in the profession of historian. I cherish those exciting moments of collecting and examining records never before seen by a historian, and of writing from a new perspective or revising an earlier one. As I approach the sunset of my career, I have one haunting regret. I would cherish an opportunity to read the revisions of younger historians appraising the works of historians of my era. Future scholars will have greater access to larger volumes of primary materials and will have the electronic and technological devices to facilitate their searches. Will they come nearer to the truth? Therein resides the virtue, or lack of it, of every individual who has borne the title "historian."

INDEX